THE NEW
AMERICAN
COMMENTARY

An Exegetical and Theological
Exposition of Holy Scripture

THE NEW
AMERICAN
COMMENTARY

Volume
27

ROMANS

Robert H. Mounce

BROADMAN
& HOLMAN
PUBLISHERS

Subject Heading: Bible. N.T. Romans
Printed in the United States of America

Editors' Preface

God's Word does not change. God's world, however, changes in every generation. These changes, in addition to new findings by scholars and a new variety of challenges to the gospel message, call for the church in each generation to interpret and apply God's Word for God's people. Thus, THE NEW AMERICAN COMMENTARY is introduced to bridge the twentieth and twenty-first centuries. This new series has been designed primarily to enable pastors, teachers, and students to read the Bible with clarity and proclaim it with power.

In one sense THE NEW AMERICAN COMMENTARY is not new, for it represents the continuation of a heritage rich in biblical and theological exposition. The title of this forty-volume set points to the continuity of this series with an important commentary project published at the end of the nineteenth century called AN AMERICAN COMMENTARY, edited by Alvah Hovey. The older series included, among other significant contributions, the outstanding volume on Matthew by John A. Broadus, from whom the publisher of the new series, Broadman Press, partly derives its name. The former series was authored and edited by scholars committed to the infallibility of Scripture, making it a solid foundation for the present project. In line with this heritage, all NAC authors affirm the divine inspiration, inerrancy, complete truthfulness, and full authority of the Bible. The perspective of the NAC is unapologetically confessional and rooted in the evangelical tradition.

Since a commentary is a fundamental tool for the expositor or teacher who seeks to interpret and apply Scripture in the church or classroom, the NAC focuses on communicating the theological structure and content of each biblical book. The writers seek to illuminate both the historical meaning and contemporary significance of Holy Scripture.

In its attempt to make a unique contribution to the Christian community, the NAC focuses on two concerns. First, the commentary emphasizes how each section of a book fits together so that the reader becomes aware of the theological unity of each book and of Scripture as a whole. The writers, however, remain aware of the Bible's inherently rich variety. Second, the NAC is produced with the conviction that the Bible primarily belongs to the church. We believe that scholarship and the academy provide an indispensable foundation for biblical understanding and the service of Christ, but the editors and authors of this series have attempted to communicate the findings of their research in a manner that will build up the whole body of Christ. Thus, the commentary concentrates on theological exegesis while providing practical, applicable exposition.

THE NEW AMERICAN COMMENTARY's theological focus enables the reader to see the parts as well as the whole of Scripture. The biblical books vary in content, context, literary type, and style. In addition to this rich variety, the editors and authors recognize that the doctrinal emphasis and use of the biblical books differs in various places, contexts, and cultures among God's people. These factors, as well as other concerns, have led the editors to give freedom to the writers to wrestle with the issues raised by the scholarly community surrounding each book and to determine the appropriate shape and length of the introductory materials. Moreover, each writer has developed the structure of the commentary in a way best suited for expounding the basic structure and the meaning of the biblical books for our day. Generally, discussions relating to contemporary scholarship and technical points of grammar and syntax appear in the footnotes and not in the text of the commentary. This format allows pastors and interested laypersons, scholars and teachers, and serious college and seminary students to profit from the commentary at various levels. This approach has been employed because we believe that all Christians have the privilege and responsibility to read and seek to understand the Bible for themselves.

Consistent with the desire to produce a readable, up-to-date commentary, the editors selected the *New International Version* as the standard translation for the commentary series. The selection was made primarily because of the NIV's faithfulness to the original languages and its beautiful and readable style. The authors, however, have been given the liberty to differ at places from the NIV as they develop their own translations from the Greek and Hebrew texts.

The NAC reflects the vision and leadership of those who provide oversight for Broadman Press, who in 1987 called for a new commentary series that would evidence a commitment to the inerrancy of Scripture and a faithfulness to the classic Christian tradition. While the commentary adopts an "American" name, it should be noted some writers represent countries outside the United States, giving the commentary an international perspective. The diverse group of writers includes scholars, teachers, and administrators from almost twenty different colleges and seminaries, as well as pastors, missionaries, and a layperson.

The editors and writers hope that THE NEW AMERICAN COMMEN-

TARY will be helpful and instructive for pastors and teachers, scholars and students, for men and women in the churches who study and teach God's Word in various settings. We trust that for editors, authors, and readers alike, the commentary will be used to build up the church, encourage obedience, and bring renewal to God's people. Above all, we pray that the NAC will bring glory and honor to our Lord who has graciously redeemed us and faithfully revealed himself to us in his Holy Word.

SOLI DEO GLORIA
The Editors

Author's Preface

Many of the best things in life happen when you least expect them. I was comfortable in retirement when a call came from Ray Clendenen asking if I would be interested in contributing a commentary on Romans to the *The New American Commentary* from Broadman & Holman. Obviously I said yes. Who wouldn't jump at the chance to spend the next several years immersed in one of the pivotal books of the New Testament?

In the same phone call Ray suggested an approach that struck me as innovative and perhaps a bit presumptuous: Why don't you write the first draft on your own? After that you can read all the commentaries and other relevant sources. The idea was appealing, not because I felt that I was so well informed, but because it promised a freedom to write about those specific issues that seemed to me to be absolutely central.

So I took the Greek text and went to work. At various points I made use of lexicons and theological wordbooks, but for the most part what I wrote was what the text was saying to me. My first discovery was that I had in fact stumbled into an approach where others were not determining the specific issues with which I wanted to deal. It was an exciting year. Paul became like an elder brother who directed me verse by verse through what he had written under the inspiration of the Spirit. I was amazed at the clarity of his presentation of justification by faith. I found myself wanting a faith like Abraham's. When it came to reckoning oneself dead to sin, I prayed that it would be true in my life. Chapter 8 left me almost breathless in adoration of God's incredible love. The experience continued right through the greetings of chap. 16.

The next step was to read the literature. The next year or so was spent with the great names who have written on Romans. Who was the most helpful? You will discover my favorite mentors if you check the index. It would be difficult, however, not to call special attention to Cranfield, Morris, Dunn, Moo, and Fitzmyer. Each in his own way added depth and insight to my study. I found Luther and Calvin still relevant and exceptionally helpful. In all I read some thirty or so commentaries. Supporting these were the many helpful journal articles. Much of the material from the second year of study shows up in footnotes rather than the body of the text. Throughout this second draft I tried to remember that the commentary was to be written primarily for pastors. I wanted to help them in very practical ways as they prepared their sermons from week to week. The commentary, however, is not loaded with an endless series of illustrations. I believe the role of a good commentary is to highlight the relevance of a passage rather than to provide a supply of generic illustrations. The best illustrations always come from the preacher's own experience anyway. When a specific truth really lays hold of you, you will have no trouble providing examples of how it works out in real life.

My purpose for the third time through was to be sure that I had said what I wanted to say and that I had said it clearly. I have always felt that it is the writer's responsibility to remove ambiguity and make the reader's experience as simple and enjoyable as possible. The reader will be the judge of how well that has been done.

I am thankful, then, for the invitation to write. I also appreciate editors Linda Scott and Marc Jolley for working so tirelessly on the text. If the reader finds this commentary to be helpful, I have accomplished my goal. My prayer is that God may use our combined efforts to bring understanding to the believer and new life to those who are just learning that God accepts us not on the basis of our performance but because Christ died for our sins.

Bend, Oregon
1995

Abbreviations

Commonly Used Sources

AB	Anchor Bible
ACNT	Augsburg Commentary on the New Testament
AJT	*American Journal of Theology*
AJTh	*Asia Journal of Theology*
ANF	Ante-Nicene Fathers
ATR	*Anglican Theological Review*
ATRSup	*Anglican Theological Review Supplemental Series*
AusBR	*Australian Biblical Review*
AUSS	*Andrews University Seminary Studies*
BAGD	W. Bauer, W. F. Arndt, F. W. Gingrich, and F. Danker, *Greek-English Lexicon of the New Testament*
BARev	*Biblical Archaeology Review*
BDF	F. Blass, A. Debrunner, R. W. Funk, *A Greek Grammar of the New Testament*
Bib	*Biblica*
BJRL	*Bulletin of the John Rylands Library*
BK	*Bibel und Kirche*
BR	*Biblical Research*
BSac	*Bibliotheca Sacra*
BT	*The Bible Translator*
BTB	*Biblical Theology Bulletin*
BZ	*Biblische Zeitschrift*
CBQ	*Catholic Biblical Quarterly*
CNTC	Calvin's New Testament Commentaries
CO	W. Baur, E. Cuntiz, and E. Reuss, *Ioannis Calvini opera quae supereunt omnia,* ed.
Conybeare	W. J. Conybeare and J. S. Howson, *The Life and Epistles of St. Paul*
CJT	*Canadian Journal of Theology*
CSR	*Christian Scholars' Review*
CTM	*Concordia Theologial Monthly*
CTQ	*Concordia Theological Quarterly*
CTR	*Criswell Theological Review*
Did.	*Didache*
DNTT	*Dictionary of New Testament Theology*
DownRev	*Downside Review*
DSB	Daily Study Bible
EBC	Expositor's Bible Commentary
EGT	*The Expositor's Greek Testament*
ETC	English Translation and Commentary
ETL	*Ephemerides theologicae lovanienses*
EvT	*Evangelische Theologie*
EvQ	*Evangelical Quarterly*

ETR	*Etudes théologiques et religieuses*
ETS	Evangelical Theological Society
Exp	*Expositor*
ExpTim	*Expository Times*
FNT	*Filologia Neotestamentaria*
GAGNT	M. Zerwick and M. Grosvenor, *A Grammatical Analysis of the Greek New Testament*
GNBC	Good News Bible Commentary
GTJ	*Grace Theological Journal*
HBD	*Holman Bible Dictionary*
Her	Hermeneia
HNTC	Harper's New Testament Commentaries
HeyJ	*Heythrop Journal*
HTKNT	Herders theologischer Kommentar zum Neuen Testament
HTR	*Harvard Theological Review*
HUCA	*Hebrew Union College Annual*
IB	*The Interpreter's Bible*
IBS	*Irish Biblical Studies*
ICC	International Critical Commentary
IDB	*Interpreter's Dictionary of the Bible*
Int	*Interpretation*
INT	Interpretation: A Bible Commentary for Preaching and Teaching
ISBE	*International Standard Bible Encyclopedia, Revised*
JAAR	*Journal of the American Academy of Religion*
JANES	*Journal of Ancient Near Eastern Studies*
JAOS	*Journal of the American Oriental Society*
JBL	*Journal of Biblical Literature*
JES	*Journal of Ecumenical Studies*
JETS	*Journal of the Evangelical Theological Society*
JJS	*Journal of Jewish Studies*
JR	*Journal of Religion*
JRE	*Journal of Religious Ethics*
JRH	*Journal of Religious History*
JRS	*Journal of Roman Studies*
JSNT	*Journal for the Study of the New Testament*
JSOT	*Journal for the Study of the Old Testament*
JSS	*Journal of Semitic Studies*
JTS	*Journal of Theological Studies*
LouvSt	*Louvain Studies*
LS	Liddel and Scott
LTQ	*Lexington Theological Quarterly*
LW	Luther's Works
LXX	Septuagint
MCNT	Meyer's Commentary on the New Testament

MDB	*Mercer Dictionary of the Bible*
MNTC	Moffatt NT Commentary
MQR	*Mennonite Quarterly Review*
MT	Masoretic Text
NAC	New American Commentary
NBD	*New Bible Dictionary*
NCB	New Century Bible
NIC	New International Commentary
NPNF	Nicene and Post-Nicene Fathers
Neot	*Neotestamentica*
NovT	*Novum Testamentum*
NRT	*La nouvelle revue théologique*
NTS	*New Testament Studies*
NTD	Das Neue Testament Deutsch
NTI	*New Testament Introduction*, D. Guthrie
NTM	*The New Testament Message*
NTS	*New Testament Studies*
PC	Proclamation Commentaries
PEQ	*Palestine Exploration Quarterly*
PRS	*Perspectives in Religious Studies*
PSB	*Princeton Seminary Bulletin*
RB	*Revue biblique*
RelSRev	*Religious Studies Review*
RevExp	*Review and Expositor*
RevQ	*Revue de Qumran*
RevThom	*Revue thomiste*
RHPR	*Revue d'histoire et de philosophie religieuses*
RSPT	*Revue des sciences philosophiques et théologiques*
RSR	*Recherches de science religieuse*
RTP	*Revue de théologie et de philosophie*
RTR	*Reformed Theological Review*
SBLMS	Society of Biblical Literature Monograph Series
SEAJT	*Southeast Asia Journal of Theology*
SPCK	Society for the Promotion of Christian Knowledge
SJT	*Scottish Journal of Theology*
SNTU	*Studien zum Neuen Testament und seiner Umwelt*
ST	*Studia theologica*
SWJT	*Southwestern Journal of Theology*
T.Ash	*Testament of Asher*
TB	*Tyndale Bulletin*
TBC	Torch Bible Commentaries
TBT	*The Bible Today*
TDNT	G. Kittel and G. Friedrich, eds., *Theological Dictionary of the New Testament*
Theol	*Theology*

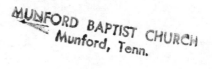

Contents

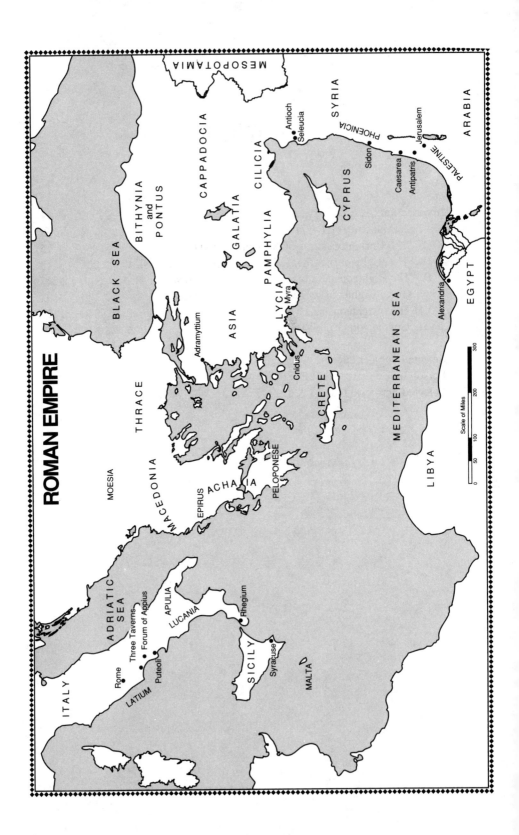

ROMAN EMPIRE

MESOPOTAMIA

SYRIA

ARABIA

Antioch
Seleucia

PHOENICIA

Jerusalem

PALESTINE

Sidon

Caesarea
Antipatris

CAPPADOCIA

CILICIA

CYPRUS

BITHYNIA
and
PONTUS

EGYPT

BLACK SEA

GALATIA

PAMPHYLIA

ASIA

LYCIA
Myra

Adramyttium

Cnidus

Alexandria

THRACE

CRETE

MEDITERRANEAN SEA

MOESIA

MACEDONIA

ACHAIA

PELOPONESE

LIBYA

EPIRUS

ADRIATIC
SEA

ITALY

Three Taverns
Forum of Appius

APULIA

LUCANIA

Rhegium

Rome

Puteoli

LATIUM

SICILY

Syracuse

MALTA

Scale of Miles

0   50 100   200   300

Romans

────────── **INTRODUCTION** ──────────

1. Authorship

As was the common practice in ancient letter writing, Romans opens with a statement identifying the author. The letter says that it was written by "Paul, a servant of Christ Jesus, called to be an apostle and set apart for the gospel of God" (1:1). It is rarely questioned today that the

Paul who wrote the Epistle to the Romans was the apostle of that name whose conversion to Christ is told in Acts 9 and whose missionary activities dominate the latter half of that book. The style and language of the letter is consistent with that of Galatians and 1 and 2 Corinthians, the other unquestioned letters of the apostle.

The only legitimate question about authorship relates to the role of Tertius, who in 16:22 writes, "I Tertius, who wrote down this letter, greet you in the Lord." We know that at that time in history an amanuensis, that is, one hired to write from dictation, could serve at several levels. In some cases he would receive dictation and write it in down immediately in longhand. At other times he might use a form of shorthand (tachygraphy) to take down a letter and then later write it out in longhand. In some cases an amanuensis would simply get the gist of what a person wanted to say and then be left on his own to formulate the ideas into a letter. Unless Tertius was the amanuensis for all of Paul's unquestioned letters, it would be hard to agree to this third option. The stylistic and semantic similarities with Paul's other letters calls for a tighter control on what was actually written down. Beyond that, it is highly questionable that Paul would have turned over such an important task to another. A. M. Hunter is undoubtedly right, "No one outside Bedlam seriously doubts that Romans was written by St. Paul."[1]

2. Destination

In the opening chapter Paul indicated that he was writing his letter to believers "in Rome" (1:7). That would seem to put the issue of destination beyond question except that several manuscripts omit *en Rōmē*. This omission has led some scholars to conjecture that the letter was originally intended to go elsewhere. The most reasonable suggestion of those who hold to an alternate destination is that it was a circular letter intended for a number of congregations throughout the Christian world. Each letter would be accompanied by a special section for the church to which it was written. For example, T. W. Manson thought that the manuscript $\mathfrak{P}^{46}$ (which places the doxology of 16:25–27 at the close of chap. 15) was the letter sent to Rome while at the same time another copy without "in Rome" and including chap. 16 went to Ephesus.[2]

---

[1] A. M. Hunter, *The Epistle to the Romans,* TBC (London: SCM, 1955), 12.
[2] T. W. Manson, *Studies in the Gospels and Epistles* (Philadelphia: Westminster, 1982), 225–41.

Although there are legitimate literary questions regarding the last two chapters of Romans, internal evidence strongly supports the view that Paul was writing specifically to Christian converts in the capital city of Rome. Since he intended to go there in the near future (Rom 15:23–24; cf. Acts 19:21), and especially in view of the role he was hoping the Romans would play in his missionary activities to the West, it is reasonable that he would write ahead of time.

That Paul had nothing to do with the founding of the church at Rome is quite certain. In 1:13 he said that he had often planned to visit them but up until that time had been prevented from coming to them. Likewise there is no evidence that Peter had been in Rome prior to his martyrdom several years later. Only later tradition refers to Peter as the founder and first bishop of the Roman church. If Peter had founded the church at Rome, certainly Paul would have referred to him in some way in his letter. Assuming that chap. 16 belongs to the original letter, Paul's "failure" to include Peter among those greeted is unexplainable if in fact Peter served as a bishop in the Roman church at that time. Paul's determination not to build on someone else's foundation (15:20) also makes it highly unlikely that Peter had anything to do with the founding of the church at Rome.[3]

Some have suggested that Christianity was carried to Rome by Jewish visitors present in Jerusalem at Pentecost (Acts 2:10,14). The assumption is that many of them were converted and were among the three thousand who were baptized that day (Acts 2:41). It is generally acknowledged that the Jews in Rome had a close connection with those in Jerusalem. For example, Marcus Julius Agrippa (the "Herod" of Acts 12) had lived in the imperial court in Rome for the first twelve or so years of his life. Although some of the "visitors from Rome" may well have been among those converted at Pentecost, the text does not specifically say so.

Another suggestion is that Rome was evangelized by the missionary outreach of Antioch, but there is no evidence of this. A more reasonable suggestion is that the church at Rome was founded by believers, both Jewish and Gentile, who for a variety of reasons traveled back and forth to the capital city or who had taken up residence there.

---

[3] It probably is misleading to speak of the church (sing.) at Rome because the word εκκλησία is never used in Romans with reference to the entire Christian community. There is reason to believe that the "church" at Rome consisted of a number of decentralized house-churches.

By whatever means the Christian faith was brought to Rome, it clearly took root and grew within the Jewish community. It has been estimated that by the first century B.C. there were some fifty thousand Jews in Rome grouped in several synagogues. From Suetonius (private secretary to the emperor Hadrian) we learn that in A.D. 49[4] Claudius had "expelled from Rome Jews who were making constant disturbances at the instigation of Chrestus" (*Life of Claudius* 25.2). This was the edict that caused Aquila and Priscilla to leave Rome and go to Corinth (Acts 18:2). Although Chrestus could have been the name of some Jewish agitator, it is more likely a corruption of the Greek *Christos* ("Christ"). Apparently there were serious disputes in the Jewish community over the claim of some who had converted to the Christian faith. Their belief that Jesus was *Christos,* the Messiah, had led to a mass expulsion of the Jewish population from Rome. From that point forward the church became predominantly Gentile. Part of Romans is directed to a Jewish minority (e.g., 2:17–24), but specific references and the overall tone of the letter argue a Gentile majority (see 9:3–5; 11:13–32).

D. G. Miller finds three general groups in the church at Rome: the legalists, who thought that righteousness was a human achievement; the libertines, who abandoned the law even as a guide for the response of faith; and the spiritualists, whose pride destroyed the true sense of community and made them indifferent to the demands of civic order.[5] From the greetings in 16:3–16 we may garner some interesting details about the membership in the church at Rome. For example, some had been Christians longer than Paul (v. 7), others had houses large enough to serve as meeting places (v. 5), and although many undoubtedly were slaves, some probably came from the higher echelons of society. One example would be Pomponia Graecina, the wife of the Roman general who commanded the British expedition in A.D. 43, who was tried and acquitted on the charge of having embraced a "foreign superstition," most likely Christianity.

3. Date and Place of Origin

In Romans 15 Paul described his current situation and laid out his plans for the future. He had completed his work in the eastern regions (v. 23), "from Jerusalem all the way around to Illyricum" (v. 19). Since

---

[4] The date comes from a fifth-century Christian historian by the name of Orosius.
[5] *ISBE* 4.225.

it had always been his ambition "to preach the gospel where Christ was not known" (v. 20), he planned to go west to Spain and visit the church in Rome as he passed through (v. 24). There he would enjoy their company and receive from them some help for his journey. First, however, he had the responsibility of taking the contribution from the churches in Macedonia and Achaia to the poor saints in Jerusalem (vv. 25–26). When that task was over, he would go to Spain and visit there on the way (v. 28).

Broad agreement exists that this corresponds to the period near the close of Paul's third missionary journey. We know that Paul had ministered in Ephesus for two to three years (Acts 19:8,10). From there he traveled through Macedonia and Achaia (19:21; 20:1), arriving in Greece, "where he stayed three months" (20:3). It was at this time that Paul wrote his letter to the Romans.

Also quite certain is that Paul's time in Greece was spent either at Corinth or its port city of Cenchrea. In a letter to the church at Corinth written toward the end of his stay in Ephesus (and less than a year before; cf. 1 Cor 16:8), Paul wrote: "After I go through Macedonia, I will come to you. . . . Perhaps I will stay with you awhile, or even spend the winter" (1 Cor 16:5–6). Also supporting Corinth as the place of origin for Paul's letter to the church in Rome are several indications in the greetings of chap. 16. In v. 23 Paul passed along the greetings of Gaius, his host. This could well have been the Gaius Paul baptized in Corinth (1 Cor 1:14). Erastus, whom Paul called the "city's director of public works" (Rom 16:24), probably is the same Erastus mentioned in a Corinthian inscription as "procurator of public buildings." The identity is strengthened by Paul's statement in 2 Timothy that "Erastus stayed in Corinth" (2 Tim 4:20). And Phoebe, whom Paul commended to the church at Rome, is called "a servant of the church in Cenchrea" (Rom 16:1). These considerations have led the vast majority of scholars to accept Corinth as the city from which Paul wrote to the believers in Rome.

When it comes to the question of a specific date for the writing of Romans, there is less certainty. We know that it falls between the time when Gallio was proconsul at Corinth (Acts 18:12,14,17) and the replacement of Felix by Festus as procurator in Palestine (24:27). The first date is established by an inscription at Delphi that shows that Gallio became proconsul in A.D. 51 or 52. Since senatorial proconsuls held office for one or two years and because we do not know whether the inscription was made early or late in his term of office, the best we can judge is that he served sometime during the period of A.D. 50–54. Since a period of some four years separates the two visits to Corinth (18:1–18; 20:3), Romans apparently was written between A.D. 54 and 58. Numismatic evidence indicates that Felix became procurator of Judea in A.D. 59, at which time Paul was in custody in Caesarea (23:33–27:2). Allowing time for the journey from Corinth to Jerusalem and the subsequent activity prior to his appearance before Festus, a date somewhere around A.D. 56 would be most likely for the composition of Romans.[6]

4. Occasion and Purpose

When Paul wrote to the church at Rome, he had completed his evangelism of Asia Minor and the Aegean world. It was now time to look further west to regions where Christ was not known (Rom 15:20). Spain was the Roman province farthest west and was an important center of Roman civilization.[7] So it was to Rome that Paul decided to go. That had been his intention for some time, but always before something had hindered him from carrying through his plan (Rom 15:22). One thing remained—taking the contribution given by believers in Macedonia and Achaia to the needy at Jerusalem. Then it was off to Spain with a stop in Rome.

Paul wrote Romans by way of preparation for his projected visit there in the capital city. He was hopeful that Rome would serve as a base for his mission to Spain somewhat as Syrian Antioch had for his first two missionary journeys. It also would have been helpful for them to provide him material support as well ("assist me on my journey there," Rom 15:24). Beyond that, it is true that Paul's opponents had misrepresented his message and vilified his character (Acts 15:1–2; 2 Cor 10:10; Gal 4:17). It was important that he lay before the church at

---

[6] D. Guthrie says that "sometime between A.D. 57 and 59 would fit all the known data" (*IDB* 3.1348); C. E. B. Cranfield holds that the book was "most probably written either during the period comprising the last days of 55 and the early weeks of 56 or during that of the last days of 56 and the early weeks of 57" (*The Epistle to the Romans,* 2 vols., ICC [Edinburgh: T & T Clark, 1975], 1:16); and C. H. Dodd writes that "the most probable date for the Epistle to the Romans is in the first quarter of A.D. 59, but a year or two earlier is possible" (*The Epistle of Paul to the Romans,* MNTC [London: Hodder & Stoughton, 1932], xxvi).

[7] Barclay speaks of Spain as producing at that time "a scintillating galaxy of greatness"—Marital, the master of the epigram; Lucan, the epic poet; Quintilian, the master of Roman oratory; Seneca, the greatest of the Roman Stoic philosophers; and others of like calibre (W. Barclay, *The Letter to the Romans,* rev. ed., DSB [Philadelphia: Westminster, 1978], 4).

Rome the message that he proclaimed. They needed to have a systematic statement of the gospel as Paul understood it[8] as well as his position on the relationship between the Gentiles and the Jewish community. Paul's emphasis on faith apart from the works of the law seemed to degrade God's ancient people Israel, and this concern needed careful qualification. His aim in chaps. 9–11 was to reconcile the righteousness of God with what appeared to be his rejection of Israel, his ancient people, an issue of great importance to Jewish Christians everywhere. These concerns[9] explain the general nature of the letter. Although written to a specific church, it would prove to serve the broad interests of the Christian faith everywhere.

Immediately after Paul presented his plans to go to Spain following his mission of taking the collection for the poor to Jerusalem, he requested prayer for his safety, specifically that he might "be rescued from the unbelievers in Judea" (Rom 15:30–31). At Miletus he shared with the Ephesian elders his concern about going to Jerusalem. He told them, "In every city the Holy Spirit warns me that prison and hardships are facing me" (Acts 20:23). Perhaps he would not come through the Jerusalem trip alive. Then would it not have been appropriate for him to write down a relatively comprehensive statement of the gospel he proclaimed so that those in Rome might carry out his plan to evangelize Spain?[10]

5. The Original Form of Romans

Although every extant Greek manuscript of Romans contains the full text (chaps. 1–16), it appears that in the second and third centuries the

---

[8] Melanchthon's oft-quoted view that Romans is "a summary of all Christian doctrine" overlooks the fact that the apostle said little or nothing about such important subjects as the nature of the church, the Lord's Supper, and the second advent.

[9] J. D. G. Dunn stresses that Paul had several purposes in writing. He categorizes them as (1) a missionary purpose—to bring in "the full number of the Gentiles," (2) an apologetic purpose—to gain acceptance for the gospel in the capital of the empire, and (3) a pastoral purpose—to introduce Phoebe and name individuals for her to call on (*Romans,* 2 vols., WBC [Dallas: Word, 1988], 1:lv–lvii).

[10] For an excellent survey of why Paul wrote Romans, see J. A. Fitzmyer's chapter "Occasion and Purpose," in *Romans,* AB (New York: Doubleday, 1993), 68–84. Extended discussions on the subject may be found in K. P. Donfried, *The Romans Debate,* rev. ed. (Peabody: Hendrickson, 1991); specifically, G. Bornkamm, "The Letter to the Romans as Paul's Last Will and Testament" (pp. 16–28); G. Klein, "Paul's Purpose in Writing the Epistle to the Romans" (pp. 29–43); A. J. M. Wedderburn, "Purpose and Occasion of Romans Again" (pp. 195–202); and P. Stuhlmacher, "The Purpose of Romans" (pp. 231–42).

letter also circulated in a shorter form that lacked the two final chapters (except for the doxology in 16:25–27). The question is whether Paul wrote a short version as a kind of circular letter he later expanded for Rome by adding chaps. 15 and 16 or whether he wrote the long version as we know it and then he or someone else for reasons not clear dropped the two final chapters. The problem is complicated by several other considerations: the location of the doxology, the omission of "in Rome" at 1:7,15 in certain manuscripts, and the question of the "grace" in 16:20,24.

Although the doxology is traditionally printed at the close of chap. 16, a number of manuscripts place it at the end of chap. 14. In 𝔓⁴⁶ (the oldest text of Romans, ca. A.D. 200) it is at the end of chap. 15. A few manuscripts place it at the end of both chaps. 14 and 15, and two or three omit it altogether (however G leaves a space for it at the end of chap. 14). A further complication is the omission of *en Rōmē* in 1:7 and *tois en Rōmē* in 1:15 in certain manuscripts. Only two verses in the epistle specifically indicate the destination of the letter. The omission is found in the manuscript tradition that closes the letter at 14:23. Another consideration is the "grace" that in the Byzantine text occurs at both 16:20 and 16:24. In some manuscripts it is omitted in v. 20 (where it forms part of the verse) and in others in v. 24 (where it comprises the entire verse). A few manuscripts place v. 24 after v. 27.

Our task is to work through these various considerations and arrive at the most reasonable solution to the question of the original form of Romans. Since the question has been dealt with at such length in numerous more technical discussions, we will be content to summarize the arguments with no attempt to include every minor issue that can be raised.

The short form is thought to have been written by Paul for circulation among churches he had not founded. It did not include the references to Rome in 1:7,15. At a later date Paul adapted it for the church in Rome by adding the material found in chaps. 15–16. While all extant manuscripts include chaps. 15–16, the evidence is fairly strong that the shorter form did exist. (1) Early Latin chapter headings designate 14:22–23 as chap. 50 followed by the doxology as chap. 51. Our chaps. 15 and 16 (up to the doxology at vv. 25–26) are not represented. (2) In his commentary on Romans, Origen mentioned that Marcion dropped not only the doxology but everything after chap. 14. (3) Irenaeus, Cyprian, and Tertullian never quote from chaps. 15 and 16. Such evidence argues the possibility of a fourteen-chapter form of Romans that with or without the doxology was in circulation in the early centuries of the Christian era.

The shorter recension, however, does have problems. (1) Romans 14:23 is a most unlikely ending for a letter by Paul. Even when a doxology is added, it fails to bring the argument of chap. 14 to a satisfactory conclusion. (2) Romans 1:8–13 contains statements so personal and direct as to be highly unlikely in a general letter to a number of churches. (3) Paul's discussion of the weak and the strong runs right on into chap. 15 and ends with v. 6.

How then did the shorter version originate? (1) It is very improbable that Paul would have mutilated his own work, although some think he may have shortened it to make a more general copy available for a wider audience. (2) It could have been the work of Marcion, the second-century eccentric, who dropped the two final chapters because of the many Old Testament quotations used there. The omission of "in Rome" in most of the shorter recensions would then be Marcion's rebuttal to the church at Rome, who considered his views unacceptable. (3) The end of a papyrus roll is easily damaged, and the final two chapters could have been torn off or mutilated by accident.

A variation of the shorter-version theory is that Paul wrote chaps. 1–15 to Rome but at a later time sent a copy of it to Ephesus along with chap. 16, a letter of commendation for Phoebe. This relatively popular view is given credence by the Chester Beatty Papyrus ($\mathfrak{P}^{46}$), an important manuscript discovered in this century. It includes chap. 16, but it places the doxology after 15:33. The implication is that there were in circulation at that time manuscripts that ended with chap. 15. Since there are no extant manuscripts that end at that point, the theory must remain speculative.

The question of the nature and destination of chap. 16 has been discussed at great lengths. Many arguments have been raised in support of an Ephesian rather than Roman destination. (1) Paul would not have been able to send so many greetings to a church he had never visited. Since his ministry in Ephesus was longer than in any other city, it is more likely that is where he would have so many friends. (2) In 16:3–5 Paul spoke of the church that met in the house of Priscilla and Aquila. The last we heard of them they were living in Ephesus, and a church was meeting "at their house" (1 Cor 16:19). We also know from Acts 18 that en route from Corinth to Syria, Paul left them in Ephesus (vv. 18–19) and that later they invited Apollos "to their home" to explain to him the way of God more adequately (v. 26). Later, when writing to Timothy in Ephesus (cf. 1 Tim 1:3), Paul asked him to greet Priscilla and

Aquila (2 Tim 4:19). Unless they had homes in both Rome and Ephesus, these references support an Ephesian destination for Romans 16. (3) Paul referred to Epaenetus in 16:5 as "the first convert to Christ in the province of Asia," which seems to favor Ephesus since it is the capital of that Roman province. (4) The harsh tone of 16:17–18 is more in keeping with the situation in Ephesus (cf. Acts 20:28–30).

Over against these arguments may be raised a series of counterarguments. (1) Chapter 16 by itself would be a strange letter, to say the least. The suggestion that it is a mere fragment of a larger letter to Ephesus is strictly conjecture. (2) For Paul to have sent such a long list of greetings to friends in a church he knew would have been out of character for the apostle. In his other letters he did not send individual greetings (except in Colossians, a church to which he was a stranger). On the other hand, Paul had reason to establish as many individual contacts as possible in the church in Rome. (3) The statement that "all the churches of Christ send greetings" (16:16b) is more natural if addressed to Rome than to Ephesus. Writing to the church in the prestigious capital of the Roman Empire, it would have been highly appropriate to send greetings from all the Christian congregations where Paul had ministered. (4) We do not actually know enough about Priscilla and Aquila to disallow their having a home in Rome in between their two journeys east. In that they were expelled from Rome by the edict of Claudius (Acts 18:2), it is not impossible that they left a home there when they settled in Ephesus. (5) It is far easier to explain how chap. 16 could be omitted in some copies sent at a later time to other congregations than to explain how it could have originated elsewhere and attached to a shorter form of Romans. (6) A number of names in the list inferentially connect it with Rome (Rufus, the households of Aristobulus and Narcissus, Ampliatus, and Nereus).[11]

We conclude that chap. 16 was an original part of Paul's letter to the church at Rome and that the several related problems are explained most convincingly from this point of view.

6. A Thematic Overview of Romans

Paul wrote his letter to the church at Rome while he was in Corinth (or perhaps the nearby seaport of Cenchrea) toward the end of his third missionary journey. We know from the opening paragraphs of his letter

---

[11] See Dodd, *Romans,* xxii–xxiii, for an expansion of this point.

that he was very desirous of going to Rome and spending some time with the Christians there. He wrote that he longed to see them so that they might be "mutually encouraged by each other's faith" (1:12). He also was "eager to preach" the gospel to those who lived in the capital city (1:15). But Paul had another agenda in mind as well. Toward the close of the letter he wrote about his plan to visit them on his way to Spain (15:28). In addition to enjoying their company, he hoped they would assist him on his journey. As he looked forward to evangelizing Spain, he trusted that Rome would be for him in the west what Antioch had been in the east.

From previous experience Paul knew that his enemies were skilled in twisting his message. Galatians is proof of that. So important were his plans for taking the gospel to the far reaches of the western empire that he could not afford to have his message jeopardized in the very place that he intended to use as a base of operations. So he wrote a rather full and complete presentation of the message he had been preaching. The result is the Book of Romans—a magnificent presentation of the gospel, the good news that God has provided a righteousness based not on what we can do for ourselves but on what God has already done for us in sending his Son as a sacrifice for sin. Paul's purpose was to set forth in a systematic fashion the doctrine of justification by faith and its implications for Christian living. The gospel had to be kept free from legalism; equally important was that it did not fall into the opposite error of antinomianism.

It is not our intention in this section to treat every topic touched on by the apostle. Nor is it our plan to provide the reader with a condensed biblical theology of Romans. The topics to be discussed have been selected on the basis of the emphasis Paul gave to each as he wrote to the church in Rome. The sequence has been determined by the order in which the apostle himself treated each subject as he wrote about how people are set right with God and what that implies about a whole series of issues related to faith and conduct.[12] Each of the topics plays an important role in Paul's overall understanding of God's redemptive self-revelation. Each is discussed primarily in terms of the context in which it is first found.[13] For textual matters related to the various themes and

---

[12] The material in this section draws heavily upon my earlier monograph, *Romans: Themes from Romans* (Ventura: Regal, 1981).

[13] An exception to this is the discussion of Rom 1:16–18, which is found in the opening paragraph of the section on 3:21–26.

an understanding of their historical contexts, the reader will want to consult the commentary itself at the appropriate places.

(1) Natural Revelation (1:18–20)

The Bible never bothers to prove the existence of God; that is everywhere taken for granted. Anthropologists confess that they are unable to find a tribe of people anywhere in the world who do not worship some sort of divine being. Atheism is not a natural state. People find it next to impossible to accept the presence of design in the world without assuming the prior existence of a Designer. If there were no creator, the only other option would be to admit candidly that what is—that is, matter itself—has always been. But the very idea of the eternality of matter boggles the mind.

But what can we know about the Creator God? Are his actions, and beyond that his essential being, unknowable? Or has he revealed himself in some way? In Rom 1:19–20 Paul clearly stated that "what may be known about God is plain to them [i.e., to "men who suppress the truth," 1:18], because God has made it plain to them." God has not left the created order without the slightest idea of who he is. Obviously our knowledge is partial. Human beings in their finiteness could no more grasp all that God is than a child could understand the intricacies of the molecular theory. Such knowledge lies beyond human ken. But the fact that people cannot know everything about God does not imply that they cannot know anything or that what they do know is necessarily distorted and unreliable. What natural man can know about God "lies plain before their eyes" (1:19, NEB).

To guarantee the process God himself took the initiative. He is the one who has "made it plain to them." It was important to God that there be a moral basis for judgment. Had he not revealed himself, he could hardly hold his creation responsible for not knowing who he is or what he requires. God does not judge people for failing to respond to what they never had a chance to know. In the second chapter Paul taught that those who sin apart from the law will not be judged by the law (1:12). The demands of God are that people respond on the basis of the degree of knowledge and insight available to them in their own cultural and historical setting. Obviously Paul was not talking about some sort of universal salvation. He was stressing that people are judged in terms of the light they have received. However, all are responsible because all have been exposed to God's self-revelation in creation.

In Rom 1:20 Paul set forth two of God's "invisible qualities" that are clearly seen by all—his "eternal power and divine nature." By this Paul meant that the evidence of creation moves a person persuasively toward the conclusion that the Creator is a powerful being and that this power is not in any sense limited in time. Rational observation of the universe in which we live provides all the proof necessary that creation does not furnish the key to its own existence. What it does reveal is the existence of a power great enough to bring it into existence. Such a power cannot be impersonal. Design calls for intelligence, and intelligence speaks of personality. So the "power" is not some inanimate force but a personal being. It is God. Creation also reveals that the Creator belongs to a higher sphere of existence. Our imperfect concepts of justice, love, and wisdom demand someone who is perfectly just, perfectly loving, and perfectly wise. In the world that God created we see evidence of a perfect God. There is no rational option but to confess his deity and commit ourselves to obey the ethical implications that flow from that postulate.

Since God is by definition spirit (John 4:24), he must be "observed" in what he has made and what he has done. Elsewhere Paul spoke of God as "the King eternal, immortal, *invisible*" (1 Tim 1:17, italics added). It is Christ Jesus the Son who "has made him known" (John 1:18). He is the visible imprint of the nature of God (cf. Heb 1:3). As trees bent by the wind give evidence of an invisible force (i.e., the wind), so does nature bear the unmistakable signs of an invisible Creator. But this Creator was not satisfied with such a minimal revelation of himself, so in time he entered his own creation through the incarnation of his Son and explained to all who would listen exactly what he is like. It is not on the basis of this fuller knowledge, however, that God holds people responsible. People are "without excuse" because they reject the basic knowledge of God that is available to everyone (1:20).

(2) The Wrath of God (1:21–32)

In Rom 1:18–20 Paul clearly established the responsibility of all people everywhere to acknowledge the existence and basic character of God. There is no excuse for the rebellious who turn from the light of revelation. Their headlong pursuit into "godlessness and wickedness" (1:18) calls down upon them the wrath of God. The section that follows (1:21–32) describes in detail the reasons for and results of this wrath. It is not a pretty picture. It depicts in graphic detail the downward course of human conduct as God withdraws his presence and restraining influence. Obviously not everyone is as grossly sinful as the section portrays. Culture at times makes at least an outward difference. Social taboos sometimes prevent a society from degenerating as rapidly as it would in a totally nonrestrictive situation. The passage is, however, an accurate account of the human penchant for sin and willful rebellion. When people turn from God, the path leads inevitably downward into degeneracy.

Paul was not at all skittish when it came to discussing the wrath of God. In eight of the sixteen chapters in Romans he had something to say about it. Although many of these references speak of the wrath of God as an eschatological event, this first mention considers it as God's displeasure that is being worked out in the present against all those who "suppress the truth by their wickedness" (1:18–32).

Running throughout the passage is the constant reminder that all people have knowledge of God (1:21,25,28). But having knowledge does not necessarily mean acting accordingly. The basic problem of the human race is not ignorance of the truth but rebellion against the one who is the truth. From the very first, humans have been rebels. Adam and Eve chose to believe Satan's lie that God was withholding something from them by not allowing them to eat from the tree of the knowledge of good and evil (Gen 2:17). So our first parents rebelled, and the entire human race has suffered the effects of that rebellion.

The rebellion continues in that although people by nature know God, they neither glorify him as God nor give thanks to him (1:21). They exchange the glory of the immortal God for idols (1:23), the truth of God for a lie (1:25), and natural sexual relations for unnatural ones (1:26). As a result they incur the wrath of God. This wrath, however, is not some violent expression of divine displeasure but the rather quiet withdrawal of the divine presence. The ominous phrase "God gave them over" is three times repeated in vv. 24–28. Paul stated that God gave them over[14] to "sexual impurity" (v. 24), "shameful lusts" (v. 26), and a "depraved mind" (v. 28). His wrath is revealed in his decision to allow people to pursue what they think they want. Unfortunately we cannot get enough of what we really do not want. Although God is the father of prodigal children and waits with forgiveness for the return of the wayward, he does not force people against their will to do what is ultimately in their best interests. Human freedom carries with it an awesome

---

[14] The *EGNT* takes παρέδωκεν in these three verses in the sense of "to abandon" (3.20).

responsibility. To be free means to be able to determine one's own destiny. God has never bullied a person into accepting his love.

But what happens if a person refuses to believe? Then a process of hardening sets in that gradually develops a resistance to divine favor from which the rebel cannot escape. In Hosea's charge against Israel the prophet said, "Ephraim is joined to idols; leave him alone!" (Hos 4:17). People become hopelessly entrapped by their own decisions. They forge their own chains. By repeatedly deciding to disregard truth, they determine their own fate. From a human perspective it is the normal result of continuing rebellion against God. Yet it is more than the inevitable process of cause and effect. God actively decides to withdraw. His wrath is seen in his reluctant willingness to allow people to reap the just rewards of their folly.

The passage under consideration condemns a number of vices that call down the wrath of God—among them the failure to glorify God (Rom 1:21), thanklessness (v. 21), intellectual pride (v. 22), idolatry (vv. 23,25), and lack of integrity (v. 25). The one receiving the greatest attention, however, is sexual impurity (vv. 4–27). *The Living Bible* translates v. 24, "So God let them go ahead into every sort of sex sin, and do whatever they wanted." Paul's emphasis on sexual sin makes clear that in that day (and certainly in ours) sexual promiscuity was a major factor in the moral degeneration of society. Homosexuality is singled out as the prime example of "disgraceful passions" (Phillips). Paul wrote that it is degrading (v. 24), it is contrary to nature (v. 26), it results from an inflamed and indecent lust (v. 27),[15] and it involves a penalty (v. 27). At the moment Paul was not speaking of final judgment but the natural penalty that accompanies the flouting of God's moral requirements. The wrath of God is at work in the present sinful world.

On the other hand, the wrath of God as an eschatological reality is strongly emphasized throughout the Book of Romans. In 2:5 Paul spoke of the stubborn and unrepentant "storing up wrath" against themselves for "the day of God's wrath" when God's righteous judgment will be revealed. A few verses later Paul said that for the self-seeking who reject the truth and follow evil "there will be wrath and anger" (2:8). They are "objects of [God's] wrath—prepared for destruction" (9:22). Those who are right with God, however, will be "saved from God's wrath" through the redemptive work of Christ (5:9). They are not to take revenge on oth-

---

[15] Montgomery's translation speaks of those who are "ablaze with passion for one another."

ers but "leave room for God's wrath"—he will repay (12:19).

The idea of divine wrath is distasteful to some. It seems to assign to God an emotion that runs contrary to what we know of him as a God of love. The problem here stems from a misunderstanding of the anthropomorphic nature of all language used in reference to God. For example, God is a "jealous God" (Exod 20:5; Deut 4:24; etc.), but no informed reader understands that to mean that he is caught up in a frenzy of resentment toward some supposed rival. God's "wrath" is his attitude of permanent opposition to all that is contrary to his holy and just nature. Without wrath he could not be holy. By definition virtue denounces its moral antithesis. Righteousness must of necessity oppose all that stands over against it. If God could compromise with wickedness, he would not be God. His wrath is proof of his unyielding commitment to holiness. Were he incapable of wrath, his love would be little more than sentimentality.

Dodd is most certainly wrong when he writes that Paul "retains the concept of 'the Wrath of God' [which Dodd claims to be absent from the teaching of Jesus] . . . not to describe the attitude of God to man, but to describe an inevitable process of cause and effect in a moral universe."[16] God's wrath is personal and active. It stems from the reality of the nature of God as a holy being. But the personal nature of God's wrath does not mean that he is vindictive or cruel. Such an interpretation reads into God's character qualities that unfortunately are all too true of much of human wrath.

Strange as it may seem to the unregenerate mind, love and wrath are not mutually exclusive in God. He does not display love in certain situations and wrath in others. Rather, when his love is resisted by ungodliness, it expresses itself as wrath. God is not victimized by conflicting emotions. His nature is unchanging. His love would not be love if it were able to accommodate itself to that which violates its very essence. The Book of Revelation portrays most vividly the final outpouring of the wrath of God on Satan and his demons. Those who find their place with those nefarious beings will share in the eschatological wrath of a holy God (Rev 14:9–10).

(3) A Righteousness from God (3:21–26)

In the first chapter of Romans, Paul established the pivotal importance of the gospel. He was not ashamed of the gospel because it is the

---

[16] Dodd, *Romans*, 23.

instrument of God's power leading to the salvation of all who believe
(1:16). But on what basis can the gospel accomplish this remarkable
feat? It is because the gospel reveals "a righteousness *that comes from
God*" (Weymouth; italics added). From the dawn of history people have
struggled in many different ways somehow to merit acceptance by God.
Later (in Rom 10:3) Paul acknowledged that his own people tried but
failed to establish their own righteousness. But to stand before God as
righteous cannot be achieved by meritorious activity. Righteousness is a
gift from God. It is a gift given by him to those who live by faith. As the
prophet Habakkuk declared, "The righteous will live by faith" (Hab
2:4).

But what exactly is intended by the expression "a righteousness from
God?" Is it an activity of God or a status of humans resulting from that
activity? C. E. B. Cranfield provides an excellent summary of the various aspects of the question.[17] He argues that justification is the bestowal
of a righteous status and does not in itself involve any reference to
moral transformation. Justification is followed by sanctification, but the
latter is not an integral part of the former. He concludes that "the righteousness of God" refers to humans' righteous status, which results
from God's redemptive action rather than to that action itself. This is
what the gospel reveals—that God has provided a right standing for
people that has nothing to do with their ethical achievements or religious activity. The righteousness of God is a right standing that God
bestows upon people of faith.

A tremendous amount of theology is compressed into the six verses
of Rom 3:21–26. In these verses Paul laid the foundation for his theology. Everything else flows from this theological center. The two previous verses (3:19–20) sum up an extended section (that began with 1:18)
on the hopeless condition of people apart from God. Paul's conclusion
was that "no one will be declared righteous in [God's] sight by observing the law." People of every nation have always tried to gain favor
with their gods by doing what they believed would please them. Hindus
have prayer wheels, and Muslims bow down five times daily toward
Mecca. Demon worshipers cut themselves in a frenzy of religious
excitement, and Christians all too often count on regular attendance at
church and deeds of kindness to their neighbors. According to the vast

---

[17] Cranfield, *Romans*, 1:91–99. On p. 98 Cranfield concludes that "we regard the interpretation which takes θεοῦ as a genitive of origin and δικαιοσύνη as referring to the righteous status which is given by God as being much more probable."

majority of people who inhabit the globe, righteousness is something we must earn.

Not so, said Paul. It cannot be earned; it can only be received. No one will ever stand before God on the basis of what the person has done. The righteousness that comes from God is "apart from the law." That is, it has nothing to do with our moral earnestness or religious fervor. It is absolutely unearned. It comes as a gift, and a gift is not a gift if it can be earned. That is why God's way of setting people right with him had to be revealed (1:17). It is so radically opposed to our normal way of thinking that it would never have entered the human mind. The gospel is the "good news" that no matter how helplessly mired in our own self-centeredness we are, there is a way to gain a right standing before God. The gospel is for those who have come to the end of themselves and, laying aside their pride, receive God's gracious gift by faith.[18]

In vv. 24–25 Paul provided some profound insights into the redemptive work of God. His metaphors were taken from the practice of law (acquittal of the guilty), the custom of buying slaves (redemption), and the ritual practices of sacrifice (atonement). First, to be "justified" (v. 24) means to be "acquitted," to be "given a right standing." Justification frees guilty people from paying the just penalty for their sins. It declares them totally exonerated. All charges are dropped. When God decided to free us from the guilt of our sin, he devised a plan whereby he could justify us and still remain a moral being. Christ died for our sin, and the value of that death becomes effective for us the moment we accept him by faith. Our only option is to accept or reject. There is no other way (cf. John 14:6).

One would think that the sinner would love to be forgiven at no cost. Unfortunately that is not the case. After all, sinners have their pride. They desperately want to claim some role in their own redemption. Unacceptable, says God. Sin is a quicksand that increases its hold the more one struggles. Why is God so insistent on doing it all? Because in heaven all glory and honor and praise belong to him. There will be no swapping of stories about how we helped him out.

Second, justification is ours "through the redemption that came by Christ Jesus" (3:24). The basic meaning of the Greek word *apolutrōsis* is "freed by ransom" or "redemption" (of prisoners or slaves).[19] "To redeem" means "to buy back." "You are not your own," said Paul; "you

---

[18] The theme of faith will be treated more fully in the following section.
[19] *EDNT* 1.138; cf. *TDNT,* abr., 543–44.

were bought at a price" (1 Cor 6:19–20). To be redeemed means to have
been freed from the marketplace of sin by the payment of a ransom.
That price was paid by the one who came not to be served but "to give
his life as a ransom for many" (Mark 10:45).

The third image is drawn from temple practice. "God presented him
as a sacrifice of atonement" (3:25). The term *hilastērion* (translated
"sacrifice of atonement") has been understood either in the sense of
"propitiation" (in which the righteous anger of God is satisfied) or
"expiation" (a covering of the sins of humans). In the Greek Old Testament it translates a Hebrew term for the lid of the ark (the mercy seat).
In Jewish practice the high priest entered the holy of holies once a year
and sprinkled blood above the ark for the atonement of Israel's sins.
Paul was saying that Jesus is that "mercy seat"—that meeting place
between God and humans where the great and final sacrifice has been
made. The death of Christ expiates or covers the sins of the human race
and at the same time propitiates the righteous anger of God against sin.
What we are called upon to believe is that by that death forgiveness of
sin is available through faith. It is by faith in this eternal act that those
who believe may gain a right standing before God.

(4) Abraham, Man of Faith (4:1–25)

Although Paul had written of the essential role of faith in justification, he knew the advantage of moving the discussion from the concep-
tual to the concrete. Truth becomes more clear and persuasive when it is
seen embodied in real life. So he turned to Abraham, that stalwart patriarch and exemplar of faith and obedience. He was, as James put it,
"God's friend" (Jas 2:23). So when Paul quoted Gen 15:6 ("Abraham
believed God, and it was credited to him as righteousness") in support
of his view that people are declared righteous on the basis of faith and
not works, his Jewish contemporaries saw him playing into their hands.
Did not the Lord also say that the promise to Abraham would be fulfilled "*because* Abraham obeyed me and kept my requirements" (Gen
26:5, italics added)? Does this not prove that Abraham was declared
righteous because of something he did?

Not so, said Paul. By quoting this basic proof text of Judaism he
showed that when properly interpreted it supports the exact opposite of
what they understood it to mean. Genesis 15:6 says nothing more than
that Abraham "believed God," and it was credited to him as righteousness. God had taken Abraham outside the tent and had shown him the

innumerable stars of heaven. Count them if you can, God challenged. "So shall your offspring be" (Gen 15:5). Then follows immediately the crucial statement that "Abram believed the Lord, and he credited it to him as righteousness." If something beyond believing were required, it would have been mentioned. Scripture is perfectly clear—it is not by doing but by believing that people are declared righteous.

It follows that since justification depends upon faith, Abraham must be the father of all who believe, whether Jew or Gentile. Paul's argument hinges on the fact that Abraham was circumcised after he had been declared righteous (cf. Gen 15:6 with Gen 17:11,24–26). In other words, he was still a Gentile when God pronounced him righteous. This was an unanswerable argument, a decisive blow against the cherished idea that God's blessings came automatically to the Jew and that circumcision was the essential proof that one belonged to the favored few. It jolted Paul's Jewish protagonists into the realization that the very first Jew, the venerable Abraham, father of the Jewish race, was indeed a Gentile when God pronounced him righteous. The Jewish point of view was that Gentiles could enter their company only if they would undergo circumcision, be baptized, and accept the ceremonial obligations of Judaism. Now the tables are turned. The Gentiles are accepted on the basis of faith alone, and if the Jews want to join the company of Abraham, they too will have to come by the way of faith. The promise that Abraham received was not contingent upon keeping the law. It was based on faith. Otherwise it would not be applicable to those outside the law. Since Abraham was "the father of many nations" (4:17), the promise of righteousness must rest upon faith so as to be available to all.

From a human standpoint the idea that Sarah, Abraham's wife, could bear him a child even though she was ninety years of age was preposterous. And Abraham himself was a hundred years old. When he was told the news, he fell down laughing (Gen 17:17). And Sarah thought, "After I am worn out and my master is old, will I now have this pleasure?" (Gen 18:12). Yet Abraham chose to believe "the impossible." He remained confident that God was able to do what he had promised. He believed that the promise of God was absolutely certain regardless of any apparent obstacle that life might place in the way.

Note, however, that Abraham's faith was not irrational. It was not a leap into the dark. Certainly it is not unreasonable to believe that the Creator of all is able to do something out of the ordinary. God is not a prisoner of the "laws of nature" he established. When God enters the equation, anything is possible. Abraham believed God, and this confidence was "credited to him as righteousness" (4:22). People of faith live with the complete assurance that what God has promised he will always accomplish. What he has promised in the gospel is that those who place their faith in what he did in and through Jesus Christ will be declared righteous.

(5) The Benefits of Believing (5:1–11)

The theme of chaps. 1–4 has been justification by faith. We enter now into a second stage in Paul's presentation. In the next four chapters Paul clarified the relationship between theology and conduct. At a later point (chaps. 12–15) he would deal more specifically with the practical implications of the new life in Christ, but first he must show the logical connection between justification and sanctification. He began by pointing out the benefits that accrue to those who believe.

Pride of place goes to "peace with God" (5:1). The first human who sinned and rebelled against God became an enemy of God. But Christ died for the ungodly, and reconciliation is now possible. When people turn back to God in faith, they find that the hostility has been removed. They find themselves at peace with God. In Scripture peace is not tranquillity but, as the Hebrew word *shalom* suggests, a state of well-being. To be at peace with God means that the hostility caused by sin has been removed.

Another benefit is access into his presence (5:2a). The image is that of being ushered into the presence of royalty. Remember that by basic temperament we are enemies of God. But he has paid the price for our rebellion and now freely offers us access. The door is open. The King is on his throne. The heralds have sounded their trumpets, and we may step into his presence to enjoy forever the inheritance of eternal joy.

Along with access comes hope (5:2b). In the culture of ancient Greece hope was little more than subjective projections about the future. It had no basis in reality. It might provide comfort in distress, but even then it was deceptive and uncertain.[20] Hope in the New Testament is radically different. It is not a fragile expectation about an uncertain future but the confident anticipation of that which will most certainly come to pass. It is not based on human expectation but on divine declaration. Christian hope is based squarely on the character of God himself. Paul said that our hope is that of "actually becoming all that God

---

[20] *TDNT*, abr., 229–30.

has had in mind for us to be" (TLB).

Paul mentioned other specific benefits (such as God's love, his death on our behalf, justification, and freedom from wrath), but they are all integral parts of the more inclusive benefit of reconciliation (5:10–11). "To be reconciled" means to be brought back into a friendly relationship with someone. It assumes a prior separation, a state of previous hostility. Reconciliation is a personal matter. For that reason it was not part of other first-century religions. Humans and their gods were not related in any intimate way. At the heart of the Christian faith lies a personal relationship. To believe in Christ is not to subscribe to a set of theological affirmations; it is to trust in a person—Jesus Christ, the Son of God, who died for my sins, rose again from the grave, and now lives in a real and personal way in my heart. By his redemptive death on the cross Christ opened the way for sinners to return to God's favor and friendship. Reconciliation is complete when we take this crucial step of faith. With hostility a thing of the past we may now live in a state of continuing fellowship with God our Father and Jesus Christ our elder brother.

(6) Does Justification by Faith Promote Sin? (6:1–25)

The argument of chap. 6 is structured around two basic questions that an opponent of the doctrine of justification by faith would be sure to raise. The questions are intended to point out the unacceptable implications that, from the detractor's point of view, must necessarily follow from the idea that a person can be considered righteous on the basis of faith alone.

Paul had just written that "where sin increased, grace increased all the more" (5:20). If that be so, would it not be reasonable to ask, "Shall we go on sinning so that grace may increase" (6:1)? Certainly the more God's grace increases the better. Paul's antagonists, however, weren't posing the question in order to learn the truth. Their purpose was to undermine his basic teaching by pointing out the ridiculous conclusions to which they felt it would lead.

Paul's immediate response was, "By no means!" (6:2). Choosing to sin is not a viable option for believers because those who have been justified by faith have "died to sin." To be baptized into Christ means to become one with him in his death. His death for sin becomes the believer's death to sin. Although Paul said the believer died to sin, he did not say that sin died to the believer. The seductive lure of sin remains operative throughout life. Devotional literature over the years bears ample evidence that even (perhaps especially) the great Christian saints struggled against the dark sides of their human natures. What Paul was saying is that in Christ we have received forgiveness for sin and are no longer at its mercy. It need not control our lives. We need to remember that we are dealing with an analogy, and all analogies break down when pressed beyond certain limits. Paul was pointing out a relationship between the actual death of Christ for sin and our "death" to sin as that power that has held us captive.

But our union with Christ in his death is only part of the story. As he was raised from the dead in a glorious manifestation of the power of God, so also do we share his resurrection in the sense that we are raised to an entirely new kind of life. This "life after death" has no obligations to sin. The "man we once were" (NEB) was put to death with Christ. The "man we are to be" has become a reality because as Christ was raised from the dead so also have we been raised to a new life in which the power of sin has been forever broken. Christianity is a new way of life. It is eminently practical. We are no longer to let sin control our lives but are to turn all our human faculties over to God as instruments of righteousness (6:12–13). In short, we need live no longer under the control of sin. Justification by faith does not lead to the absurd conclusion that we ought to sin as much as possible so that God's grace can be magnified.

Since believers are under grace rather than law, argues the detractor, does it not follow that it no longer matters whether or not we sin (6:15)? If sin is the transgression of law and believers are no longer under law, then what difference does it make if we decide to sin? Once again Paul's resounding response was, "By no means!" (6:15). The idea that freedom from the law provides a license to sin is central to the ancient heresy called antinomianism. To be under grace does not mean to be free from all obligation. What the believer is free from is the enslaving power of the law. The law itself is holy (7:12), but its role is to underscore and make specific the sinfulness of humans. It prepares the way for salvation by grace.

The idea of arbitrary freedom is a myth. Paul drew upon the general principle that all people are slaves to the one they obey. They have the option of serving either sin or righteousness, but they do not have the option of serving neither. What the believer has done is to change masters. Paul wrote, "You have been set free from sin and have become slaves to righteousness" (6:18). To be under grace means to be responsible to God, to live that kind of life that is consistent with all it means to have been freely forgiven and adopted into the family of God. Sin is no more an option for the believer than treason is for the patriot. Rather than sinning, Paul called on believers to "put themselves at the service of righteousness, with holiness as [their] goal" (6:19, Weymouth).

So both of the detractor's arguments fall by the way. It is spurious to think of sinning as a laudable practice because it magnifies the grace of God. Sin is not even an option because the believer by definition has died to sin. Nor does the fact that believers are no longer under law make sin a matter of no consequence. Salvation is not getting rid of all restraint but exchanging one master (sin) for another (God).

(7) Life in the Spirit (8:1–17)

The Greek word for "spirit" (*pneuma*) occurs twenty-one times in chap. 8, and in only two of the references does it clearly refer to anything but the Holy Spirit. Paul's concern in this chapter was not so much to provide his readers a theology of the Holy Spirit as to show how the Spirit is meant to function in the life of the believer. To get a good grasp on Paul's teaching on the Spirit is to have the secret of how to live victoriously while surrounded by sin and impaired by human frailty. It is the single most important lesson the Christian can learn.

Romans 8 begins with the joyous declaration, "Therefore, there is now no condemnation for those who are in Christ Jesus." The "therefore" refers back to 7:6 and continues its line of thought: "We have been released from the law . . . therefore, there is now no condemnation." Because we have been set free from the demands of the law, we are no longer under the condemnation it imposes. Since Christ has fulfilled the righteous demands of the law, those who are in Christ are no longer under its condemnation. In Christ we have been set free (cf. John 8:36).

It is helpful to distinguish between condemnation as an objective fact and condemnation as a sense of guilt because of past sins and the apparent inability to live the Christian life more successfully. Although believers are freed from objective condemnation (the necessary consequence of sin), many unfortunately continue to be plagued by psychological guilt. They find themselves in the Romans 7 predicament— wanting to do what is right but unable to do it; not wanting to do what is wrong but continuing to do it (7:18–19). The good news Paul declared is that not only has the condemnation of the law (objective guilt) been removed but also that all our subjective guilt has no further basis in reality. We need not go through life carrying the heavy burden of sorrow for sins that already have been forgiven.

In v. 2 Paul spoke of two different laws (or principles)—the "law of sin and death" and "the law of the Spirit of life." Phillips calls the first law "the old vicious circle of sin and death," and A. M. Hunter understands the second as "the law of the Spirit, that is, life in Christ Jesus."[21] Verses 3 and 4 explain how the law of the Spirit sets the believer free from the law of sin. The Mosaic law was unable to accomplish its goal because sinful human nature robbed it of its power. But what the law could not do, God did by sending his Son "in the likeness of sinful man to be a sin offering" (v. 3). That is, Christ took upon himself the flawed nature of humans with all its propensity to sin. Yet he lived a sinless life and thus fulfilled the demands of the law. His redemptive mission was brought to completion when he offered himself as a sacrifice for sin. The power of sin was broken by Christ's perfect obedience, and all who are in Christ share in that victory. We have been given the Spirit and empowered to live in such a way that the quality of life prescribed by the law is fulfilled in our daily experience. By walking in the Spirit we become what in fact we already are in Christ.

In the final analysis there are only two ways to live. People can follow the dictates of their fallen nature or obey the promptings of the Spirit. Apart from Christ people are controlled by their human nature. They think and act in a way that is consistent with what they are. But those who belong to Christ are controlled by a new nature. They are led by the Spirit and give their attention to those things that are spiritual. The problem for believers is that although the Spirit has taken up residence in their lives, the old nature is not removed. Thus a conflict is set up between the old person (what we were when dominated by our sinful nature) and the new person (what we are becoming as we live under the control of the Spirit). It is the complete dissimilarity between unredeemed human nature and the Spirit of God that accounts for the intensity of the struggle against sin.

What then is the answer to the disturbing fact that the believer is, as it were, morally schizophrenic? While both natures compete for control, they are not equally powerful. The old nature is deceitful. It tries to gain control through subterfuge and illicit appeal. The new nature draws its strength from the abiding presence of the Holy Spirit. Sin was defeated once for all on the cross. Consequently it may now be defeated on a daily basis in the life of the believer. Our responsibility is not to strug-

---

[21] A. M. Hunter, *The Epistle to the Romans,* TBC (London: SCM, 1955).

gle against sin (a recipe for disaster) but to call upon the Spirit to provide the victory. It is "by the Spirit" that we "put to death the misdeeds
of the body" (8:13). Our role is to say no to the intrigues of the old
nature and yes to the promise of the new. Freedom from the law of sin
and death comes when we live "according to the Spirit." The only real
question is whether or not we will allow him the opportunity to rid our
lives of sin.

The best definition of what it means to be a child of God is found in
v. 14, "For all who are led by the Spirit of God are children of God"
(NRSV). The verb is present tense and may be translated "are being
led." To be a child of God one must be continually led by God's Spirit.
Our status as God's children is expressed by the way we live. If we are
God's children, we will allow God's Spirit to lead us. If we continue to
resist the Spirit's leading, we show that we are not members of his family. A true child inevitably bears a family resemblance to the parent. The
person who continues in sin reveals a filial relationship to Satan; a life
of obedience to the Spirit is proof positive that we belong to God.

(8) The Triumph of Believing (8:18–39)

Paul would be the last person in the world to say that once you become
a Christian all your problems will be over. In his lifetime he had several
times been thrown into prison. He had been flogged and exposed to death.
He had been stoned, shipwrecked, and placed in all sorts of dangers (cf.
2 Cor 11:23–29). Paul certainly could attest that the life of faith is no bed
of roses. Yet, said Paul, all such suffering in the present time is not worthy
of comparison with the glory that awaits the child of God. The problems
of this life are trivial when compared with the glory that is about to "burst
upon us" (Goodspeed). This glory Paul spoke about is the glory of the
coming age. In that burst of glory the divine radiance lost in the fall will
be restored to all who believe.

The day is almost here when we will discard the rags of our mortality and don the robes of immortality. Darkness will turn to day, and we
will become in fact what God intended us to be—his glorious creation,
children of God reflecting the perfection and love of our Heavenly
Father. And we are not the only ones who await this day of transformation. The creation as well "waits in eager expectation for the sons of
God to be revealed" (8:19). The created universe is personified as frustrated by human sin and involved in the death and decay that sin
brought about. It too awaits that great day when it will share in the glo-

rious freedom of the children of God (8:19–21).

Clearly, living as a Christian in a world dominated and controlled by sin will inevitably involve suffering (cf. 2 Tim 3:12). Yet we are not left alone in our trials. Romans 8:26–30 points out two major sources of help. First is the intercessory prayer of the Holy Spirit. Caught up in the trials of life, we often do not know what we ought to pray for. So the Spirit intercedes on our behalf "with groans that words cannot express" (8:26). The expression depicts the intensity and earnestness of the Spirit's prayer. Although the intercessory work of Christ, the great High Priest in the order of Melchizedek, is well known to most (Heb 7:17,25), we sometimes forget that the Holy Spirit also pleads our case. In our perplexity about what we ought to pray for, the Spirit joins us in prayer and intercedes on our behalf with a level of fervor that far surpasses our own. We are strengthened in our suffering by realizing that not only does the Spirit pray for us but that God understands his prayers completely and can answer them because they are always in accordance with his will (Rom 8:27).

Our second source of help is the realization that "in all things God works for the good of those who love him" (8:28). This translation is preferable to those that read "all things work together for good," although even in that case the Christian would understand that it was God, not "things" (impersonal by definition and unable to do anything), who would "work for the good." Paul was not subscribing to the secular hope that goodness will somehow prevail over evil. He would not agree with the rabbi who claimed that "for the godly man all things, even though for others they are evils, are beneficial." God is the one in control of all that takes place, and he is fully able to work out the "present sufferings" so that the end result is for the good of those who love him.

God's ultimate control is seen in the five-step sequence of vv. 29–30. What Paul wrote is not a rigid and deterministic theology but a "lyrical expression of Christian experience."[22] To read it with the mind alone is to miss its major import. The foreknowledge of which the apostle spoke was not prior information but the necessary result of the decrees of the God, who exists outside of time. Predestination is not to salvation but to conformity to the likeness of Christ. With God's call we enter historical time. God's call is effectual; that is, it achieves its purpose. The called are justified, set right with God; and the justified are glorified—an event so certain that it can be spoken of as if it has already taken place.

[22] Barclay, *Romans*, 114.

The chapter ends with a series of rhetorical questions that rise from the apostle's existential involvement in the wonder of God's provision for those he allows to go through suffering. "What, then, shall we say in response to this?" With God on our side it could not matter less who might be against us. He is the one who gave us his Son. Will he not with him lavish upon us every good thing as well? Who can successfully lodge a charge against someone chosen by God? With the penalty for sin paid in full, who can possibly condemn? Certainly not Christ Jesus because he is the one who died for us. Furthermore, there is absolutely nothing that can separate us from the love of God—not trouble, hardship, persecution, famine, nakedness, danger, the sword, death, life, angels, demons, things present or future (the list is endless). Nothing can separate us from the love of God revealed in Christ Jesus, our Lord!

(9) What about the Jews? (9:1–11:36)

Earlier in the epistle Paul asked what advantage there is in being a member of the Jewish race or undergoing the rite of circumcision (3:1) since "a man is not a Jew if he is only one outwardly" (2:28), and circumcision is of no benefit to the Jew who breaks the law (2:25). After citing one advantage (see 3:2) Paul put the issue aside until he arrived at chap. 9. Even there the issue is not so much the advantage of being a Jew as it is the character of God in his relationship to his ancient people and the promises he gave them. The gospel has opened the way of righteousness to all people everywhere. How are we to understand this in respect to God's age-long involvement with the people of Israel? Has God failed to keep his promises? Has he acted in a capricious and arbitrary fashion? If so, what kind of a God is he?

Paul opened his discussion by revealing his great distress over the plight of his kinsmen by race. Although commissioned an apostle to the Gentiles (Gal 2:8), he carried in his heart an unceasing anguish for his Jewish brethren. God's blessings to them had been great beyond comparison. Yet they had failed. Israel's rejection of God, however, does not mean that God has failed to keep his promise. He has not severed his ties with the true Israel. It should be clear that not everyone who is descended from Israel is a true Israelite (9:6). Abraham's line of descent ran through Isaac, the son of promise, not through Ishmael, although both were natural children of Abraham. The same is true of Isaac's line of descent. Even before they were born, God chose Jacob over his twin brother, Esau (9:13). God's selection rests not on what a person has done but on God's sovereign will.

But the question arises, Doesn't such a highly arbitrary procedure imply injustice on God's part? Is God unfair? Not at all, replied Paul. Citing Exod 33:19, he reminded his readers that in his sovereignty God is free to show mercy on whomever he will. He owes no one anything. Whatever God does for anyone, he does out of mercy and compassion. His selection of some does not make him unjust to others.

A second question follows: But if God does whatever he wants, then why does he still blame us? After all, no one can resist his will (9:19). Paul's straightforward answer, "Who are you, O man, to talk back to God?" (9:19), has offended many contemporary writers. But the point is that God is the potter, and he alone has the responsibility to determine what he will make out of the clay. We have no right to quibble, since we forfeited everything by our sin. Only by the mercy of God are any selected for divine favor.

The gospel is the proclamation that God himself has done everything required to provide a right standing for humans. Our responsibility is to accept it by faith. Israel had confidence in their own ability to gain God's favor by meritorious actions. Their determination to establish their own righteousness blinded them to the righteousness that God offers as a free gift to those who will accept it by faith. Disregarding God's way, they plunged ahead in a vain attempt to establish their own. They did not realize that "Christ is the end of the law" (10:4). Of course Moses had said that anyone who did all the law commanded would live by it (10:5), but the obvious problem is that no one can meet that standard. By contrast, the righteousness of faith is within the reach of all. All that is required is a faith that accepts the resurrection of Christ and acknowledges him to be Lord (10:9–10). Since righteousness comes by faith, it matters not whether the believer is Jew or Gentile.

Then came Israel's excuse, "We did not have a chance to hear." "Oh yes you did," said Paul. "Your own prophet Isaiah described the messengers who came bearing the good news. You all heard but not everyone responded" (10:16). "But what if they did not understand?" "Unlikely," said Paul. "If a nation that was 'not a nation' understood the concept of righteousness by faith, how can you possibly argue that it was too difficult? The real problem, as Isaiah said, was that Israel was a "disobedient and obstinate people" (10:21).

Does all this mean that for all practical purposes God has rejected his people Israel? "By no means!" answered Paul. "I myself am an Israelite, and God has not rejected me" (11:1, author's paraphrase). Historically there has always been a believing remnant. Without question the Jews have stumbled, but by no means are they beyond recovery. Quite the opposite. It is because of their disobedience that salvation has come to the Gentiles.

In 11:25 Paul referred to God's plan for Israel as a "mystery"—a truth once hidden but now disclosed to all who will hear. It involves three stages. The first was the hardening of a part of Israel. That took place when the nation rejected God's way to attain righteousness. The second stage has been the bringing in of the Gentiles. When that number is complete, then "all Israel will be saved" (11:26). This crucial passage is best understood to mean that it is only in this way—by turning to the Gentiles and inciting their envy as recipients of the divine favor—that the nation of Israel as a whole (not necessarily every individual) will be saved.

The argument of chaps. 9–11 is complete. God did elect Israel and blessed them in many ways. But their insistence on seeking righteousness by works led to a rejection of all but a remnant. In turning to the Gentiles, God not only fulfilled Old Testament promises but provided the motivation for Israel's return. In the end they will respond in faith and be saved. Small wonder that the chapter ends in a rhapsody of praise (11:33–36). "To him be glory forever! Amen."

(10) Practical Christianity (12:1–2,9–13)

With chap. 12 Paul shifted his attention from the broader sweep of theology to the more specific and practical concerns of daily living. Obviously this is not to be understood as a retreat from "justification by faith" back into a new legalism. The obedience expected is not intended as a way of gaining God's favor but is, as Paul later called it, an "obedience inspired by faith" (16:26, Williams). It is not what we must do in order to be justified but what we are unable not to do because we are justified.

Verses 1 and 2 are among the best known and most often quoted passages of the New Testament. The "therefore" that begins the chapter ties together all that Paul had said (the theological base) with all he was about to say (the ethical consequences). The "mercies of God" (AV) are his redemptive activity (3:25), "peace with God" (5:1), reconciliation (5:10–11), freedom from the power of sin (6:18), the abiding presence of the Spirit (8:11), adoption into his family (8:15–16), a love from which we can never be separated (8:38–39), and the assurance that God never goes back on his word (chaps. 9–11), to name some of the more prominent ones. These "mercies" provide not only the basis but also the incentive for all moral effort on the part of the Christian.

Because of these acts of divine compassion Paul could now urge the believers at Rome to offer themselves as a "living sacrifice" to God. The tense of the infinitive (aorist) calls for decisive action. Our dedication to God should not rest in the lofty realm of theory and ideal but must be carried out on the practical plane of where we actually live. This kind of sacrifice fulfills our reasonable and spiritual obligation to love and serve the one who brought us into newness of life.

Unfortunately, the power of contemporary culture to "squeeze [us] into its mold" (Phillips) is greater than we are apt to realize.[23] Paul called on his readers no longer to conform to the "pattern of this world" (its practices, fashions, priorities, and goals). We have been rescued from "this present evil age" (Gal 1:4) and should therefore no longer conform to its pattern for living. Instead, we should allow God to transform us by giving us a totally new way of looking at things. Our moral consciousness is to be reoriented by the power of the indwelling Spirit.

The final purpose of this wholehearted surrender to God is that we may discover that what God has willed for us is "good" (of intrinsic value and moral worth), "pleasing" (acceptable to God, meeting all his requirements), and "perfect" (completely attaining its appropriate end). God's will for us is not designed for our discomfort. The mean-spirited deity who inhabits the heavens of much ill-informed popular thought is not the God of love revealed by Christ Jesus.

Verses 9–13 are representative of the "rules" by which we are to live. Incomplete as they are, they still provide a general idea of the kind of life God would have us live. Although rules are normally seen as legalistic limitations on life, these "rules" are gracious indications of that which brings pleasure to God and the greatest amount of satisfaction to us if we follow them. Paul listed an even dozen.

"Love must be sincere" (12:9). Up until this point *agapē* has been used only of God's love for us (cf. 5:5,8; 8:35). But now it is used to describe the relationship the believer is to sustain to others. In the context of biblical revelation *agapē* love is best defined as "the voluntary giving of oneself for the welfare of others." This kind of love is "sincere," that is, free from all hypocrisy or pretense. Thus we are to "hate what is evil [and] cling to what is good." Weymouth says we are to

---

[23] See H. Blamires, *The Christian Mind,* for a persuasive presentation of this point.

"regard evil with horror." The best defense for the Christian against wickedness is never to get over being shocked by it.

To "be devoted to one another in brotherly love" (12:10) is to create within the community a bond of tender affection. Paul called on his readers to "honor one another above yourselves." He was not telling them to pretend that everyone they met was intrinsically superior. What he was saying was that they were to consider others as worthy of preferential treatment. Put their welfare ahead of our own. Give them top priority.

"Never be lacking in zeal" (12:11). The new life in Christ Jesus has no place for laziness. It calls for an intensity appropriate to the urgency of the issues involved. Since the church holds the only answer for the human predicament, now is not the time to sit by and watch while the world hastens on toward self-destruction. But zeal alone cannot accomplish the task. "Be aglow with the Spirit" (RSV), said Paul. Our "spiritual life" is simply the presence and life of God's Spirit within us. We are to allow ourselves to be set on fire by the Spirit. The church at Laodicea had permitted the fires of devotion to dwindle, and the resulting lukewarmness made the risen Lord feel nauseated (Rev 3:14–18). Paul's dictum in 1 Thessalonians is relevant, "Do not put out the Spirit's fire" (1 Thess 4:19). Our job is not to stir ourselves into a blaze but rather to allow the Spirit's fire to maintain in our lives a spiritual glow. Lest someone think that Paul was placing an overly high premium on spiritual excitement, he added, "Serve the Lord." While buoyed along by the presence of the Spirit, Christians are called to carry out in practical ways the will of the Lord.

"Be joyful in hope" (12:12). The source of Christian joy is the hope (the firm conviction of what will certainly come to pass) that finds its fulfillment in the return of Christ, the vindication of the righteous, and the establishment of God's eternal reign. Since that time is still future, we are to be "patient in affliction." One of Jesus' last words to his disciples was, "In this world you will have trouble" (John 16:33). Stay the course and be "faithful in prayer." Prayer is not a way to secure release from adversity but a way to draw upon the divine strength necessary to let it fulfill its purpose in our lives. It allows us to see behind the problem of the moment and discern in every adverse situation the hand of God.

"Share with God's people who are in need" (12:13). The true measure of people is demonstrated by their relationship to those who are less fortunate. The essence of love is giving. When we actually share what we have with others who are in need, we are reflecting the love of God and his compassion for them. Finally, to "practice hospitality" is more than to entertain friends on festive occasions. The Greek participle means "to pursue." Not only are we to bring in the stranger at the door, but we also are to go out and actively pursue those who would benefit from our kindness and concern.

(11) The Obligations of Love (13:1–14)

Although some scholars hold that the first seven verses of chap. 13 are an independent fragment that somehow got into Paul's letter, it is preferable to see them as an integral part of the apostle's line of thought. In the preceding chapter Paul discussed the believers' relationships first with one another (12:9–13) and then with those outside the church (12:14–21). In the subsequent chapter he discussed the relationship between the stronger and the weaker brother. That Paul should also at this point include a section on the relationship between the Christian and governing authorities is not at all surprising. You will remember that a major problem for the early church—lasting until the Roman edict of toleration in A.D. 312—was the hostility of the Roman Empire toward Christianity. Taking v. 8 as the central theme of the chapter ("Let no debt remain outstanding, except the continuing debt to love one another"), vv. 1–7 represent one of the "debts" incurred by our relationship to those in positions of authority. Tertullian, the third-century Roman apologist, wrote that the Christian is to look up to the emperor because he "is called by our Lord to his office."[24] Obedience to duly constituted rules of society is an obligation of love.

In this section Paul taught that all authority has been established by God (13:1), that to rebel against existing authority is to rebel against God (13:2), that rulers are servants of God and authorized to punish the wrongdoer (13:4), and that those in authority are due proper respect and honor (13:7). The problem is that while all this would be fine in an ideal society, history has demonstrated with regularity that the wrong people frequently become the governing authorities. In Paul's day a crazed Nero set fire to Rome and laid the blame on Christians. In our day it was a Nazi führer who ordered the mass execution of six million Jews (and many others of different ethnic and religious backgrounds). How can it be said that such authorities are servants of God to do his will?

---

[24] Tertullian, *Apology*, 30.

The obvious answer is that at some point a leader may become such a despot that he forfeits his authority to rule. Paul was laying down a relationship to governing authorities that operates within acceptable boundaries. At what point rulers step outside their duly established role is a question that must be decided by each individual. "Civil disobedience" is assumed throughout Scripture. For example, Peter and John boldly declared to a hostile Sanhedrin: "Judge for yourselves whether it is right in God's sight to obey you rather than God. For we cannot help speaking about what we have seen and heard" (Acts 4:19–20). When the demands of governing authorities run counter to our understanding of the will of God and what is morally right, we have no option but to disobey. The war crimes trials at Nuremberg show that in contemporary jurisprudence it is, under certain circumstances, wrong to obey the demands of the state.

Our continuing debt, said Paul, is to love one another (13:8). Unlike other debts, the debt of love requires constant payment yet can never be paid in full. Love is the consummate moral responsibility in that it fulfills everything required by the law (13:8–10). For example, sincere love for another will preclude adultery. It makes murder impossible. Love rules out all stealing and coveting. Love establishes a relationship in which all the Commandments of the second table of the Decalogue are unnecessary. To love is to bring to completion the deepest intent of the Old Testament moral legislation. Love fulfills the law.

An important point in v. 8 often slips by unnoticed. The NIV's "he who loves his fellow man has fulfilled the law" leaves the impression that love for others is a general obligation. The Greek text, however, has a definite article and reads "the other." The love that fulfills the law is a love that goes out to the specific person who at that particular moment confronts us in need, the one whom God has brought across our path and who therefore has a claim on our service. A good case can be made for the proposition that love exists only in actual deeds of love. Abstractions are convenient for philosophical discourse but are without substance and have no value for those in need. We are to love the other, the neighbor who is there—whose need has a claim on our time and energy because God brought that person across our path at that particular moment in time.

It is the brevity of each person's time on earth that gives life both its urgency and its grandeur. The widely known psychoanalyst Professor R. May teaches that by accepting the limits of human mortality people are set free to live. Paul brought another kind of limitation on time into the picture. He wrote that "the night [this present age] is nearly over; the day [the coming age of God's universal and eternal reign] is almost here" (13:12). The time for compassionate concern will not continue indefinitely. Opportunities for kindness are running out. Those who would love must love while there is still time. In vv. 12–14 Paul counseled his readers to "put aside the deeds of darkness" (a form of self-love) and "put on the Lord Jesus Christ" (which cannot help but issue in genuine love for others). The "obligations of love" will be fulfilled when we so completely identify ourselves with him that he who is pure love is allowed freely to express that love in practical ways through those who bear his name.

(12) Getting Along for the Glory of God (14:1–15:13)

No matter who you are or where you live, you will always have to put up with two kinds of people: those who are more conservative than you and those who are more liberal. In every church there are those who are able to do with a free conscience what would cause us pangs of guilt. And there are others who do not have the freedom of conscience to do what we do. Although for everyone many things are clearly wrong (e.g., selfishness, cruelty, hatred) and many other things are always right (e.g., kindness, helpfulness, love), a number of things are morally neutral, neither right nor wrong. The Stoics used the term *adiaphoron* for that middle sphere between virtue and vice, that which is ethically indifferent.[25]

In this closing section of his letter Paul dealt with some first-century Christian *adiaphora*. He wrote, "One man's faith allows him to eat everything, but another man, whose faith is weak, eats only vegetables" (14:2). In the congregation at Rome were some who had come from a Jewish background with its strict dietary laws. Although they had become Christians, they would quite naturally bring along from their background a certain abhorrence of ceremonially unclean foods. Paul referred to them as "weak" in faith, not meaning that they were unsure about their faith in God but that they did not have the inner assurance that certain relatively unimportant things (e.g., eating with ceremonially unwashed hands) were now permissible. Others were "strong" in that they had grasped the fact that since Christ is the fulfillment of the law they were no longer obliged to keep its ceremonial prescriptions. How

---

[25] *TDNT* abr., 1253.

are these two types to get along together in the same Christian fellow-ship?

The natural tendency of the weak is to judge the conduct of the strong. But just because the mind-set of the weak kept them from eating meat they thought was still in some way unclean, they had no right to judge others who no longer shared their qualms of conscience. The important thing for the weak is that they not violate their own con-science. It is not their responsibility to judge the conduct of others.

The tendency of the strong is to run roughshod over the sensitivities of the weak. To them Paul urged restraint. They are not to allow their own freedom in Christ to carry them to the place where they are unable to understand and accept their brethren who find it impossible to shake off the feeling that the former restrictions may still be in force. The strong should accept the weak for the same reason the weak should not judge the strong, "Each of us will give an account of himself to God" (14:12). The primary obligation of the strong is never to do anything that would cause a brother to stumble or fall (14:13). Love, not free-dom, is the rule of Christian conduct. What we do must always be con-sidered in light of its effect on others. Even that which is morally neutral and acceptable before God must be set aside if it would cause another to act against his conscience and so undermine his personal integrity.

The first verses of chap. 15 highlight several responsibilities of the strong. (Note that Paul spent much more time speaking to the strong than to the weak!) First, he said, the strong are to "put up with the weakness of those who are immature" (15:1, Goodspeed). Love demands patience and understanding. Second (and Paul identified him-self with the strong), we are "not to insist on having our own way" (15:1, Knox). Our lives are to be governed by the needs and welfare of others, not by an intense desire to focus on what's in it for me. And third, "Every one of us must try to please his neighbor, to do him good, and help in his development" (15:2, Goodspeed). Our lives are to serve the best interests of the other person. This goal cannot be reached if we go through life insisting on "Christian freedom" as a rule of conduct.

In the closing verses of this section Paul addressed both the weak and the strong: May God "give you a spirit of unity among yourselves as you follow Christ Jesus" (15:5). Jesus did not please himself but bore the insults of human hostility toward God. If he was willing to go that far in not pleasing himself, surely we ought to be able to lay aside our personal preferences in insignificant matters and have patience with one another. Paul wrote, "Accept one another, then, just as Christ accepted you" (15:7). He welcomed you into the family of God with all your imperfections, and you must be willing to accept one another even though you may understand the implications of the faith somewhat differently. Then the God of hope will fill you with all joy and peace so that "your whole life and outlook may be radiant with hope" (Phillips).

OUTLINE OF THE BOOK

  I. Introduction (1:1–17)
      1. Salutation (1:1–7)
      2. Paul's Desire to Visit Rome (1:8–15)
      3. Theme: Righteousness from God (1:16–17)
 II. The Unrighteousness of All Humankind (1:18–3:20)
      1. The Gentiles (1:18–32)
      2. The Jews (2:1–3:8)
          (1) God's Righteous Judgment (2:1–16)
          (2) Authentic Jewishness Is Inward (2:17–29)
          (3) The Faithfulness of God (3:1–7)
      3. All People (3:9–20)
III. The Righteousness Only God Can Provide (3:21–5:21)
      1. Received through Faith in Christ (3:21–31)
      2. Abraham, the Great Example of Faith (4:1–25)
      3. The Results of Faith (5:1:21)
          (1) Peace and Hope (5:1–8)
          (2) Reconciliation (5:9–11)
          (3) The Gift of Righteousness (5:12–21)
 IV. The Righteousness in Which We Are to Grow (6:1–8:39)
      1. No Longer Slaves to Sin (6:1–23)
          (1) Dead to Sin, Alive in Christ (6:1–14)
          (2) Slaves to Righteousness (6:15–23)
      2. No Longer Condemned by Law (7:1–25)
      3. Living in the Spirit (8:1–39)
  V. God's Righteousness Vindicated (9–11)
      1. The Justice of Rejection (9:1–29)

I. INTRODUCTION (1:1–17)
1. Salutation (1:1–7)
2. Paul's Desire to Visit Rome (1:8–15)
3. Theme: Righteousness from God (1:16–17)

I. INTRODUCTION (1:1–17)

1. Salutation (1:1–7)

¹**Paul, a servant of Christ Jesus, called to be an apostle and set apart for the gospel of God— ²the gospel he promised beforehand through his prophets in the Holy Scriptures ³regarding his Son, who as to his human nature was a descendant of David, ⁴and who through the Spirit of holiness was declared with power to be the Son of God by his resurrection from the dead: Jesus Christ our Lord. ⁵Through him and for his name's sake, we received grace and apostleship to call people from among all the Gentiles to the obedience that comes from faith. ⁶And you also are among those who are called to belong to Jesus Christ.**

⁷**To all in Rome who are loved by God and called to be saints:**

Grace and peace to you from God our Father and from the Lord Jesus Christ.

1:1 Paul[1] began his letter by identifying himself in three different ways.[2] First, he was a "servant of Christ Jesus." He belonged without reserve to the one who confronted him on the Damascus road. Although cultured Greeks would never refer to themselves in such a demeaning fashion, the Old Testament designation "servant of the LORD" was a title of honor given to Moses and other prominent leaders (Josh 14:7;

---

[1] The name "Paul" is derived from a Latin word that means "little." According to the *Acts of Paul and Thecla,* he was small of stature (3). First-century Jews often had Roman or Greek names in addition to their Hebrew names. Paul's Hebrew name was Saul (cf. Acts 7:58; 8:1).

[2] D. Moo notes that the three designations identify "his master, his office, and his purpose" (*Romans 1–8,* WEC [Chicago: Moody, 1991], 34).

24:29). Then Paul said that he was "called to be an apostle." God initiated the process. Paul did not choose the role for himself. And even
before he was called, he had been "set apart"[3] to serve in the interests of
the gospel of God.[4] All three statements reflect the subordinate role the
apostle played. Not for a moment did he elevate himself above his
assigned position as a servant of God, set apart and called to serve in
the interests of the proclamation of the gospel.

Christians in leadership positions must recognize the servant nature
of their roles in the work of the kingdom. What the world calls success
has led many gifted leaders gradually to assume a celebrity posture. But
with pride, the original sin, comes spiritual disaster. It would be well for
Christian leaders to begin each day acknowledging before God that they
are his servants. And even that role is a result of God's decision to call
them into service.

1:2 The gospel comes in fulfillment of a promise. In Genesis, God
spoke of the heel of the woman's offspring crushing the serpent (Gen
3:15). Messianic psalms portray the coming deliverer (Pss 45; 72). Jeremiah spoke of a new covenant (Jer 31:31–34). The Old Testament continually points beyond itself to a time of fulfillment, the age to come.
God made his promise "through his prophets" in the Old Testament. He
entrusted his message to men chosen to speak for him. Beyond that, he
allowed his message to be written down. What the prophets wrote
became "Holy Scriptures." Here we have a brief summary of the
method God chose in order to communicate with his people. Scripture
originated with God. He used prophets to communicate his will, and
they accomplished that purpose by writing down what God was pleased
to reveal. The result was Scripture that is holy.[5]

1:3–4 The gospel is "centered in God's Son" (Goodspeed). In him
are brought into focus all the hopes of God's people in the Old Testament (v. 3). God's Son is the Father's "game plan" for the reconciliation

---

[3] Note that ἀφωρισμένος is perfect tense emphasizing the continuing effect of the
action. Paul had been set apart from birth for his ministry among the Gentiles (Gal 1:15).

[4] F. F. Bruce defines the εὐαγγέλιον of God as "the joyful proclamation of the death
and resurrection of his Son, and of the consequent amnesty and liberation which men and
women may enjoy through faith in him" (*Romans,* 2d ed., TNTC [Grand Rapids: Eerdmans, 1985], 68). K. Barth stresses the otherness of the gospel, commenting that "the Gospel is not a religious message to inform mankind of their divinity or to tell them how they
may become divine. The Gospel proclaims a God utterly distinct from men" (*The Epistle to
the Romans,* trans. E. Hoskyns [London: Oxford, 1933], 28).

[5] The absence of an article before ἁγίαις stresses the character of the writings as "holy."

of lost humanity. Ethics and theology are all subordinate to the Christ event. God's Son enters[6] the scene of history by natural descent. He belonged to the lineage of David.[7] His human nature resulted from genuine participation in the human family.[8] He was truly man. His blood line may be traced back to David. The AV inserts the final clause from v. 4 at this point, "Concerning his Son Jesus Christ our Lord." Translators apparently were anxious to assure readers that while Jesus as to his human nature came from David, he was at the same time "Jesus Christ our Lord." The transposition of this clause from v. 4 is grammatically allowable but weakens its place of emphasis in the Greek text.

Theology teaches that Jesus was both God and man. Verse 3 declares his humanity; v. 4 proclaims his deity.[9] Jesus was designated Son of God "by his resurrection from the dead."[10] It is the resurrection that sets him apart and authenticates his claim to deity. Had Jesus not risen from the dead, he would be remembered today only as a Jewish moralist who had some inflated ideas about his own relationship to God and made a number of ridiculous demands on those who wanted to be his disciples. On the other hand, if it is true that he rose from the dead, then his teachings about himself are true and his requirements for discipleship must be taken with all seriousness. C. S. Lewis wrote: "A man who was merely a man and said the sort of things Jesus said would not be a great moral teacher. He would either be a lunatic—on a level with the man who says he is a poached egg—or else he would be the Devil of Hell. You must make your choice. Either this man was, and is, the Son of God: or else a madman or something worse."[11]

---

[6] The use of γενομένου ("came") rather than γεννηθέντος ("born") has been taken as an indication that Paul was acquainted with the tradition of Jesus' unusual birth.

[7] That Jesus came ἐκ σπέρματος Δάυιδ would qualify him as fulfilling the messianic hopes of Israel (Isa 11; Jer 23:5–6).

[8] It is commonly held that vv. 3–4 are a confessional formula to which Paul made additions. Note the intentional contrast between κατὰ σάρκα and κατὰ πνεῦμα ἁγιωσύνης. See G. R. Beasley-Murray, "Romans 1:3f: An Early Confession of Faith in the Lordship of Jesus," *TynBul* 31 (1980): 147–54.

[9] J. Stott, however, holds that Paul was not referring to the two natures of Jesus Christ (human and divine) "but to the two stages of his ministry, preresurrection and postresurrection, the first frail and the second powerful through the outpoured Spirit" (*Romans* [Downers Grove: InterVarsity, 1994], 50–51).

[10] Although the Greek text does not specifically say "his" resurrection, the phrase obviously refers to that event. A number of commentators take it as referring to the general eschatological resurrection of which the resurrection of Jesus is the first fruit.

[11] C. S. Lewis, *Mere Christianity* (New York: Macmillan, 1958), 41.

Verse 4 has three parallel prepositional phrases: "in power," "according to a spirit of holiness," and "by a resurrection of dead persons" (literal translation). It is clear that the third phrase completes the major
clause. He was "declared . . . to be the son of God . . . by his resurrection from the dead." The other two phrases are variously understood.
The first ("in power") is best taken as describing the powerful status of
the resurrected Christ. He was installed as Son of God with power. The
location of "in power" in the Greek text immediately following "Son of
God" supports this interpretation. Some writers take it as describing the
manner in which Jesus was declared Son of God. Goodspeed has "decisively declared." The NEB has "declared Son of God by a mighty act."
The second phrase ("spirit of holiness") refers to Christ's own inner
spirit.[12] He lived his life in complete and perfect holiness.

Verse 4 ends with a clear declaration that this Son of God is none
other than "Jesus Christ our Lord." Jesus is the Christ, the promised
Messiah, God's anointed Redeemer. He is also "our Lord." He is our
master; we are his subjects.

1:5 The universal scope of the gospel is expressed in Paul's definition of his task as "call[ing] people from among all the Gentiles to the
obedience that comes from faith"[13] (v. 5). The promised Messiah did
not come for the benefit of the Jewish nation alone. The gospel is good
news for all who will respond in faith. But faith inevitably issues in
obedience. Faith is not intellectual assent to a series of propositions but
surrender to the one who asks us to trust him. To surrender is to obey.
Biblical faith is not some mild assent to a collection of ethical maxims
but an active commitment of one's life. Obedience is the true measure

---

[12] Some think the expression is a reference to the Holy Spirit (e.g., C. E. B. Cranfield,
The Epistle to the Romans, ICC [Edinburgh: T & T Clark, 1975], 1:62–64). Stott, however,
holds that Paul was not referring to the two natures of Jesus Christ (human and divine) "but
to the two stages of his ministry, pre-resurrection and post-resurrection, the first frail and
the second powerful though the outpoured Spirit" (*Romans* [Downers Grove: InterVarsity,
1994], 50–51).

[13] ὑπακοὴν πίστεως has been understood in various ways. Some read "obedience to
the [Christian] faith" (unlikely due to the lack of the article in Greek); others take πίστεως
epexegetically, i.e., "obedience which consists in faith." D. B. Garlington holds that Paul
deliberately coined ὑπακοὴ πίστεως as an ambiguous phrase that expresses both ideas at
the same time ("The Obedience of Faith in the Letter to the Romans: Part I: The meaning
of ὑπακοὴ πίστεως (Rom 1:5; 16:26)," *WTJ* [1990]: 201–24). In any case, faith and obedience are inseparable: true faith always expresses itself in obedience, and genuine obedience inevitably stems from faith. ὑπακοή is a compound built on ἀκούω, "hear."
Obedience is portrayed as the response to a verbal statement.

of a person's faith. E. Best comments that "faith and obedience go inextricably together. Only in obedience is there faith, for faith is not emotional feeling or intellectual acceptance but active response to a person."[14] Paul's desire was to take the gospel to the entire world and see the nations turn to God in a faith that changes conduct. Any other response would be inadequate. Apart from a changed life there is no real faith.

Through Jesus Christ, Paul and the other apostles received their commission.[15] Along with apostleship came the grace that made it possible.[16] When people from every nation profess Christ and demonstrate their faith by the obedience it brings forth, then will his name be honored.

1:6 Paul began his letter by identifying himself as a servant of Christ Jesus who had been "called to be an apostle" (v. 1). Then he told the believers in Rome that they too had been called[17] (v. 6). They were "called to belong to Jesus Christ." God's call is not an invitation but a powerful and effective reaching out to claim individuals for himself.[18] To accept Christ as Savior is to give up all rights to oneself. Christians belong to Christ. Paul the apostle was the servant of the Lord. We who believe have placed ourselves at Christ's disposal to be used as he sees fit. There is little room here for the mistaken idea that people can accept Christ as Savior without also allowing him to be Lord of their lives. As we learned in v. 5, we have been called to "the obedience that comes from faith."

1:7 Paul addressed his letter to the Christian believers in the city of Rome.[19] They are described in Greek by two verbal adjectives: they

---

[14] E. Best, *The Letter of Paul to the Romans,* CBC (Cambridge: University Press, 1967), 11.

[15] Many take "we" as an editorial "we," but Paul, in writing to a church that others had founded, would have been sensitive to the fact that he was not alone in ministering to the Gentiles.

[16] Some writers take "grace" and "apostleship" as a hendiadys and translate "the grace [or divine gift] of apostleship."

[17] The NIV takes ἐν οἷς ἐστε with what follows rather than referring back to τοῖς ἔθνεσιν of the preceding verse. It is better to place a comma after ὑμεῖς and read "among whom [that is, the Gentiles] are you also, you who are called of Jesus Christ." This would indicate that the church at Rome was predominantly Gentile.

[18] On this point see W. W. Klein, "Paul's Use of *Kalein:* A Proposal," *JETS* 27 (1984): 53–64.

[19] The ninth-century uncial known as G and several other manuscripts omit ἐν Ῥώμῃ here and in v. 15, probably so as not to limit the epistle to the Roman church alone (see the Introduction).

were "loved" by God and "called"[20] to be saints. God loves the entire human race (John 3:16), but those who respond to him in faith are loved in a special way. They have experienced the love of God and become new creations (2 Cor 5:17). They are called to be holy.[21] The ultimate purpose of God's calling is that redeemed humanity becomes like him in holiness. That single goal directs the life and conduct of every true believer.

The salutation "grace and peace" combines a Christianized form of the Greek and Hebrew greetings.[22] Grace and peace are intricately related.[23] Real peace comes only as a result of the grace of God. Grace is what we receive; peace is what we experience as a result of the activity of God on our behalf. This combination of spiritual blessings comes from "God our Father" and from the "Lord Jesus Christ." The Son takes his place with the Father as the giver of spiritual blessings.[24] His full title marks out his deity ("Lord"), his life on earth ("Jesus"), and his redemptive role ("Christ"). God is not portrayed as a remote deity but as the Father of those who believe. This supports the earlier statement in v. 7 that believers are "loved by God." He loves us as only a true father can love. We are members of a family distinguished by love.

2. Paul's Desire to Visit Rome (1:8–15)

⁸First, I thank my God through Jesus Christ for all of you, because your

---

[20] ἀγαπητοῖς, κλητοῖς.

[21] ἅγιος is an adjective meaning "dedicated to God, holy." Used as a noun it could refer to a believer as one who is consecrated to God, thus a "saint." In the NT, however, when used of believers it always occurs in the plural. The idea of individual saints is an ecclesiastical misuse of the term. Most writers note that "called to be saints" refers primarily to a status before God. Although that is true, the designation certainly implies a certain kind of ethical behavior.

[22] The ordinary Greek greeting was χαίρειν (cf. Paul's χάρις). εἰρήνη reflects the common greeting in the Semitic world (Judg 19:20; 1 Sam 25:5–6).

[23] W. Sanday and A. C. Headlam note that χάρις and εἰρήνη are both used in the full theological sense: "χάρις = the favour of God, εἰρήνη = the cessation of hostility to him and the peace of mind which follows upon it" (*A Critical and Exegetical Commentary on the Epistle to the Romans*, ICC [Edinburgh: T & T Clark, 1902], 15).

[24] A. M. Hunter asks us to "note how this born-and-bred monotheist can set Jesus unequivocally on that side of reality which we call divine; and that too within thirty years of the Crucifixion" (*The Epistle to the Romans*, TBC [London: SCM, 1955], 26). On the significance of this verse for the doctrine of the deity of Christ, see B. B. Warfield, *Biblical Doctrines*, 213–20.

faith is being reported all over the world. ⁹God, whom I serve with my
whole heart in preaching the gospel of his Son, is my witness how con-
stantly I remember you ¹⁰in my prayers at all times; and I pray that now
at last by God's will the way may be opened for me to come to you.

¹¹I long to see you so that I may impart to you some spiritual gift to
make you strong— ¹²that is, that you and I may be mutually encouraged
by each other's faith. ¹³I do not want you to be unaware, brothers, that I
planned many times to come to you (but have been prevented from doing
so until now) in order that I might have a harvest among you, just as I
have had among the other Gentiles.

¹⁴I am obligated both to Greeks and non-Greeks, both to the wise and
the foolish. ¹⁵That is why I am so eager to preach the gospel also to you
who are at Rome.

1:8–10   One of the first lessons of effective leadership is the importance of setting priorities. Not only must things be done right (manage-
ment) but the right things must be done (leadership). People reveal by
their priorities what is genuinely important in their lives. Paul wrote,
"First,[25] I thank my God." (Phillips has, "I must begin by telling you
how I thank God.") Thanksgiving and praise to God were at the center
of Paul's religious experience. Consequently ten of his thirteen epistles
open with some form of "I thank my God" (Rom 1:8; 1 Cor 1:4; Phil
1:3; Col 1:3; 1 Thess 1:2; 2 Thess 1:3; 2 Tim 1:3; Phlm 4) or "Praise be
to God" (2 Cor 1:3; Eph 1:3).

In v. 7 Paul spoke of God as "our Father." In v. 8 he spoke of "my
God." Religion, for Paul, was an intensely personal relationship. God is
not a ruling deity far removed from his people. The true believer views
God as a close companion. David cried out, "O God, you are my God"
(Ps 63:1).

Paul's thanksgiving was "through" Jesus and "for" the believers in
Rome. Because of who Jesus is and what he accomplished on the cross,
Paul was able to give thanks to God. Apart from that redemptive event
both the content and the occasion for giving thanks would be missing.
Apart from the work of the Son there would be no thanksgiving.

Specifically Paul gave thanks that the faith of the believers in Rome
was being proclaimed throughout the ancient world. From Rom 15:20–
22 we may assume that the capital city itself had not yet been evange-

---

[25] That Paul never got around to a "second" is unimportant. Some say the problem lay
with the transcription by a secretary. More likely Paul simply neglected to follow through
with an additional point.

lized. The church there was made up primarily of believers who had heard the message elsewhere. But the story of how they came to faith was widely known throughout the world.[26] The growth of the church has always been contingent upon the openness of believers to express their faith.

Verses 9–10 provide insight into the prayer life of the apostle. Paul told the believers in Rome that he never failed to remember them when he prayed.[27] Realizing how many lives the apostle had already touched, we marvel that he was able to include in his prayers believers he had not as yet met. Their faith was known throughout the ancient world (v. 8), and that alone would move the apostle to pray for them. The intensity of Paul's prayers on their behalf is seen in his statement, "How constantly I remember you in my prayers[28] at all times." We are reminded that the real work of the ministry is prayer. Preaching is more a result of the ministry of prayer than it is a ministry itself. A sermon that does not rise from intense and heart-searching prayer has no chance of bearing real fruit. F. Laubach has said that it is the preacher's business to look into the very face of God until he aches with bliss. Preaching that does not grow out of a life of prayer is like "fruit" from an artificial tree. Where there is no life, there will be no real fruit.

It was important for the believers in Rome to be sure that Paul was not using idle rhetoric regarding his concern for them. So he called God to be his witness that what he was saying about his constancy in prayer for them was true.[29] His specific prayer at this point was that it be in the will of God for him to come to them at last.[30] Later, in 15:23, he told the Roman Christians that he had longed for many years to see them.

---

[26] "All over the world" is obviously hyperbole (cf. 1 Thess 1:8, "Your faith in God has become known everywhere"). That there were Christian believers in the capital city was known wherever the gospel had been preached.

[27] W. H. G. Thomas writes, "Prayer is one of the most definite and genuine proofs of sincere Christian affection" (*St. Paul's Epistle to the Romans* [Grand Rapids: Eerdmans, 1953], 55). And Luther was quick to note that "Christian prayer is complete only when we intercede for the common good of all and not merely for ourselves" (*Commentary on the Epistle to the Romans*, trans. J. T. Mueller [Grand Rapids: Zondervan, 1954], 22).

[28] The NIV "in my prayers" translates ἐπὶ τῶν προσευχῶν μου. The phrase means "at [the time of] my prayers" and suggests that in keeping with his Jewish upbringing Paul maintained specific times for prayer (Jewish custom called for three periods each day; cf. Dan 6:11; Acts 10:3; *Did* 8.2).

[29] Cf. 2 Cor 1:23; Gal 1:20; Phil 1:8; etc. Paul invoked God as his witness because what he said concerned the inner life and therefore could not be verified by the readers.

[30] εἴ πως ἤδη ποτὲ is a complex expression. It reflects Paul's eagerness to get to Rome.

The will, or good pleasure, of God was the determining factor in all of Paul's plans. As the servant of God, he worked within the framework of the divine will. All too often believers formulate their own plans and then attempt to co-opt God into them.

Almost in passing, Paul designated God as the one whom he served "with his whole heart" (v. 9).[31] Real faith results in total surrender. Paul's service stemmed from a whole-hearted commitment to God. It was not a duty but a privilege. Some translators take the word for "service" in the equally acceptable sense of "worship." Knox has "to whom I direct the inner worship of my heart." Service and worship translate the same Greek word.[32] To serve is to worship; to worship is to serve. Genuine worship takes place more often in acts of service (taking the term in a wider sense than "ritual service") than in what we tend to call the Sunday morning worship service. While not disparaging the weekly gathering of believers (Heb 10:25 warns us not to give up meeting together), it is important to grasp that whatever we do in helping to carry out the redemptive mission of Christ is by definition an act of worship.

1:11–13 Paul longed to see the believers in Rome. Commitment to a common Lord draws people together. To be servants of the same master is to be in harmony with one another. Paul's special concern was that he would be able to share with them some spiritual favor that would provide encouragement and strength. The apostle was not at this point speaking of spiritual gifts such as those listed in 1 Corinthians 12.[33] He was concerned that believers in Rome become increasingly established in their faith. To this end he wanted to share with them some spiritual insight or gift he had received from the Spirit. His visit with them would provide the opportunity to accomplish that purpose. Here again we see the focus of Paul's ministry. A visit to Rome would not be for personal advantage or pleasure. It would serve to strengthen the faith of those who recently had turned from idols to serve the living God (cf. 1 Thess 1:9).

A person's true character is more often than not revealed in the

---

[31] ἐν τῷ πνεύματί μου has been understood in various ways: (1) the Spirit of God that dwelt in Paul, (2) Paul's spirit with reference to his prayer life, or (3) wholeheartedly. The NIV ("with my whole heart") is probably best.

[32] Moo notes that λατρεύω "focuses attention on [Paul's] service in its vertical aspect as an offering of worship to God" (*Romans 1–8,* 52).

[33] Since a χάρισμα is a gift bestowed by the Spirit of God (1 Cor 12:7–11), little is added by the adjective πνευματικόν. J. D. G. Dunn translates "a truly spiritual gift" (*Romans,* WBC, 2 vols. [Dallas: Word, 1988], 1:30).

unplanned and spontaneous moments of life. Prepared statements rarely display the real person. Verse 11, taken by itself, could be interpreted to make the apostle appear rather conceited. He wanted to be with them to give them a spiritual gift that would make them strong. But he quickly added a qualifying statement.[34] What I mean to say is that when we are together we will be mutually encouraged by one another's faith. I will be of help to you, but you also will be of encouragement to me. Your faith strengthens my faith, and I am a stronger person as a result. In this aside Paul revealed a genuine sense of appreciation for the spiritual life of others. Although he was an apostle, sent by God to proclaim the good news throughout the known world, he valued and would profit from the faith of other believers.

Paul wanted the believers in Rome to understand that he had not intentionally neglected them.[35] After all, Rome was the major city of the known world at that time. One might think that the "apostle to the Gentiles" (Gal 2:8; Rom 11:13) would have tried to visit there as soon as possible. So Paul wrote that he had "planned many times" to come to them, but up until then he had "been prevented" from carrying through with his plans (v. 13). There is no indication about what had hindered his visiting them. *The Living Bible* assumes divine intervention, "But God did not let me."[36] Other suggestions include the pressing needs of the churches Paul recently had established, Satanic opposition (cf. 1 Thess 2:18), and the organization of the collection (Rom 15:26). Perhaps there is no need to choose between God's direction and the circumstances of life, since God works through everyday circumstances to carry out his will.[37]

Paul's purpose in going to Rome was that he might "have a harvest" among the people there. Since he went on to say that this harvest would

---

[34] Verse 12 is not a correction of v. 11. Paul did not take back what he had just said. Nor is the qualification a "pious fraud" (Erasmus) or "a cumbersome qualification of v 11" (J. A. Fitzmyer, *Romans,* AB [New York: Doubleday, 1993], 248). It is a genuine expression of humility.

[35] οὐ θέλω δὲ ὑμᾶς ἀγνοεῖν is a standard formula Paul used when he wanted to emphasize that what he was about to say was especially important (cf. 1 Cor 10:1; 12:1; 1 Thess 4:13). It is always followed by the vocative ἀδελφοί.

[36] Taking ἐκωλύθην as a "divine passive."

[37] Calvin wrote, "We learn from this that the Lord frequently upsets the purposes of his saints in order to humble them, and by such humiliation to teach them to look to His providence, on which they are to depend" (*The Epistles of Paul the Apostle to the Romans and to the Thessalonians,* trans. R. Mackenzie [Grand Rapids: Eerdmans, 1961], 25).

be a continuation of the harvest he had had among other Gentiles, we conclude that he was referring to an evangelistic outreach that would bring people to faith in Christ. That he calls it a "harvest" is significant (cf. Jesus' use in John 4:34–38). We often reap what has already been sown. In a very real sense God had prepared the hearts of people for the message of the gospel. The ancient gods of Greece and Rome had no personal interest in mere mortals. As a result many Gentiles had turned to the mystery religions but had found little satisfaction. Ritual has an emotional value, but that fades rather quickly. Only the true God, ultimately revealed in the person of Jesus Christ, can satisfy the deepest longings of the human heart. He made us for himself, and nothing less than a personal redemptive encounter and continuing fellowship can meet that basic spiritual need. The gospel produced a harvest because hearts had been prepared.

1:14–15 As a servant who is called and set apart (v. 1), Paul was under obligation not only to God but also to those who would hear the message. In 1 Cor 9:16 he spoke of being compelled to preach ("Woe to me if I do not preach the gospel"), and in the following verse he added that if he preached voluntarily, he was simply discharging a trust that was committed to him. Paul had no option but to take the good news far and wide to people of every nation regardless of their ethnic or cultural orientation.

"Greeks and non-Greeks"[38] include both the nations where the Greek language was spoken fluently and other nations that either did not speak Greek or spoke it poorly. Dunn calls it "a standard phrase to include all races and classes within the Gentile world."[39] The parallel "wise and foolish" made good sense from the Greek perspective. Knox calls them the "learned and simple."[40] Most important was Paul's obligation to carry the message throughout the world irrespective of national origin or intellectual sophistication. The truth that all people are sinners before God levels the only ground of any eternal significance. All come with the same need of forgiveness. Those who accept the grace of God stand together on even ground. God shows no partial-

---

[38] βαρβάριος is an onomatopoeic word meaning "to make unintelligible sounds." From the Greek perspective this would designate anyone speaking a non-Greek language (*EDNT* 1.197).

[39] Dunn, *Romans*, 1:33.

[40] Commentators differ considerably on whether the two pairs are different ways of portraying the same group or whether the two groups are to some extent different. It is best to take them in a general sense of different degrees of culture and learning.

ity, an insight that needs to be heard once again in churches where social position and secular skills tend to determine leadership.

Paul's sense of obligation to carry the message of Christ was not a burden. To the contrary, he was "eager to preach" to those who were in Rome.[41] "Obligation to him who died produces obligation to those for whom he died."[42] Obligation need not be joyless commitment to an unpleasant task. Paul's eagerness grew out of his own transforming experience on the Damascus road coupled with the realization that he was privileged to share the good news with others. The NIV's "that is why I am so eager to preach" is a fairly interpretive translation of the Greek text[43] but fits the context well. Others translate, "And so, for my part" (TCNT) and, "So, as far as I can" (Williams).

3. Theme: Righteousness from God (1:16–17)

[16]I am not ashamed of the gospel, because it is the power of God for the salvation of everyone who believes: first for the Jew, then for the Gentile. [17]For in the gospel a righteousness from God is revealed, a righteousness that is by faith from first to last, just as it is written: "The righteous will live by faith."

1:16–17 Verses 16–17 are pivotal verses in the New Testament. They state concisely and with unusual clarity a fundamental tenet of the Christian faith. The heart of v. 16 is that the gospel is the saving power of God. Salvation is not only initiated by God but is carried through by his power. To say that the gospel is "power" is to acknowledge the dynamic quality of the message. In the proclamation of the gospel God is actively at work in reaching out to the hearts of people. The gospel is God telling of his love to wayward people. It is not a lifeless message but a vibrant encounter for everyone who responds in faith. Much religious discourse is little more than words and ideas about religious subjects. Not so the gospel. The gospel is God at work. He lives and breathes through the declaration of his redemptive love for people. To really hear the gospel is to experience the presence of God. The late evangelist Dwight L. Moody commented that the gospel is like a lion. All the preacher has to do is to open the door of the cage and get out of the way!

---

[41] Thomas comments, "These two confessions, 'I am debtor,' 'I am ready,' are at the heart of all true work for God" (*Romans,* 58).

[42] P. S. Minear, *The Obedience of Faith* (London: SCM, 1971), 104.

[43] οὕτως τὸ κατ᾿ ἐμὲ πρόθυμον.

The gospel is not simply a display of power but the effective operation of God's power leading to salvation. It has purpose and direction.[44] The salvation Paul spoke of is more than forgiveness of sin. It includes the full scope of deliverance from the results of Adam's sin. It involves justification (being set right with God), sanctification (growth in holiness), and glorification (the ultimate transformation into the likeness of Christ; cf. 1 John 3:2). The gospel serves the eternal purposes of God, who before the creation of the world chose to create for himself a people who would respond to his love. Becoming a child of God requires deliverance from what we are as children of Adam. It is not something we can do for ourselves. It requires the power of God himself working through the gospel.

The gospel does not negate a person's free will but is God's power for "everyone who believes."[45] God does not force himself upon people against their will. For the power of the gospel to effect salvation, the hearer must respond in faith. Our faith is in no way meritorious, but without faith there can be no individual salvation.[46] Paul noted the universal nature of salvation by faith when he added "first for the Jew, then for the Gentile." Historically God worked through his people Israel. They were first. Now the message goes out to everyone everywhere.[47]

The opening statement of v. 16 is Paul's declaration that he was not ashamed of the gospel. Why would he have been ashamed? Some have suggested that since Rome was the leading metropolitan center of the world, a more timid soul might be intimidated bringing to the sophisticates of that city the story of a Jewish carpenter who rose from the dead and claimed to be the very Son of God.[48] Moffatt has restated the clause

---

[44] Note that the gospel is the power of God εἰς σωτηρίον. It leads in a specific direction. In fact, it leads right up into salvation; it brings about salvation (taking εἰς as strongly as possible).

[45] That πιστεύοντι is present tense rather than aorist suggests that Paul wanted to stress that the faith that saves is not simply the initial act of trust but a continuing reliance upon the redemptive work of God.

[46] To emphasize the nonmeritorious nature of faith, Cranfield (*Romans,* 1:90) writes, "For Paul man's salvation is altogether—not almost altogether—God's work; and the faith spoken of here is the openness to the gospel which *God Himself creates*" (italics added).

[47] ῞Ελληνι here refers to anyone who is not a Jew.

[48] L. Morris cites Hunter as saying: "The gospel of a crucified carpenter in the streets of Imperial Rome—is not the idea so incongruous as to make one ashamed at the prospect? No, he is not ashamed, for the gospel is a divine POWER" (*The Epistle to the Romans* [Grand Rapids: Eerdmans, 1988], 66, n. 158). O. Michel says that Paul "shrinks neither from Jewish Christians who may slander him, nor from charismatics who may look down upon him" (quoted by Fitzmyer, *Romans,* 255).

in a more positive way, "I am proud of the gospel."[49] The statement also may be taken in the sense of the gospel not putting Paul to shame. That is, it did not let him down; the gospel did not put him to shame. These suggestions are interesting, but it is better to see in vv. 16–17 two specific reasons why Paul was not ashamed of the gospel: (1) it is the power of God, and (2) it reveals a righteousness from God.

The gospel reveals a righteousness of God that is distinct from human righteousness. But what exactly is this "righteousness"? The issue has been debated from earliest times. Stott notes that it has "attracted an enormous, even unmanageable, literature" with the result that the debate is "not easy to summarize, let alone to systematize."[50] Fitzmyer favors the view that it is best understood as an attribute of God. He argues (1) that the expression is paralleled by the "power of God" in 1:16 and the "wrath of God" in 1:18, (2) that Paul's argument reaches its climax in 3:26 with the statement "to show that he [God] is upright," and (3) that other attributes mentioned in chap. 3 ("the fidelity of God," v. 3; "the truthfulness of God," v. 7) are virtual synonyms of "God's uprightness."[51]

A second view is that the righteousness of God is God's activity whereby he declares to be righteous those who turn to him in faith.[52] The argument runs as follows: (1) the "righteousness" of God in 3:25–26 is most certainly an activity, (2) the parallel expressions in v. 16 ("the power of God") and v. 18 ("the wrath of God") suggest activity on God's part, and (3) "the righteousness of God" is a technical term in Jewish apocalyptic literature for God's saving power.[53]

Cranfield's view is that the righteousness of God refers to humans' righteous status that results from God's justifying activity. He argues (1) that a number of occurrences of "righteousness" in Paul's letters support that view (e.g., Rom 5:17; 10:3; Phil 3:9; 1 Cor 1:30; 2 Cor 5:21), (2) the emphasis on faith in v. 17b favors the view that righteousness is a status conferred on persons rather than an activity of God, (3) the quotation from Habakkuk focuses attention on the one justified and not on God's justifying activity, and (4) the structure of the argument that lays

---

[49] Taking the expression as a figure of speech (litotes) in which a positive confession is actually intended. Some find in it an echo of a primitive confessional formula (cf. Mark 8:38).

[50] Stott, *Romans*, 61.

[51] Fitzmyer, *Romans*, 262.

[52] Taking θεοῦ as a subjective genitive rather than a genitive of possession.

[53] See E. Käsemann, *Commentary on Romans* (Grand Rapids: Eerdmans, 1980), 25–30.

heavy emphasis on the status of one who has received God's gift of justification.[54]

Of the four possibilities listed, I believe Cranfield's position is the most persuasive. It may be, however, that the three positions are not mutually exclusive. There is no question that righteousness is an attribute of God, and God clearly is actively involved in declaring righteous those who turn to him in faith. The result is that people of faith are declared to be righteous. They have laid hold of the "righteousness from God."[55] With the major emphasis remaining on the status of the one declared to be righteous, there is no reason to deny that the other two aspects are integrally related and should not be excluded from the larger view of the issue.[56]

By nature we view righteousness as something we can achieve by our own meritorious action, the result of what we do. The righteousness of God is totally different. It is a right standing before God that has nothing to do with human merit. It is received by faith. We sing, "Nothing in my hands I bring; simply to thy cross I cling" (A. M. Toplady). The Greek "out of faith into faith" has been taken in many ways: "from the faith of the OT to the faith of the NT," "from God's faithfulness to man's faith," "from one degree of faith to another," and so on. Most probably it points to faith as the origin of righteousness and the direction in which it leads.[57] This radical departure from conventional wisdom had to be "revealed." It runs contrary to all the basic instincts of fallen human nature. Virtue has, since the beginning of time, been thought of as an achievement by human endeavor. But God's righteousness is a right standing he freely gives to those who trust in him. The

---

[54] Cranfield concludes, "We regard the interpretation which takes θεοῦ as a genitive of origin and δικαιοσύνη as referring to the righteous status which is given by God as being much the more probable" (*Romans,* 1:98).

[55] Moo's position regarding the righteousness of God in the OT is that it denotes God's character as one who will always do right, his activity of establishing right and the state of those who have been put right (*Romans 1–8,* 81).

[56] A related question that has divided scholars is whether (as many Roman Catholic scholars believe) or not (the Protestant interpretation) righteousness as a status includes moral regeneration. Cranfield represents the latter view, "There seems to us to be no doubt that δικαιόω as used by Paul, means simply 'acquit,' 'confer a righteous status on,' and does not in itself contain any reference to moral transformation (*Romans,* 1:95).

[57] Righteousness is ἐκ πίστεως—it is based on faith, and εἰς πίστιν—it leads to an ever-increasing faith. For a thorough study see the appendix "From Faith to Faith," in J. Murray, *The Epistle to the Romans,* 2 vols., NICNT (Grand Rapids: Eerdmans, 1965), 1:363–74.

lack of an article before "righteousness" (in the Greek text) emphasizes the qualitative aspect of the noun. That is, the kind of righteousness God provides and is revealed in the gospel is available by faith alone and leads on to greater faith.

In support of his declaration that righteousness comes by faith, Paul turned to words of the Old Testament prophet Habakkuk, "The righteous will live by faith" (Hab 2:4). In Gal 3:11 Paul used the same quotation to prove that no one is justified by keeping the law. The prophet Habakkuk used the term "faith" in the sense of faithfulness or steadfastness. The righteous will be preserved through times of difficulty by their steadfast loyalty to God. Paul used the passage in a slightly different way to make it mean that those who are righteous by faith will receive life. Bruce comments that "the terms of Habakkuk's oracle are sufficiently general to make room for Paul's application of them."[58]

That the righteousness providing life is based solely on faith is central to the New Testament teaching on salvation. *Sola fide* became the central theme of the Reformation in the sixteenth century. Whenever ecclesiastical teaching begins to compromise with the pagan notion that righteousness can be earned, there needs to be a clear reaffirmation that God's righteousness comes from faith, not works. "Just as it is written" translates a Greek verb in the perfect tense (*gegraptai*). This emphasizes the permanence and authoritative nature of Scripture. If it is true that Scripture is "holy" (see Rom 1:2)—and it is—then it follows that it is also true and unchanging. While the application of God's Word requires an understanding of contemporary culture, it is not true that it must change with the passing scene. Truth remains. Its relevance to a particular point in time requires informed and sensitive application.

---

[58] Bruce, *Romans,* 76.

II. THE UNRIGHTEOUSNESS OF ALL HUMANKIND
   (1:18–3:20)
   1. The Gentiles (1:18–32)
   2. The Jews (2:1–3:8)
      (1) God's Righteous Judgment (2:1–16)
      (2) Authentic Jewishness Is Inward (2:17–29)
      (3) The Faithfulness of God (3:1–8)
   3. All People (3:9–20)

II. THE UNRIGHTEOUSNESS
OF ALL HUMANKIND (1:18–3:20)

1. The Gentiles (1:18–32)[1]

[18]The wrath of God is being revealed from heaven against all the godlessness and wickedness of men who suppress the truth by their wickedness, [19]since what may be known about God is plain to them, because God has made it plain to them. [20]For since the creation of the world God's invisible qualities—his eternal power and divine nature—have been clearly seen, being understood from what has been made, so that men are without excuse.

[21]For although they knew God, they neither glorified him as God nor gave thanks to him, but their thinking became futile and their foolish hearts were darkened. [22]Although they claimed to be wise, they became fools [23]and exchanged the glory of the immortal God for images made to look like mortal man and birds and animals and reptiles.

[24]Therefore God gave them over in the sinful desires of their hearts to sexual impurity for the degrading of their bodies with one another. [25]They exchanged the truth of God for a lie, and worshiped and served created

---

[1] That this section does not refer exclusively to the Gentiles is favored by the observation that those who suffer the wrath of God are called ἄνθρωποι rather than ἔθνη. In addition, v. 23 condemns their idolatry in language that reflects such OT passages as Ps 106:20 and Jer 2:11. C. E. B. Cranfield holds that 1:18–32 pictures *all* persons under the judgment of the gospel and that 2:1–3:20 teaches that the Jew is no exception (*The Epistle to the Romans,* 2 vols., ICC [Edinburgh: T & T Clark, 1975], 1:104–6, 137–38).

things rather than the Creator—who is forever praised. Amen. ²⁶Because of this, God gave them over to shameful lusts. Even their women exchanged natural relations for unnatural ones. ²⁷In the same way the men also abandoned natural relations with women and were inflamed with lust for one another. Men committed indecent acts with other men, and received in themselves the due penalty for their perversion.

²⁸Furthermore, since they did not think it worthwhile to retain the knowledge of God, he gave them over to a depraved mind, to do what ought not to be done. ²⁹They have become filled with every kind of wickedness, evil, greed and depravity. They are full of envy, murder, strife, deceit and malice. They are gossips, ³⁰slanderers, God-haters, insolent, arrogant and boastful; they invent ways of doing evil; they disobey their parents; ³¹they are senseless, faithless, heartless, ruthless. ³²Although they know God's righteous decree that those who do such things deserve death, they not only continue to do these very things but also approve of those who practice them.

1:18 In v. 17 Paul wrote that in the gospel "a righteousness of God" is being revealed. Then he added that from heaven the "wrath of God" is being revealed.[2] There is an essential relationship between God's righteousness and his wrath. If God responded to wickedness with no more than a benign tolerance, his righteousness could be called into question. That which is right necessarily stands over against and defines by contrast that which is wrong. We recognize that divine wrath is not the same as human wrath, which normally is self-centered, vindictive, and intent on harming another. God's wrath is his divine displeasure with sin.[3] We call it "wrath" because it shares certain basic characteristics of human wrath. But because it is God's wrath it can

---

[2] J. C. O'Neill is uncomfortable with this section of the chapter and notes that at least twenty-nine words in vv. 18–32 occur nowhere else in Paul's writings. Then he concludes, "I doubt very much whether Paul wrote these verses" (*Paul's Letter to the Romans* [Middlesex: Penguin, 1975], 41). To understand the wrath of God as "the holy revulsion of God's being against that which is the contradiction of his holiness," however, is to understand the severity of Paul's denunciation of pagan degradation (J. Murray, *The Epistle to the Romans*, 2 vols., NICNT [Grand Rapids: Eerdmans, 1965], 1:35).

[3] Some writers tend to depersonalize the wrath of God by defining it in more general terms. C. H. Dodd refers to God's wrath as "an inevitable process of cause and effect in a moral universe" (*The Epistle of Paul to the Romans* [London: Hodder & Stoughton, 1932], 23). C. K. Barrett is more correct in his emphasis that "wrath is God's personal (though never malicious or, in a bad sense, emotional) reaction against sin" (*A Commentary on the Epistle to the Romans*, HNTC [New York: Harpers, 1957], 33).

have none of the sinful qualities of its analogical counterpart.[4] Berkeley calls it God's "indignation" (MLB) while the NEB chooses the expression "divine retribution."

Although the wrath of God is primarily eschatological, it is at the same time a present reality. The use of the present tense (*apokalyptetai*, "is being revealed") indicates something that is taking place in the present. Furthermore, vv. 24–32 describe divine wrath as currently operative in the lives of the ungodly. That God's wrath is present does not mean that it will not also be eschatological. God's present wrath anticipates his final withdrawal from those who do not respond to his love.

The wrath of God is being revealed against every sort of "godlessness and wickedness." C. Hodge takes these two terms to mean impiety toward God and unjustness toward humanity.[5] Lack of respect for God leads to a lack of justice for people. History demonstrates that nations that forsake God lose their concern for the rights of the individual. To forsake God is to forsake his creatures. As a national policy, atheism grinds its people under the collective heel of "what's best for society."

The people of whom Paul spoke were those who by their wicked and sinful lives "suppress the truth." Truth cannot be changed, but it can be held down or stifled. Wickedness "denies . . . truth its full scope" (Knox). We will learn in the verses that follow that God has revealed to all humans something of his eternal power and nature. Yet people refuse to believe, and as a result their understanding is darkened. To turn willfully against God is to move from light into darkness. The blindness that follows is self-imposed.

1:19–20   Verses 19 and 20 tell why the wrath of God is being revealed. God, in his creation, has provided sufficient evidence of himself to hold accountable all who reject that revelation. What can be known of God is perfectly clear. God himself[6] made it plain. Theolo-

---

[4] E. Best writes that God's anger "does not mean that God is subject to outbursts of passion or dominated by a slow sulky desire to get even with those who offend him" (*The Letter of Paul to the Romans,* CBC [Cambridge: University Press, 1967], 19). J. R. W. Stott calls God's wrath "his pure and perfect antagonism to evil," "his holy hostility to evil" (*Romans* [Downers Grove: InterVarsity, 1994], 37, 72).

[5] C. Hodge, *Commentary on the Epistle to the Romans* (Grand Rapids: Kregel, 1882), 53. Another way of stating the same position is to say that ἀσέβεια refers to religious sins and ἀδικία to moral sins. These two categories would cover the first four Commandments and the last six respectively. Another possibility is that the two terms form a hendiadys that summarizes the terrible sinfulness of humans.

[6] The phrase ὁ θεός stands in the emphatic position in the clause.

gians call this natural revelation (as distinguished from special revelation). Attempts by the medieval church to prove the existence of God on the basis of creation are commonly held to fall short of their goal. There is no doubt, however, that creation is the work of a Creator. To demand some sort of absolute proof of God's existence is simply an indication of the recalcitrant nature of fallen humanity.

Verse 20 explains that certain invisible attributes of God have been clearly perceived since the world[7] began, specifically, his "eternal power and divine nature."[8] They are understood from what has been made. The NEB says they are "visible . . . to the eye of reason."[9] God has revealed himself in nature in such a way as to hold all people responsible.[10] They are "without excuse." Seeing the beauty and complexity of creation carries with it the responsibility of acknowledging the Creator both as powerful and as living above the natural order. Disbelief requires an act of rebellion against common sense. It displays fallen humanity's fatal bias against God. Although the created order cannot force a person to believe, it does leave the recipient responsible for not believing.

The text says that people are without a defense for their unwillingness to believe. The Greek word translated "without excuse" (*anapologētous*) suggests that from a legal standpoint people had been stripped of any defense. The age-old question about the salvation of the "heathen" is clearly answered in this verse. Nature holds people responsible to believe in a God of eternal power. The question of what may or may not constitute the minimum requirements for salvation is not dealt with here. To rebel against God's self-revelation in nature is to incur the results of that rebellion. Things visible call for a power that is invisible. The idea that matter has always existed is an impossible premise for the logical mind. The view that behind the visible world there must exist an

---

[7] By κόσμος Paul meant the entire universe. The term originally designated an "ornament," and the universe was described as a great jewel.

[8] At this point Paul was using language common to Stoic thought, which entered Hellenistic Judaism by means of the Jewish wisdom tradition. ἀΐδιος, δύναμις, and θειότης are terms normally associated with deity.

[9] That God exists and has certain properties that distinguish him from mere mortals is clearly perceived through what he has created. Murray says that this passage is "a clear declaration to the effect that the visible creation as God's handiwork makes manifest the invisible perfection of God as its Creator" (*Romans,* 1:40).

[10] εἰς τὸ with the infinitive occurs forty-three times in Paul, almost always to express purpose. God's intention was to make people responsible by his self-revelation in nature.

invisible Being is far more reasonable. So those who do not believe are without excuse.

1:21–23 We can reasonably expect that knowing God should lead to honoring him as God and giving thanks. But by nature people neither give[11] him glory for who he is nor give him thanks for what he has done. In the Sermon on the Mount, Jesus spoke of sun and rain benefitting both the righteous and the unrighteous (Matt 5:45; cf. Acts 14:17). God gives to all the basic requirements for life irrespective of their relationship to him. The proper response should be gratitude. But people choose to ignore God and come up with their own version of reality. By rejecting the knowledge of the true God, religion is born. F. J. Leenhardt calls it "the triumph of gods over God."[12] That line of foolish speculation leads to futility. Paul said that "their misguided minds are plunged into darkness."[13] To turn from the light of revelation is to head into darkness.[14] Sin inevitably results in a darkening of some aspect of human existence. In a moral universe it is impossible to turn from the truth of God and not suffer the consequences. Ignorance is the result of a choice. People who do not "know" God are those who have made that choice. Understanding God requires a moral decision, not additional information.

In rejecting the knowledge of God available in creation, people claimed to be wiser than God (v. 22). Self-deification lies at the heart of human rebellion. But although they claimed to be wise, they became fools.[15] One cannot turn from knowledge with impunity. The rejection of truth marks the rebel as a fool. There are two contrasts here—light and darkness, wisdom and foolishness.

People participated in an unfortunate exchange. Their "wisdom" led them to barter the majesty of the immortal God for "images made to

---

[11] Beginning with v. 21 Paul used the aorist tense. He was not, however, referring to pagans of some former period. The aorists are gnomic and describe what is true at all times of pagan conduct.

[12] F. J. Leenhardt, *The Epistle to the Romans* (London: Lutterworth, 1961), 68.

[13] "Once man had fallen from his true relation with God, he was no longer capable of truly rational thought about him" (Barrett, *Romans*, 37).

[14] A. Nygren writes, "When man attempts to escape from God into freedom, the result really is that he falls a prey to the forces of corruption" (*Commentary on Romans,* trans. C. C. Rasmussen [Philadelphia: Muhlenberg, 1949], 111).

[15] L. Morris notes that ἐμωράνθησαν "has the notion of insipidity about it, . . . those who in their 'wisdom' reject God's revelation do not enter a wonderfully exciting new life, but a life which, in comparison with the service of God, is flat, tasteless, insipid" (*The Epistle to the Romans* [Grand Rapids: Eerdmans, 1988], 86).

look like mortal man" (v. 23). In fact, they even exchanged the glory[16] of God for images of birds, beasts, and creatures that crawl along the ground.[17] This threefold classification (cf. Gen 1:20–25) as well as terms such as "image" (Gen 1:26) suggest strongly that Paul was describing the wickedness of humans in terms of the Genesis account of the fall of Adam and Eve.[18] The worship of gods in the form of animals was common in the pagan world. In the ancient Near East people worshiped such animals as bulls, jackals, hawks, and serpents.[19] Paul's denunciation brings to mind Ps 106:20 ("They exchanged their glory for an image of a bull"), which alludes to the Israelites' worship of the golden calf at Sinai (Exod 32).

Although God is "immortal" (*aphtharton*), humans are only "mortal" (*phtharton*). To exchange the one who exists outside of creation, not subject to its inevitable demise, for that which at the very moment is caught in the process of decay indicates the abysmal ignorance of fallen humans. In Deut 4:16–18 God prohibited the Israelites from making images shaped like a man, any animal on earth, or any creature that moved along the ground. Paul used these same categories to describe the flight of sinners away from the knowledge of God. This decline from idols shaped like humans, to images of beasts, and even to creeping things shows that a debased mind gravitates to the lowest possible level.[20]

1:24–25 People cannot turn their backs on God with impunity. They exchanged the majesty of God for images made by their own hands, so God "gave them over[21]... to sexual impurity." The verb has a certain judicial quality. The NIVSB note on 1:24 says, "God allowed sin to run its course as an act of judgment." God's wrath mentioned in Romans 1 is not an active outpouring of divine displeasure but the removal of restraint that allows sinners to reap the just fruits of their rebellion. F. Godet writes that God "ceased to hold the boat as it was dragged by the current of the river."[22] The TCNT says that God has "abandoned them to impurity."

---

[16] The δόξαν τοῦ ἀφθάρτου θεοῦ in v. 23 refers not so much to his majesty and perfection as it does to his self-revelation in nature as described in vv. 19–22.

[17] ἑρπετῶν is from ἕρπω, which means "to creep" (LS).

[18] Cf. M. D. Hooker, "Adam in Romans 1," *NTS* 6 (1959–60): 297–306.

[19] J. B. Pritchard, *Ancient Near Eastern Texts* (Princeton: University Press, 1950), 129; and *The Ancient Near East in Pictures* (Princeton: University Press, 1954), 185–89.

[20] Luther noted four steps or stages of perversion: (1) ingratitude, (2) vanity, (3) blindness, and (4) total departure from God (*Commentary on the Epistle to the Romans,* trans. J. T. Mueller [Grand Rapids: Zondervan, 1954], 29–30).

[21] παρέδωκεν. Note the identical clause in vv. 26 and 28.

Moral degradation is a consequence of God's wrath, not the reason for it.[23] Sin inevitably creates its own penalty. "One is punished by the very things by which he sins" (*Wis* 11:16). Through the psalmist God declared, "My people would not listen to me . . . so I gave them over to their stubborn hearts to follow their own desires" (Ps 81:11–12). Divine judgment is God permitting people to go their own way.

The text speaks of "the sinful desires of their hearts." Although the Greek word translated "desires" (*epithumiais*) may be taken in a good sense (as in Phil 1:23; 1 Thess 2:17), it normally is used of desires that are evil. Scripture is clear that the human heart is fatally inclined toward evil. What the "sexual impurity" consists of is clearly delineated in the verses that follow. It is described as "degrading . . . their bodies with one another."[24] By practicing the abnormal vices listed in vv. 26–27, men and women actually degrade their own bodies. Our physical bodies were meant for better and more noble purposes. Sin is a virus that invades the human soul and takes its toll throughout a person's entire being. The Greek infinitive translated "degrading" (*atimazesthai*) is present tense, suggesting the continuing practice of dishonoring the body.

In v. 23 pagans are said to have bartered away the glory of God. Now v. 25 says they have bartered away the truth of God. The truth Paul spoke of is God's self-revelation through creation. And what did the pagans get in exchange? Hardly a bargain! In exchange for the glory of God they acquired idols. They traded the truth of God for "a lie." Calling attention to the definite article, Morris writes that Paul was "not thinking of idolatry as no more than one falsehood among many. It is the lie."[25] To turn from God is to head straight for theological and moral bankruptcy. The lie they bargained for led them to worship and serve[26] that which is made instead of the Maker.

God created humans for fellowship. To deny that intended purpose is

---

[22] F. Godet, *Commentary on St. Paul's Epistle to the Romans*, 2 vols. (Grand Rapids: Kregel, 1977), 1:177. J. Ziesler notes that God's wrath "operates not by God's intervention but precisely by his not intervening, by letting men and women go their own way" (*Paul's Letter to the Romans* [London: SCM, 1989], 75).

[23] Cf. E. Käsemann, *Commentary on Romans* (Grand Rapids: Eerdmans, 1980), 47.

[24] The articular infinitive τοῦ ἀτιμάζεσθαι is variously understood as final (designating purpose), consecutive (indicating result), or epexegetic (explaining the previous expression).

[25] Morris, *Romans*, 90.

[26] J. A. Fitzmyer says that σεβάζομαι "denotes general religious veneration," and λατρεύω "refers to cultic worship" (*Romans*, AB [New York: Doubleday, 1992], 285).

to enter the darkness of paganism. Moral direction is lost. The rebel worships himself in the form of idolatrous images. Either the Lord is God or people assume that role. The first option brings spiritual wholeness; the latter, a hopeless and fraudulent self-deification. It is the Creator, not that which he creates, who is "forever praised."[27] Both the RSV and the NEB see v. 25 as providing the reason for v. 24. God gave them over because they exchanged the truth for a lie. But the relative pronoun with which the sentence begins is qualitative.[28] Verse 25 describes what people of that sort do.

1:26–27   Again it is stated that "God gave them over" (cf. v. 24). God's anger against sin leads him to withdraw from the sinner who willfully continues in wickedness. The penalty for sin is sin itself with all its inevitable consequences. Because people failed to glorify God and give him thanks, God gave them over "to sexual impurity" (v. 24). Because they exchanged the glory of God for a lie, he gave them over to the "passions that bring dishonor" (v. 26).[29]

Romans 1:26–27 contains the clearest teaching in the New Testament on homosexuality. In this section Paul described the practice as "shameful," "unnatural," indecent," and as a "perversion." By contrast, the Greco-Roman society of Paul's day tolerated homosexuality with considerable ease.[30] Among some advocates it was viewed as superior to heterosexuality. Barclay notes that "fourteen out of the first fifteen Roman Emperors were homosexuals."[31]

In Jewish culture, however, it was regarded as an abomination. Barrett comments that "no feature of pagan society filled the Jew with greater loathing than the toleration, or rather admiration, of homosexual practices."[32] The Old Testament specifically prohibits homosexuality. Leviticus 18:22 says, "Do not lie with a man as one lies with a woman;

---

[27] Cf. Rom 9:5 and 2 Cor 11:31 for the identical phase.

[28] It begins with οἵτινες.

[29] ἀτιμίας is a genitive of quality. πάθη ἀτιμίας means "passions that bring dishonor." In the NT πάθος is always used in a bad sense. Here it refers to unnatural lust.

[30] H. Rhys says that Aristophanes found homosexuality "sufficiently widespread in Athens to say in one of his comedies that the audience contained a clear majority of sodomites" (*The Epistle to the Romans* [New York: Macmillan, 1961], 26).

[31] W. Barclay, *The Letter to the Romans* (Edinburgh: St. Andrews, 1957), 32. A. M. Hunter quotes Suetonius's remark that Julius Caesar was "every woman's man and every man's woman" (*The Epistle to the Romans*, TBC [London: SCM, 1955], 33). Cf. Plato's *Symposium* and Plutarch's *Lycurgus* on homosexuality in ancient times.

[32] Barrett, *Romans*, 39.

that is detestable." The penalty for both participants was death (Lev 20:13).[33] In 1 Cor 6:9–10 Paul specifically said that "homosexual offenders"[34] will not "inherit the kingdom of God." Against this background it is difficult to understand why some contemporary teachers—even some who claim to be biblical—make allowance for a practice clearly condemned in both the Old and the New Testaments.[35] Achtemeier writes that the kind of life Paul described in vv. 26–27 "cannot be understood as an alternative life-style, somehow acceptable to God" but rather as "a sign of one of the forms God's wrath takes when he allows us free reign to continue in our abuse of creation and in our abuse of one another as creatures."[36]

Several specifics in this section call for attention. The NIV and several other translations say that "even the women" are caught up in the unnatural practice of lesbianism. Even they have turned from natural to unnatural sexual practices. God did not intend women to "have sex" with other women. It is the shameful result of willful moral disobedience. Stuhlmacher calls lesbian love "a sinful reversal of Gen. 1:27f."[37] Men, as well, have abandoned natural relations with women and are "inflamed with lust for one another."[38] The sexual drive itself is wholesome and good. It is God's way of providing both pleasure and progeny. When directed toward a person of the same sex, it abandons its God-given purpose and becomes a degrading passion.

When men commit "indecent acts with other men," they receive back "the due penalty for their perversion" (Rom 1:27). Once again we see the necessary relationship between sin and its consequences. To put it in terms of Newton's third law of motion, every sin calls for an "equal and opposite" response. The "inevitable recompense"[39] for homosexuality

---

[33] Cf. also Gen 19:1–10; 1 Cor 6:9; 1 Tim 1:9–10; Jude 7.

[34] The term is μαλακοί, lit., "soft ones," commonly explained as males who let themselves be sexually used as women.

[35] J. Boswell understands Paul as viewing homosexual acts as peculiar, but not as "morally reprehensible" (*Christianity, Social Tolerance and Homosexuality* [Chicago: University of Chicago Press, 1980], 112). See the insightful response by R. B. Hays, "Relations Natural and Unnatural: A Response to John Boswell's Exegesis of Romans 1," *JRE* 14 (1986): 184–215.

[36] P. Achtemeier, *Romans* (Atlanta: John Knox, 1985), 41.

[37] P. Stuhlmacher, *Paul's Letter to the Romans,* trans. S. J. Hafemann [Louisville: Westminster, 1994], 37.

[38] ἐκκαίω means "to set on fire." In the passive it means "to be consumed by fire." Cf. Paul's use of πυροῦσθαι ("to burn") in 1 Cor 7:9.

[39] Zerwick, *Analysis,* 460

is to receive back the regular consequence of that practice. Since we live in a moral universe, moral failure must of necessity carry a penalty. Homosexuality, as a perversion of God's intended relationship between man and woman, carries its own destructive penalty.

1:28–32   For the third time in five verses Paul wrote that when people disregard God's revelation in nature, he gives them over to the normal consequences that follow. Here in v. 28 he is said to give them over to "a depraved mind" (cf. vv. 24 and 26). Truth rejected leaves its mark. One's ability to think clearly about moral issues is undermined.[40] Turning from the light of revelation disqualifies a person to think correctly about the issues of life. God's will and his ways with humans are crucial factors in understanding the moral world in which we live. Secular education, which rules out the hand of God in history, is seriously flawed because it attempts to understand the whole without acknowledging the most significant part.

God gave these people over to a reprobate mind, since they came to the conclusion that God was not necessary as one of life's basic presuppositions. As a result they "do what ought not to be done."[41] This expression refers not only to the debased sexual activity outlined in vv. 24–28 but also to the twenty-one negative qualities (cf. vv. 29–32) of those abandoned to their own sinful natures. This list of sins was undoubtedly part of Paul's rhetorical arsenal to be used in pressing home the need for righteousness on the part of the Gentile sinner. A common practice in antiquity was to assemble catalogs of vices.[42]

Paul's list seems to divide somewhat naturally into three parts. The first four vices are abstract nouns in the dative singular. They are all quite general. The next five are in the genitive singular and relate to envy and its consequences. The final twelve are in the accusative plural and include a variety of sins that pagan society would condemn as dan-

---

[40] The ἀδόκιμος νοῦς is a mind so depraved that it is unable to think with any clarity about moral issues. Note the wordplay between what the pagans did (ἐδοκίμασαν) and what they received as a result (ἀδόκιμον νοῦν).

[41] τὰ μὴ καθήκοντα is a technical term taken from Stoic philosophy. It designated actions that were not considered proper. Schlier says that Paul used the term to refer to "what even natural human judgment regards as vicious and wrong" (*TDNT* 3.440). By using the language of Stoicism, Paul broadened his appeal from the ethics of Jewish tradition to the broader agreement of all people that there are some things that simply should not be done.

[42] A typical example from Judaism is found in *Wis* 14:25–26. For other lists in the NT see Matt 15:19; Gal 5:19–21; 1 Tim 1:9–10; 1 Pet 4:3.

gerous to the social fabric. Each term is worthy of serious study, but for that the reader will want to consult Greek lexicons, New Testament word study books, and more technical commentaries. Here we will simply list the words and comment briefly on certain ones.

Paul first described the Gentile sinner as being "full" of a number of sinful characteristics. "Wickedness" is the lack of moral uprightness.[43] "Greed" is the insatiable desire to have more,[44] normally to the disadvantage of others. Morris comments that "envy reminds us that evildoers are not just one happy band of brothers."[45] A number of commentators have taken "malice" in the rather specific sense used by Aristotle: "the tendency to put the worst construction upon everything."[46] But Paul probably would have used it in the broader sense of malignity. Goodspeed calls it "ill-nature." Grundmann says it is "conscious and intentional wickedness."[47]

Then Paul continued by listing twelve additional character flaws of the unregenerate person. Phillips translates "slanderers" as "stabbers-in-the-back." "God-haters" may be either those who hate God or those who are "loathed by God" (Moffatt), although most scholars prefer the former. Rienecker notes that the Greek word translated "insolent" "contains a mixture of cruelty and pride."[48] "Arrogant" people are those who in their self-sufficiency elevate themselves over all others. They are "boastful." Natural humans are said to "invent ways of doing evil" (they are "ingenious in evil," Goodspeed). To be "senseless" means to be "devoid of conscience" (Moffatt).[49] The Greek term translated "faithless" designates those who are false to their word.[50] The "heartless" are those devoid of "natural affection" (AV).

A more depressing catalog of vices would be difficult to find. Yet who can deny that turning from God leads inexorably down the trail

---

[43] Some emphasize the comprehensive nature of ἀδικία and feel that it encompasses all twenty vices that follow.

[44] Dodd understands πλεονεξία as "ruthless, aggressive self-assertion" (*Romans,* 27).

[45] Morris, *Romans,* 96. Note the assonance between φθόνου ("envy") and φόνου ("murder"). There may well be a logical connection also.

[46] This is the meaning of κακοηθεία in *Rhet.* 1389[b]20 and 1416[b]20.

[47] *TDNT* 3.485

[48] Rienecker, *Key,* 2:5. ὑβριστάς is related to the English word "hubris."

[49] The NJB translates the final four vices as "without brains, honor, love or pity."

[50] ἀσυνέτους is compounded from the alpha privative σύν ("with") and τίθημι ("to place"). It designates those who do not keep a covenant—that which has not been "put in place with" another.

into moral darkness? Although people know well that those who do such things deserve the penalty of death, they not only continue to do them but also applaud others who follow the same course of action.[51] Willful rejection of divine revelation hardens the heart to the point where the rebel takes delight in the sinfulness of others. At this point wickedness has sunk to its lowest level.[52]

Was Paul a bit too severe in his opposition. Were all nonbelievers in his day that vile? What about contemporary America? Don't we all know people who although they are not believers are at the same time kind and thoughtful? The answer to the latter question is yes. Consider, however, that they are the benefactors of a civilization shaped to a great extent by its Judeo-Christian heritage. Remember also that Paul was establishing the important point that outside of Christ there is a critical need for righteousness. He would not say that everyone to whom he was writing was equally sinful or that everyone was guilty of every sin listed.[53] Using a rhetorical method well known to ancient orators, he was pressing home the crucial point that all outside of Christ are in need of salvation.

2. The Jews (2:1–3:8)

(1) God's Righteous Judgment (2:1–16)

¹You, therefore, have no excuse, you who pass judgment on someone else, for at whatever point you judge the other, you are condemning yourself, because you who pass judgment do the same things. ²Now we know that God's judgment against those who do such things is based on truth. ³So when you, a mere man, pass judgment on them and yet do the same

---

[51] *T. Ash.* 6:2 has an interesting parallel: "The two-faced are doubly punished because they both practice evil and approve of others who practice it."

[52] E. F. Scott comments: "This is really the darkest stroke in the whole picture. Not only were all those vices practised but the public conscience was dead, and evil could exhibit itself as if it were good. This is the final and deadliest phase of utter social corruption" (*Paul's Epistle to the Romans* [London: SCM, 1947], 32).

[53] E. F. Harrison, commenting on the problem raised by the sweeping nature of the charges made in this portion of the letter, writes, "Sinful man is capable of committing all [the offenses mentioned], but not every individual is necessarily guilty of every one" ("Romans," EBC 10, ed. F. E. Gaebelein [Grand Rapids: Zondervan, 1976], 27). J. Denney's wise counsel is, "It is a mistake to read these verses as if they were a scientific contribution to comparative religion, but equally a mistake to ignore their weight" ("Romans," 2:594).

things, do you think you will escape God's judgment? [4]Or do you show
contempt for the riches of his kindness, tolerance and patience, not realizing that God's kindness leads you toward repentance?

[5]But because of your stubbornness and your unrepentant heart, you are
storing up wrath against yourself for the day of God's wrath, when his
righteous judgment will be revealed. [6]God "will give to each person
according to what he has done." [7]To those who by persistence in doing
good seek glory, honor and immortality, he will give eternal life. [8]But for
those who are self-seeking and who reject the truth and follow evil, there
will be wrath and anger. [9]There will be trouble and distress for every
human being who does evil: first for the Jew, then for the Gentile; [10]but
glory, honor and peace for everyone who does good: first for the Jew, then
for the Gentile. [11]For God does not show favoritism.

[12]All who sin apart from the law will also perish apart from the law, and
all who sin under the law will be judged by the law. [13]For it is not those
who hear the law who are righteous in God's sight, but it is those who obey
the law who will be declared righteous. [14](Indeed, when Gentiles, who do
not have the law, do by nature things required by the law, they are a law
for themselves, even though they do not have the law, [15]since they show
that the requirements of the law are written on their hearts, their consciences also bearing witness, and their thoughts now accusing, now even
defending them.) [16]This will take place on the day when God will judge
men's secrets through Jesus Christ, as my gospel declares.

2:1–4   Chapter 2 begins with "therefore," a term that normally
introduces the result of that which immediately precedes. In this case,
however, the connection with chap. 1 is not clear.[54] The final section of
that chapter (vv. 18–32) established the need for righteousness among
Gentiles. By the time we reach 2:17 it is obvious that Paul was addressing his remarks to Jews. But to whom were the intervening verses
directed? Some think Paul was for the moment addressing his remarks
to certain Gentiles known for their superior morality.[55] Others think the

---

[54] Barrett's suggestion is that the particle Διὸ connects with 1:32a (v. 32b being a parenthesis): "Men know God's verdict on such sinners as are described in i. 29 ff.; *therefore* the
man who judges proves himself to be without excuse, for he sins . . . and in the act of judging proves that he knows what is right" (*Romans,* 43).

[55] The NIV misses the force of ὦ ἄνθρωπε by translating simply "You." The exclama-
tory ὦ is used to express emotion (BDF, par. 146.1b). "You, sir!" would supply the vitality
inherent in the phrase. This section, along with others, takes on the style of a diatribe, in
which the speaker puts arguments in the mouth of the opponent and then answers them with
a flourish. See S. K. Stowers, *The Diatribe and Paul's Letter to the Romans,* SBLDS 57
(Chico, Cal.: Scholars Press, 1981).

verses refer to anyone, Jew or Gentile, who was inclined to judge others. Stott says Paul "seems to be confronting every human being (Jew or Gentile) who is a moralizer, who presumes to pass judgment on other people."[56] However, the entire second chapter probably was a warning to the Jews not to assume that their national identity was sufficient to provide them a right standing before God.[57]

Earlier we learned that Gentiles who rejected the revelation of God in nature were without excuse (1:20). Now we learn that Jews who passed judgment on their pagan neighbors had "no excuse" (2:1).[58] In the very act of condemning others they automatically condemned themselves because they were guilty of doing the same things.[59] In fact, they "habitually practice"[60] (Montgomery) them. It is psychologically true that people tend to criticize in others those negative traits of which they themselves are guilty. Psychologists call this "projection." Nothing blinds a person more than the certainty that only others are guilty of moral faults.[61]

Jesus warned against condemning others. In the Sermon on the Mount he said, "Do not judge or you too will be judged" (Matt 7:1). The kind of judging both Jesus and Paul referred to was not a sane appraisal of character based on conduct but a hypocritical and self-righteous condemnation of the other person. In the same context Jesus told his followers to watch out for false prophets (v. 15), who are to be

---

[56] Stott, *Romans*, 81.

[57] Cranfield lists seven reasons in support of the position that Paul had the Jews in mind right from 2:1 (*Romans*, 1:138). E. Brunner says that "Paul is now thinking—especially, yet not exclusively—of the Jews" (*The Letter to the Romans* [Philadelphia: Westminster, 1959], 20).

[58] TCNT translates ἀναπολόγητος with, "You have nothing to say in your own defense."

[59] Although idolatry and homosexuality are not commonly associated with the Jews of Paul's day, the other vices listed in 1:21–32 are sins into which anyone can slip with considerable ease. Best does not think Paul had in mind the actual sins listed in 1:29–31. Rather, "he may have in mind a deeper conception of sin" such as in Matt 5:21–48, where Jesus showed that "sin cannot be limited to outward actions or words but involves also the inner motive, though it may never be realized in actual behavior" (*Romans*, 24). Although that is a true conception of sin, at this point Paul certainly was talking about transgressions that took place in what we tend to call the "real world."

[60] πράσσεις is present tense.

[61] Luther noted that while "the unrighteous look for good in themselves and for evil in others ... the righteous try to see their own faults and overlook those of others" (*Romans*, 36).

recognized by their fruit (vv. 16–20).[62] That would be difficult, to say
the least, apart from determining which actions are moral and which are
not. Evaluation is not the same as condemnation. It is the latter that
passes sentence.

In v. 2 Paul established a point of agreement with his Jewish readers.
Both agreed that God is absolutely right in passing judgment on the
wickedness of those described in the latter half of chap. 1. God's judgment is "based on truth," that is, it is "utterly impartial" (Phillips). It is
in accordance with the facts. But now comes the catch. The Jews were
guilty of the "same things." So to pass judgment on the sins of others,
while at the same time practicing those very same sins, was to pass
judgment on themselves. Paul's readers would have to agree that they
could not "escape God's judgment."

We are reminded of the encounter between David and the prophet
Nathan (2 Sam 12:1–14). David agreed that the rich man who killed the
poor man's pet lamb deserved to die. But having passed judgment on
another, he quickly learned from Nathan that he had judged himself. "You
are the man!" declared the prophet. You have taken the lamb (Bathsheba)
of the poor man (Uriah) for your own pleasure. In judging another, you
have judged yourself. God's judgment is based on truth. It is impartial
and makes no distinction between rich and poor, king or pauper.

The answer to the question in Rom 2:3 ("Do you think you[63] will
escape God's judgment?"[64]) would have to be no. That God judges
fairly (v. 2a) leads necessarily to the conclusion that those who do what
they condemn in others must receive the same penalty.

Romans 2:4 comprises two parallel questions. Honest answers to
each would have to be yes. "Are you not, by your hypocritical involvement in the very sins you condemn in others, holding the kindness,[65]
tolerance,[66] and patience of God in contempt?"[67] "Don't you realize
that in withholding punishment, God is trying[68] to lead you to repen-

---

[62] Cf. 1 Cor 5:9; 2 Cor 11:14; Phil 3:2; 1 Thess 5:21; 1 John 4:1 on the subject of "judging." Scripture does not urge a benign tolerance for all regardless of their moral conduct.

[63] The "you" is emphatic (ὅτι σὺ ἐκφεύξῃ τό κρίμα τοῦ θεοῦ).

[64] κρίμα here, and normally in Paul, refers to the judicial verdict of condemnation.

[65] χρηστότητος is not so much the goodness of God viewed as an attribute as it is his
acts of benevolence on behalf of the sinner (see *TDNT* 9.490).

[66] ἀνοχῆς ("tolerance") is not forgiveness but the temporary suspension of punishment.

[67] J. D. G. Dunn finds in v. 4 four reasons Paul had a *Jewish* interlocutor in mind
(*Romans,* 2 vols., WBC [Dallas: Word, 1988], 1:81–83).

[68] ἄγει is conative present, "trying to lead."

tance [paraphrase]?"[69] God's gracious dealing with his own people should have taught them of his kindness and patience. But, true to human nature, such things are rather quickly forgotten. They are "known" yet "forgotten" and must be brought to mind repeatedly.

2:5–6 Instead of turning from their sinful ways, those to whom Paul was writing continued to resist God's kindness. Their stubborn[70] hearts were hardened.[71] Ironically, the delay in divine retribution gave them even more time to accumulate a store of wrath.[72] This wrath will be brought against them on the day when God's righteous judgment will be revealed. The wrath of God spoken of in 1:18 is being revealed in the present time. In 2:5 it is eschatological.[73] It belongs to the end time when God will reward righteousness and punish wickedness. That day of wrath is prophesied in Psalm 110 and recognized as being fulfilled in Rev 6:17. This truth has serious implications. The person who knows but resists truth does not go away from the encounter morally neutral. Truth resisted hardens the heart. It makes it all the more difficult to recognize truth the next time around. Life is not a game without consequences. By our response to God's revelation we are determining our own destiny.

God, whose judgments are absolutely fair and just (v. 5), will render to every person on that day of final reckoning that which is appropriate in accordance with his or her deeds (v. 6). Here we have a basic principle of divine judgment.[74] God will "give[75] to each person according to what that person has done" (cf. Ps 62:12; Prov 24:12; Matt 16:27).[76] But you say, I thought Paul taught clearly that a person is saved by

---

[69] Cf. *Wis* 11:23, "You overlook men's sins that they may repent."

[70] The English word "arteriosclerosis" is derived from σκληρότης ("hardness"). R. Earle speaks of the "hardening of the spiritual arteries" (*Word Meanings in the New Testament, III, Romans* [Grand Rapids: Eerdmans, 1974]). That stubbornness was characteristic of the nation Israel is seen in passages such as Deut 9:27; 31:27.

[71] Jewish readers would be familiar with the dangers connected with hardening the heart (cf. Jer 4:4; Ezek 3:7; *I Enoch* 16:3).

[72] The Greek verb θησαυρίζεις pictures a person storing away wrath as in a treasure.

[73] K. Barth, however, takes the latter part of the verse beginning with ἐν ἡμέρᾳ with θησαυρίζεις. Even in the present time, when God's wrath is being revealed (1:18), the readers are storing up wrath for the future (*A Shorter Commentary on Romans* [Richmond: John Knox, 1959], 34).

[74] Murray writes that v. 6 enunciates three features of God's righteous judgment: universality, "to each one"; the criterion, "according to works"; and the certain and effective distribution of award, "who will render" (*Romans*, 1:62).

[75] ἀποδώσει ("pay back") was used in papyri for the paying of a debt (J. H. Moulton and G. Milligan, *VTGT,* 61.

[76] The principle of judgment based on works runs throughout the OT and NT: cf. Jer 17:10; Hos 12:2; Matt 7:21; 2 Cor 5:10; Eph 6:8; 2 Tim 4:14; 1 Pet 1:17; Rev 2:23; 22:12.

faith. That is true. A bit later he affirmed that a person "is justified by faith apart from observing the law" (Rom 3:18). But in the immediate context Paul was not teaching how we are made right with God but how God judges the reality of our faith. Faith is not an abstract quality that can be validated by some spiritual test unrelated to life. God judges faith by the difference it makes in how a person actually lives. A. M. Hunter is right in saying that "a man's destiny on Judgment Day will depend not on whether he has known God's will but on whether he has done it."[77] That is why Jesus taught that those who respond to the needs of the hungry, the thirsty, the stranger, the sick, and the prisoner will be rewarded with eternal life; but those who fail in these down-to-earth tasks will "go away to eternal punishment" (Matt 25:31–46).

2:7–8 These verses consist of two couplets, the second of which follows in reverse order and expands the first (A-B-B-A).[78] In v. 7 we learn of "those who . . . seek glory, honor and immortality." They are set over against "those who are self-seeking and who reject the truth and follow evil" (v. 8).[79] These descriptions help us understand what Paul said about God judging on the basis of a person's actions. The first group has directed their lives toward the qualities that ennoble humans. By a steadfast commitment to doing good they seek to share in the glory, honor, and incorruptibility that finds its source in God. But not the second group. Their lives are controlled by selfish ambition. They have rebelled against truth and allowed themselves to be persuaded[80] by that which is wrong, "always resisting the right and yielding to the wrong" (Williams).

And what are the destinies of these two radically different groups of people? Paul said that God will give eternal life[81] to the first, but for the second there will be wrath and anger.[82] Actions determine destiny.

---

[77] Hunter, *Romans*, 36. Similarly, Stuhlmacher writes that "in the final judgment, one's works, as a visible expression of the nature of a person, are evaluated. What is pleasing before God is rewarded; what is evil or was neglected, will be punished" (*Romans*, 46).

[78] D. Moo notes that unlike some chiastically structured paragraphs, the main point of vv. 6–11—that God will judge every person impartially—lies at either end rather than in the middle (*Romans 1–8*, WEC [Chicago, Moody, 1991], 134–35).

[79] Cranfield writes that the first element in the threefold description may be taken to refer to "the basic egotism of sinful men which lies behind their disobedience to the truth and their obedience to unrighteousness" (*Romans*, 1:148).

[80] Note that πειθομένοις is middle voice, "to let oneself be persuaded."

[81] This is Paul's first mention of "eternal life" in Romans. It is life that is qualitatively different from the life of this present age. It is the life of the αἰών to come.

[82] ὀργή and θυμός are the two standard NT words for wrath and anger. ὀργή normally refers to a deep-seated antagonism; θυμός usually describes sudden anger. θυμός may be the outward expression of ὀργή. The NEB combines them, "a fury of retribution."

Some have questioned whether Paul was saying that if people pursue the right goal in life (glory, honor, and immortality) they will be rewarded with eternal life apart from faith. When the question is posed in this fashion, the answer obviously is no. Paul did not teach mutually contradictory truths.[83] It is beside the point to interpret the verses to mean that if a person did persist in good deeds God would grant eternal life because no one can live a perfect life. It is better to assume that only those who have placed their trust in God through Jesus Christ are capable of, or even want to, seek godliness.[84] Paul was clear that "no one seeks God" (Rom 3:11).

2:9–10 These verses reverse the order of vv. 7–8. They treat first the evildoer and then the one who does good. In addition the order within each statement is reversed. This puts the emphasis on the results of what is done rather than on the one who acts. For the first group there will be "trouble and distress."[85] This group consists of those who persist in wrongdoing.[86] As the wise man of Israel declared, "There is a way that seems right to a man, but in the end it leads to death" (Prov 14:12; 16:25). This is true of all people. As Paul put it, "First for the Jew; then for the Gentile." Ironically, priority in blessing (Rom 1:16) results in priority in judgment. Israel was privileged to be the first to receive the revelation of God. But spiritual privilege carried with it spiritual responsibility. Failure brought "trouble and distress." Concerning

---

[83] M. Black says there is no necessary contradiction between this teaching of Paul and his doctrine of justification *sola fide*. "The Pauline doctrine deals with the conditions of entering on the Christian life—that life rooted and grounded on faith alone. But in the life that follows, 'works,' as the spontaneous expression of the life of faith … are no less an integral part of the life which will one day be judged by God—only they are no longer simply the result of conformity to an external code" (*Romans*, 2d ed., NCBC [Grand Rapids: Eerdmans, 1989], 47). Noting that Protestantism has always found serious difficulty with the idea of eschatological retribution according to works, Käsemann comments that "Roman Catholics have seized on it, not without malicious joy, as support for their dogmatics" (*Romans*, 57).

[84] "The reward of eternal life, then, is promised to those who do not regard their good works as an end in themselves, but see them as marks not of human achievement but of hope in God" (Barrett, *Romans*, 46–47).

[85] Both θλῖψις and στενοχωρία carry the idea of being constrained or pressed in by outward circumstances. The latter comes from στενός ("narrow") and χῶρος ("space"). Goodspeed has "crushing distress and anguish." The NEB combines the two words and translates "grinding misery." Some writers think that when Paul used the two words together, θλῖψις refers to outward affliction and στενοχωρία to inner distress.

[86] The NIV's "does evil" fails to convey the emphasis of the present participle (κατεργαζομένου). The TCNT has "who persists in wrongdoing."

Israel, God said, "You only have I chosen of all the families of the earth; therefore I will punish you for all your sins" (Amos 3:2).

The end result is radically different for those who do good. For them there will be "glory, honor and peace." The redeemed will be participants in the glorious reconciliation between God and humans. People will bask in the honor that God so rightly deserves and that, at the dawn of eternity, will be universally recognized (Phil 2:10–11). They will experience the *shalom,* the peace, that only God can give.

The section ends with the assertion that God shows no favorites (v. 11).[87] Ethnic background or racial privilege will not deter God from blessing those who do good or from punishing those who do evil. As Paul stated earlier (v. 6), God will reward each person on the basis of what that person has done.

2:12 Once again Paul compared two groups of people—those who were apart from the law and those were are under the law.[88] The Gentiles were "apart from the law" in the sense that they had no responsibility to obey the commands and ordinances given to Israel through Moses. Israel was "under the law" because they were the recipients of God's revelation through Moses, the great law-giver. Although both groups had sinned,[89] the basis for judgment was different. The Gentiles would "perish[90] apart from the law," while the Jews would be "judged[91] by the law." The Mosaic legislation will play no part in the judgment of those who have not heard. God judges the "heathen" on the basis of the light they have received. In the case of those who have heard, however, the law will serve as the standard for judgment.[92] From a Jewish standpoint the Gentiles,

---

[87] προσωπολημψία (from πρόσωπον, "face," and λαμβάνω, "to take"), found only in Christian literature, reflects the ancient custom of a superior "lifting up the face" of one who had bowed down out of respect. It was a way of showing partiality. In the NT it is always used in a negative sense.

[88] This is Paul's first mention of νόμος, "law." Fitzmyer reminds us that Paul used νόμος in four different senses: (1) figuratively, as a "principle," (2) generically, to mean "a law," (3) the OT or some part of it, and (4) the Mosaic law (*Romans,* 131–35, 305–6). In the majority of cases νόμος refers to the Mosaic law, the Torah.

[89] The aorist ἥμαρτον summarizes sins of an entire life viewed from judgment day.

[90] ἀπόλοῦνται is used in John 3:16 and 1 Cor 1:18 to designate the ultimate destiny of nonbelievers.

[91] κριθήσονται (a "theological passive," God will do the judging) means not simply that those under the law will be judged but that they will receive a negative verdict, they will be condemned.

[92] Käsemann remarks, "Gifts granted to the Jew in salvation history do not protect him against universal judgment" (*Romans,* 61).

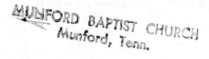

who were outside the law, would certainly perish. But Jews considered themselves to be safe because of the law that had been given to them.[93] They were familiar with passages such as *Wis* 15:2 ("Even if we sin we are thine"). What Paul was about to tell them was that obedience to the law, not possession of the law, was required.

2:13 Paul said that it was those who obeyed the law who were declared righteous, not those who merely heard it read.[94] Obviously Paul was not teaching salvation by works. Later, in his summary of this entire section (3:20), Paul clearly stated that "no one will be declared righteous in [God's] sight by observing the law." In the immediate context Paul adopted for the moment the perspective of Judaism. What needs to be added is that no one could ever keep the law so perfectly as to be considered righteous before God. People have a fatal tendency to substitute passive agreement for action. But God does not pronounce people righteous because their doctrine is correct. Only those who do what God requires are declared righteous (cf. Lev 18:5).[95] Hearing what the law requires is only the first step. Unless hearing becomes doing, it has no particular benefit (Jas 1:22–23,25). This point would be broadly accepted among the Jews. Rabban Simeon (son of Gamaliel I, under whom Paul studied) is cited as saying, "Not the expounding [of the Law] is the chief thing but the doing [of it]: and he that multiplies words occasions sin" (*'Abot* 1.17).

2:14 At this point Paul inserted a parenthetical remark,[96] underscoring for his Jewish audience the critical importance of actually doing what the law said. Whenever Gentiles[97] by natural instinct did what the law required,[98] they demonstrated the existence of a guiding principle within themselves. Twice in v. 14 Paul stressed that non-Jewish people had no

---

[93] Nygren comments, "Far from being safe because he knows the law, the Jew will stand under the judgment of the law" (*Romans,* 121).

[94] ἀκροαταὶ comes from the verb ἀκροάομαι, "to listen." In the present context it pictures a person listening to the law as it is being read.

[95] "What the law requires is ultimately neither ceremonial nor moral conformity ... but believing obedience, or obedient faith" (Barrett, *Romans,* 51).

[96] K. Barth calls it "a strangely obscure and provocative piece of information" (*The Epistle to the Romans,* trans. E. Hoskyns [London: Oxford, 1933], 65).

[97] Note that there is no definite article before ἔθνη. Paul was speaking about *some* Gentiles, not *all* Gentiles. Some scholars, troubled by what they understand Paul to have been saying about Gentiles doing by nature what the law required, take ἔθνη as designating "Gentile Christians." The argument is not persuasive.

[98] Taking φύσει with what follows. Cf. Cranfield for the view that φύσει goes with the preceding words and describes "Gentiles which do not posses the law by nature, i.e., by virtue of their birth" (*Romans,* 1:135–37).

specific knowledge of the Mosaic legislation. They did "not have the law."[99] Yet in certain cases they did instinctively the kinds of things required by the Jewish law (e.g., they cared for the sick and elderly, showed kindness to strangers). They were, as Paul put it, "a law for themselves." That does not mean that law was irrelevant in their case but that their conduct revealed a general knowledge of God's requirements for a principled and virtuous life. Not only did God reveal himself to them in nature (Rom 1:19–20) but he created them with a sense of moral obligation. This moral impetus encouraged a conduct that at many points overlapped what was taught in the laws of God given to Israel.

2:15   The Gentiles by their conduct showed that what the law required[100] was written on their hearts. Paul was not saying that God's specific revelation to Israel through Moses was intuitively known by pagan peoples. He was saying that in a broad sense what was expected of all people was not hidden from those who did not have the revelation given to Israel. Their own conscience acknowledged the existence of such a law.[101] Thrall suggests that Paul was saying that in the pagan world the conscience performed roughly the same function as the law performed in the Jewish world.[102] The conscience, however, is not a norm for action but an inner witness that judges whether or not an act is right or wrong.[103] It is customary to point out that in v. 15 Paul distin-

---

[99] It probably is best to take τὰ μὴ νόμον ἔχοντα in a causal sense, "since they do not have the law," and νόμον μὴ ἔχοντες as concessive, "although they do not have law."

[100] By the "work [ἔργον is singular] of the law" Paul referred to that which the law produced. The plural (ἔργα νόμου, "works of the law") usually has a derogatory sense (3:20; Gal 3:2).

[101] Murray correctly observes that "conscience is an evidence of our indestructible moral nature and is proof of the fact that God bears witness to himself in our hearts" (*Romans*, 1:75, n. 29). Calvin speaks of the conscience as being "equivalent to a thousand witnesses" and notes that "men are sustained and comforted by their consciousness of good actions, but inwardly harassed and tormented when conscious of having done evil" (*The Epistles of Paul the Apostle to the Romans and to the Thessalonians*, trans. R. Mackenzie [Grand Rapids: Eerdmans, 1961], 49).

[102] See M. E. Thrall, "The Pauline Use of Συνείδησις," *NTS* 14 (1967): 124.

[103] The concept of conscience does not come from the OT. Neither does it stem from classical Greek. F. F. Bruce notes that it belonged to the vernacular tongue, attaining literary status shortly before the Christian era (*The Letter of Paul to the Romans*, 2d ed., TNTC [Grand Rapids: Eerdmans, 1985], 86). Dodd says the Stoics invented the term "conscience," which he defines as a person's "consciousness of himself as a rational and moral being," and goes on to say that "neither for Paul nor for the Stoics is conscience a legislative faculty: it does not make the law; it recognizes it and judges conduct by it" (*Romans*, 36). For a definitive work on συνειδήσεως see C. A. Pierce, *Conscience in the New Testament*, SBT 15 (London: SCM, 1955).

guished three ways in which the pagan was apprised of moral responsibility—the law, the conscience, and thoughts that accuse or defend.[104] But since Gentiles were "apart from the law" (v. 12), law in their case hardly could function for them in that sense. Further, two parallel clauses with which the verse closes are closely related. Although the conscience is not specifically the thoughts that accuse and defend, it is not wrong to say that they represent the way they function. The second clause clarifies and explains the first. In other words, one ought not separate the conscience from the inner thoughts that alternatively accuse or defend. The picture is that of people inwardly debating an issue of moral conduct.[105]

2:16 The NIV considers vv. 14–15 to be a parenthetical remark. Thus v. 16 continues the thought of v. 13 and specifies the time when God will declare righteous those who have obeyed the law. The Greek text is less clear. It appears to link v. 16 with what immediately precedes.[106] This latter alternative is preferable and means that one's conscience will bear witness on the day when God judges[107] the things that they have kept secret. God's judgment will be fair because there is absolutely nothing, not even the secrets of people's hearts, that are not known to him.[108] That judgment will be "through Jesus Christ" in the sense that God has entrusted all judgment to the Son (John 5:22).[109] This agrees with the gospel Paul preached. He called it "my gospel"

---

[104] κατηγορέω ("to bring charges against [someone]") and ἀπολογέομαι ("to defend oneself") are both legal terms. They picture a courtroom scene in which charges are brought against a person and a defense is offered. Some understand this as part of final judgment, but it is better taken as an ongoing experience. ἤ καί ("or even") implies that the Gentiles' inner thoughts accused more often than they defended.

[105] The NIV has chosen not to translate the words μεταξὺ ἀλλήλων, "with one another." Knox understands this in a social sense ("when they dispute with one another"), but it is preferable to take the expression in reference to the conflicting thoughts within a person's moral consciousness.

[106] V. 15 ends with a comma, not a period. The relative pronoun ἥ has as its antecedent ἡμέρα, which in turn modifies the participle συμμαρτυρούσης.

[107] κρίνει (pres. tense) should be taken as a future in that Paul had the final judgment in view.

[108] Cf. such passages as Jer 17:10 ("I the LORD search the heart and examine the mind, to reward a man according to his conduct, according to what his deeds deserve") and Heb 4:13 ("Nothing in all creation is hidden from God's sight. Everything is uncovered and laid bare before the eyes of him to whom we must give account").

[109] That final judgment is the work of the exalted Christ is clearly taught in such verses as Matt 25:31–33; Acts 10:42; 1 Cor 4:5; 2 Tim 4:1; and Rev 22:12.

because it was given to him by revelation from Jesus Christ (Gal 1:12).[110]

Paul's attachment to the gospel was profound. Some of his harshest words were for those who would twist the good news for personal benefit (see Gal 1:7–9). The gospel remained at the very center of his ministry of reconciliation. To the Corinthian church he wrote that he was resolved to know nothing while he was with them "except Jesus Christ and him crucified" (1 Cor 2:2). In a day when so much preaching has sold its birthright for a pot of psychological porridge, the need for renewed focus on the essential gospel has never been greater. The gospel is to be *your* gospel. God has entrusted it to *you* (2 Cor 5:19).

(2) Authentic Jewishness Is Inward (2:17–29)

[17]Now you, if you call yourself a Jew; if you rely on the law and brag about your relationship to God; [18]if you know his will and approve of what is superior because you are instructed by the law; [19]if you are convinced that you are a guide for the blind, a light for those who are in the dark, [20]an instructor of the foolish, a teacher of infants, because you have in the law the embodiment of knowledge and truth— [21]you, then, who teach others, do you not teach yourself? You who preach against stealing, do you steal? [22]You who say that people should not commit adultery, do you commit adultery? You who abhor idols, do you rob temples? [23]You who brag about the law, do you dishonor God by breaking the law? [24]As it is written: "God's name is blasphemed among the Gentiles because of you."

[25]Circumcision has value if you observe the law, but if you break the law, you have become as though you had not been circumcised. [26]If those who are not circumcised keep the law's requirements, will they not be regarded as though they were circumcised? [27]The one who is not circumcised physically and yet obeys the law will condemn you who, even though you have the written code and circumcision, are a lawbreaker.

[28]A man is not a Jew if he is only one outwardly, nor is circumcision merely outward and physical. [29]No, a man is a Jew if he is one inwardly; and circumcision is circumcision of the heart, by the Spirit, not by the written code. Such a man's praise is not from men, but from God.

In the previous section Paul addressed his Jewish readers in a relatively restrained manner. But here the mood changed. Once again he employed the diatribe style that he used in the opening verses of chap. 2. His tone became quite severe as he laid out before them the

---

[110] See Rom 16:25 and 2 Tim 2:8 for other occasions of τὸ εὐαγγέλιόν μου.

absolute necessity of bringing their conduct into line with their profession.[111] From this point on to the end of the second major division (Rom 3:20), we hear Paul the preacher convincing his listeners of their need for a different kind of righteousness. Although in another letter he claimed that his preaching was not eloquent (1 Cor 2:1–5), it is hard to deny that here in Romans we are dealing with the dynamic rhetoric of an evangelist bent on persuasion.

2:17–18   Verse 17 begins with a series of conditional clauses, each of which assumes its premise to be true.[112] Paul addressed his listeners directly: "Now you, if you call yourself a Jew"[113]—and of course they did! To be a member of the Jewish race was to enjoy certain religious advantages over other nations. Gradually, however, privilege gave birth to self-righteousness. Paul understood the sentiments of those to whom he wrote because prior to conversion he himself was among those who were the most zealous for their Jewish heritage (Gal 1:14). They relied on the law.[114] After all, God had revealed himself to Israel through the great law-giver Moses and laid out his expectations for the nation. Their national identity was inextricably bound up with Mosaic legislation. They boasted[115] of their unique relationship to God. He was theirs and theirs alone. No other nation had been so blessed. God was the father of Israel (Exod 4:22; Isa 63:16). Another advantage for the Jews was their knowledge of the will of God (v. 18). God had clearly revealed to the nation what he expected of them. Because they were "instructed by the law,"[116] they were able to distinguish that which was morally superior.[117]

---

[111] Dodd writes: "Paul now turns directly to the Jew, with a fiercely satirical attack upon his complacent self-satisfaction, which elaborates the charge made in v. 3" (*Romans,* 38).

[112] It is difficult to know how Paul intended his readers to understand the structure of vv. 17–24. Some think vv. 21–24 are meant to be taken as the apodosis of the conditional clauses in vv. 17–20. Others think at v. 20 Paul simply abandoned the conditional mode.

[113] Ἰουδαῖος originally designated a person from the land in which Judah and his descendants lived. Later it served to identify anyone who belonged to the people of Israel.

[114] ἐπαναπαύομαι means "to rest upon." Here the meaning is "to rest one's hopes on."

[115] Probably an allusion to Jer 9:24 ("Let him who boasts boast about this: that he understands and knows me, that I am the LORD." Cf. 1 Cor 1:31; 2 Cor 10:17. καυχάομαι occurs thirty-seven times in the NT and in only two cases is it used by someone other than Paul.

[116] Zerwick (*Analysis,* 2:463) has "teach by word of mouth" for κατηχούμενος. Goodspeed translates "from hearing the Law read." Our word "catechism" (instruction given to new converts) is derived from this verb.

[117] The TCNT translates "have learned to appreciate the final moral distinctions." If Paul used τὰ διαφέροντα in conscious contrast to ἀδιάφορα, a technical term in Stoicism for "things indifferent, neither good or bad" (Dunn, *Romans,* 1:111), he would have been saying that the Jews were able to distinguish the things that really mattered.

2:19–20 Self-righteous Jews had persuaded themselves that they were superior to people of other nations. They pictured themselves as guides for the blind[118] and lights for those in darkness (v. 19). There is no one quite so blind as those who are confident they can see. Jesus' most severe words were directed against the Pharisees. He called them "blind guides" (Matt 23:16,24). Instead of being a light to those living in the darkness of paganism, the Jewish nation had withdrawn from other cultures. The less contact with those who disregarded ceremonial distinctions the better. The Gentiles were "foolish"[119] and in need of instruction, "infants"[120] who needed to be taught.[121] The Jews to whom Paul was writing considered them to be devoid of spiritual perception. They needed guidance and instruction from the spiritually mature.

Jewish self-righteousness stemmed from a basic misunderstanding of what it meant for them to have been the favored recipients of the law. It is true that in the law they had the "embodiment[122] of knowledge and truth." But knowledge and truth were intended to be carried out in the affairs of life. They were never meant to be co-opted into the service of personal self-aggrandizement. The Jewish audience to whom Paul wrote fell miserably short of God's intention for those so blessed with divine favor. They serve as a type of all believers who prostitute the blessings of God to serve their own selfish instincts.

2:21–23 Paul continued his diatribe with a series of pointed questions (2:21–23).[123] You, then, O teacher of others,[124] do you not teach yourself? The assumption, of course, was that they were not carrying out what they were teaching. Thus the TCNT translates, "Why, then, you teacher of others, do you not teach yourself?" You who denounce stealing, do you steal (cf. Matt 23:3–4)? You who condemn adultery, are you not guilty of the same offense?[125] You who loathe idols, have you not

---

[118] The role of the Messianic Servant was "to open eyes that are blind" (Isa 42:7).

[119] Denney comments that the ἄφρονες are "persons without moral intelligence" ("Romans," 2:599).

[120] νήπιοι is used in a patronizing way of those considered immature in issues of religious significance.

[121] παιδευτής may carry to some degree the idea of correction (cf. Heb 12:9, the only other occurrence in the NT). Fitzmyer provides a literal translation of the entire phrase, "a schoolmaster of fools" (*Romans,* 317).

[122] μόρφοσις here refers to the "full content" or "embodiment." Conybeare translates "perfect pattern."

[123] One would expect the apodosis at this point, but instead the syntax is broken (the NIV uses a dash), and five questions follow.

[124] The participles in the series of questions may be taken as vocative (GAGNT 2.463).

[125] Cf. *Pss. Sol.* 8:12, "[Israel] committed adultery, every man with his neighbor's wife."

plundered treasure from heathen temples?[126] Do you who pride your-selves in the law habitually dishonor God by transgressing the law?[127]

2:24 Throughout the Gentile world the Jews' hypocritical conduct had led others to blaspheme the name of God.[128] Intended to represent God to the nations, they had caused others to hold him in contempt. By their conduct they had disgraced the God they professed to worship.[129] In recent years a number of religious leaders have been publicly exposed for sexual sins. The impact upon those who trusted them as spiritual guides is great. Thousands have been disillusioned by the conduct of the thoughtless few. To bear the name of God is a sacred trust. To violate that trust has severe repercussions for those leaders themselves and for those whose spiritual growth is harmed by their actions. Jesus' severe denunciation of those who cause others to sin (Luke 17:1–2) is appropriate at this point.

2:25–27 Paul continued his emphasis on obeying the law rather than simply knowing what it teaches. In the previous paragraph Paul demonstrated that the possession of the law in and of itself did not grant the Jew a position of privilege. Now he said the same thing about circumcision[130] unaccompanied by an observance of the law. Circumci-

---

[126] Although the evidence that Jews were involved in robbing pagan temples is hard to come by, Deut 7:25–26 suggests that it was not unknown. Josephus reports an incident in which several Jews appropriated for their own use a gift from a recent convert intended for the temple in Jerusalem (*Ant.* 18.81–84). For protection large stores of valuable treasures often were kept in the temples of pagan gods (*TDNT* 3.255). Schrenk (*TDNT* 3.255) takes Paul's reference in a literal sense. Others take it in a figurative sense as referring to the widespread practice of failing to pay the temple tax (cf. Mal 3:8; *Pss. Sol.* 8:11–13).

[127] Because Paul changed from participles (in vv. 21–22) to a relative pronoun and the indicative (in v. 23), some translators take the fifth "question" as a statement that summarizes the previous two verses.

[128] The quotation comes from Isa 52:5 (LXX). Cf. Ezek 36:22–23; 2 Pet 2:2. In the Isaiah passage God's name was blasphemed because his chosen people were being oppressed. Paul used the quotation to prove that God's name is being blasphemed among the Gentiles because of the reprehensible conduct of the Jews.

[129] Denney pictures the heathen as saying, "Like God, like people; what a Divinity the patron of this odious race must be" (*Romans*, 600).

[130] The importance of circumcision for the Jew cannot be stated too strongly. It was the "single clearest distinguishing feature of the covenant people" (Dunn, *Romans*, 1:120). Any Jewish male who was not circumcised was to be "cut off from his people; he has broken [God's] covenant" (Gen 17:9–14). Nations conquered by Israel were to be circumcised in order to be considered part of the covenant people (cf. Josephus, *Ant.* 13.257–58, 318). At least some rabbis viewed circumcision as a guarantee of salvation; e.g., "no circumcised man will go down into Gehenna" (*Exod. Rab.* 19 [81c]).

sion did have value but only if a person continued to do what the law required.[131] Otherwise circumcision was no better than uncircumcision. Fitzmyer comments that "Paul's bold declaration, equating a good pagan with a circumcised Jew, would have been an abomination to Pharisaic ears."[132] Elsewhere Paul wrote: "Circumcision is nothing and uncircumcision is nothing. Keeping God's commands is what counts" (1 Cor 7:19; cf. Gal 6:15). The Jew who habitually breaks the law[133] has become for all practical purposes an uncircumcised pagan. What Paul taught here about circumcision for the Jew is equally true of baptism for the Christian. Both function as signs; they do not themselves effect what they signify.

It follows logically that if uncircumcised[134] people kept the righteous requirements of the law, they would be regarded as though they were circumcised.[135] It is one's actions, not one's physical features, that count.[136] In fact, people who by virtue of their birth[137] were uncircumcised Gentiles would condemn the circumcised Jew who broke the law, in spite of the fact that the latter had[138] the written code and the sacred rite of circumcision.[139] As Jesus said to his contemporaries who asked for some miraculous sign, "The men of Nineveh will stand up at the

---

[131] Scholars are divided over whether by νόμον πράσσῃς Paul meant a sincere attempt to obey the law or perfect conformity to the everything the law required. The first option fails to do justice to the apostle's clear distinction between faith and works. The second option denies any real value to circumcision because the law cannot be perfectly obeyed.

[132] Fitzmyer, *Romans,* 321.

[133] Both πράσσῃς and ᾖς are present subjunctive, emphasizing the continuing observation or violation of the law.

[134] ἀκροβυστία ("foreskin") in this context refers to the uncircumcised, the non-Jew. J. Marcus points out that ἀκροβυστία and περιτομή probably were derogatory slogans used by Jews and non-Jews to describe their opponents ("The Circumcision and the Uncircumcision in Rome," *NTS* 35 [1989]; see esp. 77–80).

[135] The question asked in v. 26 assumes a positive response (the apodosis begins with οὐχ): "Will not the uncircumcised who keep the law's requirement be regarded as though they were circumcised? Of course they will!"

[136] The identity of these uncircumcised Gentiles is variously understood. They are held to be (1) Gentiles who are saved by works apart from faith, (2) believing Gentiles, (3) hypothetical Gentiles who if they could keep the law perfectly (but of course they can't) would be acceptable to God.

[137] ἐκ φύσεως does not mean "physically" but refers to those who by birth belong to a people who do not practice circumcision.

[138] διά should be taken as indicating attendant circumstances rather than instrumentality. Paul was not saying that the Jews were lawbreakers *because* they had failed to carry out the intention of circumcision and the written code.

[139] Some take γράμματος καὶ περιτομῆς as a hendiadys meaning "literal circumcision." It is better, however, to understand the terms as two advantages of Israel.

judgment with this generation and condemn it" (Luke 11:32). Paul was not saying that obedient Gentiles would be those assigned to judge the Jews but that their conduct would serve as evidence against the disobedient Jew.[140] In the final analysis conduct prevails over doctrine. Faith that does not express itself in action is counterfeit.

2:28–29 In the last paragraph of chap. 2 Paul summarized what it meant to be a real Jew[141] and what kind of circumcision was considered authentic. People were not Jews if their Jewishness was no more than outward appearance. Going through the ceremonial activities of Judaism did not make a person a Jew. And real circumcision was not that which was merely external and physical. A person was a Jew only if he was one inwardly. The circumcision that counted was a circumcision of the heart (cf. Deut 30:6).[142] Real circumcision was the work of the Spirit.[143] It did not come through the mechanical observance of the written code.[144] Authentic Jewishness was inward and spiritual. Authentic circumcision was the cutting away[145] of the old sinful nature. It could be accomplished only by the sanctifying Spirit of God. Those who had experienced it received their praise from God, not from others.[146]

People, true to their nature, inevitably hide their real self and don a self they would like others to see. This second self is concerned to appear right before peers. The drive normally expresses itself in a legalistic battle for supremacy. Personal authenticity comes only when people surrender the hypocritical persons they appear to be and allow the persons they

---

[140] Bruce writes, "The shortcomings of an unworthy Jew will be shown up by the example of a Gentile, who, with none of the distinctive Jewish privileges, nevertheless pleases God" (*Romans*, 89).

[141] Cf. John 1:47; Rev 2:9; 3:9.

[142] The concept of a circumcised heart was well established in Jewish thought (Lev 26:41; Deut 10:16; Jer 4:4; Ezek 44:9; *1QS* 5:5; *Jub.* 1:23).

[143] This understands ἐν πνεύματι as a reference to the Holy Spirit (cf. 2 Cor 3:6) rather than one part of a contrast between the spiritual and the literal (as in the RSV). In Col 2:11 Paul compared circumcision by the hands of men and circumcision by Christ. Rom 7:6 contrasts the Spirit and the written code as two ways of serving.

[144] Older writers often took γράμμα to indicate the literal sense of Scripture and took πνεῦμα as its spiritual sense. In this context γράμμα refers to the law and πνεῦμα to the Spirit.

[145] περιτομή is from περί and τέμνω, "to cut around."

[146] Calvin comments that since the eyes of humans are fixed on mere appearance, we ought not to be satisfied with what is commended by human opinions but "should, rather, be satisfied with the eyes of God, from which the deepest secrets of the heart are not hidden" (*Romans*, 57).

to happen, hence the hypocrisy that permeates society. Believers, having acknowledged their sinfulness and accepted the gift of divine approval, are in a position to reveal themselves as they really are. This ought to make believers the most transparent and childlike people in the world.

(3) The Faithfulness of God (3:1–8)

¹What advantage, then, is there in being a Jew, or what value is there in circumcision? ²Much in every way! First of all, they have been entrusted with the very words of God.
³What if some did not have faith? Will their lack of faith nullify God's faithfulness? ⁴Not at all! Let God be true, and every man a liar. As it is written:

"So that you may be proved right when you speak
  and prevail when you judge."

⁵But if our unrighteousness brings out God's righteousness more clearly, what shall we say? That God is unjust in bringing his wrath on us? (I am using a human argument.) ⁶Certainly not! If that were so, how could God judge the world? ⁷Someone might argue, "If my falsehood enhances God's truthfulness and so increases his glory, why am I still condemned as a sinner?" ⁸Why not say—as we are being slanderously reported as saying and as some claim that we say—"Let us do evil that good may result"? Their condemnation is deserved.

3:1–2 Since racial background and the rite of circumcision did not make a person a real Jew,[147] what advantage was there in being a member of the Jewish race? And what benefit did circumcision confer on those who traced their lineage to Abraham?[148] These are serious questions that call for answers.[149] From what Paul had written in the previous chapter, the answer would seem to be, No benefit at all! But that would challenge the integrity of God, the one who had chosen the nation Israel for himself and given them circumcision as a sign of his

[147] The Greek text has τοῦ Ἰουδαίου ("the Jew"), a collective singular. Paul was not referring to any particular Jew but to Jews in a generic sense.

[148] Morris points out that "circumcision" has the article and may therefore signify "the circumcision that admits to the people of God" (*Romans*, 152).

[149] It is commonly held that Paul was writing in the style of a diatribe in which opposing arguments are raised as questions and then answered. In an important article on the subject, D. Hall challenges this position, holding that the apostle was concerned primarily with objections that arose from within ("Romans 3:1–8 Reconsidered," *NTS* 29 [1983]: 183–97). See also Achtemeier's "Paul's Dialogical Mode of Argument," *Romans*, 73–76.

covenantal relationship. Surprisingly, however, the answer to the question of benefit is, Much in every way! In the first place[150] Israel had been entrusted with the very words God had spoken.[151] Stephen, addressing the Sanhedrin, spoke of Moses on Mount Sinai having received "living words to pass on to us" (Acts 7:38). The Jewish nation was to be the guardian of all that God had revealed through his spokesmen. Of all the nations on earth God had chosen the Jews to be the custodians of his redemptive plan for the human race.[152]

3:3–4   Paul then posed the rhetorical question, What if some of the Jews did not respond in faith?[153] Did their lack of faith cancel out the faithfulness of God?[154] (The TCNT has, "Will their want of faith make God break faith?") The answer is a resounding Not at all! ("certainly not," "heaven forbid").[155] God will remain true to his promise even though every person should turn out to be a liar (cf. Ps 116:11).[156] The

---

[150] πρῶτον means either "first of several" or "of chief importance." The former probably was what he intended. Distracted for the moment, Paul did not continue his list of additional advantages. He returned to the subject in 9:4–5.

[151] τὰ λόγια has been understood in a number of ways: the promises of God, the messianic prophecies, the law, the Ten Commandments, the covenant, and the entire OT. S. L. Johnson thinks that Paul had the promises of the Abrahamic Covenant in mind ("Studies in Romans: The Jews and the Oracles of God," *BSac* 130 [1973]: 239); but τὰ λόγια, while including the covenantal promises, probably has the broader meaning of the entire OT.

[152] Harrison comments that to be "entrusted" with the divine oracles means more than simply receiving, guarding, and transmitting them. "What is called for, in light of the meaning of *logia,* is faith and obedience" ("Romans," 10:35).

[153] The UBS text considers τί γάρ a separate question (as in Phil 1:18) and places a comma after τινες, which makes the rest of the verse one question rather than two. Another and interrelated question has to do with whether the verse should be attributed to (1) an objector, (2) Paul, or (3) the first question (when nothing follows γάρ and a question mark follows τινες) to an objector and the second to Paul. The second option is the most likely. Paul seems to have been involved in an inner debate with himself.

[154] ἀπιστέω can mean either "to refuse to believe" or "to be unfaithful." The NIV chooses the first alternative, which makes the statement refer to the failure of the Jews to find in Jesus the fulfillment of OT promises. It is equally possible that Paul was referring to the unfaithfulness of some Jews to the obligations of their covenant relationship. The two meanings are closely related, and both may be intended.

[155] Fitzmyer calls this an "indignant negative" (*Romans,* 327). Murray says that μὴ γένοιτο indicates "the recoil of abhorrence" (*Romans,* 1:94, n.1).

[156] γινέσθω δὲ ὁ θεὸς should not be taken to mean that God became something he wasn't. γίνομαι often has the same meaning as εἰμι. If the imperative is maintained, the expression would mean "let God be recognized as true." Barrett comments that God's truth is to be believed "even though maintaining it (in the teeth of human unfaithfulness) leads to the conclusion that all men are liars" (*Romans,* 63).

assertion is supported with a reference to David's great prayer of penitence in Psalm 51. David confessed his sin and acknowledged that God
was justified in his judgment (Ps 51:4). Paul was saying that God will be
proven right when he speaks (in judgment). He will win the verdict when
the world goes on trial. God is always true to his word. He is faithful to
his righteous character. That God's faithfulness guaranteed his blessings
was accepted without question. But that this same faithfulness also
involved punishment for disobedience was conveniently forgotten.

3:5–8 It could be implied from vv. 3–4 that the unrighteousness of
unbelieving Jews serves to magnify the righteousness of God. In that
case, would it not be unjust of God to punish the Jew? "What shall we
say?" asked Paul. He answered his own question with a second question, this time anticipating a negative response ("God would not be
unjust in bringing his wrath on us would he?").[157] The answer (coming
in v. 6) would be a strong, Certainly not! Just before that, however, Paul
inserted "a parenthetic apology for the blasphemous thought of God as
unjust."[158] The notion that unrighteous conduct could ever serve to
enhance the righteous character of God is strictly a "human argument."[159] For Jews to reason in this way would have been for them to
deny a basic truth they held to be inviolable, namely, that "God [will]
judge the world" (cf. Gen 18:25; Ps 96:13; Isa 66:16; Joel 3:12).[160] If
punishment on God's part implied injustice, then God, who by definition is just, could not serve as the eschatological judge of all humans.
To put it in the current idiom, we cannot have it both ways.

Paul then restated the thought of v. 5b, this time in the form of
another objection (v. 7). The "antagonist" (if indeed there is one) asked,
"If my rejection of the truth serves to make the truthfulness of God
more apparent and thus increase his glory, then why am I still condemned as a sinner?"[161] In fact, why should we not say, "Let us do evil

---

[157] A question beginning with μή calls for a negative response.

[158] Dunn, *Romans*, 1:135.

[159] See Gal 3:15 for the identical expression and Rom 6:19 and 1 Cor 9:8 for comparable statements. BAGD points out that the expression "emphasizes the inferiority of man in
comparison w. God" (68, 1c).

[160] Denney writes, "That God does judge the world at last is a fixed point both for Paul
and those with whom he argues" ("Romans," 604).

[161] W. Sanday and A. C. Headlam contrast "the truthfulness of God in keeping His
promises" with "the falsehood of man in denying their fulfillment" (*A Critical and Exegetical Commentary on the Epistle to the Romans,* 5th ed., ICC [Edinburgh: T & T Clark,
1902], 73).

that good may result" (v. 8)?[162] Paul branded as "slanderous" the reports that he advocated the antinomian position that good will result from evil.[163] Those who spread such a pernicious misrepresentation deserved the condemnation that would come to them.[164]

3. All People (3:9–20)

[9]**What shall we conclude then? Are we any better? Not at all! We have already made the charge that Jews and Gentiles alike are all under sin. [10]As it is written:**

"There is no one righteous, not even one;
[11]   **there is no one who understands,**
        no one who seeks God.
[12]All have turned away,**
        they have together become worthless;
        there is no one who does good,
        not even one."
[13]**"Their throats are open graves;**
        their tongues practice deceit."
        "The poison of vipers is on their lips."
[14]   **"Their mouths are full of cursing and bitterness."**
[15]**"Their feet are swift to shed blood;**
[16]   **ruin and misery mark their ways,**
[17]**and the way of peace they do not know."**
[18]   **"There is no fear of God before their eyes."**

[19]**Now we know that whatever the law says, it says to those who are under the law, so that every mouth may be silenced and the whole world held accountable to God. [20]Therefore no one will be declared righteous in**

---

[162] Brunner comments that "it is part of God's incomprehensibly wise government of the world that he can also use man's evil doings for the purpose of his kingdom. ... But short-sighted, frivolous men stumble over this most profound truth, inferring from it that sin is not contrary to God" (*Romans,* 25). The punctuation of the UBS text separates vv. 7–8 and allows v. 8 to serve as an answer of sorts to v. 7. (See Cranfield, *Romans,* 1:185–87, for a discussion of the textual problems of these verses.)

[163] The text beginning with the first καθώς and running through λέγειν (or possibly ὅ τι) is parenthetical.

[164] This understanding takes ὧν as referring to τινες rather than to what they say. "The arrogance with which we set ourselves by the side of God, with the intention of doing something for Him, deprives us of the only possible ground of salvation, which is to cast ourselves upon His favour or disfavour" (Barth, *Romans,* 84).

his sight by observing the law; rather, through the law we become conscious of sin.

3:9–12 It was now time for Paul to draw his argument to its logical conclusion. He asked, "What shall we conclude then?"[165] The pagan, rejecting the revelation of God in nature and pursuing a lifestyle that was both idolatrous and degrading, was deserving of the wrath of God (Rom 1:18–32). The Jews, who had the law but failed to put it into practice, received no benefit from their privileged position (Rom 2:1–3). What does all this imply? It is not certain whether the Greek verb in the second question should be translated as a passive or as a middle in an active sense. The NIV takes the second option ("Are we[166] any better?"). This asks whether, in view of the dismal picture just painted, the Jew was in any way better off than the Gentile. The answer is, "Only in a limited sense." However, if the verb is taken as a passive, then the sense would be, "Are we Jews at a disadvantage?" (Weymouth), and the answer would be, "Not at all!"[167] The Jew was neither better off nor at a disadvantage since it has already been established that both Jew and Gentile are under the condemnation of sin (cf. 1 Kgs 8:46; Gal 3:22).[168] This entire section reflects a courtroom scene (the accusation in v. 9, the evidence in vv. 10–17, the courtroom setting in v. 19, and the verdict in v. 20).

To substantiate his claim that both Jew and Gentile stand accused before the bar of divine justice, Paul cited a collection of Old Testament verses.[169] Once again we hear the rhetoric of the evangelist as he urged

---

[165] V. 9 has more than its share of difficulties. Of the several alternatives, the NIV follows punctuation of the UBS text. Also present are problems of textual variants and of overall meaning. For detailed examination of the issues consult the technical commentaries.

[166] Some understand the "we" to mean "we Christians" rather than "we Jews" (e.g., Morris, *Romans,* 165). The argument that they must be distinct from the "Jews and Gentiles" later in the verse overlooks the fact that the "we" that governs that sentence is Paul's editorial "we" and distinct from the earlier question.

[167] Taking οὐ πάντως ("not altogether") in the sense of πάντως οὐ, "Certainly not!" or, "Not at all!"

[168] Commenting on ὑπὸ ἁμαρτίαν, Denney says, "The idea is that of being under the power of sin, as well as simply sinful: men are both guilty and unable to escape from that condition" (*Romans,* 606).

[169] Stringing together quotations from various books of the OT was a common rabbinic practice. It was called "pearl stringing," or more formally *testimonia.* See J. A. Fitzmyer, *Essays on the Semitic Background of the New Testament* (Missoula, Mont.: Scholars Press, 1974), 66f., for a good discussion of this phenomenon. Five of the seven citations come from the Psalms (13:2–3,5; 5:10; 9:28; 35:2; 139:4) and the other two from Isa 59:7–8 and Eccl 7:20. The text follows the LXX with minor modifications.

people everywhere to recognize their need for salvation.[170] The Jews' commitment to the truthfulness of their Scriptures would have made it extremely difficult for them to deny the obvious testimony of the Old Testament that all are under condemnation as a result of sin. "As it is written" translates a Greek verb in the perfect tense (*geqraptai*), emphasizing the authoritative character and permanent nature of the verses cited. The verses quoted by Paul are not always exactly as they are found in the Hebrew Old Testament. Several factors may explain the variations. Some quotes are taken from the Septuagint (the Greek translation of the Old Testament in use at that time), which differs somewhat from the Hebrew text. Also a New Testament author would quite often, under the inspiration of God and to accentuate a specific point, adapt an Old Testament verse to serve his immediate purpose. Furthermore, the practice of precise citation and scholarly acknowledgment is a modern phenomenon. It was not at all a customary practice in antiquity.

Paul used the Old Testament Scripture to prove the lamentable state of those outside of Christ.[171] You will not be able to find even one just or righteous individual (v. 10).[172] No one has genuine understanding (v. 11). If they fully understood the consequences of sin, they would not live as they do. By nature people simply do not seek out or search for God.[173] This insight will come as a surprise for many moderns. People throughout the world are often pictured as seeking God through the various paths offered by different religions. Paul would not agree. It is true

---

[170] Some think that this catena of quotations was already in use by Christian believers. It would serve as a handy reference to show from the OT that all people everywhere are under the domination of sin. It is more likely that Paul developed the list rather naturally as he carried out his apostolic ministry. Rhys writes that "there is no reason to suppose that they are derived from an early Christian collection of testimonies; they set forth a strict Pauline emphasis, and it is not likely that anyone other than the apostle would have selected them" (*Romans*, 39). Cranfield finds the catena constructed "with considerable care and artistry" (*Romans*, 1:191). He finds three strophes, the first consisting of two sets of three lines and the second and third each consisting of two sets of two lines. Moo takes v. 10 as a heading, vv. 11–12 as five statements on the theme of "there is none righteous," vv. 13–14 as describing sins of words, vv. 15–17 focusing on sins of violence against others, and v. 18 as exposing the root error of the sins of humans (*Romans 1–8*, 204–5).

[171] Hunter writes that the quotations "build up into a grim declaration of man's moral bankruptcy and guilt before God" (*Romans*, 43).

[172] δίκαιος here refers not only to one who is right with God but also to one who lives an upright life.

[173] The OT often speaks of "seeking God"; e.g., Isa 55:6 ("Seek the LORD while he may be found; call on him while he is near"); cf. Pss 9:10; 24:6; 27:8; Prov 28:5; Jer 29:13.

that they may be seeking some sort of religious experience, but that is not at all the same as seeking God. Scriptures teach that it is God who takes the initiative. He is the one who seeks us; not the other way around. All have "swerved from the right path" (v. 12; Montgomery). That their failure to seek God is more than an accidental omission is seen in the fact that they have deliberately turned away from God.[174] In the end their lives turn out to be useless and unprofitable.[175] "Not one of them acts honourably, no, not one" (Knox).

3:13–14 In vv. 13–14 Paul cited passages that deal with the throat, the tongue, the lips, and the mouth. The ungodly display their fallen nature when they open their mouths to speak.[176] God provided us with the gift of communication so that we may honor and praise our Creator. We tend to take the gift and place it in the service of our own sinful nature. The throat of the unrighteous is an open grave. Taylor expands the imagery and translates, "Their talk is foul and filthy like the stench from an open grave."[177] Others understand the expression as a reference to the deadly effects of the psalmist's enemies. Their tongues were used to deceive. The poison of vipers was on their lips. Their mouths were full of cursing and bitterness. Jesus said that "out of the overflow of the heart the mouth speaks" (Matt 12:34). Nowhere is this seen more clearly than in the conversation of the ungodly. Although the speech of many believers is not as gross as that of their unsaved neighbors, it often is more like the world than the courts of heaven (see Col 3:1–3).

3:15–18 The feet of the unrighteous are swift to shed blood (v. 15). Their natural instincts encourage them to kill. As a result, ruin and misery "dog their steps" (TCNT). The desire to prevail at any cost leads to suffering and disaster. Evil inevitably overreaches itself. It creates the conditions for its own collapse. In a moral universe wickedness earns its own sentence of personal retribution. The way of peace is unknown to those who turn from God. Their lives are marked by unrest and lack of genuine satisfaction. They live out their days haunted by a dim vision

---

[174] Cf. the use of ἐκκλίνω in 1 Pet 3:11 for a deliberate turning away.

[175] Commentators often mention that the verb ἀχρειόω is used in the LXX of the souring of milk. Barclay notes, "Human nature without Christ is a soured and useless thing" (*Romans*, 55).

[176] Murray writes that "the concentration upon organs of speech in verses 13,14 shows how, in the apostle's esteem, the depravity of man is exemplified in his words and how diverse are the ways in which speech betrays the wickedness of the heart" (*Romans*, 1:104).

[177] Robertson quotes Shedd as saying that "some portions of Greek and Roman literature stink like a newly opened grave" (*WP* 4:345).

that there must be something in life that would satisfy their deeper long-ings. They do not venerate God or hold him in esteem. "Reverence for God does not enter their thoughts" (NEB).[178]

Paul's portrayal of the unrighteous person may seem overly pessi-mistic to many contemporaries. After all, do we not all know certain individuals who live rather exemplary lives apart from Christ? Certainly they do not fit the description just laid out. Although it may be true that many of our acquaintances are not as outwardly wicked as the litany would suggest, we must remember that they are also benefactors of a civilization deeply influenced by a pervasive Judeo-Christian ethic. Take away the beneficent influence of Christian social ethics and their social behavior would be considerably different. Remember as well that Paul was making a specific point and was under no obligation to men-tion all the extenuating circumstances. Then, of course, we participants in this fallen world tend to minimize the difference between our own conduct and the expectations of a holy God. In view of what God intends, humans fall lamentably short (cf. Rom 3:23).

3:19–20   Paul's Jewish audience would have known that the law was applicable only to those who were under its jurisdiction (Rom 2:12).[179] What they apparently were not aware of was that the law placed them in a defenseless position. Rather than providing access to the favor of God, it served to silence any attempt on their part to argue personal righteousness. The law spoke to them "so that no one may have anything to say in self-defense" (NEB).[180] Along with the Gentile, the Jew will be held accountable to God. The whole world falls under the judgment of God.[181]

Once again Paul reiterated the theme that was so difficult for his Jewish audience to understand and accept. No human being can be brought into a right standing with God on the basis of doing what the

---

[178] Perhaps by "fear" Paul intended "terror" rather than "reverence" (see A. F. Kirk-patrick, *The Book of Psalms* [Cambridge: University Press, 1910], 184).

[179] Since ὅσα ὁ νόμος λέγει undoubtedly includes the preceding collection of verses (and they are from the Writings and the Prophets rather than the Pentateuch), ὁ νόμος should be taken as referring to the OT as a whole.

[180] ἵνα πᾶν στόμα φραγῇ pictures a defendant in court rendered speechless by the evi-dence brought against him.

[181] Some wonder how accusations against the Jews can result in the "whole world" being accountable to God. One answer is that the first half of the ἵνα clause refers to Jews alone and the second half to the entire world. More probably we are dealing with an argu-ment that says if God's people are guilty, how much more guilty is the outsider.

law requires.[182] Why? Because the law makes a person conscious of sin. It reveals that we are unable to live up to the righteous requirements of a holy God. Law encourages effort. But human effort inevitably falls short of the divine standard. The purpose of the law is to guide conduct, not to provide a method to stand before God on the basis of one's own righteousness. Phillips notes that "it is the straightedge of the Law that shows us how crooked we are."

Paul had now made his case. People have turned from the knowledge of God revealed in creation and degraded themselves. The Jew, who has the law, has not obeyed the law and is therefore no better off than the Gentile. Both Jew and Gentile fall under the condemnation of sin. Is there hope? In the verses that follow we will be introduced to the righteousness of God, a righteousness that has nothing to do with our performance but everything to do with God's provision in Christ.

---

[182] Note the allusion to Ps 143:2. The future, δικαιωθήσεται, should be understood as gnomic. The anarthrous phrase ἔργων νόμου refers to that which the [Mosaic] law requires. Fitzmyer points out that while the phrase has not been found in the OT, it has turned up in the Qumran literature, thus making Paul a "tributary to a genuine pre-Christian Palestinian Jewish tradition" (*Romans,* 338–39).

III. THE RIGHTEOUSNESS ONLY GOD CAN PROVIDE (3:21–5:21)

1. Received through Faith in Christ (3:21–31)

[21]**But now a righteousness from God, apart from law, has been made known, to which the Law and the Prophets testify.** [22]**This righteousness from God comes through faith in Jesus Christ to all who believe. There is no difference,** [23]**for all have sinned and fall short of the glory of God,** [24]**and are justified freely by his grace through the redemption that came by Christ Jesus.** [25]**God presented him as a sacrifice of atonement, through faith in his blood. He did this to demonstrate his justice, because in his forbearance he had left the sins committed beforehand unpunished—** [26]**he did it to demonstrate his justice at the present time, so as to be just and the one who justifies those who have faith in Jesus.**

[27]**Where, then, is boasting? It is excluded. On what principle? On that of observing the law? No, but on that of faith.** [28]**For we maintain that a man is justified by faith apart from observing the law.** [29]**Is God the God of Jews only? Is he not the God of Gentiles too? Yes, of Gentiles too,** [30]**since there is only one God, who will justify the circumcised by faith and the uncircumcised through that same faith.** [31]**Do we, then, nullify the law by this faith? Not at all! Rather, we uphold the law.**

3:21–24 At the very beginning of Paul's letter to the Romans we encountered the theme that runs throughout the entire epistle. Paul stated that he was not ashamed of the gospel because in it is revealed a righteousness from God that is completely dependent upon faith (Rom 1:17). After building a case against all people, showing their universal sinfulness and therefore their universal need of salvation, Paul then spelled out the only way for them to be brought into a right standing with God.

113

From a human standpoint—and by nature people are legalists—the plan was radical. It excluded anything and everything that people by themselves might do to attain righteousness. The righteousness God provides has its origin in what God did, not in what people may accomplish. It is received, not earned. It depends upon faith, not meritorious activity. God justifies the ungodly, not the well intentioned. What makes the "good news" news is that no one would have come up with a plan that excluded their own contribution toward a future salvation. This central theme is now expanded in what is generally acknowledged as the most theologically important segment of the entire New Testament.[1]

No one will be declared righteous in God's sight by keeping the law, the conclusion reached in 3:22. "But now" (v. 21) introduces God's answer to our basic dilemma. The expression is perhaps less temporal than sequential.[2] God's remedy for our lack of righteousness was enacted at a specific time (on the cross). Here, however, the emphasis falls on the qualitative difference between God's remedy and our attempt to bridge the gap. We want to earn; God will only give. God's way of providing righteousness has nothing to do with human performance. It is "apart from law."[3] Yet both the Law and the Prophets (the literature of the OT)[4] testify to it. The Old Testament itself pointed to a work of God yet future that would provide humans a way of atonement. The righteousness of God[5] comes to us through faith in Jesus Christ.[6] It

---

[1] R. Bultmann concluded that the paragraph is un-Pauline because it contains many non-Pauline words (*Theology of the New Testament,* 2 vols. [London: SCM, 1952–55], 1:46). L. Morris cites N. H. Young, who concludes that "the fragmentary hypothesis of Bultmann and Käsemann is invalid" and that "Rom. iii.24f. is a genuine insight into Paul's own peculiar thought" (*Romans* [Grand Rapids: Eerdmans, 1988], 173, n. 94).

[2] Most contemporary writers take Νυνὶ δὲ as temporal rather than logical and emphasize that it marks the transition to a new stage in salvation history.

[3] χωρὶς νόμου probably goes with the noun phrase that follows rather than the verb, although either is grammatically acceptable.

[4] The Law and the Prophets denotes the OT (E. Best, *The Letter of Paul to the Romans,* CBC [Cambridge: University Press, 1967], 40). Cf. 2 Macc 15:9; Luke 16:16; Acts 24:14.

[5] A. M. Hunter says that the righteousness of God, for Paul, meant "a divine vindicating activity whereby God confers on men a new status or standing with himself" and that in vv. 21–22 the accent falls on the status, rather than the act" (*The Epistle to the Romans,* TBC [London: SCM, 1955], 44). That the two aspects are intertwined is clear from v. 26, which speaks of God as both "just" and "the one who justifies."

[6] πίστεως Ἰησοῦ Χριστοῦ is objective genitive ("faith in Jesus Christ") rather than subjective ("faithfulness of Jesus Christ," i.e., his obedience to the Father culminating in his death on the cross). For the various arguments and related literature see D. Moo (*Romans 1–8* [Chicago: Moody, 1991], 245–46). J. D. G. Dunn (*Romans,* WBC [Dallas: Word, 1988], 1:166–67); or J. Fitzmyer (*Romans,* AB [New York: Doubleday, 1993], 345–46). Had Paul intended "the faithfulness of Christ," he probably would have used ὑπακοή ("obedience") as in 5:19.

belongs to all who believe in him.[7]

Many hold that the final clause of v. 22 and all of v. 23 form a parenthesis that explains why the righteousness of God comes to all who
believe. It is because there is no difference between Jew and Gentile.[8]
Both have sinned and fallen short of God's glory. No one can stand
before God on the basis of personal merit. All have sinned[9] and in so
doing have fallen short of "God's glorious ideal" (Montgomery).[10] In
Jewish thought humans lost their share in this glory when they broke
their relationship to God, but that relationship is to be restored in the age
to come.[11] The original intention was that people reflect the glory of
God (cf. Gen 1:26). By eating of the tree of the knowledge of good and
evil, Adam and Eve sacrificed their relationship to God and determined
the essential nature of everyone born into the human race (Gen 3). The
redemption provided by Christ enables us to be brought back into a personal relationship with God. Apart from the work of Christ we are
unable to effect that restoration.

Those who find a parenthesis in vv. 22b–23 connect "all who believe"
in v. 22 with "and are being justified freely" in v. 24. This construction,
however, contains a grammatical problem. The nominative (of v. 24) and
accusative (of v. 22b) do not fit together in a parallel structure. For that
reason it is better to connect v. 23 with what follows.[12] Although this
seems to say that all have sinned and are being justified, certainly Paul,
even though he did not repeat it, would have us understand that

---

[7] The present tense of πιστεύοντας suggests a continuing reliance on Christ rather than a
momentary acceptance of his work on our behalf. Dunn comments that the early church distinguished themselves as "the believers" (cf. Acts 2:44; 4:32) rather than "the baptized" or any
other equivalent to the rituals of the law (*Romans,* 1:167).

[8] A. Nygren, *Commentary on Romans,* trans. C. C. Rasmussen (Philadelphia: Muhlenberg,
1949), 152–53.

[9] The aorist ἥμαρτον is used as a general statement of the sins of all humans (perhaps from
the perspective of eschatological judgment). Included in that broad spectrum was the original
historical sin of Adam and Eve that predisposed the race to sin (Rom 5:12). See also A. T. Robertson, *Word Pictures,* 4:347.

[10] The NEB translates "deprived of the divine splendour." The biblical meaning of δόξα
(originally it meant "opinion") was influenced by using it to translate the Heb. קָבוֹד. Moo
comments that from the basic meaning of "be weighty" it came to mean, when applied to God,
his "weighty" and magnificent "presence" (*Romans 1–8,* 226). B. M. Newman and E. A. Nida
say that glory in this passages refers to "the likeness of God that each man is intended to bear
but which has been forfeited because of sin" (*A Handbook on Paul's Letter to the Romans* [New
York: UBS, 1973], 66).

[11] Cf. *3 Apoc. Bar.* 4.16; *Apoc. Mos.* 21.6

[12] The participle δικαιούμενοι is taken as a finite verb. It is nominative because it relates
to πάντες in v. 23.

justification[13] is contingent upon faith. Montgomery translates, "*But they are now being justified by his free grace*" (italics added).

The righteousness God provides comes as a free gift. It cannot be purchased or earned. In either case it would no longer be a gift. One of fallen humanity's most difficult tasks is to accept righteousness as a gift. With every fiber of their moral being, people want to earn God's favor. From a human perspective this sounds both reasonable and noble. The hidden agenda, however, is that it would provide a basis for boasting. God neither needs nor desires our help in doing what we could never accomplish.

We underestimate the hopelessness of our sinful state. At best, any righteousness by works would be desperately inadequate. By God's grace we are granted a right standing with him.[14] The basis for this redemptive process is Christ Jesus. The gospel centers in the atoning work of God's unique and only Son. Redemption[15] is found in him and him alone.

3:25–26   Verses 25–26 in the Greek text constitute one long relative clause that sets forth the redemptive work of God in and through Jesus Christ.[16]

Of the several problems in this theologically rich section, none has received more attention than the meaning of the Greek word translated by the NIV as "sacrifice of atonement." At the heart of the discussion is whether the term means "propitiation" (an appeasing of wrath) or "expiation" (a covering for sin).[17]

Some scholars feel that since the appeasing of divine wrath is a pagan concept, it would not be appropriate to apply it to the God of the Judeo-Christian faith. Morris, a major proponent of the view that propitiation is

---

[13] Justification, a metaphor borrowed from the law court, was one of Paul's favorite ways of portraying the work of Christ. δικαιόω means "to declare righteous." In vv. 24–25 Paul employed three metaphors; the second is taken from the institution of slavery, and the third is taken from the ritual of sacrifice. C. H. Dodd writes that Paul combined all three metaphors to describe an act of God for humanity: "In the first, God takes the part of the judge who acquits the prisoner; in the second, that of the benefactor who secures freedom for the slave; in the third, that of the priest who makes expiation" (*The Epistle of Paul to the Romans,* MNTC [London: Hodder & Stoughton, 1932], 56). This assumes, of course, that ἱλαστήριον refers to an expiatory sacrifice rather than the "mercy seat."

[14] God's grace is God acting in Christ for the benefit of sinners. Our justification stems from the unmerited favor shown to us in the gift of God's Son.

[15] ἀπολύτρωσις is a word rich with meaning. It was used of buying back prisoners of war, slaves, and condemned criminals by the payment of a ransom (λύτρον). See L. Morris, *The Apostolic Preaching of the Cross* (Grand Rapids: Eerdmans, 1965), 1–52.

[16] One view is that vv. 24–25 are a pre-Pauline formulation with several phrases added that Paul then restated in v. 26 using language of his own (Bultmann, *Theology,* 1:460). Such a view is unnecessarily speculative.

the correct understanding, presents two major reasons for rejecting the arguments of those with that position: (1) the meaning of the word ("the removal of wrath") and (2) the context (1:18–3:20) show that all are sinners and under the wrath of God. And if the term does not mean the removal of wrath, everyone is still under it.[18] If the idea of the wrath of God does not necessarily carry with it any of the negative connotations of human anger, there should be no particular reason why the appeasing of divine wrath cannot be understood in the same way.

Although the term "propitiation" may not be the best translation, the Greek term is best understood as the placating of God's wrath against sin.[19] Thus Jesus Christ is the one set forth[20] by God as a propitiatory sacrifice to be received through faith. That sacrifice involved the death of his Son. Grammatically, "in his blood" may go with "sacrifice of atonement" or complete the phrase "through faith." Although the former probably is correct, in either case the meaning of the verse remains essentially the same.

---

[17] ἱλαστήριον is related to the verb ἱλάσκομαι, meaning "to appease or to propitiate." Thus C. E. B. Cranfield holds that God set forth Christ as "a propitiatory sacrifice" (*Romans*, ICC [Edinburgh: T & T Clark, 1975–79], 1:216–17). But some argue that ἱλαστήριον is not used in this sense in either the OT or Heb 9:5 (the only other place it appears in the NT) and should therefore be understood against the background of the LXX usage of the Day of Atonement ritual and depict Christ as "the new 'mercy seat,' presented or displayed by the Father as a means of expiation or wiping away the sins of humanity" (Fitzmyer, *Romans*, 350). After a thorough study N. S. L. Fryer concludes that ἱλαστήριον is a neuter accusative substantive (rather than an adjective), and its best translation probably is "mercy seat" or "propitiatory covering" ("The Meaning and Translation of *Hilasterion* in Romans 3:25," *EvQ* [1987]: 99–116). For a concise overview of debate on ἱλασμτήριον see E. F. Harrison, "Romans," EBC 10 (Grand Rapids: Zondervan, 1976), 43–44. For a thorough study of the concept of propitiation see R. Nicole, "C. H. Dodd and the Doctrine of Propitiation," *WTJ* 17 (1954–55): 117–57.

[18] Morris, *Romans*, 180–81. For further discussion see his article, "The Meaning of *Hilasterion* in Romans iii.25, *NTS* 2 (1955–56): 33–43, chaps. 5 and 6 of his *Apostolic Preaching of the Cross*, and the literature cited there.

[19] J. Stott says, "We should not be shy of using the word 'propitiation' in relation to the cross" but struggle to reinstate this language "by showing that the Christian doctrine of propitiation is totally different from pagan or animistic superstitions" (*Romans* [Downers Grove: InterVarsity, 1994], 114–15).

[20] προέθετο means "set forth publicly" rather than "purposed" because the text is explaining how God went about establishing his redemptive program. "The Christian's *kapporet* no longer exists hidden in the holy of holies in the temple but is revealed to all in the form of Christ hanging on the cross." God has "brought to an end the sacrificial cult of atonement in the Jerusalem temple," and Christians "now encounter God directly in his Christ" (P. Stuhlmacher, *Paul's Letter to the Romans*, trans. S. J. Hafemann [Louisville: Westminster, 1994], 60). Hunter adds that if *hilasterion* refers to the lid of the ark, "the mercy seat," then "Paul is saying that Christ crucified has become for the world what the mercy seat was for Israel" (*Romans*, 47).

In setting forth his Son as an atoning sacrifice, God demonstrates his justice. In his forbearance[21] he had allowed sins of an earlier time to go unpunished. Some would argue that this amounts to a lack of justice on the part of God. A moral universe calls for sin to be punished. However, it was not neglect on God's part but a decision to allow former sins to go unpunished for a period of time. Now, by sacrificing his Son, God demonstrates his righteous nature. He does what justice requires. There must be an atonement for sin. Christ on the cross is the sacrifice that satisfies the righteous nature of God and brings salvation to humankind. God's righteousness is vindicated, and he is both just and the justifier of those who have faith in Jesus.[22] The problem of how a holy God can receive into his presence those who by nature are unholy has been solved.

The redemptive work of God through his Son Christ Jesus is the most amazing event in the history of the universe. Never would such a plan have risen in the human mind. God brings a just sentence of death upon all, for all have sinned. He then provides a sinless sacrifice, his only Son, to atone for the unrighteousness of the wayward human race. From God's standpoint forgiveness is freely offered. All that remains is for people to accept that forgiveness. The obligation is to believe, to trust in the redemptive work of Christ. The good news is good only to those who receive it. God offers his righteousness to those who will receive it, not as something to supplement their own good works but as a gift that alone can place them in a right standing with God.

3:27–31 In the final paragraph of chap. 3 Paul takes his readers through a series of rhetorical questions and answers designed to complete his argument for justification by faith. If people are set right with God through faith, what room is there for boasting? In this context "boasting"[23] should be taken not in the sense of unwarranted self-adulation for meritorious achievement but as justifiable pride on the part of the Jewish nation for having been chosen by God for a special role in

---

[21] Note that ἐν τῇ ἀνοχῇ τοῦ θεοῦ of v. 26 goes with the preceding clause in v. 25.

[22] Bengel calls this "the greatest paradox of the Gospel" (*Word Studies,* 2:50). Stuhlmacher's remark is very much to the point: "It is not that 'God is righteous and yet declares righteous the believer in Jesus,' but that 'He is righteous and also, we might almost say and therefore, declares righteous the believer" (*Romans,* 91). Some take the καί in the final clause of v. 26 as concessive, which would mean that since Christ met the full demands of God's justice, God can be true to his righteous character *even* when he is making righteous those who are unrighteous.

[23] Although there is some overlapping in use, καύχησις refers to the act of boasting rather than what is said in boasting (καύχημα). Cf. Bultmann, *TDNT* 3.649.

the drama of redemption (Rom 3:2; 9:4–5). Although the point has a wider application (faith necessarily excludes pride of achievement), Paul here had the Jewish perspective in mind. The answer, of course, is that faith by its very nature rules out[24] all boasting. People cannot boast of that which they receive through no merit of their own. Obviously, boasting is not excluded in a universe that rewards personal achievement. It is to be expected. But in the case of justification by faith, there is by definition no room for boasting.[25]

Verse 28 states in summary form Paul's basic premise—by faith we are justified quite apart from keeping the law (cf. Gal 2:16).[26] To show the universal scope of this basic truth, Paul asked, "Is God the God of Jews only?" (v. 29). No Jew of Paul's day would have denied that God was the God of all people in the sense of being their Creator and Judge.[27] The companion question, "Is he not the God of Gentiles too?" expects an affirmative response. Since there is only one God,[28] he must be the God of all. Only if one subscribes to the cavalier position that God has no interest in or connection with all the non-Jewish people in the world could it be said that he is not the God of the Gentiles as well. God is one, and his redemptive concern reaches out to all. All those whom God will justify, both Jews and Gentiles, will be justified in the same way. Faith, and faith alone,[29] is God's way of setting people right with himself.

Finally, Paul asked if the principle of faith robs law of its rightful

---

[24] The aorist passive (ἐξεκλείσθη) implies that it was God who excluded the basis for boasting and that he did it decisively, once for all.

[25] V. 27 speaks of a [νόμος] τῶν ἔργων and a [νόμος] πίστεως. The NIV (and others) take νόμος here in the sense of "principle." Alternatively it may refer to the OT law, in which case the νόμος πίστεως would be the Torah since it pointed people to faith. In either case boasting is excluded because faith removes all human involvement from the redemptive process.

[26] In response to his own question about "how the principle of faith is so rigidly exclusive of and antithetical to works of law in the matter of justification," Murray writes that "faith is self-renouncing; works are self-congratulatory. Faith looks to what God does; works have respect to what we are" (*Romans,* 1:123).

[27] In *I Enoch* 84:2 God is spoken of as "King of kings and God of the whole world," and in *Jub.* 15:31–32 it is said that "there are many nations and many peoples, and all are his." Rabbi Simeon ben Jochai said that God had told the Israelites, "I am God over all that came into the world" (*Exod. Rab.* 29:4).

[28] That God is one was the fundamental theological axiom of Israel's faith (Deut 6:4).

[29] Some writers find a slight difference in meaning between ἐκ πίστεως and διὰ τῆς πίστεως in v. 30, but they probably should be taken as no more than literary variants.

role. Does it "nullify[30] the law"? The answer is, "Not for a moment!" (Moffatt). On the contrary, faith puts law in its proper place. It plays an essential role in the divine plan, but it was never intended to make it possible for a person to earn righteousness. Faith "uphold[s] the law" in the sense that it fulfills all the obligations of the law.[31]

2. Abraham, the Great Example of Faith (4:1–25)

[1]What then shall we say that Abraham, our forefather, discovered in this matter? [2]If, in fact, Abraham was justified by works, he had something to boast about—but not before God. [3]What does the Scripture say? "Abraham believed God, and it was credited to him as righteousness."

[4]Now when a man works, his wages are not credited to him as a gift, but as an obligation. [5]However, to the man who does not work but trusts God who justifies the wicked, his faith is credited as righteousness. [6]David says the same thing when he speaks of the blessedness of the man to whom God credits righteousness apart from works:

[7]"Blessed are they
   whose transgressions are forgiven,
   whose sins are covered.
[8]Blessed is the man
   whose sin the Lord will never count against him."

[9]Is this blessedness only for the circumcised, or also for the uncircumcised? We have been saying that Abraham's faith was credited to him as righteousness. [10]Under what circumstances was it credited? Was it after he was circumcised, or before? It was not after, but before! [11]And he received the sign of circumcision, a seal of the righteousness that he had by faith while he was still uncircumcised. So then, he is the father of all who believe but have not been circumcised, in order that righteousness might be credited to them. [12]And he is also the father of the circumcised who not only are circumcised but who also walk in the footsteps of the faith that our father Abraham had before he was circumcised.

[13]It was not through law that Abraham and his offspring received the promise that he would be heir of the world, but through the righteousness that comes by faith. [14]For if those who live by law are heirs, faith has no value and the promise is worthless, [15]because law brings wrath. And where there is no law there is no transgression.

---

[30] καταργέω has a wide range of meaning, but here its specific usage is determined by the antithetical verb ἱστάνω, "to establish, confirm." Hence in this setting καταργέω means "to nullify, render ineffectual."

[31] See the discussion by Moo (*Romans 1–8*, 256–58).

16Therefore, the promise comes by faith, so that it may be by grace and may be guaranteed to all Abraham's offspring—not only to those who are of the law but also to those who are of the faith of Abraham. He is the father of us all. **17**As it is written: "I have made you a father of many nations." He is our father in the sight of God, in whom he believed—the God who gives life to the dead and calls things that are not as though they were.

18Against all hope, Abraham in hope believed and so became the father of many nations, just as it had been said to him, "So shall your offspring be." **19**Without weakening in his faith, he faced the fact that his body was as good as dead—since he was about a hundred years old—and that Sarah's womb was also dead. **20**Yet he did not waver through unbelief regarding the promise of God, but was strengthened in his faith and gave glory to God, **21**being fully persuaded that God had power to do what he had promised. **22**This is why "it was credited to him as righteousness." **23**The words "it was credited to him" were written not for him alone, **24**but also for us, to whom God will credit righteousness—for us who believe in him who raised Jesus our Lord from the dead. **25**He was delivered over to death for our sins and was raised to life for our justification.

4:1–3   Chapter 4 serves as clear proof that the principle of justification by faith apart from works of any kind was in fact the principle operative in the Old Testament. It was not some new doctrine Paul brought onto the scene.[32] He asked his readers to consider what could be learned from the experience of Abraham, the great patriarch of the Jewish nation.[33] What did he discover?[34] The Jews of Jesus' day considered Abraham the primary example of justification by works. The apostle James could ask without fear of rebuttal, "Was not our ancestor Abraham considered righteous for what he did when he offered his son Isaac on the altar?" (Jas 2:21). So the claim that God accepts people on the

---

[32] The οὖν in 4:1 indicates a logical connection between the chapters. The principle enunciated in 3:27–28 calls for a reassessment of the prevailing Jewish view of why Abraham was considered righteous. Nygren says that in chap. 4 Paul "takes Abraham away from the representatives of righteousness by the law and sets him forth as the type of those who through faith are righteous" (*Romans,* 168). M. Black calls chap. 4 "an apologetic midrash on Gen. 15:6, Ps. 32:1–2 . . . with the key word 'credited'" (*Romans,* 2d ed., NCBC [Grand Rapids: Eerdmans, 1989], 65–66).

[33] The NIV omits the phrase κατὰ σάρκα, "according to flesh," apparently because the idea of natural descent is already present in προπάτορα. It is possible to take κατὰ σάρκα with εὑρηκέναι to mean that Abraham discovered something "by human effort."

[34] εὑρηκέναι is variously located in different manuscripts. The strongest textual tradition places it immediately before Ἀβραάμ. Others place it after ἡμῶν, and still others omit it.

basis of personal trust rather than adherence to the law seems to run
counter to the principle in force with Abraham.[35]

In vv. 2–3 Paul argued as follows. Let us assume for the moment[36]
that Abraham was declared righteous as the result of what he did. (Paul
would have had no trouble convincing a Jewish reader of that!)[37] In that
case he would have something to boast about. But that cannot be
because we have already established that God's method of setting people
right excludes all boasting (3:27). Abraham may have had something to
boast about before others but certainly not "before God."[38] Scripture
says that "Abraham believed God, and it was credited to him as righteousness."[39] The quotation comes from Gen 15:6, a verse that Paul's
Jewish contemporaries would assume supported an opposite conclusion.[40] It was critical that Paul show that this proof text, far from establishing the importance of works for justification, actually proves the
opposite when properly understood.

James employed the same verse to support what appears to be an
opposite conclusion. After citing the Genesis text James added, "You see
that a person is justified by what he does and not by faith alone" (Jas
2:24). Context explains the apparent discrepancy. Paul wrote to those
deeply influenced by the Jewish emphasis on observance of the law.
They needed to learn that the righteousness of God can be received only
through faith. James spoke to those who tended to forget that saving
faith must of necessity express itself in action. For Paul, Abraham was
credited with righteousness when he believed God's promise of an offspring. For James that faith was confirmed when Abraham offered his

---

[35] E. Brunner notes the apparent contradiction between the prevailing view of Abraham as
a man of piety who fulfilled the works of the law and the scriptural emphasis on his faith as his
decisive characteristic (*The Letter to the Romans* [Philadelphia: Westminster, 1949], 34).

[36] The conditional sentence is unusually constructed. The protasis is contrary-to-fact, but
the apodosis completes the sentence as a real condition. Fitzmyer suggests that Paul's
"thoughts get ahead of his expression" (*Romans,* 372).

[37] *Kidd.* 4:14 says that because Abraham obeyed the laws and commandments of God, he
had "performed the whole Law before it was given" (cf. *Jub.* 23.10).

[38] Some commentators reject the idea of a comparison between boasting before men and
boasting before God (e.g., Cranfield, *Romans,* 1:228).

[39] λογίζομαι was a semitechnical term used in commercial dealings (*TDNT* 4.284). It
means "to place to one's account, to credit." ἐλογίσθη is a theological passive; it is God who
credits righteousness to Abraham. δικαιοσύνη here is obviously a "right standing before
God."

[40] Rabbinic Judaism held that faith itself was a meritorious act. *Mekilta* 40b speaks of Abraham's "merit of faith."

son on the altar. Paul was concerned with the basis for justification; James, with its practical expression in conduct.[41]

4:4–8 Paul was not necessarily speaking of Abraham in vv. 4–8. That alleviates the necessity of explaining in what sense it could be said that the patriarch did not work. The verses constitute a general statement that compares believing with working as the basis for justification. When people work, their wages come not as gifts but because they have earned them. The spiritual realm, however, is different. In this case those who do not work but believe are regarded by God as righteous. Rather than attempting to earn God's favor by meritorious deeds, they simply trust.[42] They are accepted by God as righteous because of their faith. God is under no obligation to pronounce righteous those who would earn his favor by working. Righteousness is a gift. God freely gives it[43] to those who believe. The disparity between legalism and grace is seen most clearly in the way God grants a right standing to people of faith.

Paul's designation of God as one who "justifies the wicked"[44] would come as a shock to his Jewish readers. In Exod 23:7 God says, "I will not acquit the guilty," and in Prov 17:15 we learn that he "detests" the practice of acquitting the guilty when carried out by others (cf. Prov 24:24; Isa 5:23). The paradoxical phrase, however, is in keeping with the remarkable fact that a holy God accepts as righteous unholy people on the basis of absolutely nothing but faith.[45] F. F. Bruce comments that God, who alone does great wonders, created the universe from nothing (1:19–20), calls the dead to life (4:17), and justifies the ungodly, "the greatest of all his wonders."[46]

---

[41] See the extended note in W. Sanday and A. C. Headlam, "The History of Abraham as treated by St. Paul and by St. James," *A Critical and Exegetical Commentary on the Epistle to the Romans,* 5th ed., ICC (Edinburgh: T & T Clark, 1902), 102–6.

[42] πιστεύοντι followed by ἐπὶ pictures faith being placed upon God. Followed by the accusative (τὸν δικαιοῦντα) it tends to emphasize the initial act of faith (J. H. Moulton, *A Grammar of New Testament Greek,* vol. I, *Prolegomena,* 3d ed. [Edinburgh: T & T Clark, 1908], 68).

[43] κατὰ χάριν means "as a favor, out of good will."

[44] Hunter calls this "Paul's gospel in a nutshell" and quotes T. Chalmers as saying, "What could I do if God did not justify the ungodly?" (*Romans,* 51).

[45] ἀσεβῆς is a strong term designating the one who lives without any regard whatsoever for God. H. C. G. Moule calls ἀσεβη "a word intense and dark" that describes "not the sinner only, but the open, defiant sinner" (*The Epistle to the Romans* [London: Pickering & Inglis, n.d.], 109).

[46] F. F. Bruce, *The Letter of Paul to the Romans,* 2d ed., TNTC (Grand Rapids: Eerdmans, 1985), 106.

To reinforce his point, Paul turned to David. Moule sees in the linking of Abraham and David an illustration of the truth that all stand unworthy before God. David was guilty of adultery and the death of a loyal follower while Abraham was known for his obedience. The conduct of neither merited God's favor.[47] David spoke of the blessedness of the person reckoned by God as righteous apart from works (vv. 6–8). In Psalm 32 (a penitential psalm) David tells of the blessedness[48] of those whose violations of the law[49] are forgiven and whose sins have been put out of sight (vv. 1–2).[50] David wrote out of his own experience. His errant behavior with Bathsheba and Uriah resulted in sorrow and remorse (see Ps 51). The forgiveness that followed relieved an enormous burden of guilt. Although it is unnecessary to sin in order to grasp fully the wonder of God's forgiveness, those who have been forgiven the most often love the most. To Simon the Pharisee, who complained about the woman who wept at Jesus' feet, Jesus said: "I tell you, her many sins have been forgiven—for she loved much. But he who has been forgiven little loves little" (Luke 7:47).

The psalmist continued, "Blessed is the man whose sin the Lord will never count against him."[51] Those who have put their faith in God are completely forgiven of their sin. Nothing can be brought up for which provision has not already been made. Believers are the most fortunate people imaginable because the question of their sin has been settled forever. "As far as the east is from the west, so far has he removed our transgressions from us" (Ps 103:12). Guilt dogs the steps of the unbeliever, but forgiveness is the sweet reward of those who trust in God.

---

[47] Ibid.

[48] Although μακαρισμός means "happiness," or "blessing" (Zerwick defines it as "pronouncement of happiness" [*Analysis,* 467]), it probably is allowable to take it, as the NIV and others do, as "blessedness."

[49] ἀνομία carries the sense of "open rebellion against God" (Cranfield, *Romans,* 1:234).

[50] Paul quoted Ps 32:1–2 just as it appears in the LXX, which in turn is almost a literal translation of the MT.

[51] Sanday and Headlam comment that μακάριος was "the highest term which a Greek could use to describe a state of felicity" (*Romans,* 102). E. Käsemann insists that "as always in the NT beatitudes μακάριος means eschatological salvation and not merely heavenly bliss" (*Commentary on Romans* (Grand Rapids: Eerdmans, 1980), 113). οὐ μὴ is an emphatic negative, "never ever, by no means" (BDF 365.3). The verb λογίζομαι occurred both in Gen 5:6 and Ps 32:2. According to a common exegetical technique known as *gezerah shewa,* "equal category," the presence of identical words allowed each to be interpreted in light of the other. The practice often led to fanciful conclusions, but not here as used by Paul. The two verses have a substantive relationship.

4:9–12 Now the question arises about the beneficiaries of forgiveness and justification. Is this blessedness only for the Jews, or does God intend it for the Gentiles as well?[52] Since Paul had just drawn from the Old Testament to strengthen his argument, Jewish readers might infer that the promise was intended for Israel alone. The premise is that Abraham's faith was regarded by God as righteousness. His confidence in God's faithfulness established him as righteous in God's sight. Now comes the critical question. Was this declaration of righteousness made before or after Abraham was circumcised? At what point in his career was it credited to him? The obvious answer is that Abraham was declared righteous before he was circumcised. According to Jewish reckoning, in fact, there was an interval of some twenty-nine years between the time when Abraham was accepted by God (Gen 15:6) and his actual circumcision (Gen 17:23–27).

What then was the purpose of circumcision (v. 11)?[53] It was both a "sign" and a "seal." As a sign it pointed beyond itself to that which it represented.[54] Conybeare refers to circumcision as "an outward sign of inward things." It was given "as a token" (Knox). As a seal it authenticated the righteousness by faith that Abraham had while he was still uncircumcised.[55] "The circumcision ceremony was a sign that Abraham already had faith and that God had already accepted him" (TLB).

Since Abraham was righteous in God's sight before he was circumcised, it follows that he is the father of the uncircumcised who believe as well as the circumcised who also walk by faith as Abraham did before he was circumcised (vv. 11b–12).[56] Circumcision itself possessed no magi-

---

[52] For use of περιτομήν and ἀκροβυστία for "Jew" and "Gentile," see commentary at 2:25–26. Dunn comments: "It is a striking fact that the difference between Jew and Gentile could be summed up and focused in the one ritual act of circumcision, and underlines the importance of circumcision for Jewish self-understanding" (*Romans,* 1:208).

[53] C. K. Barrett takes v. 11a as a parenthesis (*Romans* [New York: Harper, 1957], 90), but few have followed the lead.

[54] περιτομῆς is a genitive of apposition. Circumcision *is* the sign.

[55] σφραγῖδα, "seal," not only marked ownership but it also was a means of confirmation or attestation. The seal confirms the reality of the righteous status in which Abraham stood by virtue of his faith.

[56] The presence of the article τοῖς before στοιχοῦσιν is awkward. It was either a slip by the author or the work of a copyist so early that the entire manuscript tradition reflects it. Fitzmyer believes it points to two separate groups in v. 12, the circumcised and those who follow the faith that Abraham had before he was circumcised (*Romans,* 381–82). Cranfield says this interpretation is ruled out grammatically and rather tentatively judges that the second τοῖς was an original or early mistake (*Romans,* 1:237). ἴχνος is to be taken metaphorically as "the trace left by someone's conduct or journey though life" (*TDNT* 3.402).

cal power. It was merely a ceremonial rite that witnessed to a covenant between God and humans. The covenant was maintained by obedience, not by circumcision, the sign of that covenant (cf. Gen 18:19; 22:18; 26:4–5). Those who consider baptism as the New Testament equivalent of circumcision should take note that the comparison undermines, rather than supports, any doctrine of baptismal regeneration. If circumcision by itself was powerless to alter a person's relationship to God, the same would be true of its counterpart baptism.

Paul concluded that for Jew and Gentile alike there is only one way to be justified, and that is the way of faith.[57] God is the Father of all who place their trust in him regardless of their racial or religious background. To possess the revelation of God is of no ultimate importance apart from the walk of faith. Conduct demonstrates the reality of faith. People have a fatal tendency to elevate doctrine over behavior. Although a clear and comprehensive knowledge of the nature of God as revealed in his redemptive activity is of great importance, one cannot claim to have Abraham as father to say nothing of the God of Abraham unless that knowledge transforms life.

4:13–15 To Abraham and his offspring[58] was given the promise that he would be "heir of the world."[59] Five times in Psalm 37 David spoke of Israel as inheriting the land and dwelling therein forever (Ps 37:9,11,27,29,34; cf. Matt 5:5). This promise was not given to Abraham in the context of obedience to law.[60] It had its roots in faith. It rested on the "faith-righteousness" (Montgomery) of the patriarch. Any idea that the inheritance depended on keeping the law would have serious conse-

---

[57] "It was not for Gentiles to enter by the Jewish gateway, but for the Jews to enter by the same gateway as the Gentiles. This was indeed a striking turning of the tables on Jewish exclusiveness" (W. H. G. Thomas, *St. Paul's Epistle to the Romans* [Grand Rapids: Eerdmans, 1953], 136).

[58] σπέρματι is dative singular and refers to the physical descendants of Abraham.

[59] The singular ἡ ἐπαγγελία is used in a collective sense of all the promises made to the patriarchs in Genesis. Robertson answers his own question ("But where is the promise") by observing that the word means "not just Gen. 12:7, but the whole chain of promises about his son, his descendants like the stars in heaven, the Messiah and the blessing to the world through him" (Robertson, *WP* 4:352). Moo says that the phrase summarizes the three key provisions of the promise to Abraham—many descendants (Gen 12:2), possession of the land (Gen 13:15–17), and that he would be the medium of blessing to all people (Gen 12:13) (*Romans 1–8*, 279). The Jews held that Abraham would be heir of the world because of his righteous obedience to the law (for references see Dunn, *Romans,* 1:213).

[60] νόμος without the article refers to law in general rather than any specific commandments. However, because of the context (νόμος is used four times in vv. 14–16) many commentators hold that νόμος (v. 13) must refer to the Mosaic law.

quences. For one thing, it would invalidate the principle of faith (v. 14). What role would there be for faith if the promise were contingent on obedience to law? Furthermore, it would rob the promise of meaning. Weymouth says that it would make faith "useless," and the promise would "count for nothing." This follows from the fact that law is unable to produce a promise.[61] Its fundamental reason for being is to bring about wrath (v. 15). Ironically, the very thing the Jews were counting on to make them acceptable to God turned out to emphasize their sinfulness. By trying hard to fulfill the demands of law (and failing), their pious efforts merely turned them into conscious sinners. Dunn comments that "rightly understood, the law does not mark off Jew from Gentile but rather puts Jew alongside Gentile in need of the grace of God."[62] "Cursed is everyone who does not continue to do everything written in the Book of the Law" (Gal 3:10). Where there is no law, there can be no breaking of law. Sin would still exist, but it could not be designated as the specific transgression of a law (cf. Rom 5:13; 7:7–11).

4:16–17 Verse 16 opens with a "therefore," which probably points forward to "so that it may be by grace" rather than backward, providing the reason the promise could not come by law. The promise depends upon faith so that it may be a "matter of sheer grace" (NEB).[63] Faith is the response that makes the promise effective in a specific case.[64] It is not, however, a meritorious act. Faith is helplessness reaching out in total dependence upon God. The promise remains an act of grace.[65] God's promises flow from his nature as one who desires the very best for those he created. "Taste and see that the Lord is good" (Ps 34:8). God's promises reflect the goodness of his character. A further reason the promise rests on faith is so that it may be "guaranteed" to all of Abraham's progeny. Were the promise contingent on human achievement, it would be anything but sure. In fact, since God demands perfect righteousness, a promise conditioned on effort would be a cynical exploitation of human frailty. Since it depends on faith, it can be freely offered in

---

[61] "Law, though good in itself," writes Barrett, "is so closely bound up with sin and wrath that it is unthinkable that it should be the basis of the promise" (*Romans,* 95).

[62] Dunn, *Romans,* 1:214.

[63] The Greek text of v. 16 omits the subject, but the NIV probably is correct in supplying "the promise" (i.e., that Abraham would be heir of the world) from v. 13.

[64] Law, transgression, and wrath (v. 15) are countered by promise, faith, and grace (v. 16).

[65] Barrett writes, "God's plan was made to rest upon faith on man's side in order that on God's it might be a matter of grace" (*Romans,* 95). Note the close connection between faith and grace in Rom 3:22,24 and Eph 2:8.

good conscience. We do not earn a promise; we receive it. What we receive rests completely on what God has done.

Once again Paul stressed that the "offspring" of Abraham includes not only Jewish Christians ("those who are of the law") but also Gentile believers ("those who are of the faith of Abraham"). He is the father of all who live by faith. This accords with God's declaration to Abraham, "I have made you a father of many nations" (Gen 17:5). The NIV connects the phrase "in the sight of God" (v. 17b) to "father of us all" (repeated as "our father"). But what it means to be "our father in the sight of God" is less than clear. It may be better to take vv. 16b–17a as a parenthesis and connect the phrase with "guaranteed to all Abraham's offspring" (in v. 16). Knox follows this option and translates, "The promise is guaranteed in the very sight of God in whom he had faith."

Paul then described God in two ways. First, he is the one who is able to bring the dead to life. In the context of Abraham's faith the reference is to the promise of God to Abraham that he and Sarah would bear a child in their old age (Gen 17:15–21; 18:11–14).[66] The ability of God to quicken the dead is seen in its clearest light in the resurrection of Jesus (note vv. 24–25). God also is portrayed as the one who calls into existence things that are not. The immediate reference could be to the calling into existence of the child Isaac yet unborn at that time. The neuter plural participles, however, suggest a broader context. The point is not that God speaks of things that do not exist as though they did but that he speaks the nonexistent into existence (Heb 11:3; 2 Pet 3:5).[67] By definition the Creator brings into existence all that is from that which never was. Anything less than that would be adaptation rather than creation.

4:18–25 What Scripture considers as faith is defined by the confidence of Abraham in the inviolability of divine promise.[68] This becomes the theme of the final paragraph in chap. 4. The paradoxical quality of Abraham's faith is seen in the contrasting prepositional phrases "against

---

[66] In view of Heb 11:19 some see an allusion to Abraham's plan to sacrifice Isaac (Gen 22:1–14). Some have suggested that Paul may have been drawing upon the second blessing formula of the Jewish *Shemoneh Esreh* ("Eighteen Benedictions"), "Praise be to you, Lord, who makes the dead alive!" (see also *2 Bar.* 48.8).

[67] Phillips has the rather surprising translation "and speaks his word to those who are yet unborn."

[68] Fitzmyer defines faith not as "some inner sanctimoniousness in contrast to external deeds" but "an unwavering reliance on God's promise, which issues in hope" (*Romans,* 386–87). Moo comments that Abraham's faith was not a "leap into the dark" but a "leap from the evidence of his senses into the security of God's Word and promise" (*Romans 1–8,* 288).

all hope" and "in hope."[69] From a human standpoint there was no hope that he would have descendants.[70] Yet with God all things are possible (cf. Matt 19:26). Therefore he believed what God said. His hope was not the invincible human spirit rising to the occasion against all odds but a deep inner confidence that God was absolutely true to his word.[71] Faith is unreasonable only within a restricted worldview that denies God the right to intervene. His intervention is highly rational from the biblical perspective, which not only allows him to intervene but actually expects him to show concern for those he has created in his own image. Because Abraham believed, he became "the father of many nations." The opportunity to believe has not been assigned to any one nation or ethnic group. Belief is universally possible. The quotation from Gen 15:5 reinforces the remarkable number of those who believe and are therefore the offspring of Abraham.[72]

Abraham was fully aware that his own body was as good as dead ("utterly worn out," TCNT).[73] He was, at that time, about one hundred years old (cf. Gen 17:1). Furthermore, Sarah was "past the age of childbearing" (Gen 18:11). From a commonsense standpoint there was not the slightest possibility that she would bear a child. This, however, did not cause Abraham to weaken in his faith.[74] Faith goes beyond human potentiality. It acknowledges the existence of one who is not bound by

---

[69] παρ' ἐλπίδα could be taken as "beyond hope" in the sense that it went beyond the outer limit of human hope. Most commentators take it to mean "against hope," i.e., it flies in the face of what can be reasonably expected from a human standpoint. ἐπ' ἐλπίδι means either "on the basis of hope" or "in an attitude of hope."

[70] In classical literature ἐλπίς normally connoted uncertainty about the future. In the OT, however, it came to mean the confident expectation of that which would certainly come to pass. Like faith, it rested upon God's integrity.

[71] Barrett writes, "It is when human hope is exhausted that God-given hope (cf. viii 24f.) comes into effect" (*Romans,* 976). Calvin comments that "there is nothing more inimical to faith than to bind understanding to sight, so that we seek the substance of our hope from what we see" (*The Epistle of Paul to the Romans and to the Thessalonians,* trans. R. Mackenzie [Grand Rapids: Eerdmans, 1961], 96). Nygren notes that it is only when "without hope" and "yet with hope" stand over against each other that real faith is found (*Romans,* 160).

[72] God had just taken Abraham outside and asked him to count the stars. "So shall your offspring be" suggests a remarkable progeny.

[73] Black understands νενεκρωμένον as equivalent to the Heb. *meth* in the sense of sexually impotent (*Romans,* 73). That Abraham later bore six sons to Keturah (Gen 25:1–2) could have been possible because of his renewed reproductive ability in connection with the birth of Isaac.

[74] In v. 19 the participle (ἀσθενήσας) probably expresses the dominant idea and the finite verb (κατενόησεν) the subordinate theme. Thus Knox translates, "His faith never quailed, even when he noted the utter impotence of his own body."

the limitations of the created order. "Conscious of his own utter impotence, Abraham relied simply and completely on the all-sufficient power of God."[75] Where God is present, there is nothing that lies outside the realm of possibility.[76] The church of Jesus Christ is in desperate need of those who will insist that God is able to bring to pass anything that is consistent with his nature and in concert with his redemptive purposes. "Your God Is Too Small" is a sad epitaph inscribed on all too many ecclesiastical groups who, strange as it may seem, claim to worship the Almighty.

Abraham faced the fact that he and Sarah were beyond the age of bearing children, yet he never wavered in his confidence in the promise of God (v. 20). It is true that he fell to the ground in laughter at the idea of bearing a son at his age (Gen 17:17),[77] but that did not qualify as a departure from faith. God does not expect us to blandly assume the miraculous. The idea struck Abraham as somewhat ridiculous, but he believed it anyway. Instead of "wavering" or hesitating in his confidence in God (*diakrinō,* "to be divided in one's own mind"), Abraham's faith was strengthened through the ordeal.[78] As muscles develop when kept in tension, so was Abraham's faith strengthened by the experience he was going through. His faith rose to the occasion, and Abraham "gave glory to God."[79] He praised him for who he was and what he would do.

Abraham was "fully persuaded that God had power to do what he had promised" (v. 21).[80] This statement epitomizes what it means to believe

---

[75] Dodd, *Romans,* 70.

[76] Nygren writes that "when our own possibilities fail, faith increases; for it does not rest on ourselves and our own adequacy, but on God and His promise" (*Romans,* 181).

[77] According to *Jub.* 16.19, Abraham rejoiced because the promise filled him with joy.

[78] ἐνεδυναμώθη is a divine passive. Abraham was strengthened *by God* (1) "in respect to [his] faith" (taking τῇ πίστει as a dative of respect), or (2) "by means of [his] faith" (taking the dative as instrumental). Newman and Nida write that "because of the contrast between the first and second parts of v. 20, one may introduce the latter part by some adversative conjunction—for example, 'but rather his faith filled him with power'" (*Romans,* 88). Murray says this interpretation is not unreasonable but goes on to argue against it (*Romans,* 1:150–51).

[79] For this OT expression see 1 Sam 6:5; 1 Chr 16:28. Cranfield writes that "a man gives glory to God when he acknowledges God's truthfulness and goodness and submits to His authority" (*Romans,* 1:249). Luther cites Augustine as saying that God is glorified through faith, hope, and love, and then refers to the fact that God is directly insulted by three sins: unbelief, despair and hatred (*Commentary on the Epistle to the Romans,* trans. J. T. Mueller [Grand Rapids: Zondervan, 1954], 71).

[80] Harrison makes the interesting comment that "as far as Abraham was concerned, he was not taking a chance. He was 'fully persuaded' that God's power would match his promise" ("Romans," 10:53).

in God. It is complete confidence in his ability and integrity. God has the power—no question about it. God does what he promises. How could he do less and still be God? Faith is total surrender to the ability and willingness of God to carry out his promises. To fail him in the relatively insignificant activities of daily life is to be guilty of a sort of practical atheism. Can God? is not a valid question for the believer. Will God? is the question that drives us in prayer ever closer to his heart. "Fully persuaded" leaves no room for doubt. It calls for complete capitulation to the power and goodness of God.

It was Abraham's unwavering faith that God reckoned to his account as righteousness (v. 22).[81] However, the juridical decision "it was credited to him" was not written down for him alone. It was also written in reference to us.[82] We exercise a similar faith in the one who raised from the dead Jesus our Lord.[83] Our faith will be regarded in the same light. God will credit righteousness[84] to us as well.

Verses 24–25 show the prominence of the resurrection in the basic gospel message. It was the central theme of the apostolic kerygma and dominated the early evangelistic preaching of the apostles (cf. Acts 2:24,32; 3:15; 4:10; 13:30). It must continue to hold that central place in all preaching that reaches out to those who have never accepted Christ. Psychological insights on how to co-opt God for one's own advantage are not only powerless to effect change but obscure the real gospel in the attempt to make it relevant.

Verse 25 appears to reflect an early Christian confessional creed. The neat parallelism and the rich theological significance of the Greek nouns betray an ecclesiastical origin. Jesus is the one who was delivered up to death. Isaiah the prophet foretold that the messianic Servant would "pour out his life unto death" (Isa 53:12). Yet he was "raised to life for our justification." God's entire redemptive plan is summarized in this final verse of chap. 4. Christ died for our sins and was raised again for

---

[81] Bengel compares our faith to Abraham's noting that "Abraham's faith was directed to what would and could come to pass, ours to what has actually occurred" (*Word Studies*, 2:58).

[82] For other passages that reflect the same midrashic influence see 1 Cor 9:9–10; 10:11; 2 Tim 3:16.

[83] Normally the Christian believer is said to have faith in Christ. The reference here to faith in God may have resulted from Paul's tying together the faith of Abraham and that of his fellow believers.

[84] Some understand μέλλει λογίζεσθαι ("about to be reckoned") in terms of the eschatological validation of justification. Others take it as logical rather than temporal, in which case it is saying that whenever the condition of faith is met, justification inevitably follows.

our justification.[85] The two are inseparably bound together.[86] Without his death there would be no basis for acquittal. Without his resurrection there would be no proof of the redemptive reality of his death. Jesus Christ, crucified and raised to life, is God the Father's gracious provision for the sins of a fallen race. The simplicity of the message makes it clear for all who will hear. The power of the message is experienced by those who reach out in faith.

3. The Results of Faith (5:1–21)[87]

(1) Peace and Hope (5:1–8)

[1]Therefore, since we have been justified through faith, we have peace with God through our Lord Jesus Christ, [2]through whom we have gained access by faith into this grace in which we now stand. And we rejoice in the hope of the glory of God. [3]Not only so, but we also rejoice in our sufferings, because we know that suffering produces perseverance; [4]perseverance, character; and character, hope. [5]And hope does not disappoint us, because God has poured out his love into our hearts by the Holy Spirit, whom he has given us.

[6]You see, at just the right time, when we were still powerless, Christ died for the ungodly. [7]Very rarely will anyone die for a righteous man, though for a good man someone might possibly dare to die. [8]But God demonstrates his own love for us in this: While we were still sinners, Christ died for us.

5:1–5 The "therefore" with which chap. 5 begins connects it to what Paul had written in the previous verses. In fact, "since we have been justified through faith" (v. 1) summarizes the entire argument of chaps. 1–4. Those who have placed their trust in Christ can rest assured that their faith has been credited to them as righteousness (Rom 4:24).

---

[85] The parallel clauses with διά are variously understood. Perhaps the best option is to take the first as looking back to Christ's resurrection ("because of") and the second as looking ahead to final judgment ("for the sake of"; Moo, *Romans 1–8,* 296–97).

[86] Rhetorical considerations have played a major role in the formation of v. 25. We are not to understand the two parallel clauses as indicating separate aspects in God's redemptive program. Christ did die for our sins, but it was both his death and his resurrection that effected our justification. A resurrection without an atoning death would not have been sufficient.

[87] Many commentaries begin the second major division of Paul's letter with 5:1. Moo discusses the alternatives and gives four reasons for taking chap. 5 with chaps. 6–8 (*Romans 1–8,* 299–304). He says that "assurance of glory" is the overarching theme of this second major section (p. 302).

Their confidence is based on the fact that Christ was put to death for their sins and raised again that they might be declared just (Rom 4:25).

At this point we encounter a textual problem. The UBS text chooses the indicative ("we have peace") rather than the subjunctive ("let us have peace").[88] The NIV adopts the first option, which points to the objective state of peace with God that follows from having been granted a right standing with him. The second option understands peace as a subjective state of mind and encourages the readers to lay hold of the fact that they have been justified and to experience the peace that flows from that reality. Moffatt, for example, translates, "Let us enjoy the peace we have." In much the same way, Phillips has, "Let us grasp the fact that we have peace." Was Paul continuing to build a theological foundation, or was he moving on to the ethical implications that flow from that foundation? Perhaps the two options are sufficiently interwoven so that while we must choose between Greek variants, we do not need to limit the verse to a single emphasis.

The first consequence of justification is "peace with God." Peace is a word rich with meaning.[89] It speaks of the new relationship that exists between God and those who turn to him in faith (cf. Eph 2:14–15; Col 1:21–22). As Paul used the term, it does not primarily depict a state of inner tranquility. It is external and objective. To have "peace with God" means to be in a relationship with God in which all the hostility caused by sin has been removed.[90] It is to exist no longer under the wrath of God.[91] It is not necessary, however, in the interests of literary precision to remove all psychological connotations from the term. Peace is also the joyful experience of those who live in harmony with God, other people, and themselves.

This kind of peace is made possible through the redemptive activity of "our Lord Jesus Christ."[92] Paul delighted to dwell on the full title of his Savior. Jesus of Nazareth is the promised Messiah ("Christ"). He is

---

[88] The subjunctive ἔχωμεν has the stronger MS support, but the indicative ἔχομεν fits the context better. See Morris for a concise discussion on the issue (*Romans,* 218, n. 2).

[89] εἰρήνη should be understood in terms of its use in the LXX, where it translates the Heb. שָׁלוֹם ("positive well-being").

[90] Barrett refers to the peace Paul spoke of as "an objective status or condition" but goes on to say that this objective state "is reflected in the *feeling* of peace and security which man enjoys when he knows that he is reconciled to God" (*Romans,* 102).

[91] See Nygren, *Romans,* 192–93.

[92] That Paul referred to our peace with God as being *through* (διά) Jesus Christ supports the indicative ἔχομεν earlier in the clause.

God ("Lord"[93]). And he is "our[s]!" Through him we have been ushered into the presence of God the Father. By faith we have gained access (a second consequence of justification) into this gracious relationship in which we now find ourselves (cf. Eph 2:18).[94] It leads us to rejoice[95] in our hope[96] of sharing "the glory of God" (a third consequence).[97]

Those who chose the subjunctive ("let us have peace") in v. 1 should now translate "let us rejoice." In this case it is not a question of variants but the fact that the Greek verb can be either indicative or subjunctive in form (*kauchōmetha*). The TCNT has the unusually felicitous translation, "Let us exult in our hope of attaining God's glorious ideal." All have fallen short of that ideal, "the glory of God" (3:23); but through the rich provisions offered by God, we can move toward the goal he had in mind in creation. The fall of humankind did not put an end to God's plans once and for all but rather necessitated an eternally significant detour through the cross and the empty tomb. God's plan that we should reflect his glory is now being realized in the lives of obedient believers.

Not only do we rejoice in the hope of the glory of God, but we also rejoice in our sufferings (cf. Jas 1:2–4).[98] The believers' joy is not simply something they hope to experience in the future but a present reality even in times of trials and distress. Their joy is not a stoic determination to make the best out of a bad situation. Christian suffering is a source of

---

[93] κύριος, the LXX translation for YHWH in the OT.

[94] προσαγωγὴν means either "introduction" or "access." The first depicts a person being brought into the presence of someone of high standing while the second emphasizes the continuing availability of that privilege. Dunn points out that there is no necessity of assuming, as Käsemann does, that the dominant imagery behind προσαγωγὴν is cultic (*Romans*, 1:247–48). Luther comments that Paul "first directs himself against the arrogance of those who . . . want to have access to God by faith, yet not through Christ." He reasons correctly that "such a faith is not true, but counterfeit" (*Romans*, 74).

[95] καυχάομαι normally means "to boast," but in context the NIV's "rejoice" comes closer to what Paul was saying.

[96] J. R. W. Stott defines Christian hope as "a joyful and confident expectation which rests on the promise of God" (*Romans* [Downers Grove: InterVarsity, 1994], 140).

[97] Cranfield defines the δόξα τοῦ θεοῦ as "that illumination of man's whole being by the radiance of the divine glory which is man's true destiny but which was lost through sin, as it will be restored . . . when man's redemption is finally consummated at the parousia of Jesus Christ" (*Romans*, 1:260).

[98] Joy in the midst of suffering is a theme that runs throughout the NT (see Matt 5:4; 10–12; Acts 5:41; 14:22; 2 Cor 12:10; 1 Pet 4:13–14). Cf. *Pss. Sol.* 10:1: "Happy is the man whom the Lord remembers with reproof." Calvin notes that although tribulation "provokes a great part of mankind to murmur against God," for the person infused with an inner submissiveness by the Spirit of God tribulation becomes "the means of begetting patience" (*Romans and Thessalonians*, 106–7).

joy because its purpose is to build character in the believer.[99]

Paul argued that suffering produces steadfastness,[100] and steadfastness results in "strength of character" (TCNT).[101] The Greek term in v. 4 for "character" denotes that which has been proven by trial.[102] The NEB translates "endurance brings proof that we have stood the test." Thus it is the experience of coming through a time of testing that produces hope. Our confidence in God's ability and willingness to bring us through difficult times leads to an ever brighter hope for that which lies beyond. Hope is not superficial optimism but the confident assurance of that which will surely come to pass. It distinguishes those who have kept the faith in times of severe testing.

5:5–8 Hope never disappoints (v. 5). It does not let the believer down.[103] The reason is simple. God floods our hearts with his love[104] through the Holy Spirit, who has been given to us.[105] Hope is rewarded with a fresh awareness of the incomprehensible love of God. God's Holy Spirit, who enters our life in response to faith, is at work helping us grasp the reality of what it means to be encircled by the love of God. In another place, after speaking of things that "no eye has seen" and "no ear

---

[99] ἐν ταῖς θλίψεσιν indicates the basis of our rejoicing rather than simply the occasion.

[100] W. Barclay defines ὑπομονή as "the spirit which does not passively endure but which actively overcomes the trials and tribulations of life" (*The Letter to the Romans,* rev. ed., DSB [Philadelphia: Westminster, 1978], 73). Hunter calls it "the virtue of martyrs," a "being hammered on the anvil of trial without going to pieces" (*Romans,* 56).

[101] For no apparent reason J. C. O'Neill calls vv. 3–4 "a marginal reflection [that] has been copied into the body of the text by a later scribe" (*Paul's Letter to the Romans* [Middlesex: Penguin, 1975], 93). It is difficult to evaluate a position for which objective evidence is beside the point.

[102] δοκιμήν. No occurrence of this word has been found before Paul, and in the NT it is used only by him. Its cognates indicate its meaning to be "character proven by trial."

[103] καταισχύνω means "to put to shame, to disappoint." Cf. Ps 22:5 ("In you they trusted and were not disappointed") and 25:20 ("Let me not be put to shame"). Moo favors accenting the verb as a future (καταισχυνεῖ) and reading "hope will not put to shame" (*Romans 1–8,* 312).

[104] ἡ ἀγάπη τοῦ θεοῦ is a subjective genitive, "God's love for us." Augustine understood it as "our love for God." He distinguished between *cupiditas* (the love that seeks satisfaction in earthly things) and *caritas* (the love that is directed upward toward God) and held that true love can arise only if God creates and stirs it up in the human heart. Nygren speaks of the "unfortunate influence" of this view and concludes that "Augustine and the theological tradition that builds on him cannot correctly understand what Paul means when he speaks of love" (*Romans,* 197–99).

[105] Prophets connected the pouring out of the Spirit with the age to come (Isa 32:15; Ezek 11:19; Joel 2:28–29). The NIVSB note on 5:5 reminds us that in the first five verses of the chapter Paul moved from faith (v. 1) to hope (vv. 2,4–5) to love (v. 5).

has heard," Paul pointed out that these very things have been revealed by the Spirit to those who love God and that we have received the Spirit so "that we may understand what God has freely given us" (1 Cor 2:12).

The connection between vv. 5–6 is not clear. The Greek manuscript Vaticanus suggests a transition such as "if indeed[106] [as we believe]." The punctuation—a period at the end of v. 6 but none at v. 5—ties v. 6 to what has gone before. This would have us understand the text to say that God has poured his love into our hearts if indeed, as we believe, Christ died for the ungodly. A personal experience of God's love comes as a result of Christ's death. Most translations, however, begin a new thought with v. 6.[107] Christ died for the ungodly "at just the right time" (Goodspeed has "at the decisive moment"). Paul wrote to the Galatians that God sent his Son "when the time had fully come" (Gal 4:4). Not only was it the right time in terms of the sweep of history but it was the right time in the sense that we were powerless to break the chains of sin.[108] We were unable to help ourselves. Bound by sin and destined for an eternity apart from God, no amount of struggle could free us from condemnation. It was for us "the right time" for Christ's atoning death.

Now it is a most unusual thing for people to give up their lives even for an upright person (v. 7). Life is precious, and the yearning to live is strong. Nevertheless, once in a while a person has sufficient courage to die for a "a generous friend"[109] (Williams). The remarkable thing about the death of Christ was that it took place "while we were still sinners" (1 Pet 3:18; 1 John 3:16). God did not wait until we had performed well enough to merit his love (which, of course, no one ever could) before he acted in love on our behalf. Christ died for us while we were still alien-

---

[106] The expression is εἴ γε.

[107] The UBS text reads ἔτι γάρ, "for yet." The first ἔτι is for emphasis and the second for clarity. The NIV translates the connecting phrase, "You see."

[108] Stuhlmacher says the godless are "weak" in two respects: they cannot accomplish anything in regard to God, and they are in no position to resist temptation and sin (*Romans*, 80).

[109] Some commentators hold that δίκαιος and ἀγαθός in this context are essentially synonymous (Bruce translates, "Even for one who is righteous or good" [*Romans*, 117]). It is more probable, however, that some difference is to be seen between the two and that the second clause of v. 7 should be taken as a concession ("although some might die for a good man"). (Some, noting that ἀγαθοῦ is neuter as well as masculine, have suggested that the phrase could mean "for a good cause.") The ἀγαθός may be a more genial person than the δίκαιος who would be known for his uprightness—a "pious moralist," says Landau (Dunn, *Romans*, 1:255). Sanday and Headlam refer to Irenaeus, who says the Gnostics thought of the God of the OT as δίκαιος and the God of the NT as ἀγαθός (*Romans*, 1:128). A. D. Clarke finds a connection in Hellenistic Greek between the ἀγαθός and the benefactor. The ties of patronage in the first-century world would make it plausible that someone would give up his life for his benefactor ("The Good and the Just in Romans 5:7," *TynBul* 41 [1990]: 128–42).

ated from him and cared nothing for his attention or affection.

God is the Father who, having forgiven his prodigal son, watched daily for his return (Luke 15:20). Little wonder that the beloved disciple John exclaimed, "How great is the love the Father has lavished on us!" (1 John 3:1).[110] The proof of God's amazing love for us is the gift of his only Son (John 3:16). The cross defines what Scripture means by "love" (1 John 3:16). Love is the voluntary placing of the welfare of others ahead of one's own. It is action, not sentiment. Love is the mightiest force in the world. It is the ethical goal of human existence. God is love (1 John 4:16), and that determines the goal toward which all redemptive history moves.

(2) Reconciliation (5:9–11)

⁹Since we have now been justified by his blood, how much more shall we be saved from God's wrath through him! ¹⁰For if, when we were God's enemies, we were reconciled to him through the death of his Son, how much more, having been reconciled, shall we be saved through his life! ¹¹Not only is this so, but we also rejoice in God through our Lord Jesus Christ, through whom we have now received reconciliation.

5:9–11 In this paragraph Paul twice argued from the greater to the lesser.[111] The first premise is that we have now been declared righteous by virtue of the shedding of Christ's blood (the greater).[112] Since that is true, it is far more certain that we will be saved from wrath by him (the lesser). If the premise (which is greater in import) is true, we can be sure that the logical corollary (of lesser import) is also true. That the verb is future in tense indicates that the wrath in question is eschatological.

The second argument is parallel. The "greater" statement is that while we were enemies of God, we were reconciled by the death of his Son.[113]

---

[110] συνίστησιν ("demonstrates") in v. 8 is present tense, emphasizing that although the cross took place in the past, it continues to show forth the amazing love of God [in the present].

[111] This kind of argument is designated *a minori ad maius,* but as used here by Paul it actually moves from the major to the minor (cf. similar argument in vv. 10,15,17). It was widely used by rabbis who called it "light and heavy" (e.g., *m.ʾAbot* 1.5: "Talk not much with womankind. They said this of a man's own wife: how much more of his fellow's wife!").

[112] ἐν τῷ αἵματι αὐτοῦ means "at the price of his blood" (BDF 219.3).

[113] While justification was the language of the law court, reconciliation reflects the world of personal relationships. Reconciliation is the restoration of friendly relationships after a period of separation. The metaphor was rarely used in Hellenistic religions because the language of personal relationship would have been inappropriate in settings where worshipers and their gods were not on, what you might say, speaking terms. In an excursus on "Justification and Reconciliation," Stuhlmacher writes that "for Paul *justification and reconciliation* belong inextricably together" (*Romans,* 82).

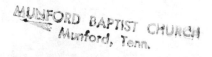

The transaction took place while we were in a state of hostility toward God (cf. Col 1:21).[114] In 2 Corinthians Paul wrote that God reconciled the world to himself in Christ, yet every person must respond in faith in order for that forgiveness to become effective in his or her case (2 Cor 5:19–20). Reconciliation is a personal relationship; it cannot be a unilateral action on the part of God alone. He has provided forgiveness for all people through the once-for-all death of his Son. Only when that forgiveness is accepted by faith is the compact completed and reconciliation takes place. God's part is finished; our part is a matter of individual decision.

It is agreed that reconciliation came through the death of Christ. The line of reasoning continues. How much more shall we be "saved through his life" (the "lesser" statement).[115] Some take this as a reference to the life of Christ in the believer (cf. Phil 1:21, "For to me, to live is Christ"; Col 1:27, "Christ in you, the hope of glory"). It is better to understand it in connection with the intercessory ministry of the resurrected Christ.[116] The author of Hebrews said that Christ "always lives to intercede for . . . those who come to God through him" (Heb 7:25; cf. Rom 8:34). In the immediate context the promised deliverance is more than eschatological. It is a daily deliverance from the power and dominion of sin. God has made every provision for us to live out our lives in holiness. His abiding presence provides the power to break free from the control of sin (6:18).

Not only is the power for deliverance available through Christ but through him we "[continue to] rejoice."[117] He is the one who made our reconciliation with God possible. At the heart of God's redemptive plan stands one solitary figure—Jesus Christ, his Son, our Savior. Through his death he has made it possible for those who believe to receive forgiveness for their sins and enter into an eternal relationship of joy with God the Father.

---

[114] ἐχθρός can be taken in a passive sense ("hateful to God") or active sense ("hostile to God"). Both may be in view in the present passage. The hostility that existed was both ours toward him and his toward us in our sinful state.

[115] Barrett notes that the contrast between reconciliation by Christ's death and salvation through his life is "rhetorical rather than substantial" (*Romans,* 108).

[116] H. Rhys says that "the *life* by which we shall be saved is the *exalted Life* of Christ. . . . His victory over the power of death [including] all the results of that victory, especially the imparting of the life of Christ to the believer" (*The Epistle to the Romans* [New York: Macmillan, 1961], 56–57).

[117] The continuous aspect of καυχώμενοι comes from its being a present-tense participle functioning as a finite verb.

(3) The Gift of Righteousness (5:12–21)

^{12}Therefore, just as sin entered the world through one man, and death through sin, and in this way death came to all men, because all sinned—^{13}for before the law was given, sin was in the world. But sin is not taken into account when there is no law. ^{14}Nevertheless, death reigned from the time of Adam to the time of Moses, even over those who did not sin by breaking a command, as did Adam, who was a pattern of the one to come.

^{15}But the gift is not like the trespass. For if the many died by the trespass of the one man, how much more did God's grace and the gift that came by the grace of the one man, Jesus Christ, overflow to the many! ^{16}Again, the gift of God is not like the result of the one man's sin: The judgment followed one sin and brought condemnation, but the gift followed many trespasses and brought justification. ^{17}For if, by the trespass of the one man, death reigned through that one man, how much more will those who receive God's abundant provision of grace and of the gift of righteousness reign in life through the one man, Jesus Christ.

^{18}Consequently, just as the result of one trespass was condemnation for all men, so also the result of one act of righteousness was justification that brings life for all men. ^{19}For just as through the disobedience of the one man the many were made sinners, so also through the obedience of the one man the many will be made righteous.

^{20}The law was added so that the trespass might increase. But where sin increased, grace increased all the more, ^{21}so that, just as sin reigned in death, so also grace might reign through righteousness to bring eternal life through Jesus Christ our Lord.

5:12–14   Beginning at v. 12 we enter Paul's extended contrast between Adam (the first man) and the results of his sin and Jesus Christ (the "second man") and the gracious provisions of his atoning life and death.[118] The contrast runs through v. 19. These two figures illustrate the central theme of the specifically theological portion of Paul's letter. Adam typifies the sinful condition of all humans (1:18–3:20). Jesus stands for the justification received by faith (3:21–5:11). Redemption is the story of two men. The first man disobeyed God and led the entire

---

[118] Williams translates, "So here is the comparison." Nygren writes that "Paul's thoughts [in vv. 12–21] leap forth . . . like a torrential mountain stream" (*Romans,* 207). For a representative bibliography of the great mass of modern literature on this section see Cranfield (*Romans,* 1:270–71). O'Neill calls it a "theological excursus of beauty and of importance" but, consistent with his approach to the composition of the epistle, assigns it to a "great but anonymous commentator on Paul" (*Romans,* 96).

human race in the wrong direction.[119] The second man obeyed God and provides justification for all who will turn to him in faith. No matter how devastating the sin of the first, the redemptive work of the second reverses the consequences of that sin and restores people to the favor of God. Only by grasping the seriousness of the first is one able to appreciate the remarkable magnanimity of the second.

S. L. Johnson, Jr., sees a close connection between this section and the preceding. The point of 1:18–3:20, he says, is the certainty and universality of condemnation. The certainty of justification is the point of 3:21–5:11. At 5:12 Paul turned to the topic of "the universal application of the saving work of Christ, its availability for all believers."[120] Like many others he regards the "therefore" (*dia touto,* "on account of this"), which begins v. 12, as drawing a conclusion from the preceding. The connection, he says, is that on account of the sure salvation we have by one man, Jesus Christ (5:1–11), there is a likeness between Christ and Adam, who introduced the world to sin and death.[121]

Adam's sin is set forth in vv. 12–14. The basic premise is that "sin entered the world through one man."[122] The story of this fateful event is chronicled in Gen 3:1–7. Satan made his appeal through Eve, but Adam rightfully bears the responsibility since he was God's appointed representative of the race. Prior to this ill-fated decision the primal pair enjoyed the blessing of God's immediate presence (Gen 3:8 pictures God walking in the garden in the cool of the day). Sin had not yet entered the picture. Marred by sin as we are, it is difficult if not impossible for us to grasp the beauty of this rich and intimate relationship between the primal pair and their Creator. But along with sin came death.[123] Death is the

---

[119] Brunner writes: "The stream of death has its origin in the fall of the first man. His fall is the fall of all, his death the death of all. Mankind is a unity, and over humanity rules the inexorable law of God that death is part of sin" (*Romans,* 44).

[120] S. L. Johnson, Jr. "Romans 5:12—An Exercise in Exegesis and Theology," in *New Dimensions in New Testament Study,* ed. R. N. Longenecker and M. C. Tenney (Grand Rapids: Zondervan, 1974), 301.

[121] Ibid. It may be better to regard the term simply as transitional. See also the study by Cranfield, "On Some of the Problems in the Interpretation of Romans 5:12," *SJT* 22 (1969): 324–41.

[122] ὥσπερ introduces a protasis but then breaks off without the expected apodosis. It is customary to take Ἄρα οὖν ὡς in v. 18a as a repetition of the original protasis with the apodosis following in v. 18b. Cf. Johnson, "Romans 5:12," 302, n. 21.

[123] Sin and death personify the powers of destruction. They probably should both be capitalized. Dodd defines death in this passage as "a comprehensive term for the disastrous consequences of sin, physical and spiritual" (*Romans,* 81–82).

natural consequence of sin. The death of which Paul spoke was, on the one hand, physical. While Adam and Eve did not die physically for a number of years, the seeds of death were planted at the moment of disobedience. More importantly, Adam and Eve died spiritually. Spiritual death is separation from God. At that point in history God and humans turned in different directions. Humans pursued the path of pride and self-concern. God pursued the path of redemptive love.

Because Adam was the first created person, his sin had consequences for all who were to be born into the human race. Paul wrote, "In this way death came to all men" (v. 12).[124] Through Adam the dread disease of sin spread to everyone. But how exactly did that happen? This brings us to the much debated clause "because all sinned." The literature on this passage is extensive, and it will be well for the person who desires a more complete discussion of the issue to turn to any of the more critical commentaries. For our purposes we will mention what I take to be the three most probable interpretations.[125]

One approach is to regard the prepositional phrase (lit., "upon which/whom"), which the NIV translates "because," as introducing a relative clause with the pronoun referring to Adam.[126] Employing the Old Testament concept of corporate personality, this would mean that death came to all because all sinned *in Adam*. Bruce writes that for Paul, Adam was not only the first man but was in a sense what his name means ("humanity"); the whole of humanity is viewed as having originally sinned in Adam.[127] The major problem with this approach is that if Paul had intended to say "in whom," he would have used a simpler and more obvious construction.[128] This construction does not take this meaning elsewhere (cf. Luke 5:25; Acts 7:33; 2 Cor 5:4; Phil 3:12; 4:10).

A second way to take the expression is to regard it as a conjunction. Death, the inevitable consequence of sin, made its way to each individ-

---

[124] Sanday and Headlam note that διῆλθεν "contains the force of distribution; 'made its way to each individual member of the race'" (*Romans*, 133).

[125] The following discussion draws heavily upon Fitzmyer, who brings to our attention eleven different possibilities and supports the final alternative (*Romans*, 413–17). See also Cranfield, "Problems in the Interpretation of Romans 5.12," 330–35.

[126] The phrase is ἐφ' ᾧ. Rhys says this is "probably the most misinterpreted phrase in the New Testament" (*Romans*, 62).

[127] Bruce, *Romans*, 119. Stott notes that although all sinned in and through Adam and therefore all died is "theologically difficult," it is "surely exegetically correct" (*Romans*, 151).

[128] This would be ἐν ᾧ. This was also Augustine's position, who was following the Latin rendering *in quo*. In addition, "one man" (i.e., "Adam") is too far back in the sentence to serve well as an antecedent.

ual member of the race because everyone, in fact, has sinned. Although Adam's transgression determined human nature with its propensity to sin, the spread of that evil virus is the result of every person's decision to sin. We are responsible not for what Adam did but for what we have done.[129] The problem with this approach is that there are no certain examples in early Greek secular literature where the words are taken as the equivalent of a causal conjunction.[130]

A third possibility, which I am inclined to follow, is that the Greek words serve as a consecutive conjunction meaning "with the result that." In this case the primary cause of our sinful nature would be the sin of Adam; the result of that sin would be the history of sinning on the part of all who enter the human race and in fact sin of their own accord. This interpretation does justice to the language involved and conforms to the apostle's theological outlook as he is building his case in the Book of Romans.

Prior to the giving of the law through Moses, sin was in the world (v. 13). But technically it was not charged to our account as sin because there was no law to define it.[131] One cannot break a law that does not exist (cf. 4:15). Nevertheless, death, the consequence of sin, was in effect from Adam until Moses, even for those who did not break a specific command like Adam's. For the purpose of comparison, Adam may be considered as a type[132] or pattern of the one to come.[133] He provides

---

[129] Best concludes, "While, then, we are responsible for our own sins and not guilty because Adam sinned, yet we do not just copy Adam in his sin but are predisposed to sin because he brought sin into the world" (*Romans,* 60). P. Achtemeier speaks of the "melancholy fact" that "humans as a race repeat the sin of their original 'ancestor'" (*Romans* [Atlanta: John Knox, 1985], 96).

[130] The conjunction διότι means "because, for."

[131] ἐλλογέω is used in the papyri as a technical term meaning "to charge to one's account" (BAGD, 252).

[132] τύπος is the impression left by a die which in turn serves as a mold to form a likeness. Here it stands for Adam as an image of Christ, the "second man" (1 Cor 15:47). He is a "type" in the sense that like Christ he is the corporate head of a race of people. While all are in Adam by virtue of birth into the human family, only those are in Christ who by faith become members of the new humanity. Cranfield writes that "Adam in his universal effectiveness for ruin is the type which—in God's design—prefigures Christ in His universal effectiveness for salvation" (*Romans,* 1:283). Dunn discusses the debate regarding Paul's source for his Adam/Christ parallel and rejects the hypothesis that he was drawing on a pre-Christian Gnostic redeemer myth. He concludes that the Adam Christology was already available in primitive Christianity (*Romans,* 1:277–79).

[133] ὁ μέλλων ("the coming one") may be a Jewish designation for the Messiah (cf. Matt 11:3) although Käsemann writes that it "is hardly a mysterious messianic predication . . . nor does it concern the future glory of Christ" (*Romans,* 151).

a basis for understanding the relationship between sin and salvation.

5:15–17 Verses 15–21 contain six comparisons between Adam and the result of his sin and Jesus and the result of his redemptive work. Verses 15 and 17 follow the pattern, "If A, how much more B." Verse 16 uses the negative form, "A is not like B." Verses 18,19,21 follow the pattern, "Just as A, so also B."

The paragraph opens with the assertion that "the gift is not like the trespass."[134] God's act of grace was out of all proportion to the offense of Adam.[135] Then comes the "If A, how much more B." The conditional premise (accepted as true) is that "many died by the trespass[136] of the one man." The Greek term translated "the many"[137] should be taken in the inclusive sense of its Hebrew counterpart to mean "all" (who are, in fact, many). Adam's sin led to the death of the entire human race. Since that is so, what should be said about the gift of God given freely in Jesus Christ? "How much more" indicates that its effect is vastly greater for all humans.[138] "God's grace is infinitely greater for good than Adam's sin is for evil."[139] Although sin extends to all who are in Adam (and all are by birth), the grace of God transforms for eternity the life and destiny of all who are in Christ (and all who turn to him in faith are).

Although v. 15 shows that "the gift is not like the trespass," v. 16 teaches that the result of "the gift . . . is not like the result of the [trespass]." The comparison takes the form of "A is not like B." Adam's one sin was followed by judgment and brought condemnation. The many trespasses (of all who stem from Adam) was followed by the gift that brought justification. "A" is the story of divine reconciliation through the obedience of the second man, Christ. "B" is the story of humankind's fall from God's favor through the disobedience of the first man, Adam. "A is

---

[134] Paul may have chosen the term παράτωμα ("a lapse, or trespass") rather than ἁμαρτία ("sin") or παράβασις ("transgression") to match phonetically with χάρισμα ("gift") in the following clause.

[135] V. 15 opens with the strong adversative ἀλλά. It serves to warn the reader not to misunderstand the nature of the typological relationship between Adam and Christ. Adam is a "pattern of the one to come" but only in a limited sense. The differences are significant.

[136] Barrett calls attention to Paul's use of three words for sin in chap. 5: ἁμαρτία, "that which determines man's nature as inimical to God," παράβασις, "an act of disobedience to a revealed command," and παράπτωμα (in v. 15), "an act of sin" (*Romans*, 113).

[137] οἱ πολλοί. It is said that to the Semitic mind a large number is more significant than the idea of totality (Zerwick, *Analysis*, 2:470).

[138] This second use of "the many" translates εἰς τοὺς πολλούς, "the rest of men." This is the same as "all men" in v. 12.

[139] NIVSB note on 5:15.

not like B." What people did was to rebel; what God did was to restore.

Verse 17 supplies the second "If A, how much more B." "A" is the premise (accepted as true) that the reign of death was set into motion by the sin of the one man.[140] Sin, with death as its consequence, entered the world through Adam (5:12). Since that is true, how much more will those receiving the abundant grace of God and his gift of righteousness reign in life through the one man Jesus Christ ("B").[141] The future tense of the verb probably points to a time yet to come when believers will join with Jesus Christ in his reign (cf. 2 Tim 2:12; Rev 22:5). It is possible, however, to understand the reign as the present experience of believers who have already passed from death unto life (cf. John 5:24). If the sin of one man caused death to reign, the obedience of one man brings triumph over death to all who believe.

5:18–19 Paul returned to the comparison he began in v. 12 but never finished. His comparison takes the "Just as A, so also B" form. The contrasting elements are clearly set over against one another:

"One trespass" — "One act of righteousness"

"Condemnation" — "Justification"

"All men [in Adam]" — "All men [in Christ]"

Just as the one sin of Adam brought condemnation,[142] so also did the one righteous act of Christ bring justification.[143] Just as condemnation spread to all, so also is the divine acquittal offered to all. Paul did not intend to imply that the result of Christ's atoning work automatically provided justification for all regardless of their willingness to accept it. Universal salvation is not taught in this text.[144] Context indicates that

---

[140] The aorist ἐβασίλευσεν is ingressive.

[141] That the righteous would reign in the age to come was a standard part of Jewish eschatology (see Dan 7:22,27; *Wis* 5:15–16).

[142] The construction of v. 18 is difficult because Paul did not use any verbs. Most translations supply verbs such as "led to" or "the result . . . was." It is possible to take the sentence as an exclamation.

[143] Because δικαίωμα normally refers to a pronouncement of some kind rather than to an action, and because earlier in the same passage it is used of the state of justification (v. 16), Morris follows Godet and understands δικαίωμα in v. 18 to mean "sentence of justification" (*Romans,* 239). ζωῆς is either an epexegetical genitive ("justification which is life") or a genitive of result ("justification that brings life").

[144] For the view that those who are not justified by faith in this life will be justified at the judgment, see A. J. Hultgren, *Christ and His Benefits* (Philadelphia: Fortress, 1987), 54–55. Käsemann writes that "all powerful grace is unthinkable without eschatological universalism" (*Romans,* 157).

Paul was comparing the fate of those who are in Adam (the position of all by virtue of their birth into the human race) and the blessings of those who are in Christ (the position of all who have responded in faith).

Paul's final contrast was between the disobedience of Adam and the obedience of Christ (v. 19). By the disobedience of the first man the entire race was constituted sinners. But by the obedience[145] of the second man "the many will be made righteous." As in v. 15 we are to understand "the many" in terms of all who are in Adam (everyone who is born into the human family) and all who are in Christ (everyone who has been born into the family of God by faith in Christ). The righteousness of which Paul spoke is a right standing before God (cf. 2 Cor 5:21). It is imputed by God as a result of faith. Righteousness as conduct (sanctification) is dealt with in chaps. 6–8. Growth in holiness is the proof that righteousness by faith has in fact been imputed. By definition, life is growth. Where there is no growth, there is no life.

5:20–21 If righteousness is by faith, it is reasonable to ask where law fits into the picture. After all, God gave the Israelites an extended code of legislation with the expectation that it would guide their life and conduct. The answer is that law was brought in so that the offense might increase.[146] Law actually makes wrongdoing all the worse. Law was "slipped in" says Moffatt, "to aggravate the trespass."[147] Later Paul would write that apart from the law we would not have known the nature of sin (Rom 7:7; cf. Gal 3:19). The law was never intended to provide salvation but to convince people of their need for it. Law increased sin. That is the sad story of humanity estranged from God. But where sin increased, "grace increased all the more" (v. 20). God lavished his grace upon us beyond all measure. His grace exceeded immeasurably the extent of human sin. Only by understanding the depths of human degradation can we hope to grasp, even in part, the surpassing wonder of divine forgiveness.

Grace "superabounded"[148] in that as the reign of sin brought death, the reign of grace brings a righteousness that issues in life eternal. Death is the fate of all who follow sin as master. Eternal life is the destiny of

---

[145] Some understand ὑπακοῆς in reference to the entire life of Christ, but Paul's focus is on the death of Christ (cf. Phil 2:8).

[146] This understands ἵνα as expressing purpose rather than result.

[147] Like Sin and Death, Law is personified as an actor on the stage of human history.

[148] ὑπερεπερίσσευσεν is translated in various ways: "surpassed by far," "exceeded immeasurably," "overflowed beyond." The preposition ὑπέρ magnifies or intensifies the verb.

those whose allegiance is to Christ. A right standing before God is a gift offered freely by God to all who will respond in faith. It is life eternal. Death—eternal separation from God, who alone possesses life immortal—is the self-inflicted penalty for pursuing sin rather than accepting salvation.

IV. THE RIGHTEOUSNESS IN WHICH WE ARE TO GROW
(6:1–8:39)
1. No Longer Slaves to Sin (6:1–23)
(1) Dead to Sin, Alive in Christ (6:1–14)
(2) Slaves to Righteousness (6:15–23)
2. No Longer Condemned by Law (7:1–25)
3. Living in the Spirit (8:1–39)

IV. THE RIGHTEOUSNESS IN WHICH WE ARE TO GROW (6:1–8:39)

Paul began his letter to the Romans by demonstrating the need of all people for righteousness, Jew and Gentile alike (1:18–3:20). Then he established that righteousness comes through faith in Jesus Christ (3:21–5:21). The righteousness of which he spoke is called "imputed righteousness." It is the work of God given freely to all who respond in faith. The doctrine is called "justification," the establishment of a right relationship between God and humans. Beginning with chap. 6 Paul moved ahead to discuss what was to happen in people's lives after their sins have been forgiven and they are declared righteous in God's sight. This process of growth in spiritual maturity is the subject of chaps. 6–8. The doctrine is called "sanctification," the lifelong process of transformation into the likeness of Christ. Any justification that does not lead to sanctification is a sham. Any sanctification not founded upon justification is an exercise in legalistic futility and does not deserve the name.

1. No Longer Slaves to Sin (6:1–23)

(1) Dead to Sin, Alive in Christ (6:1–14)

¹What shall we say, then? Shall we go on sinning so that grace may increase? ²By no means! We died to sin; how can we live in it any longer? ³Or don't you know that all of us who were baptized into Christ Jesus were baptized into his death? ⁴We were therefore buried with him through bap-

147

tism into death in order that, just as Christ was raised from the dead
through the glory of the Father, we too may live a new life.

⁵If we have been united with him like this in his death, we will certainly
also be united with him in his resurrection. ⁶For we know that our old self
was crucified with him so that the body of sin might be done away with,
that we should no longer be slaves to sin— ⁷because anyone who has died
has been freed from sin.

⁸Now if we died with Christ, we believe that we will also live with him.
⁹For we know that since Christ was raised from the dead, he cannot die
again; death no longer has mastery over him. ¹⁰The death he died, he died
to sin once for all; but the life he lives, he lives to God.

¹¹In the same way, count yourselves dead to sin but alive to God in
Christ Jesus. ¹²Therefore do not let sin reign in your mortal body so that
you obey its evil desires. ¹³Do not offer the parts of your body to sin, as
instruments of wickedness, but rather offer yourselves to God, as those
who have been brought from death to life; and offer the parts of your body
to him as instruments of righteousness. ¹⁴For sin shall not be your master,
because you are not under law, but under grace.

6:1   Paul had just written (in Rom 5:20) that where there is an
increase in sin there is an even greater increase in grace. So the question
was bound to arise, Why not continue in sin[1] so the greatness of God's
grace may be seen more fully? The question may have arisen from antinomian sources that purposively misconstrued the doctrine of justification by faith as providing an excuse for a sinful lifestyle. Against such a
perverted inference W. Barclay writes, "How despicable it would be for
a son to consider himself free to sin, because he knew that his father
would forgive."[2] Equally possible is that the question stemmed from
conscientious Jews who felt that the doctrine of salvation by faith alone
would encourage moral irresponsibility.[3] Although the latter group questioned the teaching for fear of what it might do, the former embraced the
doctrine for what they felt it would allow them to do.

6:2–3   The answer to the rhetorical question is a resounding "By no
means!"[4] How could it be possible for those who have died to sin to con-

---

[1] The NIV's "shall we go on sinning?" reflects the present tense of ἐπιμένωμεν.

[2] W. Barclay, *The Letter to the Romans,* rev. ed., DSB (Philadelphia: Westminster, 1978),
85.

[3] D. Moo thinks that "Paul himself poses this question in order to draw out the implications
of the Christian's experience of grace" (*Romans 1–8,* WEC [Chicago: Moody, 1991], 372).

[4] B. Kaye finds seventy-four rhetorical questions in Romans (*The Argument of Romans with
Special Reference to Chapter 6* [Austin: Scholars Press, 1979], 14).

tinue to live in it?[5] Death separates. Death to sin removes the believer from the control of sin. This truth finds expression throughout Paul's writings (Rom 6:6,11; Col 3:5; cf. 1 Pet 2:24). The text does not say that sin dies to the believer; it is the believer who has died to sin. Origen, the most influential theologian of the ante-Nicene period, described death to sin in this way: "To obey the cravings of sin is to be alive to sin; but not to obey the cravings of sin or succumb to its will, this is to die to sin."[6] Sin continues in force in its attempt to dominate the life and conduct of the believer. But the believer has been baptized into Christ,[7] and that means to have been baptized into Christ's death as well.[8] Christ's death for sin becomes our death to sin. Sin lies on the other side of the grave for those who have in Christ died to it. Paul asked incredulously, How can we who have died to sin "breathe its air again?" (Knox).[9]

6:4 The believer has been "buried with [Christ] through baptism into death."[10] Burial certifies the reality of death. Baptism is the ritual act that portrays this burial.[11] That Paul did not speak of faith at this point is immaterial. He was using the ritual act of baptism as a symbol of the complete redemptive event that finds its effectual cause in the death of Christ and its completion in the faith of those who believe.

But death and burial are not the end of the story. In God's redemptive

---

[5] The aorist ἀπεθάνομεν reflects a decisive step. C. E. B. Cranfield lists four different senses in which Christians may be said to have died to sin: juridical, baptismal, moral, and eschatological (*The Epistle to the Romans,* ICC, 2 vols. [Edinburgh: T & T Clark, 1975], 299–300).

[6] Cited by J. Fitzmyer, *Romans,* AB (New York: Doubleday, 1993), 433.

[7] M. Black notes that older commentaries describe this incorporation in terms of Paul's doctrine of "mystical union," but it is now recognized that "Jesus Christ" should be understood as *corporate* personality. "To be baptised 'into' Jesus Christ is to be incorporated into the Body of Christ" (*Romans,* 2d ed., NCB [Grand Rapids: Eerdmans, 1989], 87). But E. Käsemann points out that "the widespread idea that this passage too is determined by the idea of corporate personality . . . overlooks the surprising reserve with regard to this motif in general" (*Commentary on Romans,* trans. and ed. G. W. Bromiley [Grand Rapids: Eerdmans, 1980], 163–64).

[8] J. D. G. Dunn reviews the debate on the possible influence of contemporary mystery cults on Paul and the theology of Rom 6:3–4. He concludes that any direct influence is "most unlikely" (*Romans,* WBC [Dallas: Word, 1988], 1:308–11).

[9] What Paul was endeavoring to show was that "a real Christian cannot live in sin and that if he lives in sin he proves himself to be a non-Christian even though he is baptized" (F. E. Hamilton, *The Epistle to the Romans* [Grand Rapids: Baker, 1958], 93).

[10] Some commentators take εἰς τὸν θάνατον with συνετάφημεν, others take it with διὰ τοῦ βαπτίσματος. Since "buried into death" is an awkward phrase, the latter option probably is to be preferred.

[11] Βάπτισμα occurs only in Christian literature. In the NT it was used of the baptism by John, of Christian baptism, and figuratively of martyrdom.

plan burial is followed by resurrection.[12] As Christ was raised from the dead in a manifestation of the Father's glorious power, so also are we raised to an entirely new way of living.[13] The cross has as its ethical purpose a change in conduct. The Greek expression translated "a new life" is better rendered "a new sphere which is life." Apart from Christ people are dead in their sins (Eph 2:1). But raised from the dead through faith in Christ, they enter an entirely new sphere of existence. They are alive in Christ. As Jesus promised, "I have come that they may have life, and have it to the full" (John 10:10). Although contemporary use has tended to trivialize the expression "born again," the vibrant reality of new life in Christ is still portrayed most graphically by the metaphor of spiritual birth. The lives of believers are to be as different from their preconversion days as life is from death.[14]

6:5 If it is true that we have been united with Christ in his death[15] —and we have—it then follows that we are also united with him in his resurrection.[16] As he was raised victor over death, so also are we set free from the bondage of sin. Death precedes life in the realm of the Spirit. Since it is true that we are "one with Him by sharing in His death" (Weymouth), then certainly[17] we are one with him by sharing in his resurrection life. New life in Christ follows death to sin as certainly as Christ's resurrection followed his crucifixion.

---

[12] In union with Christ his followers "pass through the crucial events of his existence: his death, burial and resurrection" (E. Best, *The Letter of Paul to the Romans,* CBC [Cambridge: University Press, 1967], 67). E. F. Scott writes: "As Christ died and was buried and rose again, so the convert is plunged in the water and emerges a new man. He has reenacted in his own person the death by which Christ redeemed him, and now shares in the risen life of Christ" (*Paul's Epistle to the Romans* [London: SCM, 1947], 44). We do not believe, however, that rebirth is in any real sense connected to water baptism.

[13] περιπατέω ("to walk"; "live") used figuratively to depict a manner of living stems from a Jewish rather than a Greek background (cf. Exod 18:20; Ps 86:11). περιπατήσωμεν, an aorist, is ingressive and suggests a completely new way of living. J. Murray comments: "That believers 'walk' in newness of life indicates that the life is not conceived of as otiose possession but as engaging the activity of the believer" (*The Epistle to the Romans,* 2 vols., NICNT [Grand Rapids: Eerdmans, 1965], 1:217).

[14] The newness of the resurrected life is stressed in such texts as Rom 7:6; 2 Cor 5:17; Eph 4:22–24; Col 3:10.

[15] The NIV follows the interpretation that supplies an αὐτῷ ("with him") and takes ὁμοιώματι instrumentally. Others take τῷ ὁμοιώματι as dependent on σύμφυτοι and read "united with the likeness of his death." Although this is a bit awkward, it points out that while our death is not the same as Christ's, there does exist a symbolic relationship.

[16] The future ἐσόμεθα is logical rather than temporal. Paul was talking about the moral life of the believer.

[17] In the apodosis of a conditional sentence ἀλλά means "certainly" (BAGD, 38).

6:6–7 Our confidence in a resurrected life rests upon the fact that our old self was nailed to the cross with Jesus.[18] We were "crucified with him" (v. 6). Believers, by definition, are those who by their union with Christ died with him on the cross. That death had a definite purpose in the spiritual life history of the believer. We were crucified in order that our sinful nature[19] might be stripped of its power. "Might be done away with" translates a form of the Greek verb *katargeō,* which speaks of being "reduced to a condition of absolute impotence and inaction, as if it were dead."[20] Death fulfills the demands of sin.[21] But death opens the way for resurrection. Resurrection lies beyond the control of death. It is the victor over death. With the old self rendered powerless, it is no longer necessary for a person to continue in bondage to sin. In Christ we are set free. Since sin exhausted itself in bringing about death, from that point forward it is powerless to overcome new life.[22]

6:8 The reader will notice how often Paul repeated himself in this section. As a good teacher he knew that truth once stated is not necessarily absorbed. Remember that the book we are studying is first of all a letter written by the apostle to Christian believers in Rome. Paul stressed certain truths basic to an understanding of what it means to be united with Christ and living the new life of the Spirit. So in v. 8 he again stated the basic proposition that those who have died with Christ will also live

---

[18] We are not to think of the "old self" as the "sinful nature" with which we were born and to which a "new nature" was added at conversion but as what we were in Adam, the "old man" dominated by sin and crucified with Christ. Moo refers to the "old man" and "new man" as categories that are relational rather than ontological (*Romans 1–8,* 390–92). C. K. Barrett comments that the "old man" is "ourselves in union with Adam," and the "new man" is "ourselves in union with Christ" (*A Commentary on the Epistle to the Romans,* 2d ed. [New York: Harpers, 1991], 125).

[19] τὸ σῶμα τῆς ἁμαρτίας refers not to the physical body as inherently sinful but to the whole person under the control of sin. J. R. W. Stott favors the meaning "our fallen, self-centered nature" (*Romans* [Downers Grove: InterVarsity, 1994], 175).

[20] W. Sanday and A. C. Headlam, *A Critical and Exegetical Commentary on the Epistle to the Romans,* 5th ed., ICC [Edinburgh: T & T Clark, 1902], 158).

[21] The NIV takes δεδικαίωται in v. 7 in the legal sense of having been exonerated from a charge. The NEB has "a dead man is no longer answerable for his sin." This reflects the rabbinic principle, "When a man is dead he is freed from fulfilling the law" (*Shabb.* 151b). Others interpret the verb in the Pauline sense of "having been justified [from sin]."

[22] Calvin wisely commented that if we do not find ourselves among the number of those who have wholly crucified the flesh, there is no reason for despair because "this work of God is not completed on the day when it is begun in us, but gradually increases, and by daily advancement is brought by degrees to its completion" (*The Epistles of Paul the Apostle to the Romans and to the Thessalonians,* trans. R. Mackenzie [Grand Rapids: Eerdmans, 1961], 125).

with him. This is not a promise of life after death with Christ in heaven but of a life to be lived out here and now.[23] Death, far from being simply a negative concept, is in fact the gateway to life. Elsewhere Paul paradoxically stated, "I have been crucified with Christ . . . but . . . I live by faith" (Gal 2:20). Put simply, to live one must die.

6:9–10   Paul now appealed to a point of common knowledge among God's people.[24] Having been raised from the dead, Christ cannot die again. His resurrection was unlike that of Lazarus, who had to meet death once again.[25] But Christ's resurrection broke forever the tyranny of death. That cruel master can no longer exercise any power over him. The cross was sin's final move; the resurrection was God's checkmate. The game is over. Sin is forever in defeat. Christ the victor died to sin "once for all"[26] and lives now in unbroken fellowship with God.[27]

Many of the ancient cathedrals in the old world portray in their statuary a dead or dying Christ. But Christ crucified (if no more were said) is not the gospel. The church needs a renewed awareness of Christ as victorious over death and the grave. It is the resurrection that makes the news good news. Rising triumphant over Satan's ultimate show of force, Jesus Christ is forever crowned King of kings and Lord of lords. Join the triumphal parade! Celebrate the defeat of Satan, that rebel whose fate is now forever sealed.

6:11   Christ is our example. By his death he ended once for all his relationship to sin. Now he lives forever in unbroken fellowship with God. "In the same way,"[28] wrote Paul, we are to consider ourselves dead to sin and alive to God (cf. 1 Pet 2:24).[29] When Christ died for sin, he

---

[23] Cranfield argues that the structure of the paragraph and esp. the content of v. 11 make clear that καὶ συζήσομεν αὐτῷ refers to the present life (*Romans* 1:312–13). Others see the eschatological dimension as primary but add that it also applies to the believer's present life.

[24] Christian faith is built upon knowledge. Faith is not a "leap in the dark" but "the resting of the mind in the sufficiency of the evidence" (a favorite statement of E. J. Carnell).

[25] Nor was his death like that of a nature-god whose destiny was said to repeat forever the cycle of death and restoration.

[26] Compare ἀπεθάνομεν τῇ ἁμαρτίᾳ in v. 2. As Christ was separated from sin by death, so are we to live freed from its control. "Once for all" translates ἐφάπαξ —"an altogether decisive and unrepeatable event" (Cranfield, *Romans,* 1:314). Cf. Heb 7:27; 9:12; 10:10, where it is used to stress the once-for-all nature of the sacrifice of Christ.

[27] ζῇ is a continuous present. It is the life of eternity.

[28] Taking οὕτως to mean "just as" rather than drawing an inference from what preceded.

[29] λογίζεσθε is a present imperative, which suggests a continuing mind-set on the part of the believer. After five and a half chapters Paul exhorted his readers for the first time (the imperative in 3:4 is not relevant). Building a strong theological base before turning to the ethical implications that flow from it was important.

also died to sin. Now we are to take our place with him and regard sin as something to which we also have died. Paul was not suggesting that we imitate Christ. He was speaking of a reality that took place when we by faith were incorporated into Christ. Our responsibility is to take with all seriousness the fact that in Christ we have died to sin. Fitzmyer writes: "Ontologically united with Christ through faith and baptism, Christians must deepen their faith continually to become more and more psychologically aware of that union."[30] We are to consider ourselves "dead to the appeal and power of sin" (Phillips) and alive to God through our union with Christ Jesus.[31] The very idea of responding positively to sin's invitation should strike the believer as morbid. For the Christian to choose to sin is the spiritual equivalent of digging up a corpse for fellowship. A genuine death to sin means that the entire perspective of the believer has been radically altered.

6:12 With this verse we move from a discussion of our union with Christ in his death and resurrection (vv. 1–11) to the practical implications that flow from that relationship (vv. 12–14). We move from the "indicative" to the "imperative." The relationship between the two must neither be broken nor fused into a single unity. Sanctification separated from justification encourages legalism, while sanctification fused with justification assumes that God will do it all.[32] The imperative challenges us to become what we are. In Christ we have died to sin and are alive to God. So we should base our daily lives on that truth and live out our days from that perspective. It follows, then, that we are no longer to allow sin to reign in our mortal bodies[33] (v. 12). Sin is personified as a sovereign ruler who would make us obey the cravings of our bodies that are destined for death. But in Christ we have died to sin. Sin no longer has the authority to enforce its demands. Death has severed the relationship.[34]

---

[30] Fitzmyer, *Romans,* 438.

[31] ἐν Χριστῷ is one of the great Pauline concepts. It speaks of the intimate relationship between the believer and Christ. To be "in Christ" means to be incorporated into the one who has died to sin and is alive to God. For bibliographic information on the extensive literature see *TWNT* 2.534.

[32] See Moo, *Romans 1–8,* 398–99.

[33] σῶμα here is not simply the body of flesh but the entire person. It is θνητός in that it participates in the weakness and frailty of this age.

[34] H. C. G. Moule writes: "It is for you, O man in Christ, to say to the enemy, defeated yet present, 'Thou shalt not reign; I veto thee in the name of my King'" (*The Epistle to the Romans* [London: Pickering & Inglis, n.d.], 168).

6:13   Paul spelled out in practical terms what it means to transfer our obedience from sin to God. We are no longer to place any part of our bodies at the disposal of sin to be used as an instrument of unrighteousness.[35] If the metaphor is military, Paul was saying, "Don't let sin take command of any part of your body and use it as a weapon for evil purposes."[36] Instead, we are to present ourselves to God once for all as those who have been brought from death to life.[37] Alive with Christ, we are now to put ourselves at the disposal of God. Our bodies are to be devoted to him as instruments of righteousness.[38] "We are faced with the tremendous alternative," writes Barclay, "of making ourselves weapons in the hand of God or weapons in the hand of sin."[39]

6:14   Paul brought this section to an end with the promise that sin will not rule over believers[40] because they are not "under law, but under grace." They are not "under law" in the sense that they have been removed from the old era in which law served to intensify sin (3:20; 4:15; 5:20). Now they are "under grace"[41] in that they have entered the new era in which the power to overcome sin is readily attainable. For those in Adam law brings condemnation, not freedom. For those in Christ grace frees from the condemnation brought by failure to keep the law.[42] Believers no longer live under the condemnation of the law but

---

[35] παριστάνω has the general meaning "to put at someone's disposal," although it also serves as a technical term in the language of sacrifice (as in Rom 12:1), "to offer, to bring" (BAGD, 627–28). μέλος ("part of body") should be taken in a fairly broad sense to include any natural capacity.

[36] E. Brunner notes that "the metaphor of conquest is not strange to Paul" and speaks of a "holy war" in which "what originally belonged to God but had rebelliously turned apostate" is reconquered (*The Letter to the Romans* [Philadelphia: Westminster, 1949], 52). In John 18:3 ὅπλον is used of the weapons carried by those who came to arrest Jesus.

[37] Note the two tenses of the imperative in v. 13: παραστήσατε is aorist; παριστάνετε is present. Sanday and Headlam translate παραστήσατε "dedicate by one decisive act" and παριστάνετε "go on yielding" (*Romans,* 161). L. Morris says that "the aorist tense signifies a wholehearted and total commitment: 'once and for all present yourselves to God'" (*The Epistle to the Romans* [Grand Rapids: Eerdmans, 1988], 258). ὡσεί here means "as you really are, not as if you were." Phillips has "like men rescued from certain death."

[38] In chaps. 1–5 δικαιοσύνη refers to God's act of setting people right with himself or the result of that activity, but here it designates behavior pleasing to God.

[39] Barclay, *Romans,* 87.

[40] "Sin has neither the right nor the power" (Bengel, *Word Studies,* 2:75). Some take the future κυριεύσει in an imperatival sense ("Don't let sin continue as your master").

[41] E. F. Harrison says that to be *under* grace reflects its disciplinary power. Here in 6:14 that aspect of grace is "in line with the apostle's effort to show that grace is not license" ("Romans," EBC 10, ed. F. E. Gaebelein [Grand Rapids: Zondervan, 1976], 72).

[42] Paul did not argue that the law no longer had any validity but that what it required is now attained through grace (see Fitzmyer, *Romans,* 447–48).

with the realization that God by his grace has placed them in a totally new relationship to himself.

(2) Slaves to Righteousness (6:15–23)

[15]What then? Shall we sin because we are not under law but under grace? By no means! [16]Don't you know that when you offer yourselves to someone to obey him as slaves, you are slaves to the one whom you obey—whether you are slaves to sin, which leads to death, or to obedience, which leads to righteousness? [17]But thanks be to God that, though you used to be slaves to sin, you wholeheartedly obeyed the form of teaching to which you were entrusted. [18]You have been set free from sin and have become slaves to righteousness.

[19]I put this in human terms because you are weak in your natural selves. Just as you used to offer the parts of your body in slavery to impurity and to ever-increasing wickedness, so now offer them in slavery to righteousness leading to holiness. [20]When you were slaves to sin, you were free from the control of righteousness. [21]What benefit did you reap at that time from the things you are now ashamed of? Those things result in death! [22]But now that you have been set free from sin and have become slaves to God, the benefit you reap leads to holiness, and the result is eternal life. [23]For the wages of sin is death, but the gift of God is eternal life in Christ Jesus our Lord.

6:15 At the beginning of the chapter we encountered the question, Shall we go on sinning so that grace may increase? (v. 1). Now we meet a second and similar rhetorical question, Shall we sin because we are under grace rather than law? The first draws from 5:20 the mistaken inference that since law was added to increase the trespass, we ought to continue sinning so as to make grace increase all the more. The second mistakenly assumes that if we are not under law it does not really matter if we sin. The answer to both questions is a resounding, "By no means!" Grace does not free us to do anything we want. It does not provide the opportunity to live apart from all restrictions. Freedom is not the exercise of unlimited spontaneity. It means to be set free from the bondage of sin in order to live in a way that reflects the nature and character of God. The rhetorical question probably arose among Jews who felt that to be released from the jurisdiction of law would encourage the removal of all moral restraint. The answer to that fearful expectation is, By no means!

6:16–17 People obviously are the slaves of the one to whom they offer themselves to obey (v. 17).[43] Paul set forth two masters: one is sin,

---

[43] In Paul's day many people, especially in urban centers, sold themselves into slavery as a means of livelihood. An estimated one third of the population of Corinth were slaves.

and the other is obedience [to God]. There is no possibility of living
without an allegiance to one or the other. "There is no absolute independence for man," writes J. Denney; "our nature requires us to serve *some*
master."[44] Unbelievers may think they are free and would have to give
up that freedom should they accept Christ. Such is not the case. They are
servants of sin right now. In coming to Christ they simply exchange one
master for another. Servitude to sin is replaced with servitude to God.
The master we obey is clear evidence of whose slaves we really are.
There is no room for compromise.[45] As Jesus taught, "No one can serve
two masters" (Matt 6:24). We also are reminded of Joshua's challenge to
the Israelites at Shechem, "Choose for yourselves this day whom you
will serve" (Josh 24:15).

There is a dramatic difference in the outcomes of choosing one or the
other of these masters.[46] To choose sin as a master leads to death. To
choose obedience to God as master leads to righteousness (v. 16).[47] The
contrast in v. 16 is between sin and obedience. From this we may rightly
infer that the essence of sin is disobedience. Sin is not simply something
that we can't help doing but something we choose to do in direct violation
of the will of God. It may be forgiven but it is not something that is excus-
able due to extenuating circumstances. The righteousness to which obedience leads is the righteousness of personal growth in spiritual maturity.

Paul gave thanks that although the believers in Rome had at one time
been slaves to sin (all outside of Christ are),[48] they had broken free from
that master. They now pledged undivided allegiance to the body of teaching to which they were entrusted (v. 17).[49] Paul may have been referring

---

[44] J. Denney, "St. Paul's Epistle to the Romans," EGT 2 (Grand Rapids: Eerdmans, 1983),
636.

[45] A. Nygren writes, "There is no middle ground; if one lives in service to righteousness,
he is by that very fact *not* in the service of sin" (*Commentary on Romans,* trans. C. C. Rasmussen [Philadelphia: Muhlenberg, 1949], 254).

[46] A. T. Robertson notes that ἤτοι ("whether") has the notion of restriction (*A Grammar of
the Greek New Testament in the Light of Historical Research* [Nashville: Broadman, 1934],
1154). You must choose one or the other.

[47] θάνατος here refers to "the final and eternal exclusion from God's presence" and
δικαιοσύνη to "moral" righteousness, or "conduct pleasing to God" (Moo, *Romans 1–8,*
415–16). Some, however, understand Paul's use of δικαιοσύνη here as final or eschatological
justification (e.g., Cranfield, *Romans,* 1:322). The latter option has the advantage of maintaining the comparison with death (both are final).

[48] The clause with ἤτε is concessive. Paul did not give thanks *because* they used to be
slaves to sin.

[49] ὑπηκούσατε is an ingressive aorist and points to the occasion when the Roman Christians first placed their trust in Christ.

to a summary of the ethical teaching of Jesus drawn up for instructing new converts.[50] Later in his ministry he wrote that his message should serve as "the pattern of sound teaching" (2 Tim 1:13). To obey "whole-heartedly" requires a willing abandonment to the truth of the message. Christian obedience is never coercive; it is always voluntary. The teaching was not entrusted to the converts but the converts to the teaching. Barrett points out that unlike the rabbis, Christians are not masters of a tradition; "they are themselves created by the word of God, and remain in subjection to it."[51] The gospel message with all its ethical implications represents an existing body of truth into which new believers are brought by faith. The message is not brought to the converts but vice versa.

6:18 If Paul seems to have been repetitive, it is only because what he was teaching is so important. Once again in v. 18 the apostle reminded his readers in Rome that they had broken free from the slavery of sin and become the willing servants of righteousness.[52] The freedom brought by grace does not provide carte blanche to continue in sin. On the contrary, grace places the believer under obligation[53] to holiness and growth in righteousness.

6:19–22 Since v. 6 Paul had been personifying sin as an illegitimate slave master, one whose authority over the believer has been removed by the death of Christ. Beginning with v. 15 he expanded the analogy by contrasting the old master, sin, with the new master, righteousness. Analogies, by definition, are less than perfect. So Paul reminded his readers that he was putting the argument in human terms because of the inherent difficulties in understanding spiritual truth.[54]

---

[50] The expression τύπος διδαχῆς is held by some to be a short summary of the Christian faith passed along to the new convert at baptism. Others hold that v. 17b is a marginal gloss from church tradition that entered the text at an early stage. Without it vv. 17a and 18 form a neat comparison. (See the discussion in *EDNT* 3.374.) Fitzmyer mentions a suggestion by Lattey that the expression refers to the rites or doctrines of paganism and that all of v. 17 refers to the old status whereas v. 18 describes Christian freedom (*Romans,* 450). Since a τύπος ("the impression made by a blow") can serve as a mold, the expression may suggest the molding or formative effect of Christian teaching.

[51] Barrett, *Romans,* 132.

[52] For information on manumission in antiquity see Deissmann, *Light from the Ancient East* (1923; reprint, Grand Rapids: Baker, 1965), 320–30.

[53] Conduct pleasing to God (i.e., "righteousness") is viewed as the new power to which the believer is subject. Freedom is not the lack of all restraint but deliverance from everything that would keep a person from becoming what God intended that person to be.

[54] ἀνθρώπινον λέγειν means "to speak in humans terms," i.e., as people do in daily life (BAGD, 67). The NAB has "I use the following example from human affairs." See Rom 3:5; 1 Cor 9:8; Gal 3:15 for similar qualifying remarks.

Prior to their coming to Christ, the believers at Rome had sold their bodies in slavery to impurity and "ever-increasing wickedness."[55] But now another transaction was in order. They were to surrender their bodies again, but this time to righteousness. Freedom is not a question of whether or not we would like to serve but the choice of which master we will serve. Righteousness leads to holiness; sin as a master promotes wickedness. Righteousness reverses the moral direction taken by sin and leads to sanctification. In both cases a process is under way. Christians who entertain sin find themselves in an ethical tug-of-war they are bound to lose. The answer to this conflict is practical; surrender your body to those activities that are good and pure rather than to those that defile.

When sin was our master, we were free from the control of righteousness (v. 20). And what benefit did we reap from that lifestyle (v. 21)?[56] (We are now ashamed of how we lived.) We received no benefit at all, unless of course we consider the negative reward of death![57] But now we are set free from sin's bondage (v. 22).[58] We have become slaves of God. And is there benefit in this? Most certainly! The reward for serving God is growth in holiness and, in the end, eternal life.[59] In fact, apart from holiness there is no eternal life. The author to Hebrews counseled a holy life because "without holiness no one will see the Lord" (Heb 12:14). Slavery to sin results in death. Slavery to righteousness leads to eternal fellowship with God. Or, in the words of Jesus, the broad road (the path of sin) leads to destruction, but the narrow road (the way of righteousness) leads to life (Matt 7:13–14).

6:23 It all comes down to this: the wages paid by sin are death,[60]

---

[55] The NIV takes εἰς τὴν ἀνομίαν with τῇ ἀνομίᾳ. But since it is parallel with εἰς ἁγιασμόν, it may be better to take both phrases as pointing out the end in view. Formerly it was wickedness; now it is holiness.

[56] The punctuation that places the question mark after τότε rather than ἐπαισχύνεσθε is to be preferred. Moo points out the parallels between vv. 21 and 22 in status, result, and outcome (*Romans 1–8*, 423).

[57] Death in its fullest sense is the τέλος, the end result of a life lived under the control of sin.

[58] νυνὶ of v. 22 contrasts with τότε of v. 21. Then their fruit led to death, but now their fruit leads to holiness.

[59] The word for "holiness" is ἁγιασμός. Barclay reminds us that "all Greek nouns which end in -asmos describe, not a completed state, but a *process*. Sanctification is the road to holiness" (*Romans*, 91). A. M. Hunter writes that eternal life is "life with the tang of eternity about it" (*The Epistle to the Romans*, TBC [London: SCM, 1955], 68).

[60] ὀψώνιον is a military term for the wage paid to a soldier. In this context it connotes the stern nature of the transaction. See C. C. Caragounis, "Ὀψώνιον: A Reconsideration of Its Meaning," *NovT* 16 (1974): 35–57.

but the gift God gives is eternal life (v. 23).[61] Not only is the contrast
between death and life but also between earning and giving. Sinners earn
what they receive. By obeying the impulses of sin, they are storing up
the reward for sinning. Their severance check is death—eternal separation from God, who alone is life. By yielding to the impulses of righteousness, believers do not earn anything. They do, however, receive a
gift—the gift of eternal life, which comes by faith through Jesus Christ
their Lord.

2. No Longer Condemned by Law (7:1–25)

[1]Do you not know, brothers—for I am speaking to men who know the
law—that the law has authority over a man only as long as he lives? [2]For
example, by law a married woman is bound to her husband as long as he is
alive, but if her husband dies, she is released from the law of marriage. [3]So
then, if she marries another man while her husband is still alive, she is
called an adulteress. But if her husband dies, she is released from that law
and is not an adulteress, even though she marries another man.

[4]So, my brothers, you also died to the law through the body of Christ,
that you might belong to another, to him who was raised from the dead, in
order that we might bear fruit to God. [5]For when we were controlled by
the sinful nature, the sinful passions aroused by the law were at work in
our bodies, so that we bore fruit for death. [6]But now, by dying to what once
bound us, we have been released from the law so that we serve in the new
way of the Spirit, and not in the old way of the written code.

[7]What shall we say, then? Is the law sin? Certainly not! Indeed I would
not have known what sin was except through the law. For I would not have
known what coveting really was if the law had not said, "Do not covet."
[8]But sin, seizing the opportunity afforded by the commandment, produced
in me every kind of covetous desire. For apart from law, sin is dead. [9]Once
I was alive apart from law; but when the commandment came, sin sprang
to life and I died. [10]I found that the very commandment that was intended
to bring life actually brought death. [11]For sin, seizing the opportunity
afforded by the commandment, deceived me, and through the commandment put me to death. [12]So then, the law is holy, and the commandment is
holy, righteous and good.

[13]Did that which is good, then, become death to me? By no means! But
in order that sin might be recognized as sin, it produced death in me

---

[61] Some have suggested that χάρισμα ("gift") in this verse may refer to the *donativum,* or
"bounty," such as a new emperor might distribute to the army on his accession to the throne
(Black, *Romans,* 93).

through what was good, so that through the commandment sin might become utterly sinful.

^{14}We know that the law is spiritual; but I am unspiritual, sold as a slave to sin. ^{15}I do not understand what I do. For what I want to do I do not do, but what I hate I do. ^{16}And if I do what I do not want to do, I agree that the law is good. ^{17}As it is, it is no longer I myself who do it, but it is sin living in me. ^{18}I know that nothing good lives in me, that is, in my sinful nature. For I have the desire to do what is good, but I cannot carry it out. ^{19}For what I do is not the good I want to do; no, the evil I do not want to do—this I keep on doing. ^{20}Now if I do what I do not want to do, it is no longer I who do it, but it is sin living in me that does it.

^{21}So I find this law at work: When I want to do good, evil is right there with me. ^{22}For in my inner being I delight in God's law; ^{23}but I see another law at work in the members of my body, waging war against the law of my mind and making me a prisoner of the law of sin at work within my members. ^{24}What a wretched man I am! Who will rescue me from this body of death? ^{25}Thanks be to God—through Jesus Christ our Lord!

So then, I myself in my mind am a slave to God's law, but in the sinful nature a slave to the law of sin.

7:1–3 In the previous section Paul used the practice of slavery to illustrate by way of analogy that living under grace, far from encouraging wickedness, actually places a person under obligation to righteousness. Here he turns to the institution of marriage to illustrate a related truth. As a woman whose husband has died is free to marry another, so also are believers, since they have died to the law, free to belong to Christ.

Verse 1 states a basic principle with which all would agree, that is, legal claims are binding upon a person only during that person's lifetime. In this context Paul spoke of "law" in terms of its fundamental character rather than as a reference to the Mosaic legislation.[62] People were under the jurisdiction of law only so long as they lived. Law regulated the activities of the living, not the dead. Paul, in an aside, reminded his readers that he was writing to those who knew the law. They were acquainted with the basic precepts of legal jurisdiction. They understood what law was all about.

---

[62] Some take νόμος here as the Mosaic law and refer back to 6:14, where Paul wrote that his readers were "not under law." Fitzmyer acknowledges that the illustration Paul used in the following verses is not found in the OT but notes that it does agree with a principle enunciated in later rabbinic literature (*Romans,* 457). Other scholars hold that Paul referred to Roman law. Since νόμος is anarthrous (it has no article), it is better to take it in a general sense.

Having established the principle that death rendered law inoperative, Paul went on to illustrate how the principle applied in the case of a marriage relationship (v. 2). A married woman was bound by law to her husband while he was alive (cf. 1 Cor 7:39).[63] However, if her husband should die, she was released from the law of marriage (Goodspeed has, "The marriage law no longer applies to her").[64] If she married again while her husband was still alive, she would be designated an adulteress (cf. Luke 16:18); but if her husband died, she was free from the bond of that marriage and could take another husband without becoming an adulteress.[65]

7:4–6 The relevance of the principle is made clear in v. 4 and following. Law is the husband to which the believer was at one time married. But a death has occurred. The believer has died to the law.[66] The analogy, however, is not exact.[67] In the previous paragraph it was the husband who had died. Here it was the "wife" (the believer) who was separated from her first spouse (the law) by her own death. The important point is that the marriage relationship had been broken by the death of one of its participants. The death of the believer took place when by faith that person became identified with the crucified Christ (cf. 6:3–7).[68] Christ's death to and for sin becomes our death to sin (cf. Gal 2:19–20). The purpose of this death is that we might belong to another husband—to the one who was raised from the dead. The one in whom we died becomes the very one in whom we find our new life. Our Savior becomes our new "husband." And this, in turn, is in order that we may

---

[63] The adjective ὕπανδρος, which the NIV translates "married," means "under the power of a man." The *EDNT* has "subordinated to a man" (3.395). In Jewish society this was the actual legal standing of the wife because she could not divorce her husband.

[64] τοῦ νόμου τοῦ ἀνδρός, lit., "the law of the husband," is an unusual expression designating the legal responsibilities of a woman to her husband. Morris calls it "a husband-type law" (*Romans*, 271).

[65] B. Reicke says that in the NT χρηματίζω "denotes divine instruction by revelation" and that in Rom 7:3 it is used to indicate that the woman "is publicly reckoned an adulteress" (*TDNT* abr., 1320).

[66] The verb is a passive form of θανατόω, "to put to death," rather than ἀποθνήσκω, "to die." The passive reflects the action of God in the event.

[67] Cranfield holds that vv. 2–3 are not an allegory whose interpretation is found in v. 4 but an illustration of the principle set forth in v. 1 (*Romans*, 1:334–35).

[68] C. H. Dodd takes "the body of Christ" as Christ's mystical body, the church, and translates, "As belonging to the Body of Christ, you have died with Christ to the Law" (*The Epistle of Paul to the Romans*, MNTC [London: Hodder & Stoughton, 1932], 101–2). Consistency would require that the remainder of the verse be understood in the same way, in which case we arrive at the awkward conclusion that the church ("him") was "raised from the dead."

bear fruit to God.[69] If Paul intended us to carry on the analogy of marriage, "bear[ing] fruit" would refer to offspring. Probably a more general
idea was in mind (Phillips has "be productive for").[70]

Once again Paul drew a comparison. Verse 5 describes the preconversion days of the believers at Rome when they were "controlled by the
sinful nature."[71] Verse 6 moves ahead to the time when they were no
longer in bondage to the law. By basic inclination people are controlled
by their lower nature. Apart from this fundamental insight into human
nature it is impossible to understand the evil that has plagued the human
race. History is simply the story of humanity gone wrong. Although
made in the image of God, we inherit the propensity for wickedness
determined by the fateful choice of the first human. We are fallen creatures in dire need of hope from without. Every scheme people propose
for individual and social change is undermined by their own inclination
for personal advantage. Prior to coming to Christ the sinful cravings[72] of
our lower nature were aroused by the law (cf. 7:7b) and were at work on
a continuing basis[73] in our bodies. Law not only reveals sin (cf. 7:7), but
it also excites it to action. By nature rebels oppose restrictions. When
placed under law, people instinctively find themselves at odds with the
lawgiver and act accordingly. The response of their sinful passions is to
rebel against authority. Opposition to God inevitably ends in death.

Verse 6 completes the comparison. By dying to that which was once
in control, the believer is now released from the law and freed to serve in
a new way.[74] Formerly we were in bondage to written regulations. Law

---

[69] If the ἵνα clause is dependent on ἐθανατώθητε, the verse is saying that death to the
law is a necessary prerequisite for bearing fruit to God.

[70] F. F. Bruce characterizes as "somewhat far-fetched" the idea that the marriage metaphor
is being continued and understands "fruit" as the new life characterized by the good works God
prepared beforehand and in which we are to walk (*The Letter of Paul to the Romans,* 2d ed.,
TNTC [Grand Rapids: Eerdmans, 1985], 138).

[71] ἐν τῇ σαρκί. Barrett points out that Paul used the word "flesh" in two senses: to denote
the "physical aspect of life" and to describe "a proclivity to sin by which all men are affected"
(*Romans,* 146). "Here it is used to denote the state in which men are dominated by law, sin, and
death" (ibid., 137).

[72] ἁμαρτιῶν probably is an objective genitive ("passions that lead to sin"). Moo defines
"sinful passions" as "those desires to disobey God and His law that are, paradoxically, exacer-
bated by the law itself" (*Romans 1–8,* 444).

[73] Implied by the imperfect ἐνηργεῖτο.

[74] Commentators are divided on the question of whether ὥστε δουλεύειν expresses purpose, potential result, or actual result. The NIV follows the third option. The most natural rendering is to take it as expressing God's purpose in releasing us from the law. We are free from
law *so that we may* live in the Spirit.

was our old master.[75] But now we are set free to serve our new master in a new way, in the Spirit.[76] The shift from law to Spirit is a shift from legalism to true spirituality. How unfortunate that so many believers continue to understand their Christian experience within an ethical framework determined by law. To serve in the Spirit is to live the resurrected life, to claim our rightful place in Christ. Dead to sin and freed to live for righteousness, we now live lives that bear fruit for God.

7:7–8 Paul's teaching that we were at one time bound by the law that aroused sinful passions and led to death (vv. 4–6) quite naturally raises the question of whether the law is so hopelessly intertwined with the activities of sin as to be sinful itself. What are we to conclude from all this? "Is the law sin?" Once again (see 6:2,15) the answer is, "Certainly not!" That is not a step that logic can take. Law is not sinful because through law we came to understand what sin really is.[77] Paul used his own experience throughout this section to illustrate the general experience of all people and especially, in the latter part of the chapter, the experience of the believer. He was not providing us with his own spiritual autobiography as much as he was illustrating a general condition of all by using the first-person singular as a rhetorical device.[78]

It was the law that brought home to Paul the reality of sin. For instance, had the law not said, "Do not covet" (Exod 20:17; Deut 5:21), Paul would never have known what coveting really was.[79] Law defines sin. Apart

---

[75] "The old way of the written code" is "its strait-laced interpretation" (Black, *Romans*, 94).

[76] For other verses that compare the Spirit and the written code, see Rom 2:29 and 2 Cor 3:6. Paul's antithesis is a contrast between the old dispensation and the new.

[77] Scott calls this "a passage of marvelous psychological insight" in which "Paul describes this condition of misery which the Law discloses and can do nothing to relieve" (*Romans*, 47).

[78] Cranfield lists six ways to understand Paul's use of first-person singular in vv. 7–13 and seven ways it is used in vv. 14–25. In the present section Cranfield holds that the first person is used in a general sense but that it also reflects a desire for rhetorical vividness and a deep sense of personal involvement (*Romans*, 1:342–44). From the history of interpretation Moo lists four main identifications for Paul's ἐγώ: autobiographical, Adamic, Israelite, and existential. He opts for a combination of the first and third (*Romans 1–8*, 450–52). For a recent argument that the subject of vv. 7–13 is Adam and vv. 14–25 is those who are in Adam, see B. Witherington III, *Paul's Narrative Thought World* (Louisville: Westminster/John Knox, 1994), 24–28.

[79] In v. 7 Paul used two different words meaning "to know." γινώσκω was originally an inceptive verb representing the acquisition of knowledge, and οἶδα (in classical Greek) denoted the theoretical possession of knowledge. Horstmann holds that the "classical distinction between οἶδα and γινώσκω is generally preserved in the NT" (*EDNT* 2.494). In contrast to οἶδα, γινώσκω usually is described as knowing in a personal or experiential sense. But it is difficult to see any difference in the two verbs as used in 7:7. Both reflect an experiential relationship.

from law sin exists but cannot be designated as "sin." Without restriction there is nothing to break. Law provides the opportunity for sin's nefarious activity.[80] Sin seizes the opportunity and arouses within a person through the commandment all manner of evil desire.[81] The point is often made that only after a rule is put in place do people want to do whatever it forbids. What Paul was saying, however, goes beyond the psychological observation that stolen fruits are the sweetest. From a human perspective law is mistakenly viewed as a restriction that in turn causes resentment and gives rise to rebellion. Paul may have had the Genesis account of Adam's first sin in mind. Apart from law sin is dead in the sense that undefined, it technically does not exist (cf. 4:15). No matter how swift and straight the arrow, without a target there can be no bull's-eye.

7:9–11   There was a time, said Paul, when he was "alive apart from law" (v. 9). Some see here a reference to the time prior to his *bar mitzvah* when, at the age of thirteen, he assumed moral responsibility for his conduct before the law. Others take it in a general sense of all people before the giving of the law.[82] Paul probably referred to his preconversion days before he had grasped the full scope and power of the law's demands.[83] He was, so to speak, "alive."[84] But now he understood from experience the power of sin to use the law for its own advantage. The commandment "came home to [Paul]" (Moffatt), and sin "sprang into life" (TCNT).[85] With the coming of law, sin revived. Paul realized that

---

[80] ἀφορμή is a military term for base of operations or starting point from which an attack is launched. Black comments that the commandment against covetousness "was, as it were, a kind of bridgehead into human nature for the invading forces of Sin" (*Romans,* 97).

[81] διὰ τῆς ἐντολῆς goes with κατειργάσατο rather than ἀφορμὴν λαβοῦσα. "Paradoxically, that which the commandment forbade, it has been instrumental in producing" (Moo, *Romans 1–8,* 461).

[82] Hunter says that Paul was "thinking no doubt of his boyhood but also surely of Adam's primal innocence" (*Romans,* 72). Dunn calls it "the childhood of man, the mythical period of the human race's beginnings" (*Romans,* 382). Yet another approach is that the clause speaks of Israel prior to the giving of the Mosaic law.

[83] Those who reject the autobiographical interpretation usually concede that in some sense Paul was reflecting his own experience. Dunn, for example, who holds that "Paul is almost certainly speaking in typical terms, using the Adam narrative to characterize what is true of man in general," adds that "at the same time . . . it is difficult to believe that Paul is not speaking at least to some extent out of his own experience" (*Romans,* 1:381–82).

[84] In Phil 3:6 Paul claimed to be "faultless" regarding legalistic righteousness.

[85] Morris writes: "When the commandment 'came' it killed forever the proud Pharisee thanking God that he was not as other men and sure of his merits before God. It killed off the happy sinner, for it showed him the seriousness, not so much of sin in general as of his own sin" (*Romans,* 282). "Sin at first is there, but dormant; not until it has the help of the Law does it become an active power of mischief" (Sanday and Headlam, *Romans,* 180).

apart from Christ he was condemned to death.[86] He discovered that although the commandment was designed to bring life (Lev 18:5; Luke 10:25–28), it turned out to be a sentence to death (Rom 7:10). How did this happen? Sin deceived him (v. 11). The deceptive nature of sin runs throughout Scripture from the account of the fall (Gen 3:13) to the final days of human history (2 Thess 2:9–10).[87] Elsewhere Paul counseled us to be aware of the schemes of Satan (2 Cor 2:11). Although defeated by Jesus' death on the cross, Satan continues his wicked and deceptive plans, trying to subvert the best interests of God's people. Paul pointed out that Satan's ploy has been to convert an instrument intended for life (the law) into an instrument of death.

7:12 This verse is the definitive answer to the question raised in v. 7, "Is the Law itself a sinful thing?" (Weymouth). No, the law is holy. The commandment is "holy, righteous and good."[88] Since the law is God's law, it must of necessity reflect the nature of God. The law of a holy God must be consistent with his holy nature (Isa 6:3). A righteous God decrees commandments that are righteous. They are fair and make no unreasonable demands. The law is "good" because it intends the very best for people. In this entire discussion Paul was not depreciating law as such. His point had been that law has been used by sin as an unwilling accomplice to bring about death.

7:13 Yet another question arises: How could that which is good bring death?[89] In the previous paragraph Paul said that the commandment (law) was the occasion (v. 9) and the instrument (v. 11) of his death. But does this not involve a contradiction in terms? The good belongs by definition to a different category from death. Paul rejected the implication by pointing out that it was sin, not law, that brought about death. Law was simply the instrument used by sin to accomplish its purpose. But in so doing, sin exposed its own true character as sin. It demonstrated how unspeakably sinful it really is by using that which is

---

[86] The presence of the personal pronoun ἐγώ and its emphatic position in the sentence underscore the personal nature of Paul's understanding. That sin used law for its own wicked purposes was applied by the apostle to his own experience.

[87] Cranfield notes that the serpent deceived Eve by (1) distorting the commandment, (2) denying that disobedience would be punished, and (3) using the commandment itself to insinuate doubts about God's good will (*Romans* 1:352–53). Those who identify the "I" of vv. 7–13 with Adam should recall that it was Eve, not Adam, who was deceived (1 Tim 2:14).

[88] Paul used two words for law in v. 12: νόμος, referring to the Mosaic legislation as a whole, and ἐντολή of a specific commandment (although representative of the corpus).

[89] The two questions are related, but not the same. In v. 7 it was asked whether the law was evil. Here the question is whether the law brought about Paul's "death."

good to bring about death.[90]

7:14–25   The question that has plagued commentators for centuries is whether in this latter section of chap. 7 Paul was describing his experience before or after conversion. Both positions may be argued rather persuasively.[91] In support of the first approach are a number of phrases throughout the account that seem to reflect a preconversion setting. Paul confessed that he was "sold as a slave to sin" (v. 14). He knew that "nothing good lives in [him]" (v. 18). He was a "prisoner of the law of sin" (v. 23), a "wretched man" who called out for someone to "rescue [him] from this body of death" (v. 24). Are confessions like these what we would expect from the very apostle who said, "Follow my example, as I follow the example of Christ" (1 Cor 11:1)?

A strong argument against the opposing position (that Paul was describing his spiritual experience as a Christian) is the question that must be raised regarding the real value of a conversion that leads into a spiritual quagmire of such impotence and misery. How could this be the abundant life that Jesus came to bring (John 10:10)? Further, the dramatic contrast between chap. 7, with its continual failure, and chap. 8, which describes victory through the Spirit, argues a preconversion setting. In the former Paul was a wretched man crying out for deliverance (7:24); in the latter he had been "set free from the law of sin and death" (8:2) and was controlled by the indwelling Spirit of God (8:9).

The arguments for the alternate interpretation are equally convincing. Throughout the entire section (7:13–25) Paul used the present tense. He told his readers what was happening in his life. Repeatedly (over twenty times) he made such statements as, "I do not understand what I do" (v. 15). Had he been referring to an earlier period, would he not have said, "I did not understand what I was doing"? As the section includes

---

[90] καθ' ὑπερβολὴν means "beyond measure, to an extraordinary degree" (cf. 1 Cor 7:13; Gal 1:13). Montgomery translates "the unutterable malignity of sin."

[91] After reminding the reader that in this section Paul was primarily speaking of the law and its demands, Morris provides a convenient summary of the arguments for and against the views that the apostle was speaking of his regenerate or unregenerate state (*Romans*, 284–89). See also the excursus on "The Inward Conflict," Sanday and Headlam (*Romans*, 184–86), and P. Stuhlmacher's, "The 'I' in Rom. 7:7–25," in *Paul's Letter to the Romans*, trans. S. J. Hafemann (Louisville: Westminster, 1994), 114–16. Murray concludes his review of the subject with the decision that "for these reasons we are compelled to conclude that 7:14–25 is the delineation of Paul's experience in the state of grace" (*Romans*, 256–59). P. Achtemeier denies that Paul was speaking of the moral quandary he felt prior to his conversion or to the moral dilemma of the Christian. Rather, the discussion represents "non-Christian life under the law seen from a Christian perspective" (*Romans* [Atlanta: John Knox, 1985], 119–22).

statements that seemingly are incompatible with the experience of a Christian, other statements could never come from a nonbeliever; for example, "In my inner being I delight in God's law" (v. 22). Earlier in his letter Paul said about those outside of Christ, "There is no one righteous . . . no one who seeks God" (3:10–12). Surely such rebels do not delight in God's law in their inner being.

J. C. O'Neill solves the problem by denying that Paul wrote 7:14–25. He argues this from the general use of the word "law" and the dualism between flesh and spirit. His "best explanation" is that it was incorporated into Paul's original letter by a Hellenistic Jew to "help persuade his non-Jewish neighbours of their need of deliverance if they were to live up to the high ideals they knew they should follow."[92] All such highly speculative reconstructions fall beneath their own weight. The long and detailed history of interpretation of this crucial passage shows no tendency to give serious considerations to explanations that rely more on imagination than evidence.

In the final analysis the approach to be preferred must be the one that is more reasonable in terms of the larger context. At this point in his discussion of sanctification, would Paul have been more apt to tell his readers about his struggle with sin before he became a Christian or describe his ongoing difficulty in actually living out his deepest spiritual desires? Since elsewhere he said that in his earlier days he was "immaculate by the standard of legal righteousness" (Phil 3:6, Moffatt), it seems quite improbable that he was at that time deeply involved in a personal struggle against sin.[93] I believe that in this section Paul was revealing with considerable candor his difficulty in meeting the radical demands of the Christian faith. At the same time, he was using his own experience to describe the inevitability of spiritual defeat whenever a believer fails to appropriate the Spirit of God for victory.[94]

Romans 7 does not describe the totality of Paul's spiritual experience. In fact, it is preparatory to what follows. It sets the stage for the triumph of chap. 8. It probably is true that in the lives of most earnest Christians

---

[92] J. C. O'Neill, *Paul's Letter to the Romans* (Middlesex, Eng.: Penguin, 1975), 131–32.

[93] However, see Dodd for the argument that these verses are "an authentic transcript of Paul's own experience during the period which culminated in his vision on the road to Damascus" (*Romans,* 104–8).

[94] Stott describes the "wretched man" of v. 24 as "typical of many Jewish Christians of Paul's day, regenerated but not liberated, under the law and not yet in or under the Spirit." He rejects it as a "pattern of normal Christian experience'" but recognizes that "some churchgoers today might be termed 'Old Testament Christians'" (*Romans,* 210).

the two conditions Paul described exist in a sort of cyclical advance. Recognition of our inability to live up to our deepest spiritual longings (chap. 7) leads us to cast ourselves upon God's Spirit for power and victory (chap. 8). Failure to continue in reliance upon the power of the Spirit places us once again in a position inviting defeat.[95] Sanctification is a gradual process that repeatedly takes the believer through this recurring sequence of failure through dependency upon self to triumph through the indwelling Spirit.

In v. 14 Paul reminded his readers of the obvious fact that the law is spiritual. Since it has its origin in God, it must of necessity give expression to the holiness of God's character. In contrast, Paul acknowledged that he was unspiritual.[96] It takes very little self-examination for the Christian to agree that our life and conduct fall miserably short of the divine expectation. Even though the believer has a new nature acquired by a spiritual rebirth, the old nature continues to exert its maleficent influence. To the church at Corinth, Paul wrote that he could not address them as spiritual but as worldly, that is, unspiritual (1 Cor 3:1). Using a metaphor from slavery he confessed that he had been sold into the captivity of sin as a slave.[97] His times of defeat by the power of the lower nature made him feel like a slave to sin. He did not understand his own actions.[98] On a regular basis he failed to carry out what he meant to

---

[95] Harrison holds that the section is deliberately presented in a way that demonstrates the plight of one who, faced with the power of sin in his life, attempts to "solve his problem independently of the power of Christ and the enablement of the Spirit" ("Romans," 84). Nygren finds the "tension" of chap. 7 (free from the law yet not righteous according to its criterion) in both chap. 6 (free from sin, yet we must battle against it) and chap. 8 (free from death yet longing for the redemption of the body; *Romans,* 295–96).

[96] This contrast is more pronounced in the MSS that read οἴδαμέν, "While I know that the Law is spiritual . . . nevertheless I am 'carnal'" (see Black, *Romans,* 98). The word for "unspiritual" is σάρκινος and means "made of flesh." It emphasizes the weak and transitory nature of human existence. σάρξ is not evil in itself but has a fatal propensity toward that which is contrary to the will and nature of God. Dunn notes that it "speaks of the individual in his belongingness to the epoch of Adam, which is ruled by sin and death" (*Romans,* 1:388). Similarly, Nygren writes that "the Christian is no longer 'carnal' in the sense of 'carnal minded.' Rather he is 'carnal' in the sense that he still lives in the flesh (ἐν σαρκί) and participates in its condition" (*Romans,* 299).

[97] πεπραμένος ὑπὸ τὴν ἁμαρτίαν means "sold under sin" in the sense of "controlled by the power of sin." "Sin has closed the mortgage and owns its slave" (Robertson, *WP* 4:369). "This addresses the person who, left to his own devices, suffers the contradiction between what he wants and what he actually does" (*EDNT* 3.230).

[98] "The mystery stems from . . . the cleavage between reason-dominated desire and actual performance (Fitzmyer, *Romans,* 474). Augustine understood οὐ γινώσκω as "I do not approve," an interpretation favored by many current scholars. The NEB has "I do not even acknowledge my own actions as mine."

do;[99] instead he found himself doing the very things he despised.[100] Acting in this contrary fashion is what it means to be sold under sin.

In the very act of violating his best intentions, Paul was agreeing that the law is a noble thing (v. 16). If it were not good, he would not have had any sense of guilt when he failed to live up to its standards. His best intentions were one with the law. He concluded that when he acted against his own wishes, it must have been the work of sin that had taken up residence in him (v. 17).[101] It was not the real Paul.[102] He was not trying to escape the responsibility for his own actions but to explain how deeply lodged within him was the old corrupt nature. In his failure to live up to his own expectations, sin had taken over and dominated his life. So he confessed that nothing good dwelt in his natural self (v. 18).[103] The old man was totally corrupt. The desire to do the right thing was there,[104] but not the power to perform it. Instead of doing the good he desired, he kept on doing the evil he did not want to do (v. 19). He concluded, in v. 20, that if he did that which was contrary to his own deepest desires, the real culprit must have been sin that lived within him. In failing to live out his best intentions, he had fallen into slavery to sin.

The experiences of life led Paul to conclude that whenever he desired

---

[99] Both main verbs in 7:15b (πράσσω and ποιῶ) are present tense, indicating a continuing condition.

[100] Commentaries regularly refer to similar statements by the Roman poet Ovid ("I perceive what is better and approve of it, but I pursue what is worse") and others (Epictetus, Euripides, and the Essenes of Qumran). Dodd referred to Aristotle's four stages in the moral history possible to a human and notes that the condition Paul was describing falls into the second stage, *akrasia,* knowing what is right but failing to do it (*Romans,* 113–14).

[101] Rabbis taught that sin was like a visitor who lengthens his stay and finally becomes the master of the house (*Midrash on Genesis,* 10.6). Some think Paul's view of "sin living in [him]" may have been influenced by the rabbinic concept of יצֵר הרַע, the evil impulse that exists in every person. If so, deliverance was by the grace of God, not the יצֵר הטּוֹב ("the good impulse") as the rabbis taught (cf. W. D. Davies, *Paul and Rabbinic Judaism,* 4th ed. [Philadelphia: Fortress, 1980], 25–27).

[102] Denney's oft-quoted remark about v. 17 is, "A true saint may say it in a moment of passion, but a sinner had better not make it a principle" ("Romans," 642). Luther solved the apparent problem of how Paul could say that he was not the one who did what he did not want to do (vv. 16–17,20) by noting that "inasmuch as he resists the evil, it is not the whole person who sins, but only a part of the person (*his corrupt nature)*" (*Commentary on the Epistle to the Romans,* trans. J. T. Mueller [Grand Rapids: Zondervan, 1954], 97).

[103] Käsemann refers to σάρξ as "the workshop of sin, the whole person in his fallenness to the world and alienation from God" (*Romans,* 205). Most commentators hold that Paul was not referring to his "sinful nature" as one part of himself in contrast to some other part but to his whole self in its fallenness.

[104] παράκειται means "to lie near at hand." Paul was saying that the willingness to do the good was "well within his reach."

to do that which was good, sin reared its ugly head. His desire to do what was right was inevitably confronted by sin's insistence that he do the opposite. So regular was this opposition that Paul could designate it as a "law."[105] It was a controlling principle of life. It is true that in his inner self he joyfully concurred with the law of God (v. 22).[106] As the psalmist put it, he was the man blessed by God whose "delight is in the law of the Lord" (Ps 1:2; cf. 40:8). This confession removes the possibility that Paul was speaking about his life before coming to Christ.

Yet at the same time that other principle (v. 23) was at work through-out his body. It was at war against his desire to obey the law of God.[107] This basic conflict is nowhere better expressed than in Gal 5:17–18: "For the sinful nature desires what is contrary to the Spirit, and the Spirit what is contrary to the sinful nature. They are in conflict with each other, so that you do not do what you want" (cf. Jas 4:1; 1 Pet 2:11). Paul went on to say that this alien power took him captive to the law of sin at work in his members. Romans 7:23 speaks of three laws.[108] By the "law of [his] mind" Paul referred to the principle of rational thought. Goodspeed calls it the "law of [his] reason." It corresponds to that which Paul knew to be the right thing to do. The relationship between "another[109] law" and "the law of sin" is quite clear; they are undoubtedly to be taken as one and the same. This "law" (read "principle") is the propensity toward sin that arises from a person's lower nature. So what I am by nature is in constant conflict with what I aspire to be as a child of God in whom the Spirit of God dwells.[110] That conflict will never be settled until, seeing

---

[105] A few commentaries hold that τὸν νόμον in v. 21 refers to the Torah (cf. Dunn, *Romans,* 1:292–93), but the majority take it in the generic sense of "principle" or "law of experience." It is the ἕτερον νόμον of v. 23 that wars against "God's law" (v. 22).

[106] The term for inner self, ἔσω ἄνθρωπον, was used in Hellenistic thought of the divine or rational element in humans (in contrast to their more earthly nature). Morris points out that Paul did not use the expression in the same way as his Hellenistic contemporaries but of the regenerate person. He said that it expressed the "real Paul," who in the deep recesses of his heart delighted in the law of God, in contrast to the "other Paul," who so readily did the sin of which the real Paul did not approve (*Romans,* 294–95). In view of σύμφημι in v. 16, συνή-δομαι here probably means "I joyfully agree with the law" (*EDNT* 3.306).

[107] The NIVSB identifies the "law of [Paul's] mind" as his desire to obey God's ways (note comments on 7:23).

[108] νόμος occurs four times in vv. 22–23. I understand "the law of my mind" and "the law of sin" as more specific ways of representing "God's law" and "another law."

[109] ἕτερος may mean "another of a different kind" (e.g., Luke 23:32), but it normally carries much the same meaning as ἄλλος.

[110] K. Barth says that the person who conceals this dualism is the "supreme betrayer of religion" (Overbeck), and "the bomb, which he has so carefully decked out with flowers, will sooner or later explode" (*The Epistle to the Romans* [London: Oxford University, 1933], 268).

God, we shall be like him (1 John 3:2).

Caught up in this spiritual warfare,[111] Paul cried out: What a wretched man am I! Who is able to free me from the "clutches of my own sinful nature?" (Phillips).[112] The "body of death" was like a corpse that hung on him and from which he was unable to free himself.[113] It constantly interfered with his desire to obey the higher impulses of his new nature. Who is able to rescue the believer crying out for deliverance? The answer is, Thanks be to God, there is deliverance through Jesus Christ our Lord (v. 25).[114] Through the death and resurrection of Christ, God has provided the power to live in the freedom of the Spirit (cf. 8:2).[115]

Verse 25b (a separate paragraph in the NIV) summarizes the entire discussion of vv. 13–24.[116] Paul said that he himself (who he really was in Christ) had committed himself to serving the law of God (it was the rational thing to do) but that his lower nature was still a slave to the principle of sin. No modern translation captures the meaning better than the NEB: "In a word then, I myself, subject to God's law as a rational being, am yet, in my sinful nature, a slave to the law of sin." Although the chapter ends on this realistic observation, the positive declaration in the

---

[111] Note the military metaphors in this section: ὅπλα ("weapons") in 6:13; ὀψώνια ("wages [paid to soldiers]") in 6:23; ἀφορμή ("base of operations") in 7:8,11; ἀντιστρατευόμενον ("warring against") and αἰχμαλωτίζοντά ("taking captive") in 7:23.

[112] "A heart-rending cry, from the depths of despair" (Sanday and Headlam, *Romans,* 1:183). To those who feel that no believer could ever utter such a cry, Cranfield writes, "The farther men advance in the Christian life, and the more mature their discipleship, the clearer becomes their perception of the heights to which God calls them, and the more painfully sharp their consciousness of the distance between what they ought, and want, to be, and what they are" (*Romans,* 1:366).

[113] Bruce mentions that some commentators have referred in this connection to the Etruscan king Mezentius, who "tormented his living captives by tying them to decomposing corpses" (*Romans,* 147).

[114] The NIV places a dash after "God" and takes the remaining clause in v. 25a as a sentence fragment. This construction requires the interpreter to add an explanatory phrase. I have chosen "there is deliverance." Others suggest "God alone" with the words "has done it" understood (in answer to the question of v. 24b).

[115] While Paul seems to have been speaking primarily of victory over sin in his present situation, the exclamation of thanksgiving could have eschatological overtones. R. Banks argues rather cogently the latter position ("Romans 7:25a: An Eschatological Thanksgiving," *AusBR* 26 [1978]: 34–42).

[116] V. 25b is a rather sobering statement in between the thanksgiving of v. 25a and the freedom from condemnation in 8:1. To relieve the "awkwardness" some have considered v. 25b to be a marginal gloss (along with 8:1), while others have rearranged the sentences (Moffatt places it at the end of v. 23). Granted, such changes make the text read more smoothly, but there is nothing in the textual tradition that supports them. Better to leave the text as it is.

first part of v. 25 has prepared us for the exciting truths about to be set forth in the chapter that follows.

3. Living in the Spirit (8:1–39)

[1]Therefore, there is now no condemnation for those who are in Christ Jesus, [2]because through Christ Jesus the law of the Spirit of life set me free from the law of sin and death. [3]For what the law was powerless to do in that it was weakened by the sinful nature, God did by sending his own Son in the likeness of sinful man to be a sin offering. And so he condemned sin in sinful man, [4]in order that the righteous requirements of the law might be fully met in us, who do not live according to the sinful nature but according to the Spirit.

[5]Those who live according to the sinful nature have their minds set on what that nature desires; but those who live in accordance with the Spirit have their minds set on what the Spirit desires. [6]The mind of sinful man is death, but the mind controlled by the Spirit is life and peace; [7]the sinful mind is hostile to God. It does not submit to God's law, nor can it do so. [8]Those controlled by the sinful nature cannot please God.

[9]You, however, are controlled not by the sinful nature but by the Spirit, if the Spirit of God lives in you. And if anyone does not have the Spirit of Christ, he does not belong to Christ. [10]But if Christ is in you, your body is dead because of sin, yet your spirit is alive because of righteousness. [11]And if the Spirit of him who raised Jesus from the dead is living in you, he who raised Christ from the dead will also give life to your mortal bodies through his Spirit, who lives in you.

[12]Therefore, brothers, we have an obligation—but it is not to the sinful nature, to live according to it. [13]For if you live according to the sinful nature, you will die; but if by the Spirit you put to death the misdeeds of the body, you will live, [14]because those who are led by the Spirit of God are sons of God. [15]For you did not receive a spirit that makes you a slave again to fear, but you received the Spirit of sonship. And by him we cry, *"Abba, Father."* [16]The Spirit himself testifies with our spirit that we are God's children. [17]Now if we are children, then we are heirs—heirs of God and co-heirs with Christ, if indeed we share in his sufferings in order that we may also share in his glory.

[18]I consider that our present sufferings are not worth comparing with the glory that will be revealed in us. [19]The creation waits in eager expectation for the sons of God to be revealed. [20]For the creation was subjected to frustration, not by its own choice, but by the will of the one who subjected it, in hope [21]that the creation itself will be liberated from its bondage to decay and brought into the glorious freedom of the children of God.

[22]We know that the whole creation has been groaning as in the pains of

childbirth right up to the present time. [23]Not only so, but we ourselves, who have the firstfruits of the Spirit, groan inwardly as we wait eagerly for our adoption as sons, the redemption of our bodies. [24]For in this hope we were saved. But hope that is seen is no hope at all. Who hopes for what he already has? [25]But if we hope for what we do not yet have, we wait for it patiently.

[26]In the same way, the Spirit helps us in our weakness. We do not know what we ought to pray for, but the Spirit himself intercedes for us with groans that words cannot express. [27]And he who searches our hearts knows the mind of the Spirit, because the Spirit intercedes for the saints in accordance with God's will.

[28]And we know that in all things God works for the good of those who love him, who have been called according to his purpose. [29]For those God foreknew he also predestined to be conformed to the likeness of his Son, that he might be the firstborn among many brothers. [30]And those he predestined, he also called; those he called, he also justified; those he justified, he also glorified.

[31]What, then, shall we say in response to this? If God is for us, who can be against us? [32]He who did not spare his own Son, but gave him up for us all—how will he not also, along with him, graciously give us all things? [33]Who will bring any charge against those whom God has chosen? It is God who justifies. [34]Who is he that condemns? Christ Jesus, who died—more than that, who was raised to life—is at the right hand of God and is also interceding for us. [35]Who shall separate us from the love of Christ? Shall trouble or hardship or persecution or famine or nakedness or danger or sword? [36]As it is written:

"For your sake we face death all day long;
    we are considered as sheep to be slaughtered."

[37]No, in all these things we are more than conquerors through him who loved us. [38]For I am convinced that neither death nor life, neither angels nor demons, neither the present nor the future, nor any powers, [39]neither height nor depth, nor anything else in all creation, will be able to separate us from the love of God that is in Christ Jesus our Lord.

With chap. 8 we arrive at what may be called the inspirational highlight of the Book of Romans. Here the apostle is swept along in a wave of spiritual exaltation that begins with God's provision of the Spirit for victory over the old nature, breaks through the sufferings that mark our present existence, and crests with a doxology of praise to the unfathomable love of God revealed in Christ Jesus. Nowhere in the annals of sacred literature do we find anything to match the power and beauty of this remarkable paean of praise. Although the pinnacle of this exalted prose awaits our arrival at vv. 28–39, the earlier sections provide the setting against which the culminating truths will break forth with an even greater brilliance. We are not dealing here with mere theology. As Paul wrote, his pen gave evidence that he was caught up in an experience of profound worship and spiritual adoration.

8:1 The first verse sets forth one of the most important truths of the Christian faith. The opening word, "therefore," leads us to expect some result that flows logically from the preceding text.[117] Romans 7:25 teaches that freedom from the power of the lower nature has been provided by God through the atoning work of Jesus Christ. Therefore there is no longer any condemnation at all for those who are "in Christ Jesus," that is, who have been made one with him by faith in his redemptive sacrifice.[118] The just penalty incurred by the sins of the human race was paid by the death of Christ. The unfavorable verdict has been removed. Now all those who are in Christ are the beneficiaries of that forgiveness.[119] It follows that if condemnation as an objective reality has been removed, there is no legitimate place for condemnation as a subjective experience. To insist on feeling guilty is but another way of insisting on helping God with our salvation. How deeply imbedded in human nature is the influence of works-righteousness!

8:2 And why is there no condemnation? Because the law of the Spirit, that is, life in Christ Jesus, has set us free from the law of sin, which leads to death.[120] A quick comparison with the NIV text will indicate that Paul's answer as previously paraphrased involves considerable interpretation. Some justification is in order. The apostle was contrasting two different laws (or principles). The old law is the power of sin that inevitably results in death.[121] The new law, which sets the believer free

---

[117] Some see ἄρα referring back to the entire argument set forth in chaps. 5–7 (others to 7:1–6).

[118] "Condemnation," κατάκριμα, in the NT refers to the adverse judgment of God against sin. In the present verse it includes the execution of that condemnation as well (*TDNT* abr., 475). Black says the expression "in Christ" means "baptised Christians" but does not exclude the sense of "mystical union" (*Romans,* 109).

[119] νῦν, "now," is temporal, referring to the new epoch in human history that has replaced the former dispensation of condemnation (cf. 2 Cor 3:7–9).

[120] Cf. Weymouth's translation "the Spirit's law—life in Christ Jesus." Other translations of ὁ γὰρ νόμος τοῦ πνεύματος τῆς ζωῆς ἐν Χριστῷ Ιησοῦ are "the new spiritual principle of life" (Phillips) and "the law of the life-giving Spirit" (TCNT).

[121] The NIVSB note on 8:2 points out that Paul used "law" in several ways. Here it denotes a controlling power. Elsewhere in Romans it is God's law (2:17–20), the Pentateuch (3:21b), the OT as a whole (3:19), or a principle (3:27).

from the power of the old, is the law of the Spirit. The new law of the
Spirit says that only by living in union with Christ Jesus can believers
break the power of sin in their lives. It is the Spirit of God who provides
victory, and that Spirit is the possession of every true child of God.

When the freedom of the Spirit, celebrated in chap. 8, is compared
with the repressive power of sin in chap. 7, it seems strange that both
could be operative in the same person. Yet does not experience teach us
that every attempt to live the Christian life apart from the empowering
presence of the Spirit of God ends in defeat? We lose the battle only
when we engage the enemy without the resources supplied by the Spirit.
God never intended us to go it on our own. Did not Jesus say, "Apart
from me you can do nothing" (John 15:5)? The difficulties of the
Romans 7 experience are self-imposed. They show the natural outcome
of failing to appropriate the Spirit of God. The victory of Romans 8
results from living in vital union with Christ Jesus, sustained and
empowered by the Spirit of God.

8:3–4 The law was powerless to conquer sin (v. 3).[122] The Greek
verb in the second sentence of the verse refers not only to the pronouncement of judgment but to the execution of the sentence as well.[123]
Law was unable to overpower the malignant dynamism of sin. Legislation is ill-equipped to conquer a vital force. The problem, however, did
not lie in any inherent weakness in the law itself. Its demands were
thwarted by the debilitating influence of our fallen nature. The NEB says
that "our lower nature robbed it of all potency." Law can stimulate sin;
but when it comes to overcoming it, our sinful nature undermines its best
efforts.

But what law could not do, God did by sending his very own Son with
a nature that resembled our sinful nature. He came in the "likeness of sinful man."[124] If Christ had not taken on our nature, he could not have been
one of us. On the other hand, had he become completely like us (i.e., had
he sinned), he could not have become our Savior. Barrett translates "in the
form of flesh which had passed under sin's rule," which means that

---

[122] This takes ἀδύνατον in the passive sense rather than the active sense of "incapable."
It is necessary to add a verb such as "to do" to the first part of v. 3. The contrast is between what
the law found impossible to do and what in fact God did.

[123] Moo concludes that κατέκρινεν here refers to "a judicial action accomplished through
the sacrifice of Christ on the cross and having as its object that 'the just requirement of the law
be fulfilled' in Christians" (*Romans 1–8*, 513).

[124] ἐν ὁμοιώματι σαρκὸς ἁμαρτίας speaks of a genuine resemblance, but not a complete identity. Cf. Phil 2:7.

"Christ took precisely the same fallen nature that we ourselves have, and that he remained sinless because he constantly overcame a proclivity to sin."[125] His mission was to put an end to sin, to condemn that evil power that has, since the dawn of history, held the human race in bondage. Knox says that God "signed the death warrant of sin." In a related passage the author of Hebrews wrote that Jesus "shared in [the] humanity" of his brothers so as to "destroy him who holds the power of death—that is, the devil" and to "free those who all their lives were held in slavery by their fear of death" (Heb 2:14–15). But not only did Christ come "in appearance as a man" (Phil 2:8) but also that he might be "a sin offering."[126] Similarly, Hebrews says that he became a "merciful and faithful high priest . . . that he might make atonement for the sins of the people" (Heb 2:17). Although the NIV translates, "So he condemned sin in *sinful man*" [italics added], it is better to take the literal translation ("in the flesh") as a reference to Christ's human nature, not ours. That is where God condemned sin. It was in the person of the incarnate Son that the Father brought an end to the power of sin.

God's redemptive action in Christ was so that what the law justly demanded of us might be fully satisfied.[127] This righteous requirement is met "in us" not in the sense that we fulfilled its demands but rather that God met it through the sacrificial death of his Son.[128] The just requirement (singular in Greek, stressing the unity of OT law) of the law is summarized in 13:9 as "Love your neighbor as yourself." And who are we? We are those whose lives were once under the control of a sinful lower nature[129] but now are guided and empowered by the Spirit of God. W. H. G. Thomas illustrates the principle of living "according to the

---

[125] Barrett, *Romans,* 156. Stott writes that "his humanity was both real and sinless simultaneously" (*Romans,* 219).

[126] Here περὶ ἁμαρτίας has the special sense of "to atone for sin" (Zerwick, *Analysis* 2.475). The NEB has "as a sacrifice for sin." The phrase is regularly used in the LXX to translate the Heb. expression for "sin offering" (more than fifty times in Leviticus alone). Some, however, questioning whether Paul's readers would catch the sacrificial nuance of περὶ ἁμαρτίας, interpret the words in a more general sense, such as expressing the mission on which the Son was sent (cf. Fitzmyer, *Romans,* 486).

[127] Although δικαίωμα normally designates the result of the verb δικαιόω (thus "what is made right or right conduct"), here, corresponding to LXX usage, it means "righteous requirement" (*EDNT* 1.334).

[128] πληρωθῇ is a "theological passive." God is the one who met the righteous demand of the law. Goodspeed has "might be fully met in our case."

[129] To evade any suggestion of anthropological dualism, many commentators employ an epochal orientation when speaking of the life of the believer. E.g., "the sinful nature" of v. 4 is understood as living in the old epoch, which is "characterized by an inability to live in accordance with God's will" (Dunn, *Romans,* 424).

Spirit" by comparing the motor car that operates on the storage principle and the tram that runs on the contact principle. "It is the latter that God has adopted for holiness." We do not store up grace but stay in constant contact with the one who is the source of all life and power.[130] Our lives display the "fruit of the Spirit" (Gal 5:22–23). This kind of life demonstrates that the righteous requirements of the law have been met in us.

8:5 Paul's penchant for using comparisons as an effective method of instruction is clearly seen in this section. There are two distinct and contrasting ways of living. One is to follow the dictates of one's lower nature. Those who choose to live according to their sinful nature set their mind and heart on what that nature desires. "Their thoughts are shaped by the lower nature" (Weymouth).[131] People's decisions about how they intend to live determines how they think about things. Moral choice precedes and determines intellectual orientation. People do not think themselves into the way they act but act themselves into the way they think. Ethical decision, more often than misguided reason, lies at the heart of error.

The other way to live is to place oneself under the control of the Spirit. In this case people focus their interests on the things of the Spirit. In Galatians 5 Paul contrasted the acts of the sinful nature with the fruit of the Spirit (vv. 19–23); sexual immorality, fits of rage, and selfish ambition (to name but three of the fifteen) are set over against such qualities as love, kindness, and self-control.

8:6 Paul continued the contrast by pointing out the consequences that necessarily follow each way of thinking. The carnal mind[132] leads to death. Barclay writes that "to allow the things of the world completely to dominate life is self extinction; it is spiritual suicide."[133] On the other hand, the Spirit-controlled mind leads to life and peace.[134] The same

---

[130] W. H. G. Thomas, *St. Paul's Epistle to the Romans* (Grand Rapids: Eerdmans, 1953), 207.

[131] Cranfield notes that τά τινος φρονεῖν means "to be of someone's mind, to be on someone's side" and says that "those who allow the direction of their lives to be determined by the flesh are actually taking the flesh's side in the conflict between the Spirit of God and the flesh, while those who allow the Spirit to determine the direction of their lives are taking the Spirit's side" (*Romans*, 385–86).

[132] The NIV has "the mind of sinful man" but includes in the margin the alternate "the mind set on the flesh." The Greek text is τὸ φρόνημα τῆς σαρκός.

[133] Barclay, *Romans*, 104.

[134] Moo holds that Paul was not talking about a subjective state of mind but about the objective reality of the salvation into which the believer has entered (*Romans 1–8*, 520). But *EDNT* notes that φρόνημα τῆς σαρκος and φρόνημα τοῦ πνεύματος describe "two fundamentally different ways of orienting one's life and actions, corresponding to two mutually exclusive ways of standing— before faith . . . and in faith" (3.439).

contrast is found in Gal 6:8: "The one who sows to please his sinful nature, from that nature will reap destruction; the one who sows to please the Spirit, from the Spirit will reap eternal life."[135]

8:7–8 The approach to life that is controlled by the lower nature is hostile to God (v. 7). The old nature is antagonistic to all that God is and stands for. It refuses to submit itself to the law of God; in fact, it cannot. By nature it stands over against the nature of God. James had this radical distinction in mind when he wrote that "friendship with the world is hatred towards God" (Jas 4:4). No wonder our best intentions fail when we try to reform the old nature or reconcile it with the indwelling Spirit. The enmity between the sinful mind and the Spirit is irreconcilable. The simple truth is that individuals who are controlled by their lower nature cannot please God (v. 8).[136] How can they, since they are in bondage to a power that is in fundamental opposition to the nature and will of God? Not only are persons apart from Christ "totally depraved" (i.e., every part of their being has been affected by the fall) but also "totally disabled" — in their rebellious state they cannot please God.

8:9 Paul reminded his readers that they were not under the control of their sinful nature.[137] To the contrary, their lives were under the direction of the indwelling Spirit of God. Obviously this rests upon the assumption that the Spirit of God had taken possession of them.[138] The NIV's "if" (v. 9a) would be better translated "since" or "as is the case."[139] Unless a person has the Spirit of Christ, that person does not belong to Christ.[140] Nowhere in Scripture do we find a clearer indication that the Spirit enters a person's life at the moment of conversion (cf. also 1 Cor 12:13). If the Spirit needed to wait for some subsequent commitment to holiness, it fol-

---

[135] Compare Jesus' teaching regarding the two roads, the broad road that leads to destruction and the narrow road that leads to life (Matt 7:13–14).

[136] In this context to be ἐν σαρκί means "to be dominated by indwelling sin." σάρξ refers not simply to sexual sins but to the entire range of self-centered activities that deny God his rightful place in one's life.

[137] Ὑμεῖς is emphatic.

[138] οἰκεῖ ἐν denotes "a settled, permanent, penetrative influence" (Sanday and Headlam, *Romans*, 196).

[139] εἴπερ is a conjunction that "introduces a conditional clause which presents a new but decisive ground for the apodosis" (*EDNT* 1.393). Cranfield says "it indicates a *fulfilled* condition" (*Romans*, 1:388). But Dunn warns that since εἴπερ of itself does not imply that the condition has been met, we should not "take it for granted that Paul naively assumed it was fulfilled in this case" (*Romans*, 1:428). Many hearing his letter read would be at the inquiry stage.

[140] "'The Spirit of Christ' is none other than 'the Spirit of God' of the preceding clause and indicates that the Holy Spirit sustains to Christ a relation similar to that which he sustains to the Father" (Murray, *Romans*, 1:288). See also John 15:26.

lows that he would be absent between conversion and that later point in time. But that cannot be because Paul clearly indicated that a person without the Spirit does not belong to Christ.[141] It is because God has given us his Spirit that "we know that we live in him and he in us" (1 John 4:13). Without his Spirit there can be no assurance of salvation.

8:10–11 The presence of the indwelling Christ is the believer's guarantee of life.[142] Although believers' physical bodies are subject to death, their spirits are even now "enjoying life" (Williams).[143] Death comes as a consequence of sin; life is the reward of justification. Death is the absence of God; life is a right standing before him. Whether or not a person is indwelt by the Spirit is truly a life-and-death matter.

Throughout his writings Paul drew a close connection between the resurrection of Christ and that of his followers. To the Corinthians the apostle wrote, "The one who raised the Lord Jesus from the dead will also raise us with Jesus" (2 Cor 4:14; cf. 1 Cor 6:14; 1 Thess 4:14). In Rom 8:11 the Spirit (who lives in the believer) is the means by which God gives life.[144] The prerequisite for resurrection is the presence of the indwelling Spirit. Since that is the case in the life of the believers (and the construction in Greek indicates that it is[145]), then God, who raised Jesus from the dead, will give life to their mortal bodies.[146] Not only has

---

[141] There are no real grounds for arguing that the "Spirit of Christ" is not the Holy Spirit. Note that in the preceding sentence he is called the "Spirit of God." It will not do to take πνεῦμα Χριστοῦ as the prevailing attitude (the "spirit") of Christ. πνεῦμα is correctly capitalized in the English text here and elsewhere in the chapter.

[142] In v. 9 it was the "Spirit of God" who was said to live in the believer; now in v. 10 it is "Christ." Moo writes that "the indwelling Spirit and the indwelling Christ are distinguishable but inseparable" (*Romans 1–8*, 523). For verses emphasizing the indwelling Christ, see John 14:23; Gal 2:20; Eph 3:17.

[143] Many recent commentaries hold that πνεῦμα in v. 10 refers to the Holy Spirit (the NIV's "your spirit" translates τὸ πνεῦμα). Were Paul talking of the human spirit he would have said that it "is alive," not that it "is life." Fitzmyer comments that Paul was playing on the two meanings of πνεῦμα: "Without the Spirit, the source of Christian vitality, the human "body" is like a corpse because of the influence of sin . . . but in union with Christ the human "spirit" lives (*Romans*, 491).

[144] Following the UBS preferred reading of διά with the genitive rather than the variant in which διά is followed by the accusative. In the latter case the text would be saying that the presence of the Spirit in one's life provides a reason for the resurrection rather than that the Spirit will be the agent in resurrection.

[145] εἰ plus the indicative (οἰκεῖ) is a simple condition, which assumes the reality of the premise for the sake of the argument.

[146] Calvin holds that Paul was not here speaking of the last resurrection "but of the continual operation of the Spirit, by which He gradually mortifies the remains of the flesh and renews in us the heavenly life" (*Romans and Thessalonians*, 166).

the spirit of the Christian been made alive (v. 10), but in time the body (now under the curse of death) will be resurrected as well. The indwelling Spirit is the guarantee of the believer's future resurrection.[147]

8:12–13 Privilege involves responsibility. Paul reminded his Christian brothers that the assurance of resurrection by the indwelling Spirit placed them under obligation. That obligation, however, is not to the sinful nature, to live according to its demands.[148] What we once were no longer has any claim on us. We are not obliged to obey the desires of our old earthly nature. In fact, if we do live under the control of our lower nature, we are "on the road to death" (Moffatt).[149] But if by the power of the Spirit we keep on putting to death (the Greek verb suggests continuing action) the evil practices of the body, we will live.[150] The lower nature does not automatically fade away when a person comes to Christ. The need to put to death the evil practices of the body is ongoing. Note as well that the way to crucify the old self is to obey the promptings of the Spirit. When we walk in fellowship with the indwelling Spirit, the desires of the lower nature are not met. For all practical purposes they are put to death. It is only when we break fellowship with the Spirit that our sinful nature is able successfully to reassert its fraudulent claim on our lives. The key to freedom from what we were is constant reliance on the active presence of the Spirit.

The question sometimes arises whether Paul's warning that those who live according to their sinful nature will die means that it is possible for believers to lose their salvation. Calvinists and others correctly understand that one whose life is controlled by the lower nature is without Christ and lives constantly only a heartbeat away from the judgment of eternal death (cf. Rom 6:23). On the other hand, although a regenerate person will sin (1 John 1:8), that person will be kept by the Spirit from a

---

[147] Denney notes that "this is one of the passages in which the presuppositions of the Trinitarian conception of God come out most clearly" ("Romans," 647).

[148] The NIV translation of σάρξ as "sinful nature" does not imply an anthropological dualism but serves as a convenient way of referring to a person living under the power of the old order. τοῦ κατὰ σάρκα ζῆν probably is epexegetic ("so as to live according to the flesh") rather than consecutive ("with the result that we live according to the flesh").

[149] The periphrastic future μέλλετε ἀποθνήσκειν emphasizes the certainty of death. Stuhlmacher understands v. 13 to mean that if baptized Christians "continue to live according to the measure of the flesh, in spite of the gift of the Spirit which has been allotted to them, the sure result will be death at the day of judgment" (*Romans*, 130).

[150] σῶμα (which in itself is morally neutral) should be taken in the sense of σάρξ, "the willing instrument of sin" (BAGD, 744). Elsewhere Paul contrasted sowing to one's sinful nature and sowing to the Spirit: the former leads to a harvest of destruction; and the latter, to a harvest of eternal life (Gal 6:8).

life of sin that would give evidence of an unregenerate heart (Eph 1:13–14; 1 John 3:9; Jude 24).[151] The Christian is one in whom the Spirit is constantly at work through instruction, exhortation, and discipline to bring to an end "the misdeeds of the body." Although there may be times in a Christian's life when a snapshot would show a person living according to the flesh, over time there should be evidence of progress (Phil 1:6).[152] Clearly there is an imperative involved in sanctification, upon which this passage focuses, but there is also an indicative upon which it is based (cf. Rom 6:14; Phil 2:12).[153] Holiness is not only the standard and goal of Christians (1 Pet 1:15–16); it is also their destiny (Rom 8:29–30; cf. Phil 3:12–14; 1 John 3:2). The Arminian position is that the judgment of eternal death remains a real possibility for the Christian. Although that is a possible interpretation of this and a few other New Testament passages, it is excluded by others (see also John 10:28–29; Col 3:3–4; 1 Pet 1:3–5).

8:14 In contrast to those whose lives are controlled by their sinful nature are those who allow themselves to be led by the Spirit of God (v. 14).[154] Harrison writes that "the relation of the Spirit to the sons of God is presented as being much like that of a shepherd to his sheep. They are 'led' by him as their guide and protector."[155] These, and only these, are sons of God.[156] This may be the most succinct and specific

---

[151] See the brief but helpful discussion of the perseverance of the saints in S. J. Grenz, *Theology for the Community of God* (Nashville: Broadman & Holman, 1994), 593.

[152] C. H. Spurgeon said, "The believer, like a man on shipboard, may fall again and again on the deck, but he will never fall overboard," quoted in A. H. Strong, *Systematic Theology* (Philadelphia: Judson, 1907), 885.

[153] See H. Ridderbos, *Paul: An Outline of His Theology*, trans. J. R. De Witt (Grand Rapids: Eerdmans, 1975), 254–55.

[154] BAGD cites Rom 8:14 as an example of the passive ἄγονται ("be led, allow oneself to be led" [p. 14]). It is difficult to see the distinction Moo would like to make between being "led by the Spirit" and "as in Gal. 5:18 to have the direction of one's life as a whole determined by the Spirit" (*Romans 1–8*, 534). Käsemann translates ἄγονται as "driven by the Spirit" since it is "taken from the vocabulary of the enthusiasts according to 1 Cor 12:2" (*Romans*, 226), but the connection is less than certain.

[155] Harrison, "Romans," 92.

[156] This takes ὅσοι in a restrictive sense rather than inclusive ("only those" rather than "all those who"). Feeling that Paul may have intended to be ambiguous, Dunn translates "as many as" (*Romans*, 1:450). Among others who choose the restrictive sense are Montgomery ("only those") and Conybeare ("they alone"). H. Rhys writes, "The people who are led are the Christians, and Paul would not have thought of including anyone else" (*The Epistle to the Romans* [New York: Macmillan, 1961], 102). Sanday and Headlam distinguish between υἱός and τέκνον, pointing out that the latter "denotes the natural relationship of child to parent" while the former "implies, in addition to this, the recognized *status* and legal privileges reserved for sons" (*Romans*, 202). No such distinction is being made, however, between υἱοί in v. 14 and τέκνα in v. 16.

182

answer in Scripture to the question, Who is a child of God? While doctrinal correctness is important, no amount of theological acuity can substitute for the guiding presence of the Spirit. Not only does the Spirit guide the believer, but he initiates the action as well. While God is the Father of all in the sense of creation, and specifically the Father of Israel in a corporate sense (Deut 32:6; Isa 63:16; Jer 31:9), the only way for a person to become a child of God is through faith in Jesus Christ (John 1:12–13). The corollary is that unless people are continually being led (indicated by the Greek present tense) by the Spirit, they are not members of God's family. The NIVSB note on 8:14 says that "being led by God's Spirit is the hallmark of this relationship." Beware of the temptation to adjust this requirement to the level of common practice.

8:15 Paul contrasted slavery and adoption as children. He reminded readers that in turning to Christ they were not enslaved once again to fear (cf. 2 Tim 1:7). On the contrary, the spirit[157] they received was the consciousness that they had become adopted sons of God. Accordingly, they cried out "Abba, Father."[158] The metaphor of adoption comes primarily, but not exclusively, from the Greco-Roman world. The Greek word for "adoption" (*huiothesia*) is not found in the LXX, and the five occurrences in the New Testament are all in Paul's writings. Although adoption as a legal act was not practiced in Judaism, some Old Testament customs support the view that Paul had that background in mind as well.[159] In adoption all previous relationships are severed. The new father exercises authority over the new son, and the new son enters into the privileges and responsibilities of the natural son.[160] "Abba," the Aramaic word for "father," was used primarily within the family circle and in prayer (cf. Mark 14:36; Gal 4:6).[161] Montgomery's translation ("My Father, my dear Father!") underscores the intimate nature of the expression, which is so clearly the opposite of fear (v. 15a).

---

[157] Because the surrounding verses (13,14,16) speak of the Holy Spirit, a number of commentators take πνεῦμα υἱοθεσίας as the "[Holy] Spirit who brings about adoption." Those who hold that πνεῦμα should have the same meaning in both parts of the sentence understand πνεῦμα δουλείας as the Holy Spirit at work under the old era of the law. Others take it as rhetorical: the Holy Spirit is *not* a "spirit of bondage."

[158] Sanday and Headlam note that "the repetition of this word, first in Aramaic and then in Greek, is remarkable and brings home to us the fact that Christianity had its birth in a bilingual people" (*Romans*, 203).

[159] See F. H. Palmer's article on adoption in *IBD* 3.17.

[160] See F. Lyall, "Roman Law in the Writings of Paul—Adoption," *JBL* (1969): 458–66.

[161] Käsemann holds that in crying out αββα ὁ πατήρ "the congregation is uttering an ecstatic cry in response to the message of salvation" (*Romans*, 228).

8:16 By enabling us to cry out "Abba Father," the Spirit "endorses our inward conviction" (Phillips) that we are children of God.[162] What our own spirit assures us to be true is strengthened by the powerful inward testimony of God's Spirit. In much the same way that the hymn writer knew that Jesus lives ("He lives within my heart"), we rest assured that we are actually members of God's family because the same Spirit witnesses to our spirit that it is so.[163]

8:17 To be a child of God is to be an heir (cf. Gal 4:7; Titus 3:7). That Paul was using a metaphor does not diminish in any way the reality of what he was saying. We are co-heirs with Christ. "All that Christ claims as his will belong to all of us as well!" (Phillips). How rich in significance is the fact that we are full members of an eternal family in which God is our Father and Jesus Christ is our elder brother (cf. Heb 2:11–12). What appears to be a condition on this promised inheritance ("if indeed") is actually a simple statement of fact. Sharing the sufferings of Christ leads to sharing his glory. Obviously we do not share the redemptive suffering of Christ, but we do share the consequences in terms of opposition from the world he came to save (cf. Phil 3:10; 1 Pet 4:13). As members of the same family we share in the trials of life as well as the benefits.[164]

8:18–19 Having mentioned in v. 17 the suffering that accompanies membership in the family of God, Paul laid out three grounds of encouragement: (1) the glory that will be revealed (vv. 18–25), (2) the help of the Holy Spirit (vv. 26–27), and (3) the fact that all things work together for good (vv. 28–30).[165] First he contrasted the sufferings of believers characteristic of the present evil age with the glory that will be theirs (cf. 2 Cor 4:17).[166] To the Corinthians he wrote that he was thoroughly

---

[162] By not putting a full stop at the end of v. 15, some connect v. 15b with v. 16: "When we cry 'Abba! Father!' it is the Spirit himself witnessing with our spirit that we are children of God." E. A. Obeng writes that "Abba, Father" is an acclamatory prayer in which the Holy Spirit joins with the human spirit to bear witness to the fact that Christians are children of God ("Abba, Father: The Prayer of the Sons of God," *ExpTim* 99 [1988]: 363–66).

[163] There is a question about whether συμμαρτυρεῖ means "to witness together with" or simply "to witness to." In the former case the prefix σύν retains its normal meaning "with" rather than serving to intensify the verb (as it does in the latter case). There is no particular reason why the Holy Spirit cannot both witness *to* the regenerated human spirit and consequently *with* it.

[164] Hunter writes, "For Christ the path of suffering was the path to glory. For his JOINT-HEIRS it must be the same" (Hunter, *Romans,* 81).

[165] Cf. Murray, *Romans,* 1:300, 310, 313.

[166] The Greek text says it will be revealed εἰς ἡμᾶς, usually understood as "to us" or "in us." The NEB has "which is in store for us."

acquainted with hardships of every kind—beatings, imprisonments, sleepless nights, and hunger (2 Cor 6:4–5; 11:23–28). Yet he considered these trials not worth comparing with the glory that was "about to burst upon [him]" (v. 18, Goodspeed).[167] As a citizen of heaven (Phil 3:20) he realized that his earthly life was but a moment in time in comparison with eternity. Not only that, but the glory of the coming age will be qualitatively distinct from the trials of the present. If we allow the difficulties of life to absorb our attention, they will effectively blot out the glory that awaits us. Our focus needs to be on things above (Col 3:2), spiritual concerns of eternal significance (cf. 2 Cor 4:18).[168]

The creation itself is pictured as eagerly awaiting that time when the glorious future of the sons of God is realized.[169] Phillips's rather picturesque rendition is, "The whole creation is on tiptoe to see the wonderful sight of the sons of God coming into their own." The personification of nature would not sound strange to those who were at home with rivers that "clap their hands" and mountains that "sing together for joy" (Ps 98:8; cf. Isa 55:12).[170] Because Adam disobeyed by eating the forbidden fruit, God had cursed the ground (Gen 3:17–18; cf. 5:29). The full redemptive work of God includes the reversal of this curse.

8:20–21   Paul spoke of the creation being "subjected to frustration" (v. 20).[171] That was not because of some inherent fault in creation but because that is what God decided.[172] In punishment for his disobedi-

---

[167] μέλλουσαν denotes certainty as well as imminence.

[168] Luther laments the time wasted thinking about the creation as it now is rather than that which it is looking forward to. He quotes Seneca's observation that "we fail to know what is necessary, because we study unnecessary things" (*Romans*, 107–8).

[169] Cranfield lists eight ways that κτίσις ("creation") has been understood in this passage and provides an extensive bibliography for the history of exegesis. He understands the reference to be to "the sum-total of subhuman nature both animate and inanimate" (*Romans*, 1:411–12). H. Balz rejects the popular interpretation of ἀποκαραδοκία as a metaphor with the basic meaning "stretching forth the head." He concludes that Paul probably used the term (which he may have coined—it is not attested in non-Christian sources) "to give expression to the element of earnest and eager longing" (*EDNT* 1.132). D. R. Denton rejects the idea that the term may connote anxiety or uneasiness ("Ἀποκαραδοκία," *ZNW* 73 [1982]: 138–40). Bruce writes that the revealing of the sons of God is "their 'adoption as sons' (verse 23)" (*Romans*, 163).

[170] Denney writes that "the spirit of the passage is rather poetic than philosophical." The involvement of creation in the fortunes of humanity leads naturally to the idea of "a mysterious sympathy between the world and man" (*Romans*, 649).

[171] O. Bauernfeind notes that ματαιότης in Rom 8:20 takes up the thought of Eccl 1:2 ("Utterly meaningless! Everything is meaningless," *TDNT* abr., 572). The "frustration" of the created order lay in its inability (due to human sin) to fulfill its intended goal or purpose.

[172] The "one who subjected it" is certainly God. Because of διά with the accusative (which seems to suggest not the agent but the reason for subjection) some hold that the clause speaks of Adam or Satan. However, as in John 6:57, διά with the accusative may be used in place of διά with the genitive (*EDNT* 1.297).

ence, Adam was to garner his food from ground cursed with thorns and thistles. But the curse was not permanent. The physical universe was frustrated by Adam's sin, yet there is hope. Verse 21 states the content of that hope.[173] The day is coming when the created order will be set free from its bondage to decay. Freed from corruption, it will share in "the freedom of the glory of the children of God" (literal translation).[174] The scene is eschatological. Some have suggested that this points to life during the millennium, but it is better to see it as the entire created universe celebrating together the glorious state of final redemption and restoration. Paul's use of personification is striking. As sin brought the curse of death to the physical universe, the day is coming when a new heaven and earth will be in place (2 Pet 3:13; Rev 21:1). They will take their place with the children of God in the perfect freedom of a sinless universe.

8:22–25 Currently, however, the entire universe is in travail as if it were giving birth.[175] As in childbirth, the pain is not meaningless but "carries with it the hope of new life for all creation."[176] Likewise, we ourselves are inwardly groaning[177] as we await the final phase of our adoption[178]—the redemption of our bodies (cf. Phil 3:21). Christians are those "who have the firstfruits of the Spirit," that is, who have the "Spirit as a foretaste of the future" (Conybeare).[179] In the Old Testament firstfruits consisted of the initial portion of the harvest that was given in sacrifice to God (Exod 23:19; Lev 23:9–14). Paul used the term in reference to the gift of the Spirit as an eschatological pledge (cf. 2 Cor 5:5, where the Spirit is given "as a deposit guaranteeing what is to come"). The Spirit is evidence that at the present time we are the sons of God (vv. 14,16). He is also the "down payment" (the term *aparchēn*, "firstfruits," having essentially the same meaning here as *arrabōn* in 2 Cor 1:22; Eph 1:14) on the inheritance that will be ours as members of the family of God.

---

[173] Manuscripts that read διότι make v. 21 the reason for hope. The UBS text (4th ed. rev.) reads ὅτι, which makes v. 21 the content of the hope.

[174] The NIV and others translate τὴν ἐλευθερίαν τῆς δόξης with "the glorious freedom," but that tends to lessen the eschatological emphasis of the verse.

[175] The prefix σύν in the two compound verbs means "together with" one another, not *with* Christ or *with* us.

[176] Bruce, *Romans,* 164.

[177] Moo comments that by associating our "groaning" with that of creation, Paul characterized it as nonverbal and therefore indicative of an inner attitude of frustration at the moral and physical infirmities of the present age and of eager longing for the end of this state of "weakness" (*Romans 1–8,* 556).

[178] The NIVSB note on 8:23 calls attention to three states in the adoption process: first, God's predestination (Eph 1:5); then our inclusion as children of God (v. 14); and finally, the resurrection of the body.

[179] Taking τοῦ πνεύματος as a genitive of apposition following τὴν ἀπαρχὴν.

Our salvation involves the hope that our mortal bodies will someday be liberated from the bondage of decay (v. 24).[180] We are not saved "by hope" (as the AV has it), but our salvation is characterized by hope.[181] Since salvation, viewed in its completeness, is necessarily future, we wait for it in hope (cf. 1 Thess 5:8; Titus 3:7). But hope that is seen is not hope at all. Why would we hope for that which is in plain view? So since we are hoping for something that is still unseen (cf. 2 Cor 4:18), it falls to us to wait for it with patience (cf. 2 Cor 5:2,4).[182]

8:26–27 As it is hope that carries us through our times of suffering (vv. 24–25), so it is the Spirit who comes to our aid when we find ourselves unable to pray as we ought.[183] Paul said that the Spirit "helps us in our weakness." In context that weakness is our lack of understanding regarding prayer.[184] Prayer has always been one of the great mysteries of the spiritual life. We understand that God is listening, but we sense our inadequacy when it comes to knowing how to pray or exactly what we should pray for.[185] How many times have we wondered how to pray for a friend suffering a serious illness? Sometimes volumes of prayer have gone up to God, but the response from heaven was not what we wanted or expected. When our lack of faith undermines certainty in prayer, the Spirit himself intercedes on our behalf. So intense is his prayer that Paul described it as "groans that words cannot express." The NEB makes the believer, not the Spirit, the one who groans ("through our inarticulate groans the Spirit himself is pleading for us"). This removes the somewhat difficult image of the Spirit groaning in prayer, but in view of Gethsemane (cf. esp. Luke 22:44) there is no reason to deny emotional/spiritual involvement in prayer to the third person of the

---

[180] Note the eschatological tension of the current age (between the cross and the parousia) in the combination of the aorist ἐσώθημεν ("we were saved") and τῇ ἐλπίδι ("in this hope"), which points to that which is yet future.

[181] τῇ ἐλπίδι is a dative of reference, not of means.

[182] Williams stresses the continuous aspect of the present tense of ἀπεκδεχόμενοι, translating, "We keep on patiently waiting for it."

[183] It is less likely that Paul was here comparing the "groaning" of the Spirit with the groans of believers (v. 23). Black cites an unpublished meditation by T. W. Manson, who comments that "the prayer that comes tripping from the tongue . . . is not liable to climb very high" and that "those very longings and aspirations that reach upwards . . . where mere formal prayers can never reach . . . are themselves the work of the Spirit of God" (*Romans,* 118).

[184] Some understand "our weakness" in the wider sense of our creaturely condition in the overlap between the old and new eras.

[185] Whether Paul was speaking of *how* to pray or *what* to pray for really amounts to the same question. Certainly he had in mind the content and not the style or manner.

Trinity.[186] Here again we stand at the edge of mystery. It is better to acknowledge humbly our spiritual incapacity than to reduce the action of the Spirit to human terms.

God understands what the Spirit desires even though it is inexpressible in human terms (v. 27).[187] God is the one who has complete access to the heart. His knowledge is direct, not dependent upon one's ability to articulate concerns. God is a searcher of hearts and knows the desires of the Spirit as the Spirit intercedes for us. He knows that the Spirit is interceding for saints in harmony with his will.[188] No passage of Scripture provides greater encouragement for prayer. The Spirit comes to the aid of believers baffled by the perplexity of prayer and takes their concerns to God with an intensity far greater than we could ever imagine. Our groans (v. 23) become his (v. 26) as he intercedes on our behalf.

8:28 We come now to one of the favorite verses in Romans. How often in times of trial have believers turned to Paul's reassuring words that God has not deserted us but is at work in every circumstance of life. While the AV and other English translations follow the textual tradition that makes "all things" the subject of the sentence,[189] the NIV has chosen an alternate tradition that supplies the word "God" as subject.[190] Since "things" are incapable of independent action, the two translations actually come to the same conclusion. In both cases it would be God who is at work in the circumstances of life. God directs the affairs of life in such a way that, for those who love him, the outcome is always beneficial. The

---

[186] Some who hold that στεναγμοῖς ἀλαλήτοις ("groans that words cannot express") refers to the groaning of the believer also hold that Paul was referring to glossolalia, speaking in tongues (e.g., E. Käsemann, "The Cry for Liberty in the Worship of the Church," in *Perspectives on Paul* [Philadelphia: Fortress, 1971]: 122–37), but that is highly unlikely. ἀλάλητος means "unspoken." Stott holds that the groans are "unexpressed rather than inexpressible," the "agonized longings for final redemption and the consummation of all things" (*Romans,* 245).

[187] "The mind of the Spirit" is what the Spirit has set his mind on, what he purposes to do.

[188] This takes ὅτι in the sense of "that" rather than "because." The latter alternative (in which case the text would be telling us why it is that God knows the mind of the Spirit) also makes good sense. The lack of an article on ἁγίων, "saints," prevents our thinking of *the* saints as if they constituted a specific group of God's people. The intercessory work of the Spirit is for *all* believers. "He pleads for God's own people in God's own way" (NEB).

[189] Cranfield lists and discusses eight different interpretations of πάντα συνεργεῖ and settles on taking πάντα as subject with the understanding that "what is expressed is a truly biblical confidence in the sovereignty of God" (*Romans,* 1:424–28, esp. 427).

[190] Although the longer reading, συνεργεῖ ὁ θεός, is well attested, ὁ θεός may well have been added because συνεργεῖ implies a personal agent (see B. Metzger, *TCGNT,* 518). C. D. Osburn supports Dodd's view that "God" is the implied subject and πάντα is an inner accusative ("The Interpretation of Romans 8:28," *WTJ* 44 [1982]: 99–109).

"good" of which Paul spoke is not necessarily what we think is best,[191] but as the following verse implies, the good is conformity to the likeness of Christ. With this in mind it is easier to see how our difficulties are part of God's total plan for changing us from what we are by nature to what he intends us to be. Moral advance utilizes hardship more often than not.

The verb ("works") and the participial phrase ("those who love him") are in the present tense. Not only is God continually at work, but those for whom he works are steadfast in their love for him. The Christian faith is never presented in Scripture as a static relationship. A person's salvation is not something that took place sometime in the past with little or no impact in the present. By definition, a relationship is a continuing affair. A vital ongoing love for God is the necessary prerequisite for his active intervention in the affairs of our life. From the human side we love God. From God's side we are called in accordance with his purpose. By calling Paul meant an effectual calling—one in which our response is invariably positive.[192]

8:29–30 These verses contain a series of five verbs (all in the aorist tense) describing how God has carried out his saving purpose. The first two are foreknowledge and predestination.[193] We know that God is at work for us in the circumstances of life (v. 28) because we have been predestined to "share the likeness of his Son" (Weymouth). As Jesus "learned obedience from what he suffered" (Heb 5:8), we too should expect our share of difficulties in the process of being conformed to his image. Verse 29 is sometimes interpreted to mean that God predestines on the basis of his prior knowledge about how each of us will in fact respond.[194] But this would mean that in election God would not be sovereign; he would be dependent upon what he would see happening in the future. Theologians rightly point out that prior to knowledge must be the

---

[191] Those who think that this verse promises material wealth have missed the point.

[192] For call of God see Rom 11:29; 1 Cor 1:9; Eph 4:4; 1 Thess 2:12; 2 Tim 1:9; 1 Pet 2:9.

[193] Barrett notes that it is not easy to distinguish between these two terms: "The slightly ambiguous phraseology may serve as a warning that we are not dealing here with a rigidly thought out and expressed determinist philosophy, but with a profound religious conviction" (*Romans,* 170). In the same vein Barclay writes that "Paul never meant [the passage] to be the expression of theology or philosophy; he meant it to be the almost lyrical expression of Christian experience" (*Romans,* 114). Dodd agrees with Professor Otto that the idea of election is "a pure expression of the religious experience of grace" and adds that Augustine and Calvin "made the mistake of erecting upon it a rigid dogmatic system." He concludes that "the best commentators upon this passage of Paul are not the theologians, but the greater hymn-writers of the Church" (*Romans,* 141). On the other hand, Brunner claims that in the five-word "golden chain" we have "a summary of all Christian doctrine" (*Romans,* 77).

divine decree. Unless God determines in some sense that something will happen, he cannot "know" that it will. For God to foreknow requires an earlier decree. The etymology of the Greek verb translated "predestine" suggests marking out a boundary beforehand.[195] In the present context predestination is not concerned with election to salvation. Rather, God has foreordained that believers be brought into "moral conformity to the likeness of his Son."[196] What is predestined is that we become like Christ (cf. 2 Cor 3:18).[197] The purpose is that Christ might be the "eldest in a vast family of brothers" (Weymouth). If we were to bear no family resemblance to him, the intention of the Father would never be realized. The supremacy of Christ is reflected in the designation "firstborn" (cf. Col 1:15,18; Heb 1:6; Rev 1:5). It speaks both of his priority in time and of his primacy of rank. It also implies that there are to be others who will share in his sonship.

Verse 30 continues the sequence of divine actions (in the aorist tense). Not only did God foreknow and predestine believers, he also called, justified, and glorified them.[198] Only the final term raises a problem. Scripture teaches that glorification awaits our future resurrection (1 John 3:2). It usually is said that since future events are determined by God's prior decree, Paul could speak of glorification in the past tense. It is as certain as if it already had taken place. Another interpretation is that God has in fact "given his splendour [glory]" (NEB) to those whom he has justified. Even now we enjoy a portion of the spiritual benefits of God's redemptive work on our behalf (cf. 2 Cor 3:18).

8:31-32 What, then, are we to conclude from all of this? As children of God we have been adopted into his family (v. 15). We are co-heirs with Christ (v. 17). We have received the Spirit as the guarantee of final redemption (v. 23). Our prayers are taken up by the Spirit and laid

---

[194] Although προγινώσκω means "to know in advance," Paul's use of the word here carries the OT nuance of personal and intimate knowledge (Amos 3:2, "You only have I chosen [ἔγνων in the LXX] of all the families of the earth"). BAGD has "to choose beforehand" as the meaning for προγινώσκω in Rom 8:29 (p. 703). For a conclusive argument against the position that predestination depends on prescience, see Murray, *Romans,* 315–18.

[195] πρό (*before*) + ὁρίζω ("to mark out or bound"; cf. Eng. "horizon").

[196] Cf. NIVSB note on 8:29. The expression denotes an inward and not merely superficial conformity (Robertson, *WP* 4:377).

[197] Morris comments that "it is God's plan that his people become like his son, not that they should muddle along in a modest respectability" (*Romans,* 333).

[198] In answer to the question of why sanctification is not included in the sequence, Bruce remarks that "sanctification is glory begun; glory is sanctification consummated" (*Romans,* 168).

before God (v. 26). Though sinners by nature, through faith we have been acquitted of all wrong (v. 30). Our future glorification is so certain that God speaks of it as already having taken place (v. 30). Certainly if God is for us,[199] "what does it matter who may be against us" (Norlie).[200] Since God did not spare his own Son but delivered him over to death for us all,[201] will he not along with this gracious gift also lavish upon us everything else he has to give?[202] The argument is from the greater to the lesser. A God who sacrificed his own Son on our behalf will certainly not withhold that which by comparison is merely trivial. The immeasurable greatness of God's love is seen in the infinite nature of his sacrifice on our behalf. God is by nature a giving God.[203]

8:33–34 Paul continued by asking rather incredulously, Who is there who dares to bring an accusation against those whom God has chosen (v. 33)?[204] No one! It is God himself[205] who pronounces his people righteous.[206] There is no higher tribunal. Who is the one with the authority to condemn (v. 34)? Translations are divided on whether to take the response as a statement or a question. If a statement, the answer to "Who is he that condemns?" would be, "It is Christ Jesus [that condemns], the one who died and rose again." But Jesus said, "I did not come to judge the world, but to save it" (John 12:47). So it must be a question: "Will Christ? No! For he is the One who died for us" (TLB). If he is for us, he

---

[199] ὑπὲρ ἡμῶν here means "on our side" (cf. Mark 9:40, Phillips: "For the man who is not against us is on our side [ὑπὲρ ἡμῶν]"). ὁ θεὸς ὑπὲρ ἡμῶν is the gospel in its most succinct form.

[200] Rhys calls attention to the rhythmic structure of the final paragraph beginning with v. 31b. He feels it is so important that "no interpretation can be satisfactory unless it recognizes that Paul has formed the conclusion of this outline of redemption from quasi-liturgical material" (*Romans*, 114).

[201] Most scholars find here an allusion to Abraham's not sparing his son Isaac (the same verb, φείδομαι, is also used in the LXX of Gen 22:16), the difference being that in the case of Christ, the Son was in fact sacrificed. Cf. Newman and Nida, *Romans*, 170.

[202] Dunn takes τὰ πάντα as probably referring to creation: "What seems to be envisaged is a sharing in Christ's lordship (Ps 110:1 alluded to in v 34) over 'the all'" (*Romans*, 1:502).

[203] Cf. Jas 1:5. Note the stress on "giving" in παρὰ τοῦ διδόντος θεοῦ.

[204] ἐγκαλέω ("to bring a charge") is a legal technical term for bringing a charge against someone in a court of law (BAGD, 215). Used here in the future tense it points to the final judgment. There are a number of ways in which vv. 33–34 have been punctuated. The NIV follows the punctuation of the UBS 4th ed. rev., which has question, statement, question, statement (extended). The questions are rhetorical rather than genuine.

[205] The repetition of θέος adds additional emphasis.

[206] The present active participle δικαιῶν has led Dunn to think that the justifying activity of God is ongoing (*Romans*, 503), but it is more likely "gnomic" in a kind of titular sense (Moo, *Romans 1–8*, 584).

certainly will not condemn us. Far from condemning us, he is right now at the right hand of God interceding on our behalf.[207] Not only does the Spirit intercede for us (8:26) but the glorified Christ as well.

8:35–36 The tide of spiritual excitement rises sharply as the apostle marveled at the amazing love of Christ. Who or what could ever separate us from the love of Christ?[208] Then follows a litany of disasters, none of which can effect a separation between Christ and the believer. Far from weakening the bonds of love, trouble and hardship strengthen them.[209] Persecution drives the true believer to the arms of the one who knows from experience the full range of suffering. Famine and nakedness (perhaps a metaphor for destitution) are powerless to affect the love of Christ. Danger and the sword (possibly that of the executioner) lose their terror in view of the presence of the one in whom we find ultimate safety.[210]

8:37 Paul reflected upon the words of the psalmist (in Ps 44:22), which he found so appropriate to his situation. The troubles to be faced by the Christian are nothing new but have always been the experience of God's people. At every moment of the day we face death. We are considered no better than sheep that are marked for slaughter.[211] Nevertheless in all these difficult situations we are winning an overwhelming victory through the one who has proven his love for us (v. 37).[212] It is the love of Christ that supports and enables the believer to face adversity and to conquer it. Christians are not grim stoics who manage to muddle through somehow. They are victors who have found from experience that God is ever present in their trials and that the love of Christ will empower them to overcome all the obstacles of life.

8:38–39 The final two verses of chap. 8 call for reflection rather

---

[207] Cf. Ps 110:1 ("The LORD says to my Lord: Sit at my right hand until I make your enemies a footstool for your feet").

[208] τίς ("who") is a masculine interrogative although we might have expected the neuter τί ("what") because the following list is made up of things rather than people. Paul may have used τίς because the dangers were those of genuine adversaries. Robertson notes that χωρίσει is derived ultimately from χώρα, which means "space." "Can anyone put a distance between Christ's love and us? Can anyone lead Christ to cease loving us?" (Robertson, *WP* 4:379).

[209] θλῖψις is a strong word meaning "oppression, affliction."

[210] There may well be an eschatological orientation for all seven nouns in Paul's list. He could be referring to the final period of distress before the return of Christ.

[211] W. G. T. Shedd writes that Paul was not speaking of slaughter for sacrificial purposes but for the market. "The Romans regarded the Christian as a cheap and common victim" (*A Critical and Doctrinal Commentary upon the Epistle of St. Paul to the Romans* [1879; reprint, Grand Rapids: Zondervan, 1980]).

[212] Rather than "in spite of all these things."

than for interpretation. They supply the climax of Paul's inspired and eloquent words of praise to the love of God. The apostle voiced his confidence that there is nothing that could separate us from the love of God that comes to us in Christ Jesus our Lord. His list of ten terms moves from physical danger through the hierarchy of superhuman powers, those that now exist or ever will, powers from on high or from below, and culminates in the inclusive phrase "anything else in God's whole world" (Phillips).[213] There is absolutely nothing that can ever drive a wedge between the children of God and their Heavenly Father. It is true that life contains its full share of hardships (v. 18). But God is at work in all the circumstances of life to conform those whom he has chosen into the likeness of his dear Son. The process is God's. We are his workmanship (Eph 2:10). The process of sanctification is intended to bring us into conformity with the nature of our Creator. Although it may at times involve some serious pruning (John 15:2; cf. Heb 12:5–11), we may be sure that love is at work on our behalf. We are forever united with the one who is perfect love.

---

[213] The list is composed of four pairs interrupted by a single term after the third pair and a catch-all at the close. Commentaries discuss at length the various possibilities for each item. Some take the various designations in a general way to depict the extremes of life as we experience it, the supernatural world, time, and space.

V. GOD'S RIGHTEOUSNESS VINDICATED (9:1–11:36)
  1. The Justice of Rejection (9:1–29)
  2. The Cause of Israel's Rejection (9:30–10:21)
  3. Some Alleviating Factors (11:1–36)
     (1) The Rejection Is Not Total (11:1–10)
     (2) The Rejection Is Not Final (11:11–24)
     (3) The Salvation of All Israel (11:25–36)

—— V. GOD'S RIGHTEOUSNESS VINDICATED (9:1–11:36) ——

1. The Justice of Rejection (9:1–29)

[1]I speak the truth in Christ—I am not lying, my conscience confirms it in the Holy Spirit— [2]I have great sorrow and unceasing anguish in my heart. [3]For I could wish that I myself were cursed and cut off from Christ for the sake of my brothers, those of my own race, [4]the people of Israel. Theirs is the adoption as sons; theirs the divine glory, the covenants, the receiving of the law, the temple worship and the promises. [5]Theirs are the patriarchs, and from them is traced the human ancestry of Christ, who is God over all, forever praised! Amen.

[6]It is not as though God's word had failed. For not all who are descended from Israel are Israel. [7]Nor because they are his descendants are they all Abraham's children. On the contrary, "It is through Isaac that your offspring will be reckoned." [8]In other words, it is not the natural children who are God's children, but it is the children of the promise who are regarded as Abraham's offspring. [9]For this was how the promise was stated: "At the appointed time I will return, and Sarah will have a son."

[10]Not only that, but Rebekah's children had one and the same father, our father Isaac. [11]Yet, before the twins were born or had done anything good or bad—in order that God's purpose in election might stand: [12]not by works but by him who calls—she was told, "The older will serve the younger." [13]Just as it is written: "Jacob I loved, but Esau I hated."

[14]What then shall we say? Is God unjust? Not at all! [15]For he says to Moses,

"I will have mercy on whom I have mercy,

193

and I will have compassion on whom I have compassion."

[16]It does not, therefore, depend on man's desire or effort, but on God's mercy. [17]For the Scripture says to Pharaoh: "I raised you up for this very purpose, that I might display my power in you and that my name might be proclaimed in all the earth." [18]Therefore God has mercy on whom he wants to have mercy, and he hardens whom he wants to harden.

[19]One of you will say to me: "Then why does God still blame us? For who resists his will?" [20]But who are you, O man, to talk back to God? "Shall what is formed say to him who formed it, 'Why did you make me like this?'" [21]Does not the potter have the right to make out of the same lump of clay some pottery for noble purposes and some for common use?

[22]What if God, choosing to show his wrath and make his power known, bore with great patience the objects of his wrath—prepared for destruction? [23]What if he did this to make the riches of his glory known to the objects of his mercy, whom he prepared in advance for glory— [24]even us, whom he also called, not only from the Jews but also from the Gentiles? [25]As he says in Hosea:

"I will call them 'my people' who are not my people;
and I will call her 'my loved one' who is not my loved one," [26]and,
"It will happen that in the very place where it was said to them,
'You are not my people,'
they will be called 'sons of the living God.'"
[27]Isaiah cries out concerning Israel:
"Though the number of the Israelites be like the sand by the sea,
only the remnant will be saved.
[28]For the Lord will carry out
his sentence on earth with speed and finality."
[29]It is just as Isaiah said previously:
"Unless the Lord Almighty
had left us descendants,
we would have become like Sodom,
we would have been like Gomorrah."

At the beginning of chap. 3 the question was raised about what advantage there was in being a Jew (v. 1). It was occasioned by the previous paragraph, which established that mere membership in the Jewish nation was insufficient to warrant God's praise. To be a Jew one had to be one inwardly. Real circumcision was inward and accomplished by the Spirit, not outward obedience to a written code. In fact, the entire second chapter of Romans undermined any confidence that Paul's readers might have had that on the basis of their national identity they would receive favored treatment from God. The obvious question was what benefit there was in being a Jew. Paul started to answer the question in 3:2 but then returned to the major theme of showing that all people, regardless of their national origin, are under the condemnation of sin. It is only now in chap. 9 that we find a full answer to the earlier question. Chapters 9–11 discuss the subject of God's righteousness in view of his apparent rejection of the Jewish nation.[1]

9:1–5 Paul took special pains to let his readers know how deeply concerned he was about his kinsmen of the Jewish race. Were he to forget his roots and feel no pain for the spiritual state of his fellow countrymen, his integrity as an apostle to the Gentiles could have been called into question. What he was about to say was absolutely true. He spoke the truth "in Christ," that is, in the presence of and accountable to the one who in his very nature is truth (John 14:6). Paul's conscience, enlightened by the Holy Spirit, assured him that he was speaking the truth. The conscience of those outside of Christ, while faulty, is nevertheless their best guide for conduct. But the believer has the privilege of a conscience informed by the Holy Spirit. Only then does conscience become a reliable guide for moral conduct.

Paul was burdened with a great weight of sorrow. His heart was continually in anguish for his Jewish family.[2] In fact, he could almost wish himself cursed by God and cut off from Christ if that would in some way benefit his kinsmen by race.[3] Paul was not speaking of excommunication

---

[1] C. H. Dodd argues that chaps. 9–11 are a "somewhat earlier piece of work" by Paul—a "sermon on the Rejection of Israel"—which he "incorporated here wholesale to save a busy man's time and trouble in writing on the subject afresh" (*The Epistle of Paul to the Romans*, MNTC [London: Hodder & Stoughton, 1932], 148–50). P. Stuhlmacher, however, argues with conviction that chaps. 9–11 are "anything but a mere excursus concerning the problem of Israel . . . for in these chapters, Paul is concerned with the very life nerve of his mission and with the question of the faithfulness of God in regard to the promise that he gave to Israel" (*Paul's Letter to the Romans*, trans. S. J. Hafemann [Louisville: Westminster, 1994], 114). For a series of articles on Romans 9–11 see PSBSup 1 (1990).

[2] J. G. D. Dunn says that ἀδιάλειπτος "increases the emotional intensity still further," and "the use of καρδία reinforces the depth of sincerity Paul seeks to convey" (*Romans*, 2 vols., WBC [Dallas: Word, 1988], 2:524).

[3] ηὐχόμην is imperfect and means literally "I was praying." Rienecker notes that in Hellenistic Greek the imperfect often takes the place of the potential optative, "I could pray" (*Key*, 2:478). A. T. Robertson (*WP* 4:380) calls it an "idiomatic imperfect" ("I was on the point of wishing"). F. F. Bruce notes that ηὐχόμην "implies the unexpressed protasis, 'if such a thing were possible'" (*The Letter of Paul to the Romans*, 2d ed., TNTC [Grand Rapids: Eerdmans, 1985], 175). BDF 359 (2) translates, "I should have liked to have prayed but I did not do it." C. F. D. Moule calls it a "desiderative imperfect" and translates "'I could almost pray to be accursed'—the imperfect softening the shock of the daring statement or expressing awe at the terrible thought" (*An Idiom Book of New Testament Greek*, 2d ed. [Cambridge: University Press, 1971], 9).

from the church but of final and fatal separation from Christ in the age to come.[4] That, of course, would not be possible, but as Kuss comments, "One cannot measure the speech of the heart with the rules of logic."[5]

As Israelites, Paul's ethnic forbearers had a heritage rich with spiritual blessings (v. 4). Paul listed seven historic prerogatives that God had given to Israel.[6] The privileges of sonship belonged to them. God commanded Moses to tell Pharaoh that Israel was his "firstborn son" (Exod 4:22; cf. Hos 11:1). The splendor of the divine presence (the "shekinah of God") accompanied them throughout their desert journeys (Exod 13:21; 16:7,10). God had established covenants with them (Gen 15:18; Exod 19:5) and given them the law (Ps 147:19).[7] The regulations for worship in the temple had been entrusted to them (Heb 9:1). Their sacred literature was rich with the promises of God (e.g., Gen 12:7; Isa 9:6–7).[8] They were descendants of the great patriarchs whose moral authority and influence provided leadership for the Jewish tribes before they became a nation (Rom 9:5). And what's more, it is from them that the human ancestry of Christ is traced (1:3).

The latter phrases of v. 5 describe Christ as "God over all, forever praised!" The NIV follows the punctuation that places a comma before the final statement and understands it as a relative clause with "Christ" as the antecedent. Other translations use a full stop instead of a comma, which separates the final statement and makes it refer not to Christ but to

---

[4] ἀνάθεμα describes the object of a curse. Here it refers to being handed over to God's judicial wrath (J. Behm, *TDNT* abr., 37). The preposition ἀπό (rather than ὑπό as in several MSS) led the GNB to translate "under God's curse and separated from Christ."

[5] Quoted by Dunn, *Romans*, 2:524. W. Sanday and A. C. Headlam note that this prayer is similar to that of Moses in Exod 32:32 ("Please forgive their sins—but if not, then blot me out of the book you have written"). They quote Jowett, who says that difficulties with this passage arise from "the error or explaining the language of feeling as though it were that of reasoning and reflection" (*A Critical and Exegetical Commentary on the Epistle to the Romans*, 5th ed., ICC [Edinburgh: T & T Clark, 1902], 229).

[6] Note that Paul referred to his countrymen by their covenant name, Israelites (cf. Gen 32:28), rather than their national name, Jews. He was intent on identifying with them, not on appearing critical.

[7] Had διαθῆκαι ("covenants") been singular, the reference would have been to the covenant on Sinai. But the plural indicates that other covenants are included. It has been argued, however, that the plural could refer to the one covenant given to Abraham (Gen 15), which was at a later time renewed to Isaac (Gen 17) and Jacob (Gen 28). C. K. Barrett distinguishes three covenants within the great covenant of the Exodus (*A Commentary on the Epistle to the Romans*, HNTC [New York: Harpers, 1957], 177–78).

[8] Sanday and Headlam suggest that the promises in question are "the promises made in the O. T. with special reference to the coming of the Messiah" (*Romans*, 231).

God the Father.[9] The NEB has, "May God, supreme above all, be blessed for ever!" (cf. GNB, RSV [but see NRSV], NAB, Moffatt, Goodspeed).[10] The NRSV has reversed the position of the RSV and translates, "From them, according to the flesh, comes the Messiah, who is over all, God blessed forever." This reading of the text clearly affirms the deity of Jesus of Nazareth.[11]

9:6–9 In this paragraph Paul showed that while God had not abandoned his purpose in electing the nation Israel, a distinction must be made between the physical descendants of Abraham and the children of promise.[12] They were not one and the same. The "word" of God that had not failed was his promise to bless Israel. But not everyone descended from the patriarch Israel belonged to Israel the people of God. Nor because they have descended from Abraham are they necessarily Abraham's children (cf. Rom 2:28–29; cf. Gal 6:16). On the contrary, as it is written in Gen 21:12, "It is through Isaac that descendants shall be named for you" (NRSV).[13] This means that it will be the children who are born in fulfillment of the promise, and not those born in the course of nature, who will be regarded as Abraham's true descen-

---

[9] Since the original Greek texts had no punctuation, the alternatives are both editorial decisions.

[10] On this extensively debated issue, see C. E. B. Cranfield, *The Epistle to the Romans,* ICC, 2 vols. (Edinburgh: T & T Clark, 1975), 2:464–70; the excursus "The Punctuation of Rom. ix. 5" by Sanday and Headlam (*Romans,* 233–38); and the bibliography in J. A. Fitzmyer, *Romans,* AB (New York: Doubleday, 1993), 556–57. For a concise summary see B. Metzger (*TCGNT,* 520–23). Unfortunately, the committee decided on placing either a colon or a full stop after σάρκα because "nowhere else in his genuine epistles does Paul ever designate ὁ χριστός as Θεός (ibid., 522). Regarding this particular argument L. Morris comments: "In the last resort this is an argument from outside the passage, and it suffers from the objection that because Paul does not say something elsewhere he cannot say it here" (*The Epistle to the Romans* [Grand Rapids: Eerdmans, 1988], 350).

[11] B. Metzger presented five arguments for this interpretation: (1) τὸ κατὰ σάρκα ("human ancestry") expects a contrast; (2) "the most natural way to take the grammar of these words is to refer ὁ ὤν to the immediately preceding nominative (ὁ Χριστὸς)" (cf. 2 Cor 11:31); (3) taking it as a doxology would be contrary to Pauline usage, which always attaches a doxology to some preceding word (cf. 1:25); (4) the position of εὐλογητὸς is where it should be in a relative clause to modify Χριστὸς (in a doxology it would come before Θεὸς); and (5) a doxology would not fit the logic or the emotions of the passage (see "The Punctuation of Romans 9:5," in *Christ and Spirit in the New Testament,* ed. B. Lindars and S. S. Smalley [Cambridge: University Press, 1973], 95–112).

[12] The first "Israel" in v. 6 is ethnic Israel; the second is believing Israel (Jewish Christians). Cranfield points out that "all Jews . . . are members of God's elect people . . . but not all of them are members of the Israel within Israel" (*Romans,* 2:474).

[13] The ἐν in ἐν Ἰσαὰκ is restrictive, "only in Isaac."

dants.[14] The promise to Abraham was that about a year later the Lord would return and Sarah would have a son (Gen 18:10,14). Isaac, not Ishmael, was the child of promise. As God chose Isaac rather than Ishmael, so also does he now choose to bless those who by placing their faith in Christ become the true children of Abraham.

Spiritual kinship, not ethnic origin, determined who was a true Israelite. The modern counterpart to this truth is that the blessings of salvation extend only to those who are right with God through genuine faith in Jesus Christ. The visible church includes many who belong to "Ishmael," but salvation belongs only to "Israelites" who belong to the line of "Isaac." God has not turned his back on the nation Israel; he has simply clarified what it means to be a true child of Abraham.

9:10–13   At this point a Jewish antagonist might have questioned Paul's argument on the basis that Ishmael, as compared with Isaac, was not a true son of Abraham. His mother was Hagar, the maidservant of Sarah. So Paul strengthened his case by bringing in the account of the two sons of Rebekah. In this case there could be no question of legitimacy. Not only did Jacob and Esau have the same mother and father, they were twins as well.[15] Even before they were born or had done anything either good or bad, Rebekah was told that the older would serve the younger (Gen 25:23).[16] In his sovereignty God determined that was the way it would be. This confirms the divine purpose that election depends not upon what we may do but upon God's calling. Neither national heritage nor personal merit has anything to do with the sovereign freedom of God in assigning priority. This accords with the testimony of Scripture, "Jacob I loved, but Esau I hated" (Mal 1:2–3). This should not be interpreted to mean that

---

[14] This may reflect the birth of Ishmael, son of Abraham by Hagar, Sarah's maidservant (Gen 16:11–16).

[15] κοίτη means "bed" and by normal extension "marriage bed, sexual intercourse." As in Num 5:20 (LXX), here it means "seminal discharge." Esau and Jacob were conceived at exactly the same time.

[16] Commentaries usually note that in the Genesis oracle the children that Rebekah was to bear are pictured as two nations rather than two individuals (Gen 25:23: "The LORD said to her, "Two nations are in your womb"). Sanday and Headlam argue that the words refer "to the choice of the nation as well as the choice of the founder" (*Romans,* 246–47). Dunn is right, however, that while "the fuller oracle speaks of the two children as two nations . . . Paul evidently does not have this dimension in view . . . [He is] content to have a text . . . which shows that from the first precedence did not depend on the natural order of birth" (*Romans,* 2:544). Cf. J. Denney, "He is obviously thinking of Jacob and Esau as individuals" ("St. Paul's Epistle to the Romans," EGT 2 [Grand Rapids: Eerdmans, 1983], 661), and J. Murray (*The Epistle to the Romans,* 2 vols., NICNT [Grand Rapids: Eerdmans, 1965], 2:15–19).

God actually hated Esau. The strong contrast is a Semitic idiom that heightens the comparison by stating it in absolute terms.[17]

Paul was not building a case for salvation that in no way involves the consent of the individual. Nor was he teaching double predestination. Rather he was arguing that the exclusion of so many Jews from the family of God did not constitute a failure on God's part to maintain his covenant relationship with Israel. He had not broken his promise to the descendants of Abraham.

9:14–18 Paul then anticipated another objection.[18] If God elected with sovereign freedom, then was he not guilty of injustice? May we not infer that in choosing Jacob, God was unfair to Esau?[19] The Greek text makes clear that Paul expected a negative response. "Not at all!" God is not unjust in his actions. As Jehoshaphat told the judges of the Southern Kingdom, "With the Lord our God there is no injustice or partiality" (2 Chr 19:7). God bestows mercy on whom he chooses to bestow mercy and has compassion on whom he chooses to have compassion (Exod 33:19).[20] The point is that God's favors are not determined by anyone or anything outside of himself. God's purpose in election rests not upon human will (*thelō* in v. 16 can express desire or purpose) or effort (a par-

---

[17] Berkeley softens the contrast translating, "To Jacob I was drawn, but Esau I repudiated" (the NRSV has "chose" and "rejected"). In discussing the "hatred" of God, Michel comments that it "is not so much an emotion as a rejection in will and deed" (*TDNT* 4.687).

[18] It is not especially important to determine whether Paul's question ("What then shall we say?") was rhetorical or genuine. Cranfield's suggestion that it may be a reflective question, "that sort of question which one asks oneself, when one is trying to think one's way through a difficult matter" (*Romans,* 2:482) offers the best alternative.

[19] E. Brunner writes that "God's freedom means inequality. Inequality, however, always arouses in us men the feeling of injustice. We want to measure God by our yardstick. But God's righteousness cannot be measured by our standards. It includes his absolute sovereign freedom; else he would not be the God who freely bestows" (*The Letter to the Romans* [Philadelphia: Westminster, 1949], 86). To answer the question of whether God would predestine an unborn child to servitude, H. Rhys mentions Dodd, who "confesses that he is helpless here"; Michel, whose complex explanation resembles "double talk"; Bardenhewer, who "rushes off to deal resolutely with other dragons of less forbidding aspect"; and Barrett, who follows Augustine's position that all stand justly condemned by Adam's sin and therefore "God has no need to predestine anyone to damnation" (*The Epistle to the Romans* [New York: Macmillan, 1961], 123–24). But Rhys's rejection of the Augustinian theory of original sin leads him to conclude that "if we are damned it is our own doing" (ibid., 124–25).

[20] Calvin writes that "the predestination of God is truly a labyrinth from which the mind of man is wholly incapable of extricating itself. But the curiosity of man is so insistent that the more dangerous it is to inquire into a subject, the more boldly he rushes to do so" (*The Epistles of Paul the Apostle to the Romans and to the Thessalonians,* trans. R. Mackenzie [Grand Rapids: Eerdmans, 1961], 202).

ticiple from *trechō,* "run") but upon divine mercy. Although God elects
with sovereign freedom, it does not follow that Israel had nothing to do
with their rejection. Later in the chapter we will learn that Israel failed to
attain a right standing with God because they pursued it on the basis of
works (vv. 30–32). The sovereignty of God does not set aside human
responsibility.[21]

Paul used the case of Pharaoh (an individual rather than a nation as in
vv. 7–13) to demonstrate that God withholds mercy and hardens whomever he chooses (cf. Exod 7:3; 14:17).[22] Pharaoh, that implacable enemy
of God's people, was raised to the position of king of Egypt so that God
might display in him the evidence of his power (Exod 9:16). Although
Pharaoh's rise to a position of authority undoubtedly had a secular interpretation, God was at work in his career, bringing him to prominence.
God did it in order to display his power by bringing Pharaoh to his knees
and so that his character as the one who delivered the children of Israel
from Egyptian bondage might be known throughout the world.[23] Verse 18
summarizes the argument. It provides the principle of divine action on
which the preceding events were based. God shows mercy as he chooses,
and he hardens people's hearts as he chooses. He is sovereign in all that
he does. Although the text says repeatedly, however, that God hardened
Pharaoh's heart, it also stresses that Pharaoh hardened himself (cf. Exod
7:13–14,22; 8:15,19,32; 9:7,34–35). Morris notes that "neither here nor
anywhere else is God said to harden anyone who had not first hardened
himself."[24]

---

[21] Stott acknowledges the doctrine of election is shrouded in mystery and warns that "theologians are unwise to systematize it in such a way that no puzzles, enigmas, or loose ends are
left" (*Romans* [Downers Grove: InterVarsity, 1994], 268). Achtemeier distinguishes between
predeterminism (the idea that every thought and act is dictated by forces beyond our control)
and predestination, which sets the final outcome without determining the route by which it can
be reached (*Romans* [Atlanta: John Knox, 1985], 155). Paul was speaking of the latter here.

[22] Paul wrote that *Scripture spoke* to Pharaoh. Paul was either personifying Scripture (cf.
Gal 3:8) "as a surrogate for the name of God, who is the actual speaker" (Bruce, *Romans,* 183),
or he meant that what was said to Pharaoh would someday be embodied in Scripture. Denney
comments: "A Jew might answer the arguments Paul uses here if they were the Apostle's own;
to Scripture he can make no reply; it must silence, even where it does not convince" ("St. Paul's
Epistle to the Romans," 2:662).

[23] God's saving power, not his creative power, is in view. For the effect of the exodus on
other nations see Josh 2:10–11; 9:9; 1 Sam 4:8.

[24] Morris, *Romans,* 361. Calvin speaks of "weak exegetes" who hold that when God is said
to "harden," it implies only permission and not the action of divine wrath (*Romans,* 207). See
also Murray (*Romans,* 2:28–30). Fitzmyer says that "the 'hardening of the heart' by God is a
protological way of expressing divine reaction to persistent human obstinacy against him"
(*Romans,* 568).

God's freedom to do that which is in accordance with his will does not sit well with many moderns whose philosophy of life stems from a combination of relativism and belief in personal autonomy.[25] For the Christian, however, it is important to build one's theology not on personal perceptions of what ought to be but upon the biblical revelation of the character and purpose of God. The unalterable nature of God and the absolute justice of his actions are undoubtedly more difficult for the twentieth-century reader to understand than for those who lived in the biblical period, but a proper hermeneutic calls for us to interpret Scripture in its historical context. While its meaning will never change, how it is to be applied will depend upon the context of the reader. To fault God for showing mercy to some while hardening others is to require that he conform to our fallible and arbitrary concept of justice.

9:19–21 If God in his sovereignty has mercy on some and hardens the hearts of others, on what possible basis can he find fault with those he excludes? After all, no one resists his will. This question was bound to be raised in view of Paul's strong presentation of the freedom of God to carry out whatever he has purposed to do. Paul's "answer" in v. 20 is not really an answer but a rebuke to those who would make God answerable to humans.[26] Indeed, retorted Paul, who are you, a mere man, to "bandy words with God?" (Knox).[27] Drawing from the prophet Isaiah, he pictured the absurdity of the clay questioning the right of the potter to make of the lump whatever he wants (Isa 29:16; 45:9). Does not the potter have authority over the clay? Is it not his to mold into anything he chooses? Certainly he is free to make from the same lump of clay either an ornamental vessel or one for menial use.

---

[25] E.g., J. C. O'Neill, whose sole comment on v. 18 is "a thoroughly immoral doctrine" (*Paul's Letter to the Romans* [Middlesex: Penguin, 1975], 158).

[26] Some hold that Paul's response was less a rebuke than an attempt to help the objector understand that his questions were illegitimate in the sense that the creature has no right to question the Creator. There is a thin line, however, between correction and rebuke. Murray comments that "when we are dealing with ultimate facts categorical affirmation must content us" (*Romans*, 2:31), a position unacceptable to A. M. Hunter, who "dissent[s] emphatically" from the idea that "man . . . has no more right to talk back to his Creator than the pot to the Potter" (*The Epistle to the Romans*, TBC [London: SCM, 1955], 91).

[27] The contrast between humans and God in v. 20a (ὦ ἄνθρωπε . . . τῷ θεῷ) serves to remind us that as created beings we are in no position to question our Creator. "It is absurd and monstrous for man to question God's dealings," writes W. H. G. Thomas (*St. Paul's Epistle to the Romans* [Grand Rapids: Eerdmans, 1953], 260). Regarding Dodd's frequently quoted protest ("the weakest point in the whole epistle"), Dunn says that it "does an injustice both to Paul's integrity and to the deeper current of Paul's argument" (*Romans*, 2:557).

If Paul had said nothing more on the subject, it would be reasonable to conclude that God exercises his absolute power in an unqualified sense. But Paul had not as yet given us the entire story. God is not an arbitrary despot who does what he wishes without regard for anyone or anything. In the very next verse (v. 22) Paul told of the great patience God showed toward those who deserve wrath. And in the following chapter he discussed the liberty and responsibility of human beings. God's freedom operates within a moral framework. Human logic cannot harmonize divine sovereignty and human freedom, but both are clearly taught in Scripture. Neither should be adjusted to fit the parameters of the other. They form an antimony that by definition eludes our best attempts at explanation.

9:22–24 Up to this point Paul had insisted that God acts in sovereign freedom. The clay has no right to question the intentions of the potter. But here he added another perspective. The "objects of wrath" are not summarily dismissed with no concern for their lot as those not chosen. That God exercised great patience with them indicates that there is more to be learned about why they "deserve wrath and are maturing for destruction" (v. 22, Berkeley). God's sovereignty does not reduce humans to helpless automatons. Although it was God's will to show his wrath against sin and make known his power, he nevertheless postponed action against those who will someday experience his judicial displeasure.[28] Earlier we learned that God's kindness was intended to lead the sinner to repentance (2:4). God's patient endurance also was to make known to them his surpassing glory in dealing with the "objects of his mercy."[29] These he had prepared in advance to share his glory. Elsewhere Paul spoke of the glorious riches of God by means of which the Spirit will strengthen the inner person (Eph 3:16). The provisions of God's grace are boundless. It is his desire that they be made known in and through the lives of those who have been set apart from the beginning to reflect his glory.

---

[28] They are σκεύη ὀργῆς, "objects of wrath." They are "prepared for destruction" in the sense that they by their life and conduct have determined their own destiny. Murray comments that "there is an exact correspondence between what they were in this life and the perdition to which they are consigned. This is another way of saying that there is continuity between this life and the lot of the life to come" (*Romans,* 2:36).

[29] The NIV understands ἐπί in v. 23 in the sense of "to" rather than "upon." But it is hard to understand why God would deal patiently with unbelievers in order to make known to believers the glory they would share. It is better to understand v. 23 as giving another reason for God's patience, i.e., that unbelievers might see his glory being poured out *upon* the believers.

The grammatical structure of vv. 22–24 is difficult.[30] The NIV has chosen to separate the final clause of v. 22 along with all of v. 23 from the narrative both before and after. As a result, v. 24 would explain that even believers were at one time "objects of wrath."[31] Even though God has mercy on whom he chooses to have mercy, those who turn to him in faith, both Jew and Gentile, find themselves called by God. Far from being an arbitrary despot, God allows those who believe to take their place as "objects of his mercy."

9:25–29 Paul then turned to a number of Old Testament passages to show (1) that Gentiles are included in God's redemptive plans and (2) that only a remnant of believing Jews will be preserved. He drew first upon the prophet Hosea, through whom God said that he will call those who are not his people "my people" (Hos 2:23; cf. 1 Pet 2:10).[32] He will call the one not loved by the name "my loved one."[33] Although Hosea was speaking of the restoration of Israel, Paul freely applied the words to the Gentiles coming into the church. Quoting again from Hosea, Paul said that in the very place where they were disowned they would be called "sons of the living God" (Hos 1:10).[34]

Turning to the plight of the Jewish nation (v. 27), Paul quoted Isaiah, who declared that though the Israelites were as countless as the sands of the sea, only a remnant would be saved (Isa 10:22).[35] The Lord would carry out his judgment "fully and without delay" (TCNT).[36] Isaiah again was quoted, noting that unless the Lord Almighty had left the Israelites a few descendants, they would have been like Sodom and Gomorrah (cf. Gen 19:24–29). So Paul was saying that God had brought together in his

---

[30] It begins as a conditional sentence but is not followed up with an apodosis. J. Knox comments that "only a few passages in Paul are more obscure than this one" ("The Epistle to the Romans," *IB* 9 [New York: Abingdon, 1954], 548).

[31] Most take v. 24 as a relative clause dependent on σκεύη ἐλέους.

[32] "Lo-Ammi" means "not my people," and "Lo-Ruhamah" means "not the object of my affection." These were the names of Gomer's second and third children and stood for the Northern Kingdom when it broke its covenant with God.

[33] The perfect passive participle ἠγαπημένην emphasizes the continuing nature of the love of God.

[34] For the prophet the place was Jerusalem (or perhaps Palestine); as used by Paul it simply was part of the quotation and had no special significance. Dunn says it is "more likely theological than geographical" (*Romans,* 2:572).

[35] κράζει, "cries out," carries with it a note of urgency. E. Käsemann, sees it as indicating "inspired, proclamatory speech" (*Commentary on Romans,* trans. and ed. G. W. Bromiley [Grand Rapids: Eerdmans, 1980], 275).

[36] συντελῶν and συντέμνων are participles meaning "bringing to pass" and "cutting short." Moffatt translates "with rigour and dispatch."

new order those of faith regardless of their national background. Although he worked out his redemptive plan through his Son Jesus, a descendant of David in terms of his human nature, his new people are comprised of those who are Gentile by birth as well as Jewish. It is faith, not national origin, that brings a person into the family of God.

2. The Cause of Israel's Rejection (9:30–10:21)

[30]What then shall we say? That the Gentiles, who did not pursue righteousness, have obtained it, a righteousness that is by faith; [31]but Israel, who pursued a law of righteousness, has not attained it. [32]Why not? Because they pursued it not by faith but as if it were by works. They stumbled over the "stumbling stone." [33]As it is written:

> "See, I lay in Zion a stone that causes men to stumble
>   and a rock that makes them fall,
> and the one who trusts in him will never be put to shame."

[1]Brothers, my heart's desire and prayer to God for the Israelites is that they may be saved. [2]For I can testify about them that they are zealous for God, but their zeal is not based on knowledge. [3]Since they did not know the righteousness that comes from God and sought to establish their own, they did not submit to God's righteousness. [4]Christ is the end of the law so that there may be righteousness for everyone who believes.

[5]Moses describes in this way the righteousness that is by the law: "The man who does these things will live by them." [6]But the righteousness that is by faith says: "Do not say in your heart, 'Who will ascend into heaven?'" (that is, to bring Christ down) [7]"or 'Who will descend into the deep?'" (that is, to bring Christ up from the dead). [8]But what does it say? "The word is near you; it is in your mouth and in your heart," that is, the word of faith we are proclaiming: [9]That if you confess with your mouth, "Jesus is Lord," and believe in your heart that God raised him from the dead, you will be saved. [10]For it is with your heart that you believe and are justified, and it is with your mouth that you confess and are saved. [11]As the Scripture says, "Anyone who trusts in him will never be put to shame." [12]For there is no difference between Jew and Gentile—the same Lord is Lord of all and richly blesses all who call on him, [13]for, "Everyone who calls on the name of the Lord will be saved."

[14]How, then, can they call on the one they have not believed in? And how can they believe in the one of whom they have not heard? And how can they hear without someone preaching to them? [15]And how can they preach unless they are sent? As it is written, "How beautiful are the feet of those who bring good news!"

[16]But not all the Israelites accepted the good news. For Isaiah says, "Lord, who has believed our message?" [17]Consequently, faith comes from

hearing the message, and the message is heard through the word of Christ.
[18]But I ask: Did they not hear? Of course they did:

"Their voice has gone out into all the earth,
their words to the ends of the world."

[19]Again I ask: Did Israel not understand? First, Moses says,

"I will make you envious by those who are not a nation;
I will make you angry by a nation that has no understanding."

[20]And Isaiah boldly says,

"I was found by those who did not seek me;
I revealed myself to those who did not ask for me."

[21]But concerning Israel he says,

"All day long I have held out my hands
to a disobedient and obstinate people."

We come now to the second part of Paul's discussion on the relationship of the Jews to the gospel of justification by faith. In the earlier
verses of chap. 9 Paul reminded his readers that the Jews could not
establish a legitimate claim on God's favor based on national heritage.
Their own history demonstrated that God carries out his purposes with a
freedom uninhibited by human notions of what ought to be. Here Paul
showed that the Jews themselves were responsible for their rejection.
They thought they could gain a right standing with God on the basis of
personal performance. But they should have known that nothing they
could possibly do would ever merit acceptance by God.

9:30–33 Paul rhetorically asked, "What then shall we say?" The
same question was asked in v. 14, where it was followed by another
question. Here it leads to a somewhat paradoxical conclusion. Gentiles,
who "never had the Law's standard of righteousness to guide them"
(Phillips), nevertheless attained righteousness. Their right standing
before God was based on faith. Israel, on the other hand, pursued a righteousness based on law and failed to achieve it.[37] The reason is obvious.

---

[37]Commentaries discuss at length the specific meaning of νόμον δικαιοσύνης in v. 31.
Dunn calls "the righteousness which is based on law" an "inadmissible reversal of the terms"
(*Romans,* 2:581). Maintaining the order of words in the text yields, e.g., "the law that teaches/
demands/promises uprightness." Israel pursued the law in the sense that it "aimed incessantly
at bringing its conduct up to the standard of a law in which righteousness was certainly held
out, but was never able to achieve its purpose" (Denney, "Romans," 2:667). In the final analysis
there is little difference in this and "the righteousness that comes as a result of obeying the law."

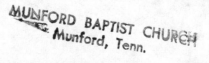

Their efforts were based not on faith but on personal performance.[38] Their efforts were doomed from the beginning because God does not accept sinners on the basis of what they do. Righteousness comes by faith and faith alone. God does not allow himself to be put in debt to people and their best efforts. The approach that says righteousness can be earned fails to grasp the enormity of sin. Our separation from God is so great that only he can bridge the gap. He chooses to do it entirely on his own. Our only responsibility is to accept by faith the finished work of Christ on behalf of sinners.

Justification by faith was a stumbling block to Israel. It stood in the way of their own popular religious philosophy of works and became the obstacle that brought about their fall. Paul mingled two passages from Isaiah to describe the situation (Isa 8:14; 28:16). In Zion was placed a stone that made people stumble and a rock that would trip them up.[39] Those who placed their trust in Christ, however, would never be disappointed.[40] What was true in Paul's day remains true today. Sinners still reject the righteousness of God because they cannot earn it. It is absolutely free. They stumble over the offer because it deprives them of any proprietary involvement in their own salvation. It is pride that brings people down. How deeply ingrained is our rebellious self-esteem! Too proud to accept God's willingness to forgive, sinners stumble headlong into eternity with their stubborn sinfulness intact.

10:1–4 Paul left no doubt about his deep affection for his fellow Israelites. He had just criticized their attempt to secure acceptance before God by performing all that the law required. They pursued righteousness but failed to achieve it because they sought it by personal merit rather than by faith. The deep longing of Paul's heart was that his countrymen experience salvation.[41] The reality of his love is seen in the

---

[38] T. Schreiner writes that to pursue the law by faith is to understand that no matter how perfectly the law is kept it cannot bring salvation; salvation comes only by believing in Christ ("Israel's Failure to Attain Righteousness in Romans 9:30–10:3," *TrinJ* 12 [1991]: 209–20). It is better to follow the NIV and supply a verb ("pursued") and an object ("it") than to supply a participle and make all but the first two words in the verse one sentence ("Because pursuing it, not by faith but by works, they stumbled . . .").

[39] σκάνδαλον originally referred to the bait stick in a trap.

[40] The antecedent of αὐτῷ is λίθον, which stands for Christ. These two verses were used in the early church to defend the messiahship of Jesus (cf. 1 Pet 2:6,8).

[41] Murray finds a "lesson of profound import" in the fact that although chap. 9 emphasized the sovereignty of God, we now learn of "the apostle's passion for the salvation of his kinsmen." He writes that "our attitude to men is not to be governed by God's secret counsel concerning them" (Murray, *Romans*, 2:47).

fact that he prayed for them. He, like they, belonged to that special race
through whom God had revealed himself in history. Reflecting on his
preconversion days, he told the Galatians of his extreme zeal for the tra-
ditions of the fathers (Gal 1:14; cf. Acts 22:3). But God met him on the
Damascus road, and his eyes were opened to God's way of righteousness. The experience did not turn him bitter against his former associates
but rather kindled within his heart a burning desire that they too might
experience the forgiving grace of God through Jesus Christ.

There is no question that his Jewish compatriots were zealous for
God, but unfortunately their zeal was not guided by knowledge (v. 2).[42]
They had no valid insight into God's plan for providing righteousness.
They failed completely to recognize the righteousness that comes from
God. "In their eagerness to set up a righteousness of their own" (TCNT)
they would not submit themselves to God's plan.[43] It is important to see
that Israel's failure resulted from its determination to achieve its objective in its own way. God would have to come to terms with them. Their
lack of knowledge was self-inflicted. Refuse the truth and God will give
you up to your own foolishness.[44]

The law, instead of providing a way to arrive at a right standing with
God, comes to an end in Christ. Paul wrote, "Christ is the end of the
law" (v. 4).[45] The law is brought to an end so that righteousness may be
within the reach of all who believe. As Paul said elsewhere, the purpose
of the law is to lead us to Christ so that we might be justified by faith

---

[42] ζῆλος is from the verb ζέω, which means "to boil." Fitzmyer notes that in postexilic and
late pre-Christian Judaism, "zeal for God, his law, or his temple was considered the characteristic of the faithful Jew" (*Romans,* 582–83).

[43] "The man who seeks to establish his own righteousness, however virtuous he may be,
can be only a rebellious creature of God" (Barrett, *Romans,* 197).

[44] Dunn comments that "ἀγνοέω could be translated here 'disregarding' . . . and therefore
imply some culpability" (*Romans,* 587). M. Black questions the approach that the Jews
ignored the righteousness of God (cf. NEB) and holds that they, "blinded by their 'zeal,' which
robbed them of their powers to discern the true nature of things, failed accordingly to recognize
the *dikaiosyne* of God when it appeared" (*Romans,* 2d ed., NCBC [Grand Rapids: Eerdmans,
1989], 141).

[45] Commentaries discuss at length whether τέλος means "end" in the sense of "termination" or in the sense of "goal." For a discussion of the first position cf. Käsemann, *Romans,*
282–83, and for the second cf. Cranfield, *Romans,* 2:515–20. Bruce understands the double
sense of τέλος to mean that Christ is the goal of the law "in that he embodies the perfect righteousness which it prescribes," and "this implies the termination of the law's function (real or
imagined) as a means of acquiring such a righteous status" (*Romans,* 190). For an extended
treatment of τέλος cf. R. Badenas, *Christ the End of the Law: Romans 10.4 in Pauline Perspective,* JSNTSup 10 (Sheffield: JSOT, 1985).

(Gal 3:24). Phillips translates, "For Christ means the end of the struggle for righteousness-by-the-Law for everyone who believes in him." As the hymnwriter A. M. Toplady put it, "Nothing in my hand I bring; simply to thy cross I cling." The only thing God requires of people is that they not persist in trying to earn what they can only receive as a totally free gift. Their problem is that pride stands in the way of receiving God's gift. Deeply ingrained in people's hostility to divine grace is a proud and stubborn self-reliance that would rather suffer loss than be deprived of an occasion for boasting.

10:5–13 In this paragraph Paul contrasted two kinds of righteousness. The first is the righteousness that has its origin in the law. Regarding this approach to righteousness Moses said, "The man who does these things will live by them" (Lev 18:5; cf. Gal 3:12). That is to say, if a person is able to perform all that the law requires, it will lead to life.[46] The problem lies in the fact that no one is able to live up to the requirements of the law. Although law points us in the right direction, it provides no power to achieve its demands. It was never meant as a way to merit God's favor. Its role was to reflect the character of God in terms of ethical goals. The Jewish legalists had perverted the divine intention of the law and made it into a way to gain God's favor based on personal merit.

The righteousness that is based on faith is quite different. It does not require valiant exploits such as bringing Christ down from heaven or up from the grave (vv. 6–7). Paul quoted freely from Deut 30:12–13, substituting a phrase from Ps 107:26 ("down to the depths") for "beyond the sea." In pesher style he interpreted the verses in reference to the incarnation and resurrection of Christ. In Deuteronomy, Moses was telling the people that they did not have to climb up to heaven or cross the sea to discover the will of God. Paul applied the passage to the availability of the message of salvation. Hunter writes: "No heroic attempts to storm the citadel of heaven or the kingdom of the dead are needed. Christ the Saviour is here, incarnate and risen."[47] Faith is readily available for those who will simply believe and confess that Jesus is Lord (Deut

---

[46] Sanday and Headlam understand ζήσεται here as "shall obtain life in its deepest sense both here and hereafter" (*Romans,* 286). Some hold that the quotation points not to the hopeless plight of the person striving to fulfill the law but to Christ, who in his sinless life and victorious death fulfilled the demands of the law and gained a righteous status before God (cf. references to Barth's *Church Dogmatics* in Cranfield, *Romans,* 2:521–22, n. 4). Black calls these ideas "curiosities of Barthian eisegesis" (*Romans,* 143, n. 1).

[47] Hunter, *Romans,* 95.

30:14). The message concerning faith is "already within easy reach of each of us" (TLB).[48]

Romans 10:9–10 has long served as one of the most helpful portions of Scripture for pointing out the way of salvation. In an *A-B-B-A* format it lays out both the necessity of believing from the heart and the role of public confession.[49] What must be believed is that "Jesus is Lord." This quintessential affirmation is perhaps the earliest Christian confession of faith (cf. 1 Cor 12:3; Phil 2:11). It proclaims in the simplest possible words that Jesus of Nazareth is in fact God. The Greek word used throughout the LXX for Yahweh (over six thousand times) is here applied to Jesus.[50] The implications of this are staggering. Primarily it means that Jesus' authority is absolute, unlimited, and universal. Those who come to Christ by faith are acknowledging that they have placed themselves entirely and without reserve under his authority to carry out without hesitation whatever he may choose for them to do. There is no such thing as salvation apart from lordship. Although our level of obedience may falter from time to time, that does not imply that we can view our responsibilities as if they did not matter. Those who say that they intend to have a good time on earth and take a back seat in heaven do not realize that there are no "back seats" for those who approach salvation with this attitude.

Outward confession stems from a profound inward conviction. Those who come to Christ must believe in their hearts that Jesus was raised from the dead by God the Father. The resurrection of Jesus Christ is the very center of the Christian faith. Apart from the resurrection Christianity would be little more than a well-intentioned ethical system. It is a

---

[48] Taking τῆς πίστεως as an objective genitive. Some understand the "word of faith" as content of the message rather than the reaction to its proclamation.

[49] E. F. Harrison comments that "'confess' (ὁμολογέω) when used of sin means to say the same thing about it that God says; when used in the creedal sense, as here in v. 9, it means to say the same thing that other believers say regarding their faith" ("Romans," EBC 10, ed. F. E. Gaebelein [Grand Rapids: Zondervan, 1976], 112).

[50] κύριος. Some think the title "Lord" as applied to Jesus originated in a Hellenistic setting (e.g., R. Bultmann, *Theology of the New Testament,* 2 vols. [London: SCM, 1952–55], 1:124). This is unlikely in view of the survival of the Aramaic *Marana* ("Our Lord") *tha* ("come") as directed to the risen Christ in the early days of Palestinian Christianity (cf. 1 Cor 16:22). Some see it as the church's intentional contrast to the acclamation κύριος καῖσαρ, an ascription of deity to the emperor. The evidence supports Cranfield's conclusion that "for Paul, the confession that Jesus is Lord meant the acknowledgment that Jesus shares the name and the nature, the holiness, the authority, power, majesty, and eternity of the one and only true God" (*Romans,* 2:529).

fact that within history God did something that defies all the laws of nature as we know them. He raised Jesus from the dead. It is the reality of this resurrection that lends credence to all that Jesus did and taught throughout his earthly life. It is God's way of authenticating to us that Jesus is the Son of God (cf. 1:4). The truth of the resurrection was at the very center of the apostolic preaching.[51]

When Paul wrote in v. 10 that believing leads to justification and that confession leads to salvation, he was not speaking of two separate processes.[52] Justification and salvation are being used interchangeably in this context.[53] To believe with one's heart means to commit oneself at the deepest level to the truth as revealed and experienced.[54] Confession is giving expression in words to that conviction. Phillips says of the one who believes, "It is stating his belief by his own mouth that confirms his salvation." Those who genuinely accept the truth of Jesus' resurrection and therefore his deity are willing to go public with their conviction.[55] That kind of commitment will never lead to disappointment. Calvin's picturesque comment regarding those who would consider the confession of the mouth as superfluous is that "it is quite nonsensical to insist that there is fire, when there is neither flame nor heat."[56] The prophet Isaiah said, "No one who places his trust in him will have cause for shame" (Isa 28:16).[57] The promise extends to Gentile as well as to Jew.[58] God does not have alternate methods of salvation for groups from diverse ethnic back-

---

[51] R. H. Mounce, *The Essential Nature of New Testament Preaching* (Grand Rapids: Eerdmans, 1960), 78.

[52] A. Nygren comments that when Paul spoke of believing with the heart and confessing with the lips he was not distinguishing between the two but "using a rhythmic parallelism of the sort very common in the Old Testament" (*Commentary on Romans,* trans. C. C. Rasmussen [Philadelphia: Muhlenberg, 1949], 383–84). Fitzmyer adds that "the chiastic balance stresses the different aspects of the one basic act of personal adherence to Christ and its effect" (*Romans,* 592). The order in v. 9 (confess-believe) reflects the order in Deut 30:14, the source of the quotation ("the word is very near you; it is in your mouth and in your heart"), while the order of logic and experience (believe-confess) is followed in v. 10.

[53] Theologically, salvation tends to be a more inclusive concept including sanctification and glorification as well as justification.

[54] The aorist πιστεύσῃς refers to the initial act of placing one's faith in Christ as Lord.

[55] "Christianity is belief plus confession," writes W. Barclay; "it involves witness before men. Not only God, but also our fellow men, must know what side we are on" (*The Letter to the Romans,* rev. ed., DSB [Philadelphia: Westminster, 1978], 139).

[56] Calvin, *Romans and Thessalonians,* 228.

[57] As Paul interpreted, Isaiah's "precious cornerstone" is Christ. Cf. 1 Cor 3:11; 1 Pet 2:4–7.

[58] Bruce comments that the phrase in 3:22 "there is no difference" had a "grim sound" because both Jew and Gentile were under the condemnation of sin, but here in 10:12 the same words have a "joyful sound" because they proclaim to both that his free pardon is for all who will claim it (*Romans,* 193).

grounds. The one Lord is Lord of all. He is rich in blessing (cf. 2 Cor 8:9; Eph 3:8) to all who call upon him.[59] Turning to the prophet Joel, Paul reminded his readers that salvation is for everyone who calls on the name of the Lord (Joel 2:32). Nowhere in Scripture is the universal scope of salvation presented with greater clarity. Although God's redemptive plan was worked out in history through one particular race, it was meant from the beginning for the benefit of all people everywhere.

10:14–15[60]   If everyone who calls upon the Lord will be saved, it is important that everyone have the opportunity to hear. Apart from hearing the message no one can believe. People do not believe in one of whom they have never heard.[61] Therefore it is necessary that a messenger be sent. Someone must come preaching the good news. Stott observes that "the essence of Paul's argument is seen if we put his six verbs in the opposite order: Christ sends heralds; heralds preach; people hear; hearers believe; believers call; and those who call are saved."[62]

The Greek word group used in both v. 14 and v. 15 reflects primarily the activity of preaching.[63] Paul once again drew on Isaiah to emphasize how welcome are those who come bearing the good news of the gospel (v. 15).[64] Although the prophet was speaking of the messengers who brought the news of Israel's imminent release from Babylonian captivity (Isa 52:7), Paul applied the verse to the apostolic bearers of the good news of the gospel. The apostolic writers were not hesitant to apply Old Testament passages to New Testament settings.[65]

---

[59] ἐπικαλέω here refers to the cry of confession that Jesus is Kyrios (*EDNT* 2.29).

[60] Sanday and Headlam suggest that vv. 14–21 are structured as a series of difficulties (four to be exact: vv. 14,16,18,19) to each of which Paul gave a short and decisive answer (*Romans*, 293–94). According to Käsemann the importance of these verses is seen in "the artistic form of the chain-syllogism in which each question retraces part of the previous one. . . . For Paul rhetoric is not a matter of verbal adornment. It is a means of substantive argument" (*Romans*, 293).

[61] Some point out that the genitive οὗ with ἤκουσαν should be understood as "whom" rather than "about whom." Morris comments, "The point is that Christ is present in the preachers; to hear them is to hear him" (*Romans*, 390). While it is true that the risen Christ is actively at work in and through the proclamation of the gospel (cf. Luke 10:16, "He who listens to you listens to me"), it is questionable that that is the point Paul was making here.

[62] Stott, *Romans*, 286.

[63] κηρύσσοντος, κηρύξωσιν. The more common verb for preaching (εὐαγγελίζομαι) emphasizes the quality of the message (R. H. Mounce, "Preaching," in *The Illustrated Bible Dictionary*, 3 vols. [Leicester, Eng.: InterVarsity, 1980], 3.1261).

[64] Fitzmyer takes ὡραῖοι in the sense of "coming at the right time" (cf. BAGD, 896) and translates, "How timely the arrival of those who bring good news." *EDNT* supports the more common understanding of the term as "lovely or pleasant" (3.508).

[65] See the excellent article by E. Ellis, "Quotations in the NT," *ISBE* 4.18–25.

10:16–21   Although the gospel had been universally proclaimed, not all had responded to it. Specifically, not all Israelites had submitted to its claims. As Isaiah lamented, "Lord, who has believed our message to be true?" (Isa 53:1). Very few Israelites had given credence to the good news of salvation by faith.[66] But faith comes from hearing the message (v. 17). As the NEB puts it, "Faith is awakened by the message." Although it is true that faith is our response to the gospel, it is also true that the message itself awakens and makes faith possible. God is at work even in our response to his gracious offer of forgiveness. The message is heard "through the word of Christ," that is, it is Christ himself who speaks when the gospel is proclaimed.[67] All effective preaching is accomplished by God himself. The messenger is at best merely the instrument used by the Holy Spirit as a necessary part of the process. It is God's own voice that confronts the sinner and offers reconciliation. This existential reality is what constitutes the gospel, "the power of God for . . . salvation" (Rom 1:16).

Paul raised two objections on behalf of the unbelieving Israelites. First, in v. 18 he questioned whether or not they had the opportunity to hear.[68] The answer is, "Of course they did." The response is based upon Psalm 19, which affirms that the heavens declare the glory of God to all who are on the earth. Paul applied v. 4 of the psalm to the proclamation of the gospel in his own time.[69] Thus the "voice" and the "words" that have gone out represent the message that awakens faith. In another place Paul said that the gospel "has been proclaimed to every creature under heaven" (Col 1:26; cf. v. 6 as well).[70] The Israelites could not be excused on the basis that they had not heard the message.

The second caveat is that although they had heard the message, they perhaps did not understand it (v. 19). The NEB has, "Can it be that Israel failed to recognize the message?" The answer implied in v. 19 is that if

---

[66] "The 'not all,' by *litotes,* really means 'only very few' (cf. 3:3 and 9:6,27f.)" (Black, *Romans,* 148).

[67] Some, however, take ῥήματος Χριστοῦ as an objective genitive, i.e., "the word about Christ" (cf. Robertson, *WP* 4:390).

[68] μὴ introduces a question that expects a negative answer. But the question itself contains a negative (οὐκ), so the anticipated response is affirmative.

[69] Bruce comments, "The dissemination of the gospel, it is implied, is becoming as worldwide as the light of the heavenly bodies" (*Romans,* 157).

[70] Obviously, we should not take this to mean that the worldwide ministry of preaching the gospel was then complete. Later in Romans we learn that Paul was planning a trip to Spain to continue his ministry (Rom 15:24,28).

unenlightened people outside of the covenant could understand the gospel, then certainly a religiously gifted and highly favored group like the Jews had no grounds for claiming that it was beyond their understanding. Paul drew upon the testimony of Moses in Deuteronomy 32, reminding his readers of God's method of using other nations as instruments in carrying out his divine intention (Deut 32:21).[71] With the spread of the gospel to the Gentiles, it follows that if they could understand the gospel, certainly the Jews could not argue that it was beyond their ability to comprehend. The same idea is strengthened by Isaiah's bold declaration (as he spoke for God) that he was found by those not seeking him, and he manifested himself to those who were not even asking about him (Isa 65:1–2).[72] It is an argument from the greater to the lesser: if the Gentiles, then certainly the Jews. There remained no basis for any Jewish claim that they could not understand the message.

Israel's rejection had nothing to do with any lack of opportunity to hear or ability to understand. It rested solely upon the nation's willful disobedience (v. 21).[73] They insisted on personal merit based on works to gain God's approval. All the time they knew that God's requirement for righteousness is faith. Denney notes that God's outstretched arms were "the symbol of that incessant pleading love which Israel through all its history has consistently despised."[74] And why today do so many people reject the gospel? It is not necessarily because they have not heard or do not understand. Perhaps one reason is that "they find it hard to see, in a man who was hanged, the master-clue to the riddle of the world."[75]

---

[71] Although Luther's comment on v. 19 may be more homiletical than exegetical, it is certainly true that "these are words of divine grace, for their purpose is to glorify God's grace. He saves only sinners, makes wise only the foolish and the weak, enriches only the poor, and makes alive only the dead" (*Commentary on the Epistle to the Romans,* trans. J. T. Mueller [Grand Rapids: Zondervan, 1954], 136).

[72] To underscore the point that the way of faith had always been open to the Gentiles, Paul "cites from both the law and the prophets to show that this was in God's plan" (Morris, *Romans,* 394).

[73] The quotation is from Isa 65:2 (LXX).

[74] Denney, "Romans," 2:675. Although the difference is slight, others understand the outstretched hands more in the sense of welcome than supplication. Calvin writes that "God stretches forth His hands to us exactly as a father stretches forth his arms, ready to receive his son lovingly into his bosom" (*Romans,* 236–37).

[75] Hunter, *Romans,* 98.

3. Some Alleviating Factors (11:1–36)

(1) The Rejection Is Not Total (11:1–10)

[1]I ask then: Did God reject his people? By no means! I am an Israelite myself, a descendant of Abraham, from the tribe of Benjamin. [2]God did not reject his people, whom he foreknew. Don't you know what the Scripture says in the passage about Elijah—how he appealed to God against Israel: [3]"Lord, they have killed your prophets and torn down your altars; I am the only one left, and they are trying to kill me"? [4]And what was God's answer to him? "I have reserved for myself seven thousand who have not bowed the knee to Baal." [5]So too, at the present time there is a remnant chosen by grace. [6]And if by grace, then it is no longer by works; if it were, grace would no longer be grace.

[7]What then? What Israel sought so earnestly it did not obtain, but the elect did. The others were hardened, [8]as it is written:

"God gave them a spirit of stupor,
  eyes so that they could not see
  and ears so that they could not hear,
to this very day."

[9]And David says:

"May their table become a snare and a trap,
  a stumbling block and a retribution for them.
[10]May their eyes be darkened so they cannot see,
  and their backs be bent forever."

11:1–6 Once again Paul posed a rhetorical question. He asked, "God did not reject his people, did he?" The answer is, "By no means!" They had been disobedient and obstinate (10:21), but they had not been repudiated as a nation. After all, Paul himself was an Israelite.[76] He was a descendant of the great patriarch Abraham (2 Cor 11:22) and a member of the tribe of Benjamin (Phil 3:5).[77] If God had rejected the entire nation of Israel, then Paul would not have been able to claim a right standing before God. The truth is that God had not rejected the nation he

---

[76] "Had God cast away His people, then above all He would have cast away the Apostle Paul, who had opposed Him with all his might" (Luther, *Romans,* 139). Cranfield thinks Paul's reference to himself is meant to argue that if God had really cast off Israel as a whole he would never have chosen an Israelite to be his apostle to the Gentiles (Cranfield, *Romans,* 2.544).

[77] Moses referred to Benjamin as "the beloved of the Lord" (Deut 33:12). Morris notes that Benjamin was the only son of Jacob born in Israel, that Jerusalem was situated on land belonging to the tribe of Benjamin, that Benjamin was the only tribe remaining faithful to Judah, and that the first king of Israel came from the tribe of Benjamin (*Romans,* 398–99). Käsemann refers to the tradition that says Benjamin was the first of the tribes to cross through the Red Sea (*Romans,* 299).

chose from the very first.[78] He had not taken unilateral action against those whom he approved from the beginning.[79]

To illustrate and strengthen his point Paul reminded them of the story of Elijah (vv. 2–4).[80] After Elijah's spectacular victory over the prophets of Baal on Mount Carmel, Jezebel's threats sent him fleeing for his life. Hiding in a cave on Mount Horeb, he complained to God against Israel. They had killed the prophets and demolished the altars. "I am the only one left," he complained, "and they are trying to kill me" (1 Kgs 19:10,14). And what was the divine response, asked Paul?[81] God answered, "I have reserved for myself seven thousand men who have not bowed the knee to Baal" (1 Kgs 19:18).[82] Sulking in a cave forty days' and nights' journey away from danger and consumed with self-pity, Elijah learned that he was not a minority of one. He was not the last prophet in the land. If he had known the whole story, he would have realized that God had reserved for himself a significant number of Israelites that had not fallen into the worship of Baal.

So it was in his own time, said Paul. There remained a remnant chosen by grace (v. 5; cf. 9:27). This remnant (Jewish Christians) did not exist because of works they had done but because they had been selected by God on the basis of his own unmerited favor.[83] Grace and works are

---

[78] ἀπωθέω means "to push aside." It conveys the idea of vigorous action. Here it is used figuratively to mean "reject" or "repudiate" (BAGD, 103). The clause as it appears in both v. 1 and v. 2 echoes the wording of Ps 94:14 in the LXX [Ps 93:14].

[79] For προέγνω see commentary at 8:29.

[80] ἐν Ἡλίᾳ means "in the passage about Elijah" (1 Kgs 17:1–2 Kgs 2:18). "The O.T. Scriptures were divided into paragraphs to which were given titles derived from their subject-matter; and these came to be very commonly used in quotations as references" (Sanday and Headlam, *Romans,* 310).

[81] χρηματισμός ("answer") occurs only here in the NT. It refers to a divine oracle (cf. 2 Macc 2:4), an authoritative answer from God.

[82] Since in Semitic thought the number "seven" carries the idea of a completed period (*TDNT* 2.628), some think that the seven thousand in v. 4 is to be taken figuratively of the full number of those chosen by God to be his own. Rengstorf says that "we cannot be sure from the context whether Paul connected with the OT number the thought of the totality of the true Israel which is certainly present in 1 K. 19:18" (*TDNT* 2.629). The Greek text combines the masculine noun βάαλ with the feminine article τῇ. This is regularly explained as representing a stage in the transmission when the word βάαλ was replaced with the feminine word αἰσχύνη ("shame"), thus accounting for the gender of the article. For examples see the LXX of 2 Kgs 21:3; Jer 2:8; 12:16.

[83] Nygren points out that the existence of a remnant in any age depends not upon the character of the people but wholly on God's purpose and election. Thus "'remnant' and 'election' (λεῖμμα and ἐκλογὴν) are interchangeable concepts. A 'remnant' is not just a group of separate individuals, taken out of a people doomed to overthrow; it is itself the chosen people, it is Israel *in nuce*" (*Romans,* 392–93).

mutually exclusive principles. If the remnant had earned their position by their works, then grace would no longer have been grace. As a remnant "chosen by grace" there was absolutely no room for personal merit or meritorious performance. Although the seven thousand in the days of Elijah were certainly worthy of commendation for their faithfulness to Yahweh, in the case of the remnant in Paul's day there was nothing they had done that would ever merit their standing as God's people.

11:7–10 "What are we to infer from all of this?" asked Paul. The answer is that Israel as a nation failed to obtain what it still was searching for.[84] The longing for righteousness based on personal merit is deeply embedded in human nature. It is not that people wish to live exemplary lives because that is the right thing to do but that such conduct is thought to provide the basis for commendation when compared with the achievements of others. When an absolute standard is removed, the goal is more readily achieved. What's more, it allows for the pride of accomplishment. All of this has no place in God's plan for setting people right. What Israel sought and could not obtain had been achieved by the chosen remnant.[85] The rest of Israel had become hardened.[86] Because they refused the way of faith (cf. 9:31–32), they had become insensitive to God's self-revelation and the promptings of his Spirit. Disobedience never leaves a person in the same condition. Obedience draws the believer into an increasingly intimate relationship with the Lord, but disobedience separates and hardens. The tragic aspect of hardening is that disobedient people are increasingly unable to grasp the serious nature of their spiritual apostasy.

The hardening of Israel is clearly seen in various passages in the Old Testament. In Deut 29:4 and Isa 29:10 we learn that God brought upon them a "numbness of spirit" (NEB) so that their eyes could not see and their ears could not hear (Rom 11:8). Their failure to trust resulted in a "state of spiritual insensitivity" (Goodspeed).[87] What's more, that torpor

---

[84] ἐπιζητεῖ is present tense and indicates a continuing activity.

[85] Note the abstract ἡ ἐκλογή ("the elect") rather than the more concrete οἱ ἐκλεκτοί ("those whom God chose"). While the term would include Gentile believers as well as Jewish converts, Paul undoubtedly had the latter group primarily in mind here. Note that "the others" (οἱ λοιποί, i.e., the rest [of the Jews]) were hardened.

[86] The verb πωρόω ("to make dull or obtuse") occurs five times in the NT and always in a figurative sense (*EDNT* 3.202). Black notes that the passive ἐπωρώθησαν should not be stressed "as if Paul was avoiding any suggestion that God did the 'hardening'; indeed, the opposite is true, and the passive here could be an idiomatic Hebraic locution to avoid the use of the divine name (*Romans,* 151).

[87] κατάνυξις ("stupor") is a late and rare word that comes from a verb meaning "to prick." Robertson says, "The torpor seems the result of too much sensation, dulled by incitement into apathy" (*WP* 4.393).

remains with them until the present time. Spiritual hardening is a terminal disorder for which, in its advanced stages, there is no remedy. In the same way, David (in Ps 69:22–23) spoke of their feasts becoming snares and traps.[88] Their celebrations proved to be hindrances and a retribution "rebounding as a boomerang upon them" (Amplified). Their eyes were dimmed so they could no longer see, and their backs were continually bent under their burden (v. 10).

(2) The Rejection Is Not Final (11:11–24)

[11]**Again I ask: Did they stumble so as to fall beyond recovery? Not at all! Rather, because of their transgression, salvation has come to the Gentiles to make Israel envious.** [12]**But if their transgression means riches for the world, and their loss means riches for the Gentiles, how much greater riches will their fullness bring!**

[13]**I am talking to you Gentiles. Inasmuch as I am the apostle to the Gentiles, I make much of my ministry** [14]**in the hope that I may somehow arouse my own people to envy and save some of them.** [15]**For if their rejection is the reconciliation of the world, what will their acceptance be but life from the dead?** [16]**If the part of the dough offered as firstfruits is holy, then the whole batch is holy; if the root is holy, so are the branches.**

[17]**If some of the branches have been broken off, and you, though a wild olive shoot, have been grafted in among the others and now share in the nourishing sap from the olive root,** [18]**do not boast over those branches. If you do, consider this: You do not support the root, but the root supports you.** [19]**You will say then, "Branches were broken off so that I could be grafted in."** [20]**Granted. But they were broken off because of unbelief, and you stand by faith. Do not be arrogant, but be afraid.** [21]**For if God did not spare the natural branches, he will not spare you either.**

[22]**Consider therefore the kindness and sternness of God: sternness to those who fell, but kindness to you, provided that you continue in his kindness. Otherwise, you also will be cut off.** [23]**And if they do not persist in unbelief, they will be grafted in, for God is able to graft them in again.** [24]**After all, if you were cut out of an olive tree that is wild by nature, and contrary to nature were grafted into a cultivated olive tree, how much more readily will these, the natural branches, be grafted into their own olive tree!**

11:11–12 The next question to be raised is whether or not Israel's failure to believe had led to their absolute ruin.[89] Had they stumbled

---

[88] David was speaking of his enemies, but Paul freely adapted the words to faithless Israel.
[89] This understands the ἵνα clause in the sense of result rather than purpose.

irretrievably? Were they beyond recovery?[90] Once again the answer is
"Not at all!"[91] In fact, because of their rejection of the gospel salvation
had gone out to the Gentiles (e.g., Acts 14:36). This in turn would make
Israel envious and incite them to do what the Gentiles had done.[92] It is
true that Israel had stumbled, but the God who "in all things . . . works
for the good" (8:28) decreed that the result of their transgression would
ultimately provide the incentive for their return.[93] If Israel's false step
had brought enrichment to the world and their defeat had proved to be
such a benefit for the Gentiles, just think how great would be the result
of their restoration. "Riches for the world" speaks of the abundant benefits that accompany adoption into the family of God. Israel's "loss"
refers to all they had sacrificed by their obstinate refusal to accept God's
way of faith.[94] Israel's "fullness" refers to the time of their full restoration (cf. vv. 25–26). The argument in v. 12 is from the lesser to the
greater, if A, how much more B (cf. Rom 5:9).

11:13–16   Although the condition of Israel has been the major
theme since the beginning of chap. 9, Paul clearly was writing primarily
to Gentile believers. Throughout the section he spoke of his Jewish kinsmen in the third person (e.g., 9:4–5,32; 10:1–3,18; 11:1,7). In 11:13 he
reminded his Gentile readers that it was to them[95] that he was talking,
and he addressed them in the second person (11:13,17–22,24–25,28,30).
Contrary to much that is written, the major theme of chaps. 9–11 is less
the fate of Israel than a warning to the Gentiles not to presume on their
fortunate position as a wild branch that had been grafted into a historic

---

[90] BAGD cites Rom 11:11 under πίπτω in the sense of *"fall* in the relig. or moral sense, *be
completely ruined"* (p. 660). Cranfield says that here it denotes "that falling which means irre-
versible ruin as contrasted with πταίειν, which denotes a stumbling from which it is possible
to recover" (*Romans,* 2:555).

[91] γένοιτο is the aorist optative of γίνομαι, and the expression μὴ γένοιτο was consistently translated in the AV as "God forbid!" Fourteen of the fifteen times it occurs in the NT it
is used by Paul, and eleven of those occurrences are in Romans (the other three being in Galatians). The expression is appropriate to the rhetorical style in which Romans was written.

[92] Nygren writes that the conversion of the Gentiles stands as a constant reminder that the
messianic hope of Israel is being realized by the Gentiles. The very name "Christian" rests on
the OT name "Messiah." Gentile believers have become "the messianic congregation." For
reasons such as these the Jews would be aroused to envy (*Romans,* 395–96).

[93] Paul used παράπτωμα as a specific sinful act. ἁμαρτία refers to sin as a controlling
power (*EDNT* 3.33). In this case it was Israel's rejection of the gospel.

[94] ἥττημα is a rare word, found only in biblical Greek. Elsewhere in Scripture it occurs in
Isa 31:8 (LXX) and 1 Cor 6:7. Cranfield says the habit of understanding ἥττημα in the sense
of "diminution or fewness" "should surely be abandoned at last" (*Romans,* 2:557).

[95] Standing first in the sentence, ὑμῖν is emphatic.

tree of Jewish origin.[96]

In writing to the Gentiles, Paul laid great stress on his office as "the apostle to the Gentiles."[97] His hope was that in this way he might stir his countrymen to envy with the result that "some of them" might be saved (v. 14).[98] This rather minimal expectation seems to run counter to the optimism of v. 12 with its confidence in the enrichment attendant upon the reinstatement of Israel. There is no verb, however, in the final clause of v. 12 (cf. v. 15). It would not be off the mark to read "how much greater riches would their fullness bring" rather than "will their fullness bring." This would be in keeping with v. 3, which says the Jews would be grafted back into the tree "if they do not persist in unbelief."

Verse 15 parallels v. 12. If the rejection of Israel led to reconciliation for the world, what would their acceptance mean but "life from the dead."[99] The note on this verse in the NIVSB suggests three possible interpretations of this phrase: (1) "an unprecedented spiritual awakening in the world," (2) "the consummation of redemption at the resurrection of the dead," and (3) "a figurative expression describing the conversion of the Jews."[100] Each position has its advocates, but it would appear that what Paul was speaking of here was a great spiritual awakening of Israel to take place at the end of human history. Fitzmyer says that the acceptance of the gospel by the Jewish people "will mean for them the passage from a status of death to life."[101] If we follow the parallelism between vv. 12 and 15, then "life from the dead" says essentially the same thing as "their fullness," that is, "the full quota of Jews" (Williams). For Israel to turn from their unbelief and embrace the gospel of

---

[96] Although his interpretation is subjective, Stuhlmacher may be right in holding that Paul "sees himself up against a group of Gentile Christians who look down upon Israel in its hardened state and maintain that God has turned himself away from Israel once and for all, and that the salvation of the Gentiles through the gospel is the crown of all his works" (*Romans*, 168).

[97] Since there is no definite article before ἀπόστολος, it would be better to read "an apostle to the Gentiles" (cf. Gal 2:7; 1 Tim 2:7). Paul did not consider himself the only one to take the gospel to the Gentiles.

[98] Harrison comments that the word "some" indicates that Paul did not expect that through his own efforts the nation would turn to Christ. The promise "all Israel will be saved" will be fulfilled in "the indefinite future" ("Romans," 120).

[99] The Amplified NT has "rejection and exclusion from the benefits of salvation." Fitzmyer (*Romans*, 612) takes ἀποβολὴ αὐτῶν as a subjective genitive (the Jew's rejection of the gospel) rather than as an objective genitive (God's rejection of them, even though temporary).

[100] NIVSB, 1723.

[101] Fitzmyer, *Romans*, 613. Stott understands "life from the dead" as an unimaginable enrichment of the world that results from Israel's acceptance and fullness (*Romans*, 298–99).

salvation by faith would be well described as a "resurrection."

Numbers 15:17–21 describes an offering made from the first grain harvested and ground. The cake presented to the Lord consecrated the rest of the batch. Paul wrote that if the dough offered as firstfruits was holy, then the entire batch was holy. In this metaphor the "dough" represents the Jewish believers who had accepted Christ (the remnant of v. 5), and the "whole batch" would be those who would come to believe. The metaphor changes to a tree with its branches. If the root is holy, so are the branches. In this case the "root" represents the patriarchs (esp. Abraham); and the "branches," the nation that follows. The point is that if the patriarchs were holy (and they were), so also were the Jewish people (in the sense that the positive effects of the patriarchs reached to them (cf. 1 Cor 7:14). God's rejection of the Jewish nation was neither complete (Rom 11:1–10) nor final (11:11–24).

11:17–21 In vv. 17–24 Paul used the figure of grafting olive trees to illustrate how the Gentiles came to share the spiritual blessings of Israel, to warn them that the arrogance of privilege would lead to their being cut off, and to remind them of God's ability to graft in the natural branches once again should they not persist in unbelief.[102] The normal process of grafting called for cultivated shoots to be joined to the branches of a wild olive tree that had been cut back. The exposed ends were smeared with clay and bound with cloth or date straw.[103] That Paul reversed the process in order to illustrate the engrafting of the Gentiles (the "wild olive shoot") into historic Israel ("the olive root") is simply the literary freedom allowed to any writer. It does not betray some critical lack of horticultural knowledge.[104] In fact, he later noted that grafting of the wild shoots into the cultivated tree was contrary to nature (11:24).[105]

Gentile believers are described as a wild olive shoot that had been grafted into a cultivated olive tree, some of whose branches had been

---

[102] In Jer 11:16 Israel is called "a thriving olive tree" (cf. Hos 14:6).

[103] J. A. Patch, "Graft," *ISBE*, rev., 2.553.

[104] Dodd calls Paul's reference to grafting a wild olive shoot to a cultivated olive tree "a truly remarkable horticultural experiment!" (*Romans*, 180). Julicher says, "Paul is a child of the city; but Jesus is a countryman." But Columella, a contemporary of Paul, spoke of a mode of grafting in which "a green slip taken from a wild olive tree" was placed tightly into a hole made in an old olive tree (cited by Fitzmyer, *Romans*, 614–15). See also A. G. Baxter and J. A. Ziesler, "Paul and Arboriculture: Romans 11.17–24," *JSNT* 24 (1985): 25–32. Sanday and Headlam comment that "the whole strength of St. Paul's argument depends upon the process being an unnatural one" (*Romans*, 328).

[105] Cranfield says that παρὰ φύσιν ("contrary to nature") in v. 24 more likely means "the grafting of a branch onto a tree to which it does not belong by nature which is being characterized as contrary to nature" (*Romans*, 2:571–72).

broken off. The NIV's "among the others" (v. 17) inadvertently substantiates Paul's earlier assertion that Israel's rejection was neither complete nor final.[106] Now the Gentiles "share in the nourishing sap from the olive root."[107] The root, which supplied the rich and nourishing life to the cultivated olive tree, represented historic Israel, specifically the patriarchs through whom God brought the nation into existence. The TCNT describes the root as "the source of the richness of the cultivated olive." Paul admonished his Gentile readers not to view themselves as somehow superior to the former branches. After all, they owed their spiritual existence to Israel; it was not the other way around. They did not support the root; the root supported them. How subtle yet powerful is the human tendency to presume that "accomplishments" in the realm of the Spirit are due to one's own persistence and acumen!

Believing Gentiles were correct in their understanding that unbelieving Jews were broken off so they could be grafted in. Paul said: "That is true. But don't forget that they were broken off because of unbelief and your permanence depends upon your continuing faith."[108] Weymouth translates, "You stand only through your faith." Therefore Gentile believers were no longer to preoccupy themselves with lofty ideas of their favored position but to be on guard. After all, if God did not spare the natural branches (Israel), what possible chance was there that he would spare branches grafted in contrary to nature (the Gentiles)?[109]

11:22–24 It would be well for the Gentile believers to consider that God is both kind and stern. Any adequate doctrine of God must include both his kindness and his sternness.[110] The liberal mind chooses to emphasize the kindness of God with less than satisfactory attention to

---

[106] For ἐνεκεντρίσθης ἐν αὐτοῖς in v. 17 the RSV has "grafted in their place."

[107] The second genitive in τῆς ῥίζης τῆς πιότητος is either adjectival ("the rich root") or appositional ("the root, that is, its fatness [its nourishing qualities]").

[108] ἕστηκας is perfect active of ἵστημι, which, when used intransitively, may carry the meaning "to stand firm."

[109] μή πως ("perhaps") is placed in square brackets by the UBS committee to show that the words are disputed. If omitted, as in the NIV, the warning is more severe. Dunn comments, "A doctrine of 'perseverance of the saints' which does not include the lessons of salvation-history has lost its biblical perspective" (*Romans*, 2:664). Rhys thinks that although Paul did not teach that "man is the author of his own salvation," the stress on faith in vv. 21–24 "is a complete refutation of the claim that once saved means always saved" (*Romans*, 144). A review of the commentaries on these verses reveals how powerful is the influence of theology on exegesis. Fortunately, no major doctrine stands or falls only upon a single verse of Scripture.

[110] See note on Rom 11:22 in NIVSB, 1723. The two qualities are found together in the OT (e.g., Ps 125:4–5). Morris writes of "a goodness which is not so much austere as kind, a kindness that is not indifferent to moral values" (*Romans*, 416).

his sternness. The overly serious concentrate only on God's sternness. In the first case God comes across as a well-intentioned but doting father. In the latter case he appears as a merciless despot. Goodness does not rule out "strict justice" (Phillips), and sternness does not rule out graciousness. The two qualities must be maintained in balance.[111] God's sternness is seen in his dealings with faithless Israel. He cut them off. God's kindness is seen in the inclusion into his family of those who at one time were "foreigners to the covenants of the promise, without hope and without God in the world" (Eph 2:12). His kindness to Gentile believers is, of course, contingent upon their continuing to be responsive to that kindness.[112] A failure in this responsibility will lead to their being cut off.[113] Goodspeed translates, "Otherwise you in your turn will be pruned away." There is no security for those who by their lives show that the grafting process of faith was apparent rather than real.

Paul said of Israel that if they did not persist in unbelief they would be grafted back into their own olive tree (v. 23). God certainly had the power to graft them in again (Matt 19:26 and parallels). The only thing that stood in Israel's way was their continuance in unbelief. God would never overpower their unwillingness to believe and force them back into his family. Verse 24 may be taken as a statement (RSV), a question (AV), or an exclamation (NIV). In any case, the logic is crystal clear. If God can take a wild olive shoot and graft it into a cultivated olive tree (as he did with the Gentiles), how much easier it would be to graft the natural branches (Israel) back into their parent tree. A warning against presumption runs throughout this section. A caution Paul left with the Corinthians is apropos, "If you think you are standing firm, be careful that you don't fall!" (1 Cor 10:12).

---

[111] Hunter writes, "Neglect his SEVERITY, and we make of the Supreme Being a weak-kneed Benevolence. Ignore his GOODNESS, and we turn the gracious Father of Christ into a ruthless Omnipotence" (*Romans*, 103).

[112] Dunn maintains that "the triple χρηστότης ["kindness"] strengthens the implication that this is the dominant divine characteristic for Paul" (*Romans*, 2:665). For the human responsibility in maintaining a vital relationship with God see such verses as 1 Cor 15:2; Col 1:23; Heb 3:6,14. Fitzmyer comments, "God's election, though gratuitous, is conditioned by Christians' responsible fulfillment of obligations to him" (*Romans*, 616).

[113] Calvin's answer to the theological awkwardness at this point (i.e., possibility of being cut off) will not satisfy those who are more Wesleyan in their soteriology. He writes that "although in the first place this cannot happen to the elect, they have need of such warning, in order to subdue the pride of the flesh" (*Romans*, 253).

(3) The Salvation of All Israel (11:25–36)

[25]I do not want you to be ignorant of this mystery, brothers, so that you may not be conceited: Israel has experienced a hardening in part until the full number of the Gentiles has come in. [26]And so all Israel will be saved, as it is written:

"The deliverer will come from Zion;
   he will turn godlessness away from Jacob.
[27]And this is my covenant with them
   when I take away their sins."

[28]As far as the gospel is concerned, they are enemies on your account; but as far as election is concerned, they are loved on account of the patriarchs, [29]for God's gifts and his call are irrevocable. [30]Just as you who were at one time disobedient to God have now received mercy as a result of their disobedience, [31]so they too have now become disobedient in order that they too may now receive mercy as a result of God's mercy to you. [32]For God has bound all men over to disobedience so that he may have mercy on them all.

[33]Oh, the depth of the riches of the wisdom and knowledge of God!
   How unsearchable his judgments,
      and his paths beyond tracing out!
[34]"Who has known the mind of the Lord?
   Or who has been his counselor?"
[35]"Who has ever given to God,
   that God should repay him?"
[36]For from him and through him and to him are all things.
   To him be the glory forever! Amen.

11:25–27 It is important that we understand this paragraph in the larger context of what Paul had been saying about Israel as a nation. All that he had taught about the unfortunate condition of faithless Israel, the grafting in of believing Gentiles and how this would arouse his countrymen to envy and lead them to salvation, is summarized in v. 26 with the statement, "And so all Israel will be saved." Paul did not want his Gentile brethren to be uninformed about this "mystery." He used the statement "I do not want you to be ignorant" when he had something to say that was especially important (cf. Rom 1:13; 1 Cor 10:1; 12:1; 2 Cor 1:8; 1 Thess 4:13). It is always accompanied by the vocative *adelphoi*, "brothers."

A great deal has been written about the word "mystery," whose Greek equivalent occurs in one setting only in the Synoptics (Mark 4:11 and parallels), not at all in John's Gospel, but some twenty times in Paul's writings. In the mystery religions the term was used of secret information that was revealed only to the devotees who underwent initiation into the cult. Paul used the word in reference to something that was formerly hidden but now is revealed by God so that all may understand.[114] In the present context the mystery referred to "God's saving activity toward Israel."[115] God had not gone back on his promises made to his ancient people. There was a future for Israel if it did not persist in unbelief (v. 23). Paul wanted the Gentiles to understand this so they would not become conceited and think too highly of themselves.[116] The hardening that Israel had experienced was limited in scope and in time.[117] It was "in part" in that some (the believing remnant) had not become callous toward God. It was also "until" the full number of Gentile believers had come to Christ—that is, the hardening was temporary (cf. Luke 21:24).[118]

"And so all Israel will be saved." It was only in this way that Israel as a whole would be restored to favor with God.[119] Obviously this was not some unilateral action of God on behalf of his people. Israel's salvation would be on the same basis as anyone else's, that is, by responding in faith to the forgiveness made possible by the death and resurrection of Jesus Christ. Earlier commentators tended to take "all Israel" to mean "spiritual Israel," that is, all believers, Jew and Gentile alike. But throughout this entire section Paul had been comparing Gentile and Jew

---

[114] G. Bornkamm defines μυστήριον as "the eternal counsel of God which is hidden from the world but eschatologically fulfilled in the cross of the Lord of glory and which carries with it the glorification of believers" (*TDNT* abr., 617). H. C. G. Moule speaks of "this mystery" as "this fact in God's purposes, impossible to be known without revelation, but luminous when revealed" (*The Epistle to the Romans* [London: Pickering & Inglis, n.d.], 307). See Dan 2:18–19,27–30 for the concept of "mystery" in the OT.

[115] H. Kramer, *EDNT*, 2.448. Kramer goes on to note that "the traditional apocalyptic expectation of the restoration of Israel is altered in that the partial hardening of Israel creates room for the conversion of the Gentiles."

[116] Cf. Prov 3:7, "Do not be wise in your own eyes; fear the LORD and shun evil."

[117] πώρωσις belongs to a word group "used medically for the 'hardening' or 'thickening' of the bone" (*TDNT* abr., 817). Barclay says that it means *callus* and writes that "when a callus grows on any part of the body that part loses feeling. It becomes insensitive" (Barclay, *Romans,* 146). Robertson understands the term in context as "obtuseness of intellectual discernment, mental dulness" (*WP* 4:398).

[118] The order of God's redemptive activity in history is reversed in the order of its proclamation: it is to the Gentile "first" and then to Israel.

[119] Harrison says "all Israel" in this context means "the nation Israel as a whole, in contrast to the present situation when only a remnant has trusted Christ for salvation" (*Romans,*123).

as separate ethnic groups. It would have been highly unlikely for him to have blurred this crucial distinction when it came time for a summarizing conclusion.[120]

Paul found indication of this final salvation of Israel in the words of the prophets.[121] Isaiah promised that a Redeemer would come to those in Zion who repented of their sins (Isa 59:20), and Paul applied the prophecy to the coming of the Messiah.[122] When he came, he would banish ungodliness from Jacob. This was the covenant he made with the descendants of Israel when he took away their sin (Isa 59:21).[123] Jeremiah described a new covenant in which the law of God would be written on the heart, controlling life from within. It stands in contrast to the old covenant, which was inscribed on stone and legislated from without (Jer 31:33–34). Paul was saying that beyond the current period of Israel's unbelief there would come a time when believing Jews would turn to Christ in faith.[124] They would join the faithful remnant and believing Gentiles to complete the family of God, which stretches throughout all of redemptive history. From the standpoint of the twentieth century, that time is yet future.

11:28–32 In terms of the spread of the gospel, Israel's failure to respond made them an enemy of God.[125] That worked for the advantage of the Gentile. Although unbelieving Jews were temporarily at odds with their God, they were, after all, his elect people and were loved by him "on account of the patriarchs." In accordance with his eternal plan, God continues to welcome them for the sake of their ancestors. Paul was not supporting the idea that merit is passed on from the patriarchs to their

---

[120] Cranfield lists four interpretations of πᾶς Ἰσραὴλ and favors as the most likely "the nation Israel as a whole, but not necessarily including every individual member" (*Romans 9–16*, 576–77).

[121] Sanday and Headlam understand σωθήσεται as an event within the course of history (*Romans*, 336), but Cranfield says that it "seems more probable that Paul was thinking of a restoration of the nation of Israel as a whole to God at the end, an eschatological event in the strict sense (*Romans*, 2:577).

[122] The reference is to the eschatological coming of the Messiah, the parousia.

[123] It is sobering for the Gentiles to realize that "it is primarily this salvation of all Israel from the hardening of unbelief that is the goal of salvation history, and not the fact that the Gentiles are already obtaining salvation" (Stuhlmacher, *Romans*, 73).

[124] Note that this passage says nothing of the reestablishment of the modern nation of Israel. What is envisioned is a dramatic fulfillment of God's ancient promise to his people Israel that will take place at or immediately following the second coming of Christ.

[125] Although Israel was hostile to God, ἐχθροὶ should here be taken passively to indicate that they were the object of divine hostility.

descendants. But they were the ones who received his call (Gen 12:1–2; Deut 7:6–7), and it was to them that he first gave his gifts. And God's gifts and call are irrevocable (cf. 1 Sam 15:29; Isa 31:2).[126] He does not change his mind regarding the nation he called and sustained with gracious acts of provision and protection.[127]

Verses 30–31 compare Gentile and Jew in terms of their disobedience and the mercy that follows.[128] The Gentile believers were at one time in a state of rebellion, but now they had received mercy as a result of Israel's disobedience. In the same way, Israel's present disobedience opened the possibility of their receiving mercy as a result of God's present mercy to the Gentiles. Mercy was extended to the Gentiles because of Israel's disobedience. Mercy would be extended to Israel because of the mercy shown to the Gentiles. The theological conclusion is that God has "locked up all in the prison of disobedience" (Montgomery).[129] Now he is able to show mercy to all alike.[130] Since "there is no difference, for all have sinned and fall short of the glory of God" (3:22b–23), no one can lay claim on the mercy of God. It is a free gift for all who believe regardless of ethnic background or ethical performance.[131]

11:33–36 God's providence at work in his redemptive relationship with all humans brought forth from Paul a doxology of praise and adoration. This doxology, thought by many to have been written by Paul himself, provides an appropriate finale for the theological portion of Romans and an effective transition to the more instructional nature of the chapters that follow.[132] Its power is felt more in hearing it read and reflecting

---

[126] The primary meaning of ἀμεταμέλητος is "not to be regretted." The implication is that "God's gifts and call are 'not things ever to be regretted by God'" (Black, *Romans,* 162). Paul placed ἀμεταμέλητα at the beginning of the sentence for emphasis.

[127] K. Berger says that χαρίσματα in Rom 11:29 refers to "the irrevocable gifts associated with Israel's election (i.e., the covenantal provisions spoken of in 9:4)" (*EDNT* 3.461).

[128] Dunn calls these two verses "the most contrived or carefully constructed formulation which Paul ever produced in such a tight epigrammatic form, with so many balancing elements" (*Romans,* 2:687).

[129] συγκλείω taken figuratively means "to confine, imprison" (cf. Gal 3:22–23).

[130] Bruce comments that "there is an unmistakable universalism in Paul's language here, even if it be . . . a representative rather than an individual universalism," which is then defined by J. Munck as "a representative acceptance of the Gospel by the various nations" (Bruce, *Romans,* 210).

[131] Best calls v. 32 "the conclusion to the whole argument: God treats all men in the same way" (*Romans,* 133).

[132] Stott reminds us that "there can be no doxology without theology" and that "there should be no theology without doxology." He cites Bishop Moule as saying we must "beware equally of an undevotional theology and an untheological devotion" (*Romans,* 311–12).

upon its truth than in comments that must be made regarding its specific meaning at various points. The commentator's role, however, is to clarify the text and make observations that may expand the reader's grasp of the text. With that caveat we proceed.

How fathomless is the depth of the wisdom and knowledge of God.[133] Who but God could have conceived a plan that would turn disobedience into an occasion for mercy and in the process reach out universally to all who would believe? How inscrutable are his judgments.[134] His decisions are beyond human ken. How unsearchable are his ways.[135] His methods are mysterious and beyond our ability to grasp. Phillips translates, "How could man ever understand his reasons for action, or explain his methods of working?" As God said through the prophet Isaiah, "As the heavens are higher than the earth, so are my ways higher than your ways and my thoughts than your thoughts" (Isa 55:9). No one grasps the mind of God or could ever serve as his counselor (cf. Isa 40:13–14).[136] No one has ever advanced anything to him so as to deserve payment in return. God is debtor to no one. It is God who has set everything in motion by his creative word. He is the source, the agent, and the goal of all that is. All things find their origin in him. Through him everything that exists is sustained and directed. All things exist for his glory.[137] Therefore to him be praise and glory forever! Amen.

---

[133] Cranfield suggests that σοφία may mean "the wisdom which informs God's purposes and His accomplishment of them" and γνῶσις "God's electing love and the loving concern and care which it involves" (*Romans,* 9–16, 589–90). Denney, however, remarks that the distinction between God's σοφία and γνῶσις "is to be felt rather than defined" ("Romans," 686).

[134] Käsemann notes that "the righteousness of God and not, as commonly assumed, his love, is the central concept in Paul's theology" (*Romans,* 320).

[135] Newman and Nida comment that "the first of these terms describes something that cannot be found by searching for it, while the other suggests footprints that cannot be tracked down" (*Handbook on Paul's Letter to the Romans,* 230).

[136] Barrett says this quotation "emphasizes the profundity and inscrutability of God's counsels" (*Romans,* 228).

[137] Many commentators see the influence of Hellenistic thought in these verses. O'Neill, e.g., believes that "the doxology contained in 11:33–36 was taken over from Hellenistic Judaism" (*Romans,* 190). Verse 32 is often compared with a passage by the Roman emperor Marcus Aurelius: "From thee, in thee, to thee are all things" (*Meditations,* 4.23). Barth raises the question, Why, if Paul simply borrowed a formula, was his use of it "so much more original than in the source from which he borrowed it?" (*Romans,* 423).

VI. HOW RIGHTEOUSNESS MANIFESTS ITSELF (12:1–15:13)

VI. HOW RIGHTEOUSNESS MANIFESTS ITSELF (12:1–15:13)

1. Among Believers (12:1–21)

[1]Therefore, I urge you, brothers, in view of God's mercy, to offer your bodies as living sacrifices, holy and pleasing to God—this is your spiritual act of worship. [2]Do not conform any longer to the pattern of this world, but be transformed by the renewing of your mind. Then you will be able to test and approve what God's will is—his good, pleasing and perfect will.

[3]For by the grace given me I say to every one of you: Do not think of yourself more highly than you ought, but rather think of yourself with sober judgment, in accordance with the measure of faith God has given you. [4]Just as each of us has one body with many members, and these members do not all have the same function, [5]so in Christ we who are many form one body, and each member belongs to all the others. [6]We have different gifts, according to the grace given us. If a man's gift is prophesying, let him use it in proportion to his faith. [7]If it is serving, let him serve; if it is teaching, let him teach; [8]if it is encouraging, let him encourage; if it is contributing to the needs of others, let him give generously; if it is leadership, let him govern diligently; if it is showing mercy, let him do it cheerfully.

[9]Love must be sincere. Hate what is evil; cling to what is good. [10]Be devoted to one another in brotherly love. Honor one another above yourselves. [11]Never be lacking in zeal, but keep your spiritual fervor, serving the Lord. [12]Be joyful in hope, patient in affliction, faithful in prayer. [13]Share with God's people who are in need. Practice hospitality.

[14]Bless those who persecute you; bless and do not curse. [15]Rejoice with those who rejoice; mourn with those who mourn. [16]Live in harmony with one another. Do not be proud, but be willing to associate with people of low position. Do not be conceited.

[17]Do not repay anyone evil for evil. Be careful to do what is right in the

eyes of everybody. **¹⁸If it is possible, as far as it depends on you, live at peace with everyone. ¹⁹Do not take revenge, my friends, but leave room for God's wrath, for it is written: "It is mine to avenge; I will repay," says the Lord. ²⁰On the contrary:**

> **"If your enemy is hungry, feed him;**
> **if he is thirsty, give him something to drink.**
> **In doing this, you will heap burning coals on his head."**

²¹Do not be overcome by evil, but overcome evil with good.

12:1–2 The "therefore" in v. 1 refers back not simply to the previous argument about God's mercy in bringing salvation to Jew and Gentile but to everything that Paul had been teaching from the beginning of the epistle. It marks the transition from the theology of God's redemptive act in Christ Jesus to the ethical expectations that flow logically from that theological base.[1] We come now to what is usually called the "practical" section of Romans.

The practical, however, must of necessity rest upon a solid theological foundation. Otherwise it is little more than advice about how to get along in a religious community. If God had not done what he did for us, there would be no compelling reason why we should now do what he says. The dynamic of God's ethical instruction arises from its logical and necessary relationship to who he is and what he has done on our behalf. Many of the living religions have an ethical code that uplifts and inspires. Only the Christian faith, rooted as it is in a supernatural act that took place in history (the incarnation, life, death, and resurrection of Jesus Christ), has the ultimate moral authority as well as the effective power to transform human life according to the divine intention. So Christian ethics are practical specifically because they do not stand alone but emerge as unavoidable implications of an established theological base. Theology in isolation promotes a barren intellectualism. Ethics apart from a theological base is impotent to achieve its goals.

In view of the many mercies of God, Paul exhorted[2] his readers to

---

[1] J. Mosier holds that chaps. 12–15 are an exhortation directed at Christian believers in Rome stressing the importance of unity in dealing with three critical problems facing the Roman churches in A.D. 57: civil disobedience, the law, and the conflict between meat eaters and vegetarians. Christians there, both Gentile and Jewish, needed a change of heart so that Paul would have a cooperative base for the extension of the Gentile mission ("Rethinking Romans 12–15," *NTS* 36 [1990]: 571–82).

[2] παρακαλέω, BAGD, 617.

offer their bodies as living sacrifices (cf. 6:13; 1 Pet 2:5).[3] C. K. Barrett comments that "'the mercies of God' forms a not inadequate summary of what is contained in chs. i–xi, and especially in chs. ix–xi" and that the proper response "is not to speculate upon the eternal decrees, or one's own place in the scheme of salvation, but to be obedient."[4] The first word of 12:1 is the verb *parakalō*, "I urge," which has a fairly wide range of meanings including "to call to one's side," "to exhort," "to implore," "to encourage." C. E. B. Cranfield says that it is a technical term for Christian exhortation, which he defines as "the earnest appeal, based on the gospel, to those who are already believers to live consistently with the gospel they have received."[5] The metaphor in the verse has as its setting the sacrificial system of the Old Testament.[6] Believers are exhorted to "make a decisive dedication" (Berkeley) of themselves as worshipers stepping forward to place their offerings on the altar. Holiness of life rarely progresses apart from deliberative acts of the will. While sanctification is gradual in the sense that it continues throughout life, each advance depends upon a decision of the will. That the sacrifice is "living" reflects the voluntary nature of the act. F. F. Bruce comments that "the sacrifices of the new order do not consist in taking the lives of others, like the ancient animal sacrifices, but in giving one's own."[7] Such sacrifices are "holy and pleasing to God." They are worthy of his acceptance. The possibility of bringing pleasure to God provides a powerful motivation for complete surrender of self.

Paul said that the offering of one's body as a living sacrifice is a "spiritual act of worship." This expression has been variously translated as "spiritual service, reasonable worship, rational service," and so on.[8] Per-

---

[3] J. D. G. Dunn comments that the σῶμα "denotes not just the person, but the person in his corporeality, in his concrete relationships within this world" (*Romans,* 2 vols., WBC [Dallas: Word, 1988], 2:709).

[4] C. K. Barrett, *A Commentary on the Epistle to the Romans,* HNTC [New York: Harpers, 1957], 230–31). E. F. Harrison says the NIV's "mercy" (sing.) is justified on the basis that οἰκτιρμῶν (pl.) reflects the Hebrew רחמים, an intensive plural meaning "great mercy" ("Romans," EBC 10, ed. F. E. Gaebelein [Grand Rapids: Zondervan, 1976], 127).

[5] C. E. B. Cranfield, *The Epistle to the Romans,* ICC, 2 vols. (Edinburgh: T & T Clark, 1975), 2:597.

[6] παρίστημι ("to present") is a technical term in the language of sacrifice (BAGD, 628).

[7] F. F. Bruce, *The Letter of Paul to the Romans,* 2d ed., TNTC (Grand Rapids: Eerdmans, 1985), 213.

[8] Bartsch says that all possibilities are exhausted in translating λογικός as "spiritual, rational, appropriate," or "reasonable" (*EDNT* 2.355). For extended discussions on the meaning of λογικός in Greek philosophy consult the more technical commentaries.

haps the best paraphrase is that of Knox, "This is the worship due from you as rational creatures."[9] In view of God's acts of mercy it is entirely fitting that we commit ourselves without reservation to him. To teach that accepting the free gift of God's grace does not necessarily involve a moral obligation on our part is a heresy of gigantic proportions. The popular cliche "He is Lord of all or not Lord at all" is absolutely right.

If v. 1 speaks of a specific act in which we offer ourselves to God, v. 2 tells us of two ongoing activities[10] that carry out the intention of the living sacrifice. The first is negative; the second, positive. Believers are no longer to conform themselves to the present age (cf. 1 Pet 1:14). As citizens of heaven (Phil 3:20) we are to "set [our] minds on things above, not on earthly things (Col 3:2). Paul reminded the Galatians that the present age is evil (Gal 1:4). It cannot, and must not, serve as a model for Christian living. Its values and goals are antithetical to growth in holiness. The church should stand out from the world as a demonstration of God's intention for the human race. To be culturally identified with the world is to place the church at risk.[11] Believers are to be salt and light (Matt 5:13–14), purifying and enlightening contemporary culture.

Rather than allowing the world to "squeeze you into its own mold" (Phillips), Paul told believers to be "transformed by the renewing of your minds." From without there is a continuing pressure to adopt the customs and mind-set of the world in which we live. Although that influence must be rejected, that alone will never create the kind of change God has in mind for his followers. Real and lasting change comes from within. We must "let ourselves be transformed."[12] The verb occurs in two other settings in the New Testament. First is Mark 9:2 (Matt 17:2), where Jesus is said to have been "transfigured" before his three disciples. Next is 2 Cor 3:18, where Paul taught that believers, as they behold the glory of the Lord, are being "transformed" into his likeness. The

---

[9] Not rational in the sense of human rationality (cf. 1 Cor 2:6–10) but rational in terms of a proper understanding of truth as revealed in Jesus Christ.

[10] Although παραστῆναι was aorist, both συσχηματίζεσθε and μεταμορφοῦσθε are present continuous.

[11] A. W. Tozer lamented that "almost everything the church is doing these days has been suggested to her by the world" (*Man: The Dwelling Place of God* [Harrisburg: Christian Publications, 1966], 166).

[12] μεταμορφοῦσθε is a present passive imperative. Although God brings about the transformation, we must voluntarily place ourselves at his disposal so it can happen. He will not "transform" us against our will. The present tense suggests that the process is to continue throughout life. Transformation is not instantaneous.

transformation of which Paul spoke in Rom 12:2 is not a change effected from without but a radical reorientation that begins deep within the human heart.

A renewed mind is concerned with those issues of life that are of lasting importance.[13] By nature our thoughts tend to dwell on the ephemeral. But that which passes quickly is normally inconsequential. As Paul said in another place, "What is seen is temporary, but what is unseen is eternal" (2 Cor 4:18). The mind renewed enables us to discern the will of God.[14] Released from the control of the world around us, we can come to know what God has in mind for us. We will find that his will is "good, pleasing and perfect." It is good because it brings about moral and spiritual growth. It is pleasing to God because it is an expression of his nature. It is perfect in that no one could possibly improve on what God desires to happen.

12:3–8 Paul was fully aware of the devastating consequences of pride in any group of believers. So he cautioned the Christians at Rome not to think of themselves more highly than they ought (v. 3), reminded them that they were all members of the one body (vv. 4–5), and encouraged them to utilize their individual gifts for the benefit of the entire church (vv. 6–8).[15] Paul offered these instructions in virtue of the office he himself held. His appointment as an apostle was a special act of divine favor. He called on his readers not to entertain an inflated view of their own importance. Rather, they should model the humility that places the rights and welfare of others above their own (cf. Phil 2:3). As J. Denney writes: "To himself, every man is in a sense the most important person in the world, and it always needs much grace to see what other people are, and to keep a sense of moral proportion."[16] That they were to think of themselves with "sober judgment" (v. 3)[17] suggests how

---

[13] J. A. Fitzmyer defines the νοῦς as "that aspect of the human being which is considered the seat of intellectual and moral judgment" (*Romans,* AB [New York: Doubleday, 1993], 641). J. Behm says the νοῦς of Christians is "the inner direction of their thought and will and the orientation of their moral consciousness" (*TDNT* 4.958).

[14] δοκιμάζω means "to put to the test or to approve as the result of testing." The second meaning fits the present context best.

[15] The view that these verses are directed exclusively toward leaders in the church cannot be sustained. Although those in positions of authority may be especially prone to pride, the need for humility extends to every member of the church.

[16] J. Denney, "St. Paul's Epistle to the Romans," EGT 2 (Grand Rapids: Eerdmans, 1983), 689.

[17] Note the play on words (φρονεῖν, ὑπερφρονεῖν, σωφρονεῖν), a fairly common characteristic of Hellenistic literature.

out of touch with reality were their opinions of themselves.[18] Since the metaphor suggests intoxication, one might say they were in danger of becoming "egoholics!"

To each member of the church in Rome, God had given a measure of faith (cf. 1 Cor 12:11; Eph 4:7).[19] Paul reminded them that as the physical body is made up of many members performing various functions, so also in Christ the many members form one body (cf. 1 Cor 12:12–31; Eph 4:25). Unity in diversity is the theme that runs through this section. This unity, however, which is spiritual, was only possible because the members were "in Christ," that is, joined by faith they had become a part of the body of Christ. Since they were all members of one body, it follows that "each member belong[ed] to all the others" (v. 5). The Christian faith is essentially a corporate experience. Although each member has come to faith by a separate and individual act of faith, the believing community lives out its Christian experience in fellowship with one another. John Donne's "No man is an island" is true of the church of Jesus Christ. "Lone Ranger Christianity" is a contradiction in terms.

The gift each believer has received is the result of the gracious outpouring of God's blessing on the church (v. 6). Berger writes: "The various charismata are understood as concrete manifestations of the one grace bestowed on all."[20] Paul mentioned seven different gifts and showed how they were to be exercised (cf. 1 Pet 4:10).[21] First is the gift of prophecy. The New Testament prophet was a person who spoke for God.[22] According to Eph 4:11 prophets served together with apostles, evangelists, pastors, and teachers in the preparation of God's people for service. Each

---

[18] C. H. Dodd stresses this point when he writes that "a fantastical estimate of one's own worth, powers, or importance is one of the most radical, and certainly one of the commonest, causes of obliquity of moral vision" (*The Epistle of Paul to the Romans,* MNTC [London: Hodder & Stoughton, 1932], 194).

[19] The NIV omits ἑκάστῳ in v. 3 but seems to carry the idea over into v. 4 ("each of us"). Cranfield discusses at some length how μέτρον is to be taken in this passage. He argues against the commonly held view that it means a measure or "quantity" and prefers "a means of measurement" (*Romans,* 2:613–16). Dunn, however, argues conclusively that μέτρον in that sense is unlikely (*Romans,* 2:721–22).

[20] *EDNT* 3.458.

[21] P. Stuhlmacher divides the seven gifts into two categories (prophetic activity and service) with the duties of the teacher and the preacher placed under prophecy (*Paul's Letter to the Romans* [Louisville: Westminster, 1994], 193).

[22] In 1 Cor 12:28, where Paul listed the gifts in order of their importance, the prophet is second only to the apostle. Fitzmyer defines prophecy as "inspired Christian preaching" and says that "it denotes not one who predicts the future, but one who speaks in God's name and probes the secrets of hearts" (*Romans,* 647).

prophet is to speak in proportion to the gift he has received.[23] If a person's gift is practical service, then he is to serve (v. 7). Since the English term "deacon" comes from this Greek word group,[24] many relate the admonition to the care of any kind of practical need that might surface in the membership. Murray refers it to the ministry of the Word.[25]

The next two gifts mentioned are teaching and encouraging. Teaching was an ancient and honorable profession in the Jewish culture. In the New Testament world teaching was primarily but not exclusively moral instruction.[26] In 1 Cor 12:28 Paul assigned a place of importance to teachers right after apostles and prophets. If teaching is your gift, then teach. If teaching provides guidance for what people ought to do, encouragement helps them achieve it.[27] If a person's gift is contributing to the needs of others, then generosity is what is called for. As Paul taught elsewhere, giving is not to be done reluctantly or under compulsion; God loves the cheerful giver (2 Cor 9:7).

Another gift of God's grace is leadership. Leaders are to carry out their responsibility with diligence. Although leadership in the contemporary world is often seen as the fruit of ambition, persistence, and good fortune (cf. Matt 8:9), biblical leadership is essentially a service carried out for the benefit of others.[28] The final gift mentioned is showing mercy. This would include such helpful activities as feeding the hungry, caring for the sick, and caring for the aging. These are to be done cheerfully.[29] The afflicted

---

[23] Some understand κατὰ τὴν ἀναλογίαν τῆς πίστεως to mean "in agreement with the faith," i.e., the Christian faith. In this case the prophet is being warned not to say anything that does not agree with that body of truth already delivered to the church.

[24] The words are διακονέω, διακονία, διάκονος.

[25] J. Murray, *The Epistle to the Romans*, NICNT (Grand Rapids: Eerdmans, 1965), 2:123.

[26] Dunn observes that since Paul thought of teaching as a *charism*, the implication is that he recognized an interpretative role for the teacher, in which the teacher must depend on the Spirit for insight (*Romans*, 2:729).

[27] "Encouraging" translates the same verb, παρακαλέω, used in 12:1. Phillips calls the gift "the stimulating of the faith in others." Luther says that "teaching is meant for the ignorant and exhortation for those who know" (*Commentary on the Epistle to the Romans*, trans. J. T. Mueller [Grand Rapids: Zondervan, 1954], 156). Teaching, however, was not simply doctrinal instruction but included guidance in ethical conduct. Its goal should be a changed life as well as an informed mind. Jesus connected teaching and obedience (Matt 28:20). H. C. G. Moule insists that teaching "first passes through the teacher's own soul into his own life" before it is given to others (*The Epistle to the Romans* [London: Pickering & Inglis, n.d.], 324).

[28] The location of ὁ προϊστάμενος between "contributing to the needs of others" and "showing mercy" has led some to understand it in reference to the person whose responsibility was to oversee the charitable work of the congregation.

[29] From ἱλαρότης ("gladness") we derive our word "hilarity."

have troubles of their own. They have no need of "helpers" who carry out their obligation as if they were great crushing burdens.

12:9–13   Nowhere else in Paul's writings do we find a more concise collection of ethical injunctions. In these five verses are thirteen exhortations ranging from love of Christians to hospitality for strangers. There are no finite verbs in the paragraph. There are, however, ten participles that serve as imperatives.[30] In the three other clauses (vv. 9,10,11) an imperative must be supplied. Each of the thirteen exhortations could serve as the text for a full-length sermon. What they deal with are basic to effective Christian living.

The series begins by calling the reader's attention to the absolute primacy of genuine love. Some view the exhortation to love as the theme that is then particularized in the following sequence of participial clauses.[31] Nygren remarks that "one needs only to make 'love' the subject throughout 12:9–21, to see how close the contents of this section are to I Corinthians 13."[32] The adjective translated "sincere" (*anupokritos*) means "without deception or hypocrisy."[33] Apparently there is a danger that in certain cases what looks like love is actually something quite distinct. Calvin comments, "It is difficult to express how ingenious almost all men are in counterfeiting a love which they do not really possess."[34] Love must never be used as a disguise for ulterior aims. True love is free from all pretense and hypocrisy.

Next, the believer is called upon to "hate what is evil."[35] E. Brunner writes that love, "if it is not to degenerate into sentimentality . . . must include a strict objectivity: hatred against evil, faithful adherence to

---

[30] Barrett holds that the argument that in Hellenistic Greek the participle could stand for the imperative is not supported by evidence. It is much more probable that they represent original Hebrew participles used to express "not direct commands, but rules and codes." If this linguistic explanation is correct, "the material in vv. 9–13 goes back to a Semitic source originating in very primitive Christian circles" (*Romans,* 239–40).

[31] Cf. Dunn, *Romans,* 2:739.

[32] A. Nygren, *Commentary on Romans,* trans. C. C. Rasmussen (Philadelphia: Muhlenberg, 1949), 425.

[33] Elsewhere it modifies brotherly love (1 Pet 1:22), faith (1 Tim 1:5), and wisdom (Jas 3:17). Murray writes, "If love is the sum of virtue and hypocrisy the epitome of vice, what a contradiction to bring these together!" (*Romans,* 2:128).

[34] Calvin, *The Epistles of Paul the Apostle to the Romans and to the Thessalonians,* trans. R. Mackenzie (Grand Rapids: Eerdmans, 1961), 271.

[35] M. Black writes that "hate" and "hold fast" ("cling to") are "both strong expressions, conveying a passionate hatred of evil and zeal for good" (*Romans,* 2d ed., NCBC [Grand Rapids: Eerdmans, 1989], 172). Barclay's comment is that "our one security against sin lies in our being shocked by it" (*Romans,* 163–64).

what is good."[36] To love God is to regard evil with horror. Unfortunately, familiarity with a culture that is shaped by the forces of Satan has lulled too many believers into a state of general tolerance for whatever deviant behavior is in vogue at present. We are to abhor evil because it is the enemy of all that leads to Christlikeness. It is worth mentioning that all ten participles, beginning with this clause, are present continuous. What God seeks in the believer is not so much a single worthy act as it is a continuing quality of life. We are to turn away from all evil and "cling to what is good." The Greek participle comes from a verb (*kollaō*) that means "to glue or join together." In 1 Cor 6:16 it is used to describe a sexual union. Holding on tightly to that which is right becomes a necessity in view or our natural inclination to fall back into sin (cf. 7:15–20).

Believers are to be tenderly affectionate with one other in the bonds of brotherly love (v. 10).[37] As a result of this affectionate relationship they will not seek their own good but outdo one another in showing honor.[38] The TCNT translates, "In showing respect, set an example of deference to one another." In a similar vein Paul encouraged the Philippians to "consider others better than" themselves (Phil 2:3). To honor the other person is one way of holding in check the innate human tendency to honor oneself unduly.

Paul warned his readers about the debilitating results of lethargy, "Never be lacking in zeal" (v. 11). In whatever they do they are to put their whole heart and soul into it (cf. Col 3:23). Believers are to be aglow with the Spirit.[39] The life-giving presence of the Holy Spirit radically alters the way a person lives. Goodspeed speaks of being "on fire with the Spirit." A Spirit-filled believer by definition cannot be dull and boring. That would be a contradiction in terms. Christians are called to serve the Lord.[40] This service is by no means drudgery. Servants of God

---

[36] E. Brunner, *The Letter to the Romans* (Philadelphia: Westminster, 1949), 106.

[37] Note φίλος in both φιλαδελφία and φιλόστοργοι. στοργή is the "natural affection" of parents and children (LS abr., 653).

[38] Cranfield lists three possible interpretations of the clause as to anticipate one another in showing honor, to surpass one another in showing honor, and "in honor preferring one another." Accepting the third alternative he says that this is appropriate because the "Son of man Himself is mysteriously present in the other person in his human need," and for that reason "I must honour him, not just as myself, but above myself" (*Romans,* 2:633).

[39] This understands τῷ πνεύματι as referring to the Holy Spirit. The NIV understands a reference to the human spirit and translates "spiritual fervor." ζέοντες is from ζέω, which means "to boil."

[40] Some manuscripts, chiefly Western, read καιρῷ rather than κυρίῳ, which would mean "meet the demands of the hour" (NEB, "Seize your opportunities").

continually rejoice in their hope. The Greek word *elpis* in the New Testament is confident trust rather than uncertain expectation. Käsemann says that hope is "confident reaching out for the eschatological future."[41] According to Calvin (commenting on "rejoicing in hope"), Paul warned us against remaining content with earthly joys and counseled us to "raise our minds to heaven, that we may enjoy full and solid joy."[42] The apostle Peter spoke of being born anew "into a living hope through the resurrection of Jesus Christ" (1 Pet 1:3). The reality of that hope brings joy. This world will have its full share of difficulties (John 16:33), but the believer is to be steadfast in time of trouble. The realization that life is to some extent an obstacle course keeps a person from being surprised when things do not go as planned. Afflictions are to be borne patiently. And the source of spiritual help during such times is prayer. So Paul counseled his readers, "Steadfastly maintain the habit of prayer" (Phillips). Barclay comments, "No man should be surprised when life collapses if he insists on living it alone."[43] Most Christians will confess the difficulty of maintaining a regular and effective prayer life. The reason is not difficult to discern. If Satan can keep us out of touch with God, he will not have to worry about any trouble we might cause for his evil kingdom.

In Gal 6:10 Paul instructed the members of the church to "do good to all people, especially to those who belong to the family of believers." In Romans 12 he added specificity to that rather general instruction: "Share with God's people who are in need" (v. 13). The level of poverty and the need for help were relatively high in the early church. It was critical for believers who had enough and more to share their abundance with those who were in need (cf. 2 Cor 8:13–14). And finally, Paul indicated the moral responsibility of showing hospitality.[44] In a day when inns were scarce and not always desirable, it was critical for believers to extend hospitality to Christians (and others) who were traveling.[45] The author of Hebrews counsels hospitality to strangers on the basis that by so

---

[41] E. Käsemann, *Commentary on Romans,* trans and ed. G. W. Bromiley (Grand Rapids: Eerdmans, 1980), 346.

[42] Calvin, *Romans,* 272.

[43] Barclay, *Romans,* 166.

[44] The Greek word translated "hospitality" (φιλοξενία) is more expressive than the English because it means "love of strangers" (φίλος, "friend," and ξένος, "stranger").

[45] Note the participle διώκοντες, "pursue." The implication is not simply that believers should be ready to extend hospitality if called upon but that they should be looking for those they can befriend in this way.

doing one may perhaps entertain angels without knowing it (Heb 13:2).

12:14–16 This paragraph contains six exhortations that are stated positively and three that take a negative form.[46] The apostle urged his readers to invoke God's blessing on behalf of those who persecute them.[47] We remember the teaching of Jesus on the Mount, "Love your enemies and pray for those who persecute you" (Matt 5:44 // Luke 6:28).[48] Stephen provided an example of this godly attitude when as he was being stoned, "Lord, do not hold this sin against them" (Acts 7:60; cf. 1 Cor 4:12). The principle of nonretaliation for personal injury permeates the entire New Testament. It provides guidance when life brings us up against those who care nothing for us and are in fact opposed to all that we stand for. Ask that they might enjoy the blessings of God! Love inevitably desires the best for other people regardless of who they may be. The old nature says, "Curse them"; God says, "Ask me to bless them."[49]

God's will is that his children become a family where the joys of one become the joys of all and the pain of one is gladly shared by all the others. The Christian experience is not one person against the world but one great family living out together the mandate to care for one another.[50] So rejoice with those who are rejoicing, and weep with those who are weeping (v. 15).[51] The elder brother in the account of the prodigal son provides an example of the failure to join in rejoicing (Luke 15:25–32). On the other hand, the Gospels record that upon meeting Mary following the

---

[46] In vv. 9–13 there were ten participles functioning as imperatives; in vv. 14–16 there are four imperatives, plus three participles and two infinitives that serve that purpose.

[47] In the Greek world εὐλογέω meant "to speak well of" (cf. the English "eulogize"). Here it carries the Hebraic sense of calling upon God to bestow his favor on another.

[48] ὑμᾶς is placed in square brackets in the UBS text indicating considerable doubt on the part of the committee about whether it should be included. Those MSS that omit ὑμᾶς broaden the exhortation to persecutors in general. Cf. Paul's words in Phil 2:2–5.

[49] Black comments that while "'blessing' and 'cursing' was a regular feature of synagogue practice, the teaching of Jesus abolished the formal practice of 'cursing' one's opponents (*Romans,* 175). Stuhlmacher comments, "Until Christianity became a state religion in the fourth century A.D., the practice of loving one's enemy remained one of the main characteristics of the Christian church within its non-Christian environment" (*Romans,* 196–97).

[50] E. Best writes that "there is no Christianity without fellowship, and this means, as in a family, entering into those experiences of others which are deepest and mean most to them" (*The Letter of Paul to the Romans,* CBC [Cambridge: University Press, 1967], 145).

[51] Commentators often quote Chrysostom, the famous fourth-century patriarch and preacher, who noted that it is easier to sympathize with those who mourn than to congratulate those who succeed and rejoice over it. For a close parallel to Paul's admonition cf. *Sir* 7:34, "Withdraw not thyself from them that weep, and mourn with them that mourn."

death of her brother, "Jesus wept" (John 11:35).

Pride sows the seeds of discord. The tendency to regard oneself as worthy of preferential treatment is universal in scope. The entire range of personal conflict, which reaches all the way from minor squabbles to international wars, reflects the misguided idea that we are better than they or that they have done something against us. So Paul counseled us to "live in harmony with one another" (v. 16).[52] This unity is less the result of accommodation to the other person's point of view than it is the result of arriving at a mutual understanding of God's way of thinking. Like spokes in a wheel that converge at the hub, the closer we are to God the closer we come to one another. Paul admonished his readers not to be proud since it is pride more than anything else that destroys the harmony of the body.[53]

At issue in the second sentence of v. 16 is the question of the gender of the two pronominal adjectives. The first is neuter, but the second is either masculine or neuter. Goodspeed takes the second as neuter and translates, "Do not be too ambitious, but accept humble tasks." Berkeley has, "Do not aspire to eminence, but willingly adjust yourselves to humble situations." Similar to the NIV (which takes the second adjective as masculine) is Phillip's, "Don't become snobbish, but take a real interest in ordinary people," and Norlie's, "Avoid being haughty; mingle with the lowly." In either case the admonition is to get off one's high horse and come to grips with reality. There are both humble tasks and ordinary people who need our attention. To withdraw from either is to allow pride to control our lives. Cranfield writes, "It is always a sign of the worldliness of the Church when its 'leaders' no longer associate as readily and freely with humble people both inside and outside the Church as with those who are socially superior."[54] So the verse ends with the cogent advice, "Don't think too highly of yourselves" (TCNT). No one is to assume complete knowledge. Isaiah spoke of the folly of those who were "wise in their own eyes" and "clever in their own sight" (Isa 5:21; cf. Prov 3:7). Morris observes that "the person who is wise in his own eyes is rarely so in the eyes of other people."[55]

12:17–21 The natural impulse is to return injury for injury. But retaliation for personal injury is not for those who claim to follow the

---

[52] Barrett translates, "Have a common mind" (*Romans,* 241).

[53] As in Rom 11:20 the warning is against arrogance or haughtiness rather than ambition.

[54] Cranfield, *Romans,* 2:644.

[55] L. Morris, *The Epistle to the Romans* (Grand Rapids: Eerdmans, 1988), 451.

one who told his disciples to turn the other cheek and go the second mile (Matt 5:39,41; cf. Gal 6:10; 1 Thess 5:15; 1 Pet 3:9). Instead, believers are to be careful[56] to do what is honorable in the sight of everyone[57] (cf. Prov 3:4). The early church understood the necessity of having a good reputation with outsiders (1 Tim 3:7). Although it is imperative that believers take pains to do what is right in God's sight, it also is important that what we do, as long as it does not violate Christian ethics, is well thought of by the world (cf. 2 Cor 8:21). In so far as it is possible, we are called to live at peace with everyone. Wickedness is to be opposed and righteousness lauded, but Christians must be careful not to allow their allegiance to God to alienate them from the world they are intended to reach with the gospel. Jesus pronounced a blessing upon the peacemaker (Matt 5:9), and the author to Hebrews wrote that we are to "make every effort to live in peace with all men" (Heb 12:14).

Christians are never to take vengeance into their own hands (v. 19; cf. Lev 19:18). Rather, we must allow the wrath of God to follow its own course. After all, it is written: "It is for me to avenge. I am the one who will repay."[58] Christians are not called upon to help God carry out divine retribution. God has promised to "pay back trouble to those who trouble you" (2 Thess 1:6). He has no need of our help or advice. Genuine trust will leave everything in his hands. Rather than to take revenge we are to feed our enemies if they are hungry and give them something to drink if they are thirsty. In this way we will "make him feel a burning sense of shame" (Moffatt).[59] Verse 21 summarizes much of what has just been said. Instead of allowing evil to get the upper hand and bring defeat, win the victory against that which is wrong by doing what is right. Bruce

---

[56] προνοέω etymologically means "to think of beforehand."

[57] Dunn writes that "Paul shows himself ready to appeal to a widespread sense of what is morally right and fitting" (*Romans*, 2:748), but Cranfield correctly observes that "the arbiter of what is good [is] not a moral *communis sensus* of mankind, but the gospel" (*Romans*, 2:646). What Paul was saying was that the believers in Rome were to live out the implications of the gospel.

[58] This emphasis is clearly indicated by ἐμοὶ and ἐγώ. The quote is from Deut 32:35 (cf. Heb 10:30).

[59] Fitzmyer lists five possible explanations for Prov 25:21–22a, a "mysterious verse" that Paul quoted in the latter part of v. 20 (*Romans*, 657–58). In addition to the understanding reflected in Moffatt's translation, two others deserve attention. One is that treating an enemy kindly will make that person liable to a more severe punishment from God. The other says that the idea of heaping burning coals on a person's head reflects an Egyptian ritual in which the penitent carried a tray of glowing coals on his head to show that he had wronged someone (see W. Klassen, "Coals of Fire: Sign of Repentance or Revenge?" *NTS* 9 [1963]: 337–50).

comments, "The best way to get rid of an enemy is to turn him into a friend."[60] Our most powerful weapon against evil is the good. To respond to evil with evil is not to overcome it but to add to it. Believers are called upon to live victoriously in a hostile world by continuing to live as Jesus lived. Right will inevitably prevail against wrong. God is on his throne, and though all is not right in this world, he is the one who will avenge the wicked and reward the righteous.

2. In the World (13:1–14)

[1]Everyone must submit himself to the governing authorities, for there is no authority except that which God has established. The authorities that exist have been established by God. [2]Consequently, he who rebels against the authority is rebelling against what God has instituted, and those who do so will bring judgment on themselves. [3]For rulers hold no terror for those who do right, but for those who do wrong. Do you want to be free from fear of the one in authority? Then do what is right and he will commend you. [4]For he is God's servant to do you good. But if you do wrong, be afraid, for he does not bear the sword for nothing. He is God's servant, an agent of wrath to bring punishment on the wrongdoer. [5]Therefore, it is necessary to submit to the authorities, not only because of possible punishment but also because of conscience.

[6]This is also why you pay taxes, for the authorities are God's servants, who give their full time to governing. [7]Give everyone what you owe him: If you owe taxes, pay taxes; if revenue, then revenue; if respect, then respect; if honor, then honor.

[8]Let no debt remain outstanding, except the continuing debt to love one another, for he who loves his fellowman has fulfilled the law. [9]The commandments, "Do not commit adultery," "Do not murder," "Do not steal," "Do not covet," and whatever other commandment there may be, are summed up in this one rule: "Love your neighbor as yourself." [10]Love does no harm to its neighbor. Therefore love is the fulfillment of the law.

[11]And do this, understanding the present time. The hour has come for you to wake up from your slumber, because our salvation is nearer now than when we first believed. [12]The night is nearly over; the day is almost here. So let us put aside the deeds of darkness and put on the armor of light. [13]Let us behave decently, as in the daytime, not in orgies and drunkenness, not in sexual immorality and debauchery, not in dissension and jealousy. [14]Rather, clothe yourselves with the Lord Jesus Christ, and do not think about how to gratify the desires of the sinful nature.

---

[60] Bruce, *Romans,* 218.

13:1 In 13:1–7 Paul discussed the divinely sanctioned role of government and the believers' responsibility to those in power.[61] Christians, like everyone else, are to submit to the governing authorities.[62] Allegiance to God does not negate responsibility to secular authority. In Paul's day all those serving as public officials probably were nonbelievers. That is to make no difference for the Christian because there is no authority apart from that which God has established. He alone is the sole source of authority, and it has pleased him to delegate authority to those in charge of the public well-being.[63] Paul clearly stated that "the authorities that exist have been established by God." When Pilate told Jesus that he had power to set free or to crucify, he was reminded that he would have no power at all if it had not been given to him from above (John 19:11). It is important to remember that government is God's way of maintaining the public good and directing the affairs of state.

13:2–3 It follows that the one who resists authority is resisting what God has ordained. Those who act in this manner will bring judgment upon themselves.[64] Rebels against authority malign the Giver of author-

---

[61] Some find a discontinuity between chaps. 12–13, which leads them to regard 13:1–7 as an independent segment that Paul inserted (e.g., J. Kallas, "Romans xiii.1–7: An Interpolation," *NTS* 11 (1965): 365–574). J. C. O'Neill says it is Stoic in origin and by giving license to tyrants has caused untold misery in the Christian world (*Paul's Letter to the Romans* [Middlesex: Penguin, 1975], 207–9). Käsemann says "it can be pointedly called an alien body in Paul's exhortation (*Romans*, 352), a position questioned by Black, who settles for "a traditional Jewish (or Jewish-Christian) body of doctrine on relations with the civil power," which Paul adapted for his immediate purpose (*Romans*, 179–80). Cranfield, however, says that it would have been surprising if Paul "had had nothing to say on a subject which must have been of great importance to Christians of the first century" (*Romans*, 2:651–53). For a recent article against the hypothesis that this is a non-Pauline interpolation see D. Kroger, "Paul and the Civil Authorities: An Exegesis of Romans 13:1–7," *AJT* 7 (1993): 344–66.

[62] ὑποτάσσω occurs thirty-eight times in the NT, most often in the middle voice, meaning "to subordinate oneself." It is used of submission to political authorities (Titus 3:1); wives to husbands (Col 3:18), the younger toward elders (1 Pet 5:5). Cranfield argues that the predominant thought is not obedience but the conduct that flows naturally from the recognition that the other person as Christ's representative has an infinitely greater claim on one than one has on oneself (*Romans*, 2:660–62). O. Cullmann argued that ἐξουσίαι denoted the angelic powers that stood behind the state (*The State in the New Testament* [London: SCM, 1957], 95–114), but most exegetes have rejected the idea and regard them as the duly constituted civil authorities (e.g., F. F. Bruce, "Paul and 'The Powers That Be,'" *BJRL* 66 [1984]: 78–96).

[63] In Prov 8:15–16 wisdom says, "By me kings reign and rulers make laws that are just; / by me princes govern, and all nobles who rule on earth."

[64] ἀνθεστηκότες is a perfect participle, which suggests that their rebellion had hardened into an established policy. The NEB translates v. 2b, "Those who so resist have themselves to thank for the punishment they receive." κρίμα is used in the sense of κατάκριμα, condemnation. Paul spoke of divine judgment, primarily but not solely eschatological.

ity. It is a dangerous thing to set oneself in opposition to a divinely ordered process. Those who rule pose no threat to those whose lives are marked with good deeds. It is the one who does evil who fears authority. Returning to the diatribe style, Paul asked his readers whether they would like to be free from fear of the one in authority. The answer was simple: practice doing what is right.[65] This brings the approval of secular society (cf. 1 Pet 3:13).

Obviously this does not happen in every instance. Government sometimes oversteps its rightful domain. When this happens, the believer will find it impossible to obey the ruler. Two clear examples of civil disobedience are found in Acts. When Peter and John were told by the Sanhedrin not to preach in the name of Jesus, they replied, "Judge for yourselves whether it is right in God's sight to obey you rather than God" (Acts 4:19). Upon being released they resumed their work and consequently were taken into custody. To the charge of the Sanhedrin that they had filled Jerusalem with their teaching they replied, "We must obey God rather than man!" (Acts 5:19). The believer's ultimate allegiance is to God. Wherever the demands of secular society clearly violate this higher allegiance, the Christian will act outside the law.[66] This, of course, must not be done in a cavalier fashion.

13:4–5   The ruler serves as an instrument of God for the benefit of society. We are reminded of Cyrus, the Persian emperor, whom God anointed to carry out his will (Isa 44:28; 45:1; cf. also Jer 25:9). It is the person who makes it a practice of disobeying who has reason to be afraid. The ruler serves as the agent of God for the punishment of the one who does wrong. The text says that "he does not bear the sword for nothing." The sword is a symbol of the power delegated to governing authorities to enforce acceptable social conduct.[67] Here we have the biblical basis for the use of force by government for the maintenance of law and order. The power to punish has been delegated by God to those who rule.[68] To disobey the laws of the land, except where they contravene the express will of God, is to violate the purpose of God himself. Obedience

---

[65] ποίει is a present imperative denoting a general rule (*Analysis* 2.489).

[66] "Whenever laws are enacted which contradict God's law," writes Stott, "civil disobedience becomes a Christian duty" (*Romans* [Downers Grove: InterVarsity, 1994], 342).

[67] Many understand this to refer to the Roman right of a magistrate to inflict the death penalty (the *ius gladi*), but Sherwin-White has shown the limited nature of that power during the first two centuries of the empire (*Roman Society and Roman Law in the New Testament* [Oxford: Clarendon, 1963], 8–11).

[68] Note the emphasis on "God" in the clause θεοῦ γὰρ διάκονός ἐστιν. Black translates, "God's servant he is" (*Romans,* 183).

to civil law is necessary not only for fear of punishment but also for the sake of conscience.[69] As Phillips puts it, one should obey "not simply because it is the safest, but because it is the right thing to do."

13:6–7 Part of what it means to submit to the authorities is to pay taxes.[70] Believers are to carry out this particular civil obligation because those who levy taxes are servants of God.[71] They devote their time and energies to governing. They are "God's servants" in the sense that it is God who has granted them the authority with which they secure and maintain civil order.[72] Believers are under obligation to those in authority in government (cf. Mark 12:16).[73] They are to pay taxes where taxes are due and "import duties" (TLB) where such charges are appropriate.[74] They are to respect and honor governing authorities, "not because they are powerful and influential *men,* but because they have been appointed by God."[75] The social benefits that come from a properly managed state place the Christian under obligation to abide by the accepted regulations. Undergirding all secular law and order is the authority of God delegated to those who rule.

13:8–10 The Christian is to allow no debt to remain outstanding except the one that can never be paid off—"the debt to love one another."[76] The obligation to love has no limit. We are to love not only

---

[69] C. A. Pierce says that conscience in this context means "the pain a man suffers when he has done wrong" (*Conscience in the New Testament,* SBT 15 [London: SCM, 1955], 71).

[70] See A. H. M. Jones, *The Roman Economy* (Oxford: Blackwell, 1974), 151–58, on taxation in the Roman Empire. The Roman historian Tacitus noted that in the year A.D. 58 there were persistent complaints against taxes and the acquisitiveness of tax collectors (*Ann.* 13).

[71] λειτουργός describes one commissioned for service whether secular or priestly. It was formed from the Ionic λήιτος, "concerning the people," and ἔργον, "work, service" (*EDNT* 2.348). In the same article Balz says that in Rom 13:6, when Paul described the Roman tax officials as λειτουργοὶ, he meant that they were "representatives or instruments commissioned by God for service" (p. 349).

[72] This is the third time in chap. 13 that Paul stressed that the authority of civil authorities comes from God (cf. vv. 1, 4).

[73] "Give everyone what you owe him" is not a general exhortation regarding our responsibility to all men but has to do with "the obligations we owe to those in authority in the state" (Murray, *Romans,* 2:155).

[74] It is customary to consider φόρος ("tribute") as a direct tax, such as a property tax or a poll tax, and τέλος ("revenue") as an indirect tax, such as customs.

[75] Barrett, *Romans,* 248. φόβος as respect toward governing authorities is considered a higher form of reverence than τιμή. Cranfield questions whether τῷ τὸν φόβον in v. 7 refers to the magistrate and suggests that exegetes not dismiss too cavalierly the possibility that it refers to God (*Romans,* 670–73).

[76] Moule says the debt of love is not like a forgotten account that is owed to a lender but like interest on capital that is continuously due and payable (*Romans,* 358).

those of the family of God but our "fellowman" as well. As God's love extended to all, so must our concern reach out to believer and nonbeliever alike (cf. Matt 5:44–45). Obviously love will take different forms depending on the recipient, but the decision to "place the welfare of others over that of our own" may not be limited to those of like faith. Paul added that whoever loves his "fellowman"[77] has satisfied all that the law requires.[78]

Verse 9 explains the previous statement. The Commandments (cf. Exod 20:13–15,17; note the order—seventh, sixth, eighth, tenth) against adultery,[79] murder, theft, covetousness—and "whatever other commandments there may be"—are all summed up in the second great commandment (Matt 22:38), "Love your neighbor as yourself" (cf. Gal 5:14; Lev 19:18).[80] As Jesus taught us in the parable of the good Samaritan (Luke 10:25–37), our "neighbor" is anyone we encounter in life who needs our help. Love is the inevitable response of a heart truly touched by God. God's love manifests itself through the loving acts of his children. Where it is absent, any claim to a family relationship is merely pretense. In our present culture, enamored as it is with the cult of self-esteem, it is necessary to point out that Jesus' words are "not a command to love oneself but a recognition of the fact that we naturally do so."[81] Stott observes that Jesus spoke of a first and second commandment but never of a third. He also argues that *agapē* is selfless love, which cannot be turned in on itself, and that self-love is the essence of sin.[82] What is commanded is that we are to have the same loving regard for others that we have instinctively for ourselves. Love never wrongs another person. It fully satisfies all that the law requires (cf. Matt 22:40).[83]

13:11–14 The need to love is supremely important in view of the

---

[77] τὸν ἕτερον follows naturally after ὁ ἀγαπῶν rather than modifying νόμον. Paul was not saying that the person who loves has fulfilled the "other law" (the "second commandment" [Mark 12:31], the "law of Christ" [Gal 6:2; 1 Cor 9:21]).

[78] "Paul's design," writes Calvin, "is to reduce all the precepts of the law to love, so that we may know we are duly obeying the commandments when we are maintaining love" (*Romans and Thessalonians*, 284–85).

[79] Commenting on adultery as a failure to discharge the debt of love, Barclay writes, "When two people allow their physical passions to sweep them away, the reason is, not that they love each other too much, but that they love each other too little; in real love there is at once respect and restraint which saves from sin" (*Romans*, 176).

[80] Rabbi Akiba called Lev 19:18 "the greatest general principle in the Torah" (*Sipra* on Lev 19:18).

[81] NIVSB note on Rom 13:9.

[82] Stott, *Romans*, 350.

[83] πλήρωμα, "that which fills," serves as the equivalent of πλήρωσις, "fulfilling." It is love in action that fulfills the law.

critical age in which we find ourselves.[84] Paul wrote from the perspective of the closing period of the present age. The fact that the fullness of the kingdom is upon us calls for godly living (cf. Jas 5:8–9; 2 Pet 3:11–14).[85] The world lives as though human history were destined to continue for ever. The Christian knows that God is in control of the events of people and nations and is directing history to a predetermined end. Since the end is near, we are to arouse ourselves from sleep, to "wake up to reality" (Phillips).[86] The critical nature of the hour calls for the Christian to be wide awake and ready for action (cf. 1 Thess 5:6). Salvation, that is, our final deliverance at the second coming of Christ, is nearer to us than when we first believed.[87] Every day brings us closer to that final day when all that we have anticipated in Christ will become a reality. The long-awaited kingdom is about to be unveiled fully and completely.

Since the night is nearly over and the day is about to dawn (v. 12), it is critical that believers rid themselves completely of the works of darkness (v. 12; cf. Eph 5:11).[88] It is time to clothe ourselves with the weap-

---

[84] The NIV's "present time" translates τὸν καιρόν. J. Baumgarten notes that while χρόνος and καιρός may at times serve as partial synonyms, the former "designates a 'period of time' in the linear sense," while the latter "frequently refers to 'eschatologically filled time, time for decision'" (*EDNT* 2.232).

[85] Cranfield refers to this section as an "appeal to eschatology as an incentive to moral earnestness" (*Romans,* 2:680) and cites such passages as Phil 4:4–7 and 1 Thess 5:1–11 for comparison. A. M. Hunter labels vv. 11–14 "Ethics of Reveille" (*The Epistle to the Romans,* TBC [London: SCM, 1955], 115).

[86] Many scholars understand the primitive church to have believed that the parousia was just around the corner and that the nearly twenty centuries of subsequent history has proven that they were wrong. Cranfield says the true explanation is that the early church was convinced that the ministry of Jesus had ushered in the end time and that all subsequent history is an epilogue with God's patience providing an interval for people to hear the gospel and make the decision of faith (*Romans,* 2:682–83).

[87] ἡμῶν should probably be taken with ἐγγύτερον ("nearer to us") rather than with σωτηρία ("our salvation"). Denney says "ἡ σωτηρία has here the transcendent eschatological sense: it is the final and complete deliverance from sin and death, and the reception into the heavenly kingdom of our Lord Jesus Christ" ("Romans," 2:699). ἐπιστεύσαμεν may be an ingressive aorist indicating our entrance into a life of faith.

[88] The antithesis between light and darkness is a regular feature of Paul's writing (2 Cor 6:14; Eph 5:8; Col 1:12–13; 1 Thess 5:4–5) as it is of John's (John 1:5; 3:19; 8:12; 12:35; 1 John 1:5; 2:8–9). Bruce calls attention to the fact that it is "one of the most obvious points of contact in concept and language between the New Testament and the Qumran texts" (*Romans,* 228–29). "Night" is the present evil age (cf. Gal 1:4); and "day," the coming age of God's kingdom fully realized. Or, as Thomas writes, "The night of Christ's absence is nearly over and the day—dawn of His appearance is at hand" (*Romans,* 361). Harrison comments that "the Christian is to live as though that final day had actually arrived, bringing with it the personal presence of Christ" (*Romans,* 143).

ons of light.[89] Our conduct is to be decent and honorable (v. 13). It must be acceptable in the open light of day. One example is Augustine. In his *Confessions* Augustine tells of his conversion to Christianity (viii.12). In A.D. 386, at a time when he was deeply moved by a desire to break from his old way of living, he sat weeping in the garden of a friend in Milan. Suddenly he heard a child singing *Tolle, lege! Tolle, lege!* ("Take up and read! Take up and read!"). He picked up a scroll lying there, and his eyes fell on Rom 13:13–14, "Not in orgies and drunkenness . . ." Immediately his heart was flooded with a clear light, and the darkness of doubt vanished. No other theologian has made a greater contribution to the theology of the Western world.

The conduct of darkness is described as "orgies," "drunken bouts," "sexual immorality[90] and debauchery."[91] In John's Gospel we learn that people prefer darkness to light because their deeds are evil (John 3:19). Darkness hides, but light discloses. Evil flourishes in darkness because its perpetrators assume, although incorrectly, that what they are doing cannot be seen. The desire for darkness is itself an admission of the wrongness of the act.

Along with the more socially repugnant acts of drunkenness and debauchery we find, rather unexpectedly, quarreling and jealousy. These too are acts of darkness. Unfortunately, the church is considerably more tolerant toward such sins. Quarreling and jealousy, while not especially polite, are more acceptable than sexual immorality. This is not to make a case for immorality but to remind ourselves that Paul placed them together as deeds of darkness.

Instead of maintaining a lingering relationship to all such activity, believers are to put on as their armor the Lord Jesus Christ (v. 14). The verb calls for a decisive action. The critical nature of the day in which we live demands that we separate ourselves unmistakably from all that

---

[89] Paul used the same word (ὅπλον) in 2 Cor 6:7 in the expression "weapons of righteousness" and in 2 Cor 10:4 in "weapons of the world." The metaphor of armor occurs often in Paul's writing (cf. e.g., 1 Thess 5:8; Eph 6:13–17).

[90] κοίτη, which literally means "bed," is used here euphemistically for "sexual intercourse" (M. Silva, "New Lexical Semitisms?" *ZNW* 69 (1978): 225.

[91] These six vices come in pairs of two with each pair so closely related that it could be considered as one basic idea; e.g., "drunkenness" and "orgies" may be taken as "drunken orgies." The plurals in the first two pairs suggest frequent repetition. Barclay calls ἀσέλγεια "one of the ugliest words in the Greek language" and says it describes not only immorality but "the man who is lost to shame" (*Romans,* 179). Luther says that "all who study history, at least that of St. Jerome, will find that the six vices at that time had gained the ascendancy in Rome and exerted an almost tyrannical sway" (*Romans,* 174).

belongs to darkness. Jesus Christ himself is our armor against wickedness. Those who are "in him" know what it means to experience victory in spiritual warfare. There is no other place of security (cf. Eph 6:11,13).

As a final word of advice, Paul counseled the believer against allowing any opportunity whatsoever for gratifying the evil desires of the lower nature.[92] New life in Christ stands diametrically opposed to the old life controlled by earthly passions. To clothe ourselves with Christ is to take off and dispose of the old clothing of sin. While the appetites of sin remain until the glorious day of our complete transformation into the likeness of Christ (1 John 3:2; Phil 3:21), we are to deny them any opportunity of expression. We are not even to consider the possibility of allowing them to fulfill their evil intentions through us.

3. Among the Weak and the Strong (14:1–15:13)

[1]**Accept him whose faith is weak, without passing judgment on disputable matters. **[2]**One man's faith allows him to eat everything, but another man, whose faith is weak, eats only vegetables. **[3]**The man who eats everything must not look down on him who does not, and the man who does not eat everything must not condemn the man who does, for God has accepted him. **[4]**Who are you to judge someone else's servant? To his own master he stands or falls. And he will stand, for the Lord is able to make him stand.**

[5]**One man considers one day more sacred than another; another man considers every day alike. Each one should be fully convinced in his own mind. **[6]**He who regards one day as special, does so to the Lord. He who eats meat, eats to the Lord, for he gives thanks to God; and he who abstains, does so to the Lord and gives thanks to God. **[7]**For none of us lives to himself alone and none of us dies to himself alone. **[8]**If we live, we live to the Lord; and if we die, we die to the Lord. So, whether we live or die, we belong to the Lord.**

[9]**For this very reason, Christ died and returned to life so that he might be the Lord of both the dead and the living. **[10]**You, then, why do you judge your brother? Or why do you look down on your brother? For we will all stand before God's judgment seat. **[11]**It is written:**

> **"'As surely as I live,' says the Lord,**
> **'every knee will bow before me;**
> **every tongue will confess to God.'"**

[12]**So then, each of us will give an account of himself to God.**

---

[92] Cranfield defines σάρξ as "the whole of our human nature in its fallenness, organized as it is in rebellion against God" (*Romans,* 2:689).

¹³Therefore let us stop passing judgment on one another. Instead, make up your mind not to put any stumbling block or obstacle in your brother's way. ¹⁴As one who is in the Lord Jesus, I am fully convinced that no food is unclean in itself. But if anyone regards something as unclean, then for him it is unclean. ¹⁵If your brother is distressed because of what you eat, you are no longer acting in love. Do not by your eating destroy your brother for whom Christ died. ¹⁶Do not allow what you consider good to be spoken of as evil. ¹⁷For the kingdom of God is not a matter of eating and drinking, but of righteousness, peace and joy in the Holy Spirit, ¹⁸because anyone who serves Christ in this way is pleasing to God and approved by men.

¹⁹Let us therefore make every effort to do what leads to peace and to mutual edification. ²⁰Do not destroy the work of God for the sake of food. All food is clean, but it is wrong for a man to eat anything that causes someone else to stumble. ²¹It is better not to eat meat or drink wine or to do anything else that will cause your brother to fall.

²²So whatever you believe about these things keep between yourself and God. Blessed is the man who does not condemn himself by what he approves. ²³But the man who has doubts is condemned if he eats, because his eating is not from faith; and everything that does not come from faith is sin.

¹We who are strong ought to bear with the failings of the weak and not to please ourselves. ²Each of us should please his neighbor for his good, to build him up. ³For even Christ did not please himself but, as it is written: "The insults of those who insult you have fallen on me." ⁴For everything that was written in the past was written to teach us, so that through endurance and the encouragement of the Scriptures we might have hope.

⁵May the God who gives endurance and encouragement give you a spirit of unity among yourselves as you follow Christ Jesus, ⁶so that with one heart and mouth you may glorify the God and Father of our Lord Jesus Christ.

⁷Accept one another, then, just as Christ accepted you, in order to bring praise to God. ⁸For I tell you that Christ has become a servant of the Jews on behalf of God's truth, to confirm the promises made to the patriarchs ⁹so that the Gentiles may glorify God for his mercy, as it is written:

"Therefore I will praise you among the Gentiles;
  I will sing hymns to your name."

¹⁰Again, it says,

"Rejoice, O Gentiles, with his people."

¹¹And again,

"Praise the Lord, all you Gentiles,
  and sing praises to him, all you peoples."

¹²And again, Isaiah says,

"The Root of Jesse will spring up,
  one who will arise to rule over the nations;
the Gentiles will hope in him."

¹³May the God of hope fill you with all joy and peace as you trust in him, so that you may overflow with hope by the power of the Holy Spirit.

14:1–4 Paul's letters were not intended as abstract treatises on matters ethical and theological but pastoral notes addressed to real life situations in first-century churches. At Rome there were Jewish Christians who were reluctant to give up certain ceremonial aspects of their religious heritage. They were uncertain about how faith in Christ affected the status of Old Testament regulations.[93] Others embraced the new freedom in Christ unencumbered by an overly sensitive regard for the past. Paul referred to the first group as "weak" (Rom 14:1) and the latter as "strong" (Rom 15:1). The terms are descriptive rather than judgmental, although as Stuhlmacher says, "the designation 'weak in faith' is based on the presupposition that strength of faith is the attitude which is really to be desired."[94]

The church at Rome was to welcome into its fellowship those Jewish believers who were finding it difficult to let go of their religious past, but not "for the purpose of passing judgment on their scruples" (TCNT). That would be an unworthy motive for bringing them into the fellowship. The church does not exist as a judiciary body to make pronouncements on issues that in the long run will prove to be of no real consequence. Those things are *adiaphora,* things that do not really matter.

Paul identified two classes of believers in Rome: the "strong," whose faith allowed them to eat whatever they wanted, and the "weak" (the overscrupulous), who ate nothing but vegetables. The tendency of those

---

[93] Cranfield devotes ten pages to a discussion of the nature of the problem Paul was dealing with. Although not entirely certain, he favors the view that the "weakness of the weak consisted in a continuing concern with literal obedience of the ceremonial part of the OT law" (*Romans,* 694). Black says this still does not account for the combination of food and wine (note also the argument about "feast-days") and suggests the possibility that in Rome there were certain "'sectarian' Jews, similar to the Therapeutai, the Egyptian Essenes, who had embraced Christianity, but wanted to retain their 'asceticism,' with regard to meat and wine, and perhaps their own views of the festival calendar" (*Romans,* 190).

[94] Stuhlmacher, *Romans,* 223. Brunner refers to them as "the nervous ones"—"a group of nervous people who observed strict food regulations for religious reasons, and also certain holy days" (*Romans,* 114).

who eat whatever they want is to look down on those who for reasons of conscience are unable to exercise the same freedom.[95] Freedom in such matters tends to create an attitude of superiority. It is tempting to hold up for ridicule those whose lifestyle is more restricted than one's own. In the broad spectrum of Christianity those to the right are often caricatured as hopelessly fundamental. The problem is that one person's "overly scrupulous neighbor" is another person's "libertarian." It all depends upon where you happen to stand along the spectrum. The Christian is not to despise or treat with contempt those who are still working through the relationship between their new faith in Christ and the psychological and emotional pressures of a previous orientation.

On the other hand, the person who does not eat everything must not sit in judgment upon the one who does (cf. Matt 7:1). A natural consequence of the more restricted perspective is to condemn those who are enjoying greater freedom.[96] What is wrong for me translates easily into what is wrong for everyone. But the fact that God has received them ought to temper one's tendency to criticize. Since God has found room for them in the fellowship, any attempt on our part to exclude them will fail to meet with God's approval. It is not up to us to judge the servant of another (cf. Jas 4:12). That prerogative belongs exclusively to that person's own master. And that master is God. The strong as well as the weak will stand because the Lord is able to make them stand.

14:5–8 There was considerable diversity in the early church. Some believers regarded certain days as more sacred than others.[97] Old Testament law had declared that feast days were consecrated to God in a special way. The Sabbath, for instance, had its own set of regulations. Other believers, however, regarded all days alike. After all, all life belongs to God, and every day offers unique opportunities for worship and service. More important is that each person be fully persuaded in his own mind. What the other person does is a matter of that person's conscience. Each

---

[95] ἐξουθενέω is a strong word meaning "to despise, disdain" (BAGD, 277). In a passage like Luke 23:11 it means "to treat with contempt."

[96] Denney says the sharpness of the rebuke in v. 4 shows that Paul with all his love and consideration for the weak was nevertheless "alive to the tyranny of the weak. . . . It is easy to lapse from scrupulousness about one's own conduct into Pharisaism about that of others" ("Romans," 2:701).

[97] Exegetes are divided about the specific kind of days to which Paul referred. Suggestions include (1) special days of OT ceremonial law (particularly the Sabbath; Dunn, *Romans,* 2:805), (2) days of abstinence (Black, *Romans,* 193), or (3) lucky and unlucky days taken over from pagan life (Käsemann, *Romans,* 370).

believer must be convinced for himself whether or not to regard some days as more sacred than others.[98] Those who observe special days do it to honor the Lord (v. 6).[99] Those who eat meat do it in honor of the Lord.[100] They bless the Lord for the provisions he supplies.[101] At the same time, those who abstain from eating meat also do it in honor of the Lord. They too give thanks to the Lord. There is no difference in their motivation. Both conduct themselves in such a way as to please their Master.

"None of us lives to himself alone" (v. 7) often has been understood in the sense of John Donne's "No man is an island." Paul's statement, however, is not a sociological observation regarding the oneness of the human race. What he was saying was that all believers live out their lives accountable to God.[102] Decisions about such matters as special days and eating meat are not made in isolation but in accordance with the will of God as understood by the individual. Even in death believers maintain their relationship to God. To live means to honor the Lord. To die is no different. Whether we live or die we belong to the Lord (cf. 1 Thess 5:10). Since each believer belongs to God, it is out of place for any to question the decisions of another in matters not central to the faith.

14:9–12 "For this very reason" (v. 9) looks forward and is explained by the final clause of the verse. The purpose of Jesus' death and resurrection was "that he might be the Lord of both the dead and the living."[103] His lordship is universal.[104] His subjects are not merely those

---

[98] Moule makes a strong case for "Christian individualism," concluding that the church "can be perfectly strong only where individual consciences are tender, and enlightened; where individual souls personally know God in Christ; where individual wills are ready, if the Lord call, to stand alone for known truth even against the religious Society" (*Romans,* 380).

[99] The Textus Receptus adds the clause καὶ ὁ μὴ φρονῶν τὴν ἡμέρα κυρίῳ οὐ φρονεῖ, apparently to match the balanced clauses later in the verse (*TCGNT,* 531).

[100] κυρίῳ occurs three times in v. 6. It is best understood as a dative of advantage, e.g., the one who "eats to the Lord" eats with the desire to serve the Lord by so doing.

[101] To "give thanks to God" in this context probably refers to a table blessing. The first example of a prayer of thanksgiving to be said before a meal is found in *Didache* 10.1–6.

[102] Cranfield points out that "the expression 'live to oneself' is used both in Greek and in Latin of living selfishly, caring only for one's own interest and comfort" (*Romans,* 2:707, n. 3). Plutarch, the late first and early second century Greek biographer, declared that it is "a disgraceful thing to live and die for ourselves alone" (*Vita Cleom.,* 31).

[103] ἔζησεν should be taken as an ingressive aorist ("came to life"). The reference is to Christ's resurrection, not his earthly life.

[104] Murray holds that the lordship of Christ dealt with here did not belong to him as a native right but had to be secured. "It is the lordship of redemptive relationship . . . achieved by mediatorial accomplishment and is the reward of his humiliation" (*Romans,* 2:182).

who are alive at the present time. All who have died previously are subject to his authority. Therefore he is the judge of all. Why then, asked Paul, do you weak believers (the abstainers) pass judgment on your brothers in Christ (those who do not abstain for the sake of conscience)?[105] God is their judge, not you. And turning to the strong believers, Paul asked why they held the weaker Christians in contempt.[106] It was wrong for them to look down on their fellow believers who were not as yet able to set aside the regulations that previously controlled their religious life. Each and every believer will stand[107] before the judgment seat of God.[108] Barclay writes, "We stand before God in the awful loneliness of our own souls; to him we can take nothing but the character which in life we have been building up."[109]

There is no room in the family of God for one group to pass judgment on another (v. 10). In the Sermon on the Mount Jesus settled the matter once and for all: "Do not judge, or you too will be judged" (Matt 7:1). This admonition, however, has often been misinterpreted to mean that we are not to disapprove of anything another person does. But how, then, would we be able to follow through on Jesus' later instruction that "by their fruit you will recognize them" (Matt 7:16)? It is harsh and censorious criticism that Jesus opposed, not insight conditioned and made possible by biblical truth.

Verse 10 states without equivocation that all believers will be judged. The judgment will not entail a decision regarding one's salvation because according to John 5:24 the believer has already crossed over from death to life. Eternal life is a present possession (cf. 1 Cor 3:10–15). There will, however, be for every believer a judgment of the quality of his or her life. In 2 Cor 5:10 Paul said, "We must all appear before the judgment seat of Christ, that each one may receive what is due him for the things done while in the body, whether good or bad." This will be a judgment based

---

[105] ἀδελφός, a term Paul had not used since 12:1, occurs five times in chap. 14 (vv. 10 [twice],13,15,21). It stresses the incongruity of treating fellow Christians in such a shameful way.

[106] For ἐξουθενεῖς cf. note on v. 3. The tendency to judge (v. 10a) leads rather quickly to contempt (v. 10b).

[107] παρίστημι may serve as a legal technical term for appearing before a judge in a court of law (BAGD, 628). Cf. Acts 27:24.

[108] βῆμα is a technical term for the official seat on which the higher Roman officials sat in their function as judge (*EDNT* 1.215). Some MSS read χριστοῦ for θεοῦ, probably due to the influence of 2 Cor 5:10.

[109] Barclay, *Romans,* 188.

on works (cf. Matt 16:27; Rom 2:6; Rev 22:12). In the long run the validity of faith is established by the quality of life it produces. What people do is the most accurate indicator of what they really believe.

Paul quoted Ps 45:23 in support of the validity of universal judgment (v. 11).[110] Every knee will bow before God, and every tongue will acknowledge him as God.[111] The same passage is quoted in Phil 2:6–11, where Christ's elevation to honor comes as a result of his obedience to the messianic mission. Verse 12 serves as an emphatic summary of the previous paragraph. "Each of us then will have to answer for himself to God" (Moffatt).[112] Since that is true, it is highly questionable, to say the least, for us to be involved in judging one another. Judging is a divine prerogative. To take up that role is to usurp the place of God himself.

14:13–18 So it was time for the believers in Rome to stop criticizing one another. If they felt they must reach a decision about something, they were not to place a stumbling block or an occasion to sin in the path of a weaker brother in Christ.[113] Paul himself was fully convinced that nothing was intrinsically unclean.[114] To Timothy he wrote, "Everything God created is good, and nothing is to be rejected if it is received with thanksgiving (1 Tim 4:4; cf. Titus 1:15). The old taboos on certain ceremonial foods were no longer in force. Jesus taught that it is not what goes into the mouth that makes a person unclean but what comes out

---

[110] Paul quoted Isa 45:23 beginning with ὅτι but preceded it with a clause from Isa 49:18 (ζῶ ἐγώ, λέγει κύριος, "'As I live,' says the Lord"). Apparently he was quoting from memory and brought the two passages together without realizing it. Black believes that Paul introduced the Isaiah passage as he did "with the clear intention of identifying 'the Lord' in the quotation with the . . . Risen and Living Lord" (*Romans,* 195). Cranfield, however, holds that it is more likely that Paul was referring to God (*Romans,* 2:710).

[111] O. Hoofs notes that Paul found in ἐξομολογέομαι "a reference to the eschatological confession of sin that every person must make before the judgment seat of God" (*EDNT* 2.9). Others follow the LXX use of the word and translate it "praise" or "give thanks." Paul used the same verb on two other occasions (Rom 15:9; Phil 2:11), and in both cases it means "to praise." Cf. Matt 11:25 for a similar use.

[112] Morris notes that "'*each*' makes the judgment universal, and '*of us*' makes it personal" (*Romans,* 484). "Every word in this sentence is emphatic" is Denney's oft-quoted remark (*Romans,* 704).

[113] Murray calls attention to the two distinct senses in which κρίνω is used in v. 13. First, κρίνωμεν means "don't judge harshly" and then κρίνατε means "determine, decide" (*Romans,* 2:186). The original stem of σκάνδαλον has the idea of trapping (*TDNT* abr., 1036), although no reference to the "trip-stick of a trap" is documented in literature (*EDNT* 3.249). In the latter article H. Giesen refers to πρόσκομμα ἢ σκάνδαλον as a hendiadys, "stumbling block to faith."

[114] κοινός was a semitechnical term describing those customs of the non-Jewish world that were forbidden to the devout Jewish believer.

(Matt 15:10–11,16–20). Nevertheless, Paul was concerned with the
affect of this new freedom on the lives of those Christians who still felt
that in some way the regulations of Judaism were not totally obsolete.
Although no food is unclean in itself, if someone regards it as unclean,
then for that person it is.[115]

We must be careful not to generalize on the principle expressed in this
teaching. Paul was not saying that sin is a matter of personal opinion. He
was not teaching that as long as we think something is okay it is okay for
us. Scripture clearly teaches that certain things are wrong. There are,
however, other matters about which there may be legitimate differences
of opinion. They are secondary issues about which Christians may be of
differing persuasions. In such cases "strong" believers are to be willing,
as an expression of Christian love, to allow the sensitivities of the
"weak" to condition how they live.[116]

If a Christian brother, unable to enjoy the freedom that is yours, is troubled by your "unrestricted diet" (Phillips) and you persist in eating whatever you wish, you are no longer acting in the spirit of love (v. 15). Paul's
instruction is clear: Do not allow your own freedom of conscience to
destroy your brother or sister for whom Christ died.[117] To influence others
to act against their conscience is a serious matter. Acting contrary to what
one perceives to be right is to weaken one's own moral structure and
undermine integrity. Since Christ died for believers with a weak conscience (as well as for all others), certainly it is not too much to ask that
strong believers not destroy them by encouraging actions of which the
weaker brothers do not approve. Elsewhere Paul discussed the same issue
and added that if a weak believer is destroyed by your knowledge, your
sin is not only against that person but also against Christ (1 Cor 8:11–12).

Stronger Christians are not to encourage misunderstanding by allowing what they consider to be permissible to be an occasion for slanderous talk (v. 16).[118] After all, the kingdom of God is not a matter of eating

---

[115] Bruce comments that "defilement is located in people's minds, not in material objects" and adds that this truth has "far reaching implications" (*Romans*, 237).

[116] Black writes, "It is better to tolerate another's prejudice than to advocate one's beliefs at the expense of a breach of *agape*" (*Romans*, 196).

[117] Note, as Bruce says, "the divine worth of a human being" (*Romans*, 238).

[118] Commentators discuss what is meant by ὑμῶν τὸ ἀγαθόν and the identity of the one who speaks evil of it. "What you consider good" probably is either the gospel or the freedom that strong believers enjoy. Those who speak evil of it probably are those outside the church. Stuhlmacher sees the verse as "a warning from the apostle not to discredit the church and the salvation obtained by it before the eyes and ears of unbelievers through an offensive dispute between the strong and weak" (*Romans*, 227).

and drinking but of righteous living.[119] For people to insist on eating whatever they want (since nothing is unclean in itself) is to reduce the kingdom to matters of dietary preference. God's kingdom simply cannot be trivialized in this way. His kingdom has to do with righteous living.[120] Its concerns are significantly broader and relate to issues such as peace and joy, which come from our relationship to the Holy Spirit.[121] Those who serve Christ in this way, that is, "by recognizing that food and drink are secondary matters," bring pleasure to God and are accepted by others.[122] Pursuing the higher priorities is something "approved by men" and "pleasing to God."

14:19–21   The conclusion is that believers are to make every effort to do those things that lead to peace and to mutual upbuilding.[123] Although peace with God was central in Paul's thought, the peace he spoke of here was peace within the family of believers (cf. Ps 34:15). "Christian history, alas, shows numerous examples of people utterly earnest about nonessentials, who have felt at liberty to break the unity of the Church for the sake of their particular fetish."[124] We are not to destroy what God is doing[125] by insisting on our right to eat what we want. "All food is clean" may have been a slogan used by the strong. If so, it should be taken in a restricted sense as applying to such things as people eat and drink.[126] While freedom is a right, it is not a guide for

---

[119] Only eight of the sixty-five occurrences of βασιλεία τοῦ θεοῦ in the NT are in Paul's letters. It has been suggested that he made little use of the concept because as an itinerant preacher traveling throughout the Roman Empire to proclaim another kingdom could lead to charges of sedition (cf. Dunn, *Romans,* 2:822). On the other hand it may have been because non-Jews did not have the OT background to comprehend it fully.

[120] Thomas says the three main principles of the kingdom of God are moral uprightness, fellowship among Christians, and the joy of genuine exaltation (*Romans,* 375).

[121] Some hold that the phrase "in the Holy Spirit" belongs only with the final term in the triad (i.e., joy). Others connect it to all three. Although the Spirit is certainly involved in both righteousness and peace, it seems better to read the phrase primarily with "joy." See Rhys for other interpretations of the triad (*Romans,* 180). Cranfield would have us remember that "the joy which is the sign of the presence of God's kingdom is specifically the joy given by God's Spirit." It must be distinguished from any joy "which is merely the temporary result of the satisfaction of one's own selfish desires" (*Romans,* 2:718). Cf. 1 Thess 1:6; Acts 13:52.

[122] Barrett, *Romans,* 265.

[123] οἰκοδομή ("building, edifice") here refers to the process of building. That which is being built is the ἐκκλησία (*EDNT* 2.496).

[124] Hunter, *Romans,* 121.

[125] κατάλυε describes an action opposite of τῆς οἰκοδομῆς. Of the many interpretations offered for τὸ ἔργον τοῦ θεοῦ the most likely is "God's work in the weak brother, the new man He has begun to create" (Cranfield, *Romans,* 2:723).

[126] However, the text does not include the word "food" (πάντα μὲν καθαρά). Morris understands it in a wider sense as including "anything that soils or corrupts" (*Romans,* 490).

conduct. Love serves that purpose. Rights are to be laid aside in the interest of love. That principle was firmly established by the incarnation (Phil 2:6–11). All food is now ceremonially clean (Titus 1:15), but it is wrong to eat if by that act others are encouraged to act against their conscience. The right course of action is to refrain from eating meat or drinking wine or doing anything else that will cause another believer to fall (cf. 1 Cor 8:13).[127] If Paul began to sound repetitive in this section it was simply because he felt the issue to be so important that it bore continual restatement. The apostle knew the difficulty of driving home a point that runs contrary to the prevailing attitude.

14:22–23 Such issues as the ceremonial condition of food offered to God are best kept as private matters between a person and God.[128] "Blessed are those who do not condemn themselves by eating certain foods that they have approved." This admonition is relevant to both the weak and the strong. What is wrong is to act in a way that contravenes one's convictions.[129] Those who eat a certain food about which they have reservations will stand condemned.[130] That is because their actions do not spring from faith. Those who doubt do not have the assurance that what they are doing is acceptable.[131]

The final clause of v. 23 ("Everything that does not come from faith is sin") is applicable on a much wider scale than the immediate context.[132] Whatever is done without the conviction that God has approved it is by definition sin.[133] God has called us to a life of faith. Trust is the willing-

---

[127] φαγεῖν and πιεῖν are both aorist participles, which suggests that the principle is to be applied in those specific instances where a weaker believer will be offended by the act.

[128] The Old Latin MSS and all the other versions omit the relative pronoun ἥν, allowing the clause to be read as either a statement or a question. The AV has, "Hast thou faith?"

[129] Bruce defines πίστις as it occurs here in the Greek text as "a firm and intelligent conviction before God that one is doing what is right" (*Romans,* 239). It is not the essential Christian faith as Paul used the term elsewhere.

[130] The perfect passive (κατακέκριται) is to be taken proleptically. Montgomery translates "condemned already."

[131] Cf. Luke 6:4 in Codex Bezae, in which Jesus said to a man working on the Sabbath, "If you know what you are doing, you are blessed; but if you do not know, you are accursed and a transgressor of the law."

[132] A number of commentators restrict this to those matters Paul had been discussing, such as eating meat, drinking wine, and related issues (e.g., Fitzmyer, *Romans,* 700; Cranfield, *Romans,* 2:728), but Dunn is correct in his assessment that the final clause is "the statement of a general principle or rule ... and not one limited to the particular issue under discussion (*Romans,* 2:828).

[133] ἁμαρτία is used fifty-three times by Paul with the general meaning of an "offense against God with a stress on guilt" (*TDNT* abr., 48). Here it is used to describe the result of acting without the necessary inner freedom to do so. Bruce comments that "an act performed against the voice of conscience can never be right" (*Romans,* 728).

ness to put all of life before God for his approval. Any doubt concerning an action automatically removes that action from the category of that which is acceptable. This principle will be of special help to the Christian in what is sometimes called the "gray area." If it is gray to you, it is wrong—not in itself necessarily but for the one who is considering it.[134]

15:1–4 Paul's concern that weak and strong Christians live in harmony carries right on into chap. 15. The apostle placed himself in the company of the strong ("we who are strong"). Their faith in Christ allowed them to partake with a clear conscience of food that earlier they had held to be ceremonially unclean. They were free from ceremonial obligations, but they remained under the obligations of love. It was not enough that the strong simply put up with the foibles of weaker Christians; they were to bear the weaknesses of the immature.[135] Rather than insisting on their own way, they were to be supportive of those whose faith was insufficiently robust (cf. Gal 6:1–2). The temptation of the strong is to pay scant attention to the timorousness of the weak. But Paul insisted that the strong be supportive and helpful to those who naturally speaking would be nonproductive in the assembly.

Rather than pleasing themselves, strong believers are to please their neighbors.[136] The goal is to help them develop into more mature Christians (v. 2). The goal is the benefit of the one in greatest need of help (cf. 1 Cor 10:24,33). The great example of self-denial for the sake of others is, of course, Jesus Christ (v. 3). If Christ, the very Son of God, did not order his life so as to please himself, how much more should we forego all personal advantage and follow the path of the Suffering Servant.[137] The selfless life of Christ is reflected in Ps 69:9, "The insults of those

---

[134] Marcion ended his edition of Romans at this point. For a concise summary of the problems of the termination of Romans, see *TCGNT,* 533–36.

[135] The literal meaning of βαστάζω is "to take up, bear." Figuratively it is used to convey the idea of enduring or putting up with. In the present context it goes beyond mere toleration. "Those who are strong in faith should be willing to experience self-denial for the sake of believers whose faith is weak" (Newman and Nida, *A Handbook on Paul's Letter to the Romans* [New York: UBS, 1973], 270). Moffatt translates, "We who are strong ought to bear the burdens that the weak make for themselves and us."

[136] Luther remarks that those set on pleasing themselves are given to scorn for others. "They do not rejoice, because they [themselves] are righteous, but rather, because others are unrighteous" (*Romans,* 192). In this context ὁ πλησίον ("neighbor") refers not to people in general but to a member of the believing community.

[137] ἤρεσεν is a constative aorist indicating how Jesus lived throughout his entire earthly life. It was not his practice to make his decisions and act in a way that would bring pleasure to himself. In the world *noblesse oblige* ("privilege entails responsibility") requires a person of importance in society to live for the benefit of those less fortunate.

who insult you have fallen on me."[138] As Paul applied the verse, Christ becomes the speaker; and God, the second person. That Christ did not live to please himself is clearly stated in Mark 10:45 ("For even the Son of Man did not come to be served, but to serve, and to give his life as a ransom for many"; cf. 1 Cor 10:33–11:1; 2 Cor 8:9; Phil 2:5–8).

Verse 4 contains a principle of great significance for the twentieth-century believer. Everything that was written in Scripture in days gone by was written for us. Not only did it serve the needs of its own day but it is still relevant in the modern world. Scripture is relevant because it speaks to our deepest needs.[139] It is through the endurance taught in Scripture[140] and the encouragement it brings that we are enabled to live in hope. Morris reminds us that "Paul is not exhorting believers to pull themselves together and manifest these qualities, but rejoicing in God who gives them" (cf. v. 5).[141] The difficulties of today are bearable because God in his Word tells us of a better time yet to come. He mediates his comfort and encouragement by speaking through his Word to the hearts of receptive believers. To separate oneself from Scripture is to turn a deaf ear to the voice of a Heavenly Father anxious to console.

15:5–6   Paul's wish was that God would grant the church at Rome a spirit of unity. His desire that they "mind the same thing among one another" (literal translation) does not mean that they should all come to the same conclusion. That is obvious from his discussion of the weak and the strong—the conscience of each is to guide the conduct of that person. It is unity of perspective that is desired. And that perspective is that of Christ Jesus, our model for Christian conduct. Think as he does. Take on his values and priorities. As each member of the church draws closer to Christ, we will at the same time draw closer to other members of the body. The experience of Christian unity produces a symphony of praise to God in which each voice blends with all the others to the glory of God. It is a family affair. We, the adopted sons of God, sing praises to

---

[138] "Ps. 69 was evidently widely used as a Christological *testimonium* in the early Church" (Black, *Romans,* 200).

[139] The contemporaneity of Scripture is seen in verses such as 1 Cor 10:11 ("These things happened to them as examples and were written down as warnings for us, on whom the fulfillment of the ages has come"), and Rom 4:23–24 ("The words 'it was credited to him' were written not for him alone, but also for us, to whom God will credit righteousness—for us who believe in him who raised Jesus our Lord from the dead").

[140] Many writers hold that the two διά clauses are independent and that τῶν γραφῶν modifies only τῆς παρακλήσεως.

[141] Morris, *Romans,* 501.

the Father of our Lord Jesus Christ.

15:7–12 This paragraph brings to a close Paul's major presentation. It highlights the overall theme of the letter, "the inclusion of the Gentiles within the promises to his people."[142] Both the weak and the strong are to accept one another.[143] That is what it means to follow Christ. He accepted us;[144] we are to accept one another. It should not be too difficult to extend the hand of friendship to one who is loved by the one we honor and worship (cf. 14:1,3,15). We might say, "Any friend of his is a friend of mine." This spirit of brotherly kindness will bring praise to God, who makes it all possible in the first place.[145]

Christ became a servant of the Jews to demonstrate the truthfulness of God (v. 8).[146] He confirmed the promises made to the patriarchs by fulfilling them. Now the Gentiles can glorify God for the mercy he has shown to them.[147] Of the many promises made by God to the children of Israel, none is more apropos in this context than Gen 22:18, "Through your offspring all nations on earth will be blessed" (cf. Acts 3:25). God's great redemptive plan was that through his Son, born a Jew as to his human nature (cf. 1:3), he might reach out in reconciling love to those of every nation under the sun.

In support of the universal scope of God's redemptive work through Christ his Son, Paul cited four Old Testament Scriptures.[148] The first is

---

[142] Dunn, *Romans,* 2:848.

[143] προσλαμβάνομαι denotes a genuine and heartfelt acceptance.

[144] Some MSS read ἡμᾶς rather than ὑμᾶς.

[145] The final clause of v. 8 completes the main clause of the sentence, although the theme of mutual acceptance would be strengthened if it were connected with the dependent clause. There is no reason the final clause cannot be understood with both.

[146] The Greek text has περιτομή, "circumcision," thus identifying the Jewish people by their distinctive covenant mark. Sanday and Headlam, however, understand διάκονον . . . περιτομῆς to mean "'a minister of circumcision' . . . i.e., to carry out the promise implied in that covenant the seal of which was circumcision" (*Romans,* 397–98).

[147] The syntactical relationship of v. 9 to the previous verse is unclear. Cf. Cranfield (*Romans,* 2:742–43) for a discussion of six different possibilities. Some take v. 9 as directly dependent on λέγω and therefore parallel but adversative to v. 8. Dunn objects that this answer provides little coherence and that reading δέ as a strong adversative separates the promises and the acceptability of the Gentiles to God (*Romans,* 2:847–48). Perhaps a better solution is to take the two aorist active infinitives (βεβαιῶσαι and δοξάσαι) as parallel. Thus Christ is said to have had two purposes in becoming a servant of the Jews: (1) to confirm the promises made to the patriarchs and (2) so that the Gentiles might glorify God (the major theme of chap. 11).

[148] The quotes come from all three divisions of the OT canon: the Law, the Prophets, and the Writings.

found in 2 Sam 22:50 and in Ps 18:49. David vowed to praise God among the Gentiles, to sing in honor of his name. Israel was to be the instrument through whom God's redemptive work would extend to the Gentiles. The second is from Moses' great hymn celebrating God's victory over Pharaoh and his army: "Rejoice, O Gentiles, in company with his people" (Deut 32:43). The third is from Ps 117:1, where the writer called upon the Gentiles to lift their voices in praise to the Lord. Paul cited the verse in support of his position that the salvation of the Gentiles was in God's mind from the very first. It was not something he decided at a later time. Finally, Paul cited the well-known messianic promise from Isaiah 11. The Messiah will come as a shoot springing up from the stump of David's family line.[149] He will rule the nations, and on him the Gentiles will "rest their hopes" (TCNT). "The Gentile mission of the early church was a fulfillment of this prophecy, as is the continuing evangelization of the nations."[150]

15:13   The mention of hope in v. 12 leads naturally to a "prayer-wish" directed to God, who is the source of all hope. The prayer was that God would fill the believers at Rome with all joy and peace.[151] Note, however, that it was "as you trust in him."[152] While it is God who provides the joy and peace, it is our continuing confidence and trust in God that enables him to bless us as he does. The joy and peace given by God results in an overflow of hope in the life of the believer. Our role is to maintain a relationship of continuing trust in God. Everything else is in his hands, and he never fails. Our experience of overflowing hope is made possible by the power of the Holy Spirit.[153] Clearly, the Christian life is God's empowering presence in the midst of life's uncertainties. It is not up to us to conjure up hope or any other spiritual quality. Our only access to empowerment is to believe. Then God steps in and does the rest. The Christian life is a supernatural life in the fullest sense of that term: "Christ in you, the hope of glory" (Col 1:27; cf. Phil 1:21).

---

[149] Dunn notes that ἀνίστημι can mean simply "arise," but since it occurs so frequently in connection with the resurrection "it would be surprising if Paul did not have in mind the double reference" (*Romans,* 2:850).

[150] NIVSB note on Rom 15:12.

[151] Luther comments that "the Apostle places joy first and then peace, because it is joy that gives peace to men, engendering it in their hearts" (*Romans,* 198–99).

[152] ἐν τῷ πιστεύειν is causal.

[153] Cranfield comments, "The existence of this hope in men is no human possibility but the creation of the Spirit of God" (*Romans,* 2:748). "There are no hopeless situations," writes Barclay; "there are only men who have grown hopeless about them" (*Romans,* 199).

At this point Paul's great argument comes to a close. From here to the end of the letter he deals with several matters of a more personal nature. He had told them in detail of the gospel he preached. It revealed a righteousness from God that justifies sinful people on the basis of faith alone. It supersedes the Jewish law but maintains the moral demands for which the law stood. The new morality it creates is God's righteousness at work in human lives.[154] These are the themes that have dominated the earlier chapters. Now it was up to the Romans to evaluate all that the apostle had written.

---

[154] This summary is from Dodd, *Romans,* 224.

VII. CONCLUSION (15:14–16:27)
    1. Paul and His Plans (15:14–33)
        (1) Paul's Ministry to the Gentiles (15:14–22)
        (2) Paul's Plan to Visit Rome (15:23–33)
    2. Some Final Items (16:1–27)
        (1) Commendation for Phoebe (16:1–2)
        (2) Greeting (16:3–16)
        (3) Warnings against False Teachers (16:17–20)
        (4) Greetings from Paul's Companions (16:21–23)
        (5) Doxology (16:25–27)

VII. CONCLUSION (15:14–16:27)

1. Paul and His Plans (15:14–33)

(1) Paul's Ministry to the Gentiles (15:14–22)

[14]I myself am convinced, my brothers, that you yourselves are full of goodness, complete in knowledge and competent to instruct one another. [15]I have written you quite boldly on some points, as if to remind you of them again, because of the grace God gave me [16]to be a minister of Christ Jesus to the Gentiles with the priestly duty of proclaiming the gospel of God, so that the Gentiles might become an offering acceptable to God, sanctified by the Holy Spirit.

[17]Therefore I glory in Christ Jesus in my service to God. [18]I will not venture to speak of anything except what Christ has accomplished through me in leading the Gentiles to obey God by what I have said and done— [19]by the power of signs and miracles, through the power of the Spirit. So from Jerusalem all the way around to Illyricum, I have fully proclaimed the gospel of Christ. [20]It has always been my ambition to preach the gospel where Christ was not known, so that I would not be building on someone else's foundation. [21]Rather, as it is written:

"Those who were not told about him will see,

    and those who have not heard will understand." [22]This is why I have often been hindered from coming to you.

15:14–16 Although Paul had never visited or ministered to the Christian congregation in Rome, he was confident that they were a healthy church (chap. 16 reveals that he knew a number of them personally).[1] Morally, they were "full of goodness," intellectually they were "complete in knowledge," and functionally they were "competent to instruct one another."[2] Williams says they were "competent to counsel." The believers in Rome were expected to help one another toward spiritual maturity. They were to advise and instruct one another.[3] None were so wise that they had nothing more to learn, and none were so inept that they had nothing of value to share. Spiritual insight is by no means the sole prerogative of those with high intelligence.

Paul reflected that in parts of his epistle he had written rather boldly (v. 15).[4] It was his way of refreshing their memory regarding certain basic tenets of the Christian faith they had previously learned. Paul did not pretend to be bringing them theological insights they never had heard. His tone was courteous. His letter to the church in Rome was in keeping with his role as the Apostle to the Gentiles (cf. 11:13; Gal 2:8). Paul's service as a priest of Christ Jesus was to proclaim the gospel of God.[5] Using the language of religious ceremony, he pictured his role as that of a priest bringing an offering to God. The offering consisted of believing Gentiles who had been sanctified by the Holy Spirit (cf. Phil 2:17 for another example of liturgical metaphor).[6]

---

[1] There is a balance between καὶ αὐτὸς ἐγὼ and καὶ αὐτοί. The first stresses the depth of his conviction regarding what he was about to say and the second an awareness that they had grown spiritually without his help. E. Käsemann explains the latter as "you yourselves without the cooperation of others (*Commentary on Romans* [Grand Rapids: Eerdmans, 1980], 391).

[2] There may be some hyperbole in this statement, but it does not follow that "the object of these complimentary references is now, as at chapter 1, to prevent the hearers from taking offence" (M. Black, *Romans,* 2d ed., NCBC [Grand Rapids: Eerdmans, 1989], 202).

[3] The stress of νουθετέω is on "influencing not merely the intellect but the will and disposition. . . . The idea is not that of punishment but of a moral appeal that leads to amendment" (*TDNT* abr., 645).

[4] ἀπὸ μέρους could mean "in some measure" or "on some points" (Goodspeed), but here it refers to "certain parts" (perhaps 12:1–15:13), not all of his letter. ἔγραψα is an epistolary aorist; it does not refer to some earlier correspondence.

[5] λειτουργός is one who performs a public service. In the NT, however, it carries religious connotations. Heb 8:2 applies the term to Christ, the true High Priest, who "serves in the sanctuary." Cranfield comes to the conclusion that Barth is correct in understanding Paul as thinking of himself as fulfilling the function not of a priest but of a Levite (*Romans,* ICC [Edinburgh: T & T Clark, 1975–79], 2:754–56), a position J. D. G. Dunn says is "too strained" (*Romans,* WBC [Dallas: Word, 1988], 2:859). See also Mal 2:7.

[6] τῶν ἐθνῶν is a genitive of apposition (cf. Isa 66:20, where the Jewish remnant is to be brought back to Jerusalem "as an offering to the Lord").

15:17–22   Paul wrote that he had reason to be proud, not of any personal achievement but of what Christ had accomplished through him. In a similar passage in 2 Corinthians he acknowledged that his "competence comes from God" (2 Cor 3:5). By faithfully carrying out his priestly duty of proclaiming the gospel to the Gentiles, Paul had served as Christ's instrument in leading the Gentiles to obedience to God.[7] Like the ancient heralds who walked throughout the city proclaiming only what the king chose to make known,[8] so Paul served as an ambassador of Christ (cf. 2 Cor 5:18–20) spreading the gospel of God. His ministry was accompanied by "signs and miracles."[9] Together they attested the power of God. Betz notes that the signs of the apostle "are not only charismatic miracles but also missionary successes visible in the life of the congregation (cf. 2 Cor 3:2)."[10] The signs and miracles that had accompanied Paul's ministry among the Gentiles revealed the presence and power of the Holy Spirit.

Paul could attest that all the way from Jerusalem to Illyricum he had fulfilled his task of preaching the gospel of Christ (v. 19).[11] To have "fully proclaimed the gospel of Christ" does not mean that he had evangelized everyone in the area indicated but that he had completed his "trail-blazing, pioneer preaching" of the gospel that he believed was his own special apostolic ministry.[12] As Acts reveals, Paul's strategy was to concentrate his missionary activity on the great urban centers of his day.

---

[7] "The main purpose of the Epistle to the Romans. Cf. 1:5" (Black, *Romans*, 203).

[8] See R. Mounce, *The Essential Nature of New Testament Preaching* (Grand Rapids: Eerdmans, 1960), 12–14, for a summary of the role of the herald in the ancient world.

[9] τέρας ("wonder") occurs sixteen times in the NT, always in the plural and always accompanied by σημεῖον ("sign"). The first term emphasizes the unusual nature of the event (contrary to nature), and the second calls attention to its significance. E. F. Harrison defines a "sign" as "a visible token of an invisible reality that is spiritually significant" ("Romans," EBC 10, ed. F. E. Gaebelein [Grand Rapids: Zondervan, 1976], 156). The two terms occur together nine times in Acts. They are the marks of an apostle (2 Cor 12:12; Heb 2:4).

[10] *EDNT* 3.241.

[11] Paul began his actual preaching in Damascus and his extended missionary journeys from Syrian Antioch, but Jerusalem was considered the heart of the Christian movement. Illyricum is the Roman province across the Adriatic Sea from Italy. κύκλῳ μέχρι ("around to") describes a broad arc that begins in Jerusalem, goes through Syrian Antioch and Asia Minor, "right up to Illyricum" (Dunn, *Romans,* 2:864). Since Acts does not mention any missionary work of Paul in Illyricum, it is customary to assume it took place in the interval described in Acts 20:1–6. But the Romans text does not say Paul preached *in* Illyricum, only that his journeys took him *that far* (μέχρι, when used of space, means "as far as" [BAGD, 515]). Cranfield raises the possibility that the reference is to that part of the province of Macedonia that was inhabited by people of Illyrian race (*Romans,* 2:761).

[12] Cranfield, *Romans,* 2:762.

He had accomplished that goal in the eastern Mediterranean world and
from that point on intended to move to the western reaches of the
empire. Paul's ambition had always been to preach the gospel in places
where Christ was not known.[13] He would rather not build on founda-
tions laid by others.[14] That was not because of some peculiar pride that
would encourage him to go it on his own but because of his intense
desire to reach the known world as quickly as possible. In support of his
modus operandi he quoted the prophet Isaiah's words concerning the
Suffering Servant (Isa 52:15).[15] It is for this reason that the apostle was
so often hindered from going to Rome. That is, his desire to fulfill his
ministry among those in the Eastern Mediterranean sector who had not
heard kept him from moving on with his subsequent plan to visit Rome
and proceed westward to Spain.

(2) Paul's Plan to Visit Rome (15:23–33)

[23]**But now that there is no more place for me to work in these regions,
and since I have been longing for many years to see you, [24]I plan to do so
when I go to Spain. I hope to visit you while passing through and to have
you assist me on my journey there, after I have enjoyed your company for
a while. [25]Now, however, I am on my way to Jerusalem in the service of the
saints there. [26]For Macedonia and Achaia were pleased to make a contribution for the poor among the saints in Jerusalem. [27]They were pleased to
do it, and indeed they owe it to them. For if the Gentiles have shared in the
Jews' spiritual blessings, they owe it to the Jews to share with them their
material blessings. [28]So after I have completed this task and have made
sure that they have received this fruit, I will go to Spain and visit you on
the way. [29]I know that when I come to you, I will come in the full measure
of the blessing of Christ.**

[30]**I urge you, brothers, by our Lord Jesus Christ and by the love of the
Spirit, to join me in my struggle by praying to God for me. [31]Pray that I
may be rescued from the unbelievers in Judea and that my service in
Jerusalem may be acceptable to the saints there, [32]so that by God's will I**

---

[13] "Not where Christ was named" (ὠνομάσθη) means where the message of Christ had not
yet been heard and Christ had not yet been acknowledged in terms of what his name implies.
H. C. G. Moule laments, "Would that the principle of it [the preaching of the gospel where it
was not known] could have been better remembered in the history of Christendom, and not
least in our own age" (*The Epistle to the Romans,* new ed. [London: Pickering & Inglis, n.d.],
412–13).

[14] If this seems inconsistent with his plans to visit Rome, remember that the visit to Rome
was simply preparatory to his continuing work in Spain (Rom 15:24,28).

[15] Paul followed the LXX interpretation in which the reference is to the Servant of Yahweh
and then applied the verse to his own ministry.

may come to you with joy and together with you be refreshed. ³³The God of peace be with you all. Amen.

15:23–29 On the basis of the principle set forth in v. 20—to preach where Christ is not known—Paul could say that no longer was there opportunity to carry out his apostolic ministry in the regions covered in his first three missionary journeys.[16] For many years he had had the desire to visit the believers in Rome. Now he had the opportunity. His trip to Spain would take him through Rome, where he would spend some time with the believers.[17] It was his desire that they would send him on his way with their support, both spiritual and material.[18] Right now, however, he was on his way to Jerusalem (cf. Acts 19:21).[19] There he would deliver the financial gift that the churches in Macedonia and Achaia had gathered for the poor among God's people (cf. 2 Cor 8:1; 9:2,12).[20] It was important for the Jewish Christians to understand that the contribution provided by the Gentile believers demonstrated their love and affection for their brethren in Christ.[21] God's love binds together all believers regardless of ethnic origin. The contribution made by the Gentile church expressed in tangible form the bond of Christian unity that surpasses the artificial barriers of race.

The believers in Macedonia and Achaia were pleased to make a contribution to their fellow believers in Jerusalem who were in need.[22] And, in fact, they owed it to them. From the Jewish church they had received spiritual blessings (v. 27). They were obligated to respond with material

---

[16] Peterson paraphrases, "Now that there is no more pioneering work to be done in these parts . . ." (*The Message,* 334).

[17] Spain (or "Iberia," as the Greeks called it) then was part of the Roman Empire. "For Paul Spain represents the unconverted world of the west" (J. A. Fitzmyer, *Romans,* AB [New York: Doubleday, 1993], 717). Kraeling holds that it was the large number of enslaved Greeks who had been sent to Spain that attracted Paul to the area (*HDB,* 932). Whether Paul ever went to Spain (following a first imprisonment in Rome) is still being debated. References to such a trip, found in Clement of Rome (*1 Clem.* 5.7) and the Muratorian Canon, are strong evidence but fall short of proving beyond doubt that Paul actually set foot in Spain.

[18] Cf. his expectations in connection with his plan to visit Corinth (1 Cor 16:6).

[19] πορεύομαι (present tense) conveys the idea he was about ready to leave for Jerusalem.

[20] τῶν ἁγίων is partitive, not epexegetic ("the poor who are the saints").

[21] Dunn comments that the reasons for Paul's desire to take the collection to Jerusalem "are not so clear as we might have hoped," but then he lists five suggestions, each of which is not without cogency (*Romans,* 2:873–74).

[22] Since the word translated "contribution" (κοινωνία) is usually rendered elsewhere "fellowship" (Acts 2:42; 1 Cor 1:9; Phil 3:10), it is possible to understand v. 26 as saying that Macedonia and Achaia "have undertaken to establish a rather close relation w. the poor" (BAGD, 439). Some conjecture that the poverty in the early church resulted from their distribution of capital in the first days of the new movement (Acts 2:44–45; 4:32,34–35).

help when the occasion called for it (cf. 1 Cor 9:11).[23] So after Paul had completed this responsibility, being sure the gift was safely in their hands, he would start for Spain and come by Rome on his way.[24] He was confident that his visit would be accompanied with the full measure of Christ's blessing.[25] Always in the mind of the apostle was the spiritual potential of every personal contact. His sensitivity to the spiritual needs of others is everywhere evident. What for many would be merely a pleasant contact becomes for the apostle an occasion to share the blessings of Christ.

15:30–33 Although Paul seemed rather confident in the preceding paragraph, he nevertheless called upon his Christian brethren to join him in his struggle by praying to God[26] for him. Paul's final meeting with the Ephesian elders reveals his sense of uncertainty about what could happen to him when he returned to Jerusalem. The Holy Spirit had continually warned him of the perils that lay ahead (Acts 20:22–23). Paul urged the believers in Rome to enter into his conflict by joining him in prayer.[27] This request reveals the true humility of the apostle. The reality of intense spiritual opposition moved him to request urgently that his friends in Christ join him in the struggle. It was pride that kept believers from sharing their need for spiritual help.

The Roman Christians were one with Paul in their love for Christ. This provided the essential motive for their entering into the problem he faced. An additional motive was the love inspired by the Spirit.[28]

---

[23] σαρκικός means "belonging to the order of earthly things, material" (BAGD, 742). Here it is not pejorative as it is in 1 Cor 3:3 and 2 Cor 10:4.

[24] "Have made sure that they have received" is literally "having sealed to them." The participle σφραγισάμενος is somewhat awkward in this setting, but BAGD understands it in connection with the practice of sealing sacks of grain, the difficulty being that the "fruit" must also be taken to Jerusalem and delivered there. BAGD suggests "when I have placed the sum that was collected safely (sealed) in their hands" (p. 796).

[25] W. Sanday and A. C. Headlam note that these words argue for the authenticity and early date of the chapter because "no one could possibly write in this manner at a later date, knowing the circumstances under which St. Paul actually did visit Rome" (*A Critical and Exegetical Commentary on the Epistle to the Romans,* 5th ed., ICC [Edinburgh: T & T Clark, 1902], 414).

[26] Note that all three persons of the Trinity ("our Lord Jesus Christ . . . the Spirit . . . God") are specifically mentioned in this one verse.

[27] συναγωνίζομαι in v. 30 means "to fight along with." It occurs only here in the NT. Black thinks the image of prayer as "an 'agonizing,' 'wrestling' with God" could go back to the account in Gen 32:22–32 of Jacob wrestling with God (*Romans,* 205). Cf. 2 Cor 1:11; Col 4:3; 2 Thess 3:1 for similar requests for prayer.

[28] J. Denney notes: διά in this construction "indicates that in which the motive is found" ("St. Paul's Epistle to the Romans," *EGT* 2 [Grand Rapids: Eerdmans, 1983], 687, 716).

Awareness of a fellow believer's difficult situation will move the authentic Christian to join that person in prayer. Paul asked that the Roman Christians pray with him that he would be rescued from those in Judea who had rejected the faith.[29] He also was concerned that his mission in Jerusalem be well received. The still somewhat fragile union in the church between Jew and Gentile will be measurably strengthened by a favorable reception of the gift.[30] Not only will it provide needed material help but will serve to bind together in a spiritual fellowship the growing number of believers throughout the known world regardless of ethnic origin. Paul desired that by the will of God he might come with joy to Rome and there together with other believers enjoy a time of spiritual refreshment. Such encounters call for earnest prayer. Satan does not intend that the work of God's servants be enjoyable.

The chapter closes with a prayer: "May the God of peace be with you all." He is the God of peace[31] in the sense that he alone can give peace. As Paul wrote elsewhere, it is a peace that "transcends all understanding" (Phil 2:7). It can be experienced and enjoyed, but not rationally explained.

2. Some Final Items (16:1–27)

As indicated in the introduction, I consider chap. 16 to be an integral part of Paul's letter to Rome. It is made up of five separate segments. First, the apostle commends Phoebe to the church at Rome (vv. 1–2). This is followed by a long list of greetings to Paul's friends and helpers living in the capital city (vv. 3–16).[32] Verses 17–20 warn against false

---

[29] ἀπειθής (derived from πείθω, "to persuade," prefixed by an alpha privative, hence "unpersuadable") is "one who will not be persuaded," and therefore "disobedient" (from Strong's *Exhaustive Concordance: Greek Dictionary*, 545, 3982). Black says "the participle 'those who are unbelieving' suggests an active disbelief" (*Romans,* 205).

[30] Cranfield rightly questions the view of "those who still labour in the shadow of the Tübingen school's continuing influence" in finding in this verse evidence of a "serious tension between Paul and the Jerusalem church" (*Romans,* 2:778).

[31] For other examples of this designation cf. Rom 16:20; 2 Cor 13:11; Phil 4:9; 1 Thess 5:23; and Heb 13:20. See also Num 6:26; Judg 6:24; Pss 4:8; 29:11; 85:8; Isa 9:6; 57:19; 66:12.

[32] E. Brunner makes the interesting observation that although it appears at first sight to be a dry list of names, "it is one of the most instructive chapters of the New Testament, provided one knows how to read it properly. . . . The relationship of these persons to one another—that alone is essential in the Christian Community [and such personal relations] are not a matter of secondary importance but belong to the substance of the letter" (*The Letter to the Romans* [Philadelphia: Westminster, 1949], 126–27).

teachers, while vv. 21–23 consist of greetings from Paul's companions to the church at Rome. The chapter closes with a doxology (vv. 25–27).

(3) Commendation for Phoebe (16:1–2)

[1]I commend to you our sister Phoebe, a servant of the church in Cenchrea. [2]I ask you to receive her in the Lord in a way worthy of the saints and to give her any help she may need from you, for she has been a great help to many people, including me.

16:1–2 Letters of commendation were well known in the ancient world.[33] Phoebe is undoubtedly the person carrying Paul's letter to the church at Rome.[34] As the bearer of the letter it would be quite natural for Paul to have commended her and made special mention of her.[35] She is described both as "our sister" (meaning a female member of the Christian community) and as a "servant"[36] in the church at Cenchrea.[37] Paul asked the Roman congregation to welcome her in a manner worthy of God's people. It is uncertain whether the emphasis should be placed on her worthiness as a believer or on the worthy manner in which they as a Christian assembly should conduct themselves. Neither should be excluded. Paul asked the church to provide her with whatever help she needed from them because she had been a staunch friend of many others

---

[33] As attested in the papyri, συνίστημι ("I commend") is a standard way of stating a recommendation.

[34] Since the name Φοίβη was used regularly in mythology, it is reasonable to infer that the Phoebe Paul spoke of was Gentile.

[35] A. M. Hunter refers to Renan's observation that if Phoebe took Paul's letter to Rome, "she carried under her robe the entire future of Christian theology" (*The Epistle to the Romans,* TBC [London: SCM, 1955], 129).

[36] The word is from διάκονος, which can be a general word meaning "servant or helper" (cf. Matt 20:26; Rom 13:4; Eph 6:21; Col 1:23,25; 1 Tim 4:6) as well as an office in the church (cf. Phil 1:1; 1 Tim 3:8,10,12). διάκονος serves as both feminine and masculine. J. Murray correctly notes that the term "can be used to denote the person performing any type of ministry" and concludes that "there is neither need nor warrant to suppose that she occupied or exercised what amounted to an ecclesiastical office comparable to that of the diaconate" (*The Epistle to the Romans,* 2 vols., NICNT [Grand Rapids: Eerdmans, 1965], 2:226). Against this, J. D. G. Dunn writes that "Phoebe is the first recorded "deacon" in the history of Christianity (*Romans,* 2 vols., WBC [Dallas: Word, 1988], 2:887). Weiser assumes that this verse indicates the presence of the deaconess at an early stage in the Pauline churches (*EDNT* 1.303).

[37] Cenchrea was a small seaport about seven miles southeast of Corinth on the Saronic Gulf. It served as the southern harbor of Corinth. Cf. Acts 18:18.

including Paul himself.[38] One is reminded of the reciprocity involved in Paul's words to the Philippians: "You sent me aid again and again when I was in need . . . And my God will meet all your needs" (Phil 4:16,19). Phoebe's help for others merits a similar response from the believers at Rome.

(4) Greetings (16:3–16)

[3] Greet Priscilla and Aquila, my fellow workers in Christ Jesus. [4] They risked their lives for me. Not only I but all the churches of the Gentiles are grateful to them.
[5] Greet also the church that meets at their house.
  Greet my dear friend Epenetus, who was the first convert to Christ in the province of Asia.
[6] Greet Mary, who worked very hard for you.
[7] Greet Andronicus and Junias, my relatives who have been in prison with me. They are outstanding among the apostles, and they were in Christ before I was.
[8] Greet Ampliatus, whom I love in the Lord.
[9] Greet Urbanus, our fellow worker in Christ, and my dear friend Stachys.
[10] Greet Apelles, tested and approved in Christ.
  Greet those who belong to the household of Aristobulus.
[11] Greet Herodion, my relative.
  Greet those in the household of Narcissus who are in the Lord.
[12] Greet Tryphena and Tryphosa, those women who work hard in the Lord.
  Greet my dear friend Persis, another woman who has worked very hard in the Lord.
[13] Greet Rufus, chosen in the Lord, and his mother, who has been a mother to me, too.
[14] Greet Asyncritus, Phlegon, Hermes, Patrobas, Hermas and the brothers with them.
[15] Greet Philologus, Julia, Nereus and his sister, and Olympas and all the saints with them.

---

[38] προστάτις is usually taken in the sense of "helper" or "one who provides support." J. A. Fitzmyer says that in the ancient Greco-Roman world προστάτις denoted a person of prominence, and Phoebe probably was an influential woman of means who could help believers who traveled to and from Corinth (*Romans,* AB [New York: Doubleday, 1993], 731). R. R. Schulz seems to have gone beyond the evidence in arguing that προστάτις here means "leader" or "president," which leads to an interesting title for his article ("A Case for 'President' Phoebe in Romans 16:2," *LTJ* 24 [1990]: 124–27).

**16Greet one another with a holy kiss.
All the churches of Christ send greetings.**

16:3–16 Nowhere else in Paul's writings do we find such a lengthy list of personal greetings.[39] Since Paul had not as yet visited the church at Rome, it is widely held that Romans 16 must have been intended for some other locality (probably Ephesus) and somehow got attached to this letter. But in a long and extensive ministry Paul undoubtedly had established a great number of personal friendships. In preparation for his visit to Rome it would be natural for him to stress his contacts with various believers there.[40] It is not surprising that so many Christians had made their way to the capital city over a period of some twenty years.[41]

Priscilla[42] and Aquila were the first to be greeted.[43] Aquila was a Jewish tentmaker, a native of the Roman province of Pontus. He and his wife Priscilla were driven out of Rome by the edict of Claudius in A.D. 49. Paul met them in Corinth, where he stayed and worked with them (Acts 18:2–3). When he set sail for Ephesus, they went with him (Acts 18:18–19). So close was the friendship that they risked their lives for Paul.[44] For that both he and all the churches of the Gentiles were deeply grateful. Paul sent his greetings to the congregation that met in their house as well (cf. 1 Cor 16:19). In the early days of the church believers

---

[39] L. Morris notes that there are twenty-four names and two who are not named. Of the twenty-six, nine are women (*The Epistle to the Romans* [Grand Rapids: Eerdmans, 1988], 531). W. Barclay notes the significance of the number of women to whom Paul sent his greetings since he is so often accused of belittling the status of women in the church (*The Letter to the Romans,* rev. ed., DSB [Philadelphia: Westminster, 1978], 211–12). Although most of the names are Greek, some are Jewish and some Latin. Readers who have a high regard for Paul's motives and integrity should question H. Rhys' view that the apostle sent greetings to so many in Rome because he was not well known there and wanted to drum up as much support as possible in order to carry out his ambitious plans (*The Epistle to the Romans* [New York: Macmillan, 1961], 197).

[40] For W. H. G. Thomas the many believers in vv. 3–16 are appropriately described as "A Galaxy of Saints" (*St. Paul's Epistle to the Romans* [Grand Rapids: Eerdmans, 1953], 421).

[41] For a fuller discussion see Introduction.

[42] Priscilla is a diminutive of Prisca. Luke always referred to her as Πρίσκιλλα (Acts 18:2,18,26) while Paul always uses the more dignified Πρίσκα (here and in 1 Cor 16:19 and 2 Tim 4:19).

[43] That Priscilla is mentioned before Aquila four times out of six usually is explained by conjecturing a strong personality or by suggesting she was an independently wealthy matron in her own right (cf. Black, *Romans,* 207).

[44] Williams understands the aorist ὑπέθηκαν to indicate a specific incident. He translates, "who once risked their very necks for my life." The incident may have occurred during the riot at Ephesus (Acts 19).

met in homes for instruction and prayer (cf. Acts 2:42–47; Col 4:15). Obviously the growth of the church is not dependent upon buildings erected for the specific purpose of worship.

Among the many to whom Paul sent his greetings was Epaenetus, the earliest convert to Christ in Asia (v. 5b).[45] Mary is identified as one who "worked very hard for you."[46] This emphasis on strenuous labor is reflected in Paul's greetings to three other women as well: Tryphena, Tryphosa,[47] and Persis[48] (v. 12). Although Priscilla and Aquila along with Urbanus are called "fellow workers" (vv. 3, 9), it is interesting that the mention of exhausting work is restricted to women.[49] Andronicus and Junia[s] are cited as "relatives" of the apostle. The second name can be understood as either masculine (Junias) or feminine (Junia).[50] Patristic commentators read Junia and considered her to be the wife of Andronicus. Since they are referred to as "outstanding among the apostles,"[51] the gender of Junia[s] is often discussed in connection with the issue of women and church leadership.[52] However, since the term "apos-

---

[45] Ἐπαίνετος is not mentioned elsewhere in the NT. Since the name is Greek, we can assume he was a Gentile believer. 1 Cor 16:15 mentions the household of Stephanas as the "first converts in Achaia."

[46] Six different Marys are mentioned in the NT. We know nothing of this Mary except that she was known to Paul. C. K. Barrett holds that here and in v. 12 the reference to hard work means "'to work as a Christian' but not necessarily 'to do Christian (that is, church) work'" (*A Commentary on the Epistle to the Romans,* HNTC [New York: Harpers, 1957], 283–84).

[47] Because it was customary to give children similar sounding names, it is often conjectured that Tryphena and Tryphosa may have been sisters, perhaps twin sisters. Their names are associated with τρυφή which means "softness, delicacy, daintiness" (LS abr., 719). Thus J. Knox writes, "One cannot fail to be slightly amused by the allusion (in vs. 12) to these workers in the Lord, 'Dainty' and 'Delicate'" ("The Epistle to the Romans," *IB* 9 [New York: Abingdon, 1954], 660).

[48] The name περσίς means "Persian woman."

[49] The verb κοπιάω in secular Greek means "to work till one is weary" (LS abr., 387).

[50] BAGD reads Ἰουνιᾶν as masculine, explaining that the name "Junias" is not found elsewhere and probably is a short form of the common name "Junianus." However, it continues, "The possibility, fr. a purely lexical point of view, that this is a woman's name Ἰυνία,ας, *Junia* . . ., deserves consideration" (p. 380). See also Fitzmyer, *Romans,* 737–38.

[51] ἐπίσημοι ἐν τοῖς ἀποστόλοις means outstanding "among the apostles" rather than "in the eyes of the apostles." Barrett translates "who are notable in the ranks of the apostles" (*Romans,* 283). There is little question that Andronicus and his wife Junia were influential "apostles" (in the wider sense of the word; note that τοῖς ἀποστόλοις in 1 Cor 15:7 is distinguished from τοῖς δώδεκα two verses earlier).

[52] Dunn is one of a number of contemporary writers who are definite in their opinion that the reference is to Junia, a woman. He writes, "We may firmly conclude, however, that one of the foundation apostles of Christianity was a woman and wife" (*Romans,* 2:895). See also R. R. Schulz, "Romans 16:7: Junia or Junias?" *ExpTim* 98 [1987]: 108–10).

tles" here should be understood in the wider sense of those who served as missionaries and evangelists,[53] the passage really contributes little to the debate. The term "relatives" is used in the wider sense of fellow countrymen, that is, Jews.[54] These two had shared imprisonment with Paul.[55] They were early believers in that they had become Christians at a time before Paul's conversion. They must have been among the earliest Palestinian believers.

Both Ampliatus (v. 8) and Stachys (v. 9) are greeted as dear friends in the Lord. In one of the oldest Christian cemeteries in Rome, the Catacomb of Domitilla, there is a burial chamber with the single inscription *APLIAT*. Decorations indicate that it is late first or early second century A.D. Some feel that there lies the believer to whom Paul sent his greetings. However, the name "Ampliatus" was a common name for slaves, so the identification is quite unlikely. Although the NIV translates "whom I love" for the first and "my dear friend" for the second, the Greek term is the same in each case. Apelles is identified as one who has been tried and found to be trustworthy. This may well refer to a specific incident in which he had proved to be a faithful believer. Goodspeed calls him a "veteran Christian." Few qualities are as important in the believer as faithfulness in carrying out the responsibilities assigned. Paul reminded the believers at Corinth that "it is required that those who have been given a trust must prove faithful" (1 Cor 4:2).

Paul sent his greetings to "the household of Aristobulus" (v. 10b). We know of a grandson of Herod the Great by the name of Aristobulus who lived as a private citizen in Rome. His brother, Agrippa I, was a friend and confidant of the Emperor Claudius. If Aristobulus enjoyed the same relationship, when he died his household would have been taken over by Claudius, as was the established practice. Collectively they would be known as "the household of Aristobulus." If we assume that the Aristobulus Paul mentioned was the one just described, then Paul would have had close friends among the household of an eminent family in the capital city. This may also have been the case in "the household of Narcissus" if the reference in v. 11 is to Tiberius Claudius Narcissus, the

---

[53] See the use of ἀπόστολος in John 13:16; Acts 14:4 (see on that verse J. B. Polhill, *Acts*, NAC [Nashville: Broadman, 1992], 311); 2 Cor 8:23 (see R. P. Martin, *2 Corinthians*, WBC [Waco: Word, 1986], 278); Phil 2:25; Heb 3:1.

[54] Herodion, in v. 11, is referred to as a "relative" as well.

[55] Sanday and Headlam comment that "metaphorical explanation of the words [καὶ συναιχμαλώτους μου] are too far-fetched to be probable" (*Romans*, 423). Clement of Rome says of the apostle Paul, "Seven times he was in bonds" (*1 Clem.* 5:6).

famous freedman of the emperor Tiberius, a man of proverbial wealth who exercised great influence at the time of the emperor Claudius.

Next to receive Paul's greetings was Rufus (v. 13).[56] He was "chosen" not in the sense of having been called to be a Christian but to a place of prominence in the local assembly of believers. Some think this was Rufus, son of the Simon from Cyrene who was forced to carry Jesus' cross (cf. Mark 15:1). Since Mark, who wrote his Gospel from Rome, was the only synoptist who identified the two sons of Simon, some commentators conjecture that they may have emigrated to Rome and become persons of importance in the church there. In any case, the mother of Rufus had been like a mother to Paul. The relationship was close and supportive.

Nine individuals are mentioned by name in vv. 14–16. First come five men "and the brothers with them" (i.e., other Christians who were associated with or met with them). Although it is not known whether their names had any particular significance, "Asyncritus" means "incomparable," and "Phlegon" means "burning." "Hermes" was the name of the god of good luck (as well as travelers, music, eloquence, etc.). "Patrobas" had the name of a confidant of Nero who was in charge of Nero's theatrical events. "Hermas" (a shortened form of several names) was a name widely used among slaves.[57] If the first two clauses of the Greek text of v. 15 are intended to be understood as parallel, Julia would have been the sister of Philologus,[58] just so an unnamed woman is the sister of Nereus. Others think Julia was the wife of Philologus, and Nereus and Olympas were their children.

Paul closed his greetings with the instruction, "Greet one another with a holy kiss" (v. 16). This ancient practice was a regular part of the worship service in the early church (1 Cor 16:20; 2 Cor 13:12; 1 Pet 5:14).[59] Morris, however, holds that Paul's reference was to the regular form of greeting of the day and not to a liturgical action such as the "kiss of peace," which was a part of the service of Holy Communion.[60] Phillips transposes the custom into contemporary Western terms with his well-known, "Have a hearty handshake all around."

---

[56] The name means "red."

[57] Both Origen and Eusebius held that this Hermas was the author of the well-known apocalypse, *The Shepherd of Hermas* (early second century), but the identification is highly improbable.

[58] "Philologus" means "fond of words."

[59] The earliest reference to the "kiss of peace" is in Justin Martyr (*1 Apol.* 65).

[60] Morris, *Romans,* 537.

(5) Warnings against False Teachers (16:17–20)

17I urge you, brothers, to watch out for those who cause divisions and put obstacles in your way that are contrary to the teaching you have learned. Keep away from them. 18For such people are not serving our Lord Christ, but their own appetites. By smooth talk and flattery they deceive the minds of naive people. 19Everyone has heard about your obedience, so I am full of joy over you; but I want you to be wise about what is good, and innocent about what is evil.

20The God of peace will soon crush Satan under your feet.

The grace of our Lord Jesus be with you.

16:17–20[61]   In every group there seems to be those intent on bringing it down. Paul urged his Christian friends at Rome to be on the watch for those who stirred up dissensions.[62] Among the "seven [things] that are detestable to [the Lord]," the writer of Proverbs listed in the most emphatic position "a man who stirs up dissension among brothers" (Prov 6:16,19). This kind of person created obstacles that caused others to stumble. Their teaching was contrary to the instruction the church had received. Jesus warned of false prophets who come in sheep's clothing but inwardly are ferocious wolves (Matt 7:15), and elsewhere Paul instructed a young preacher to have nothing to do with a divisive person after he had been warned twice (Titus 3:10). "Disassociate yourselves" is the TCNT's translation of the imperative in v. 17.[63]

False teachers are identified by their teaching. To be true their doctrine had to agree with the teaching that already had been delivered to the church. Truth does not contradict itself. Teaching that deviated from the apostolic teaching was by definition spurious. Even today the church must accept or reject that which claims to be true on the basis of its consistency with revealed truth. God's Word stands as the only absolute. All else is measured by what God has stated as true.

---

[61] E. Käsemann holds that in v. 17 Paul broke away from his greetings to deliver a "wild polemic" (*Commentary on Romans* [Grand Rapids: Eerdmans, 1980], 419; cf. 416). Cranfield responds, "The abruptness of the introduction of vv. 17–20a at this point has, in our judgment, been greatly exaggerated" (*Romans,* 2:797).

[62] σκοπέω, a strong term, here means "to look out for [so as to avoid]" (BAGD, 756). Note the definite article in τὰς διχοστασίας. Apparently the kinds of divisions threatening the unity of believers were widespread and well known. διχοστασία is included in the catalog of vices in Gal 5:20.

[63] The present active imperative (ἐκκλίνετε) may be translated "keep turning away [from them]."

Those who cause divisions are not serving the Lord but are "slaves of their own base desires" (Moffatt) (v. 18).[64] There is considerable difficulty in determining just who these trouble makers were. They have been variously identified as Judaizers, antinomians, charismatic enthusiasts, or the selfish among the strong of 14:1–15:13. Black opts for "the libertarian 'meat-eaters,' the people who boasted of 'liberty,' including independence of kosher taboos about food."[65] Paul may have had several such groups in mind. Trouble is never far away where people are concerned. These people used smooth and plausible speech to deceive the innocent. By pious talk and flattering speech[66] they attempted to seduce the minds of the unsuspecting. Peter spoke of false prophets who would "exploit you with stories they have made up" (2 Pet 2:3; cf. Col 2:4). The child of God must beware of all those who by deceptive eloquence would lead them into error. To the Corinthians Paul wrote that his preaching was not "with wise and persuasive words, but with a demonstration of the Spirit's power" (1 Cor 2:4). Beware of the glib tongue and the deceptive argument.

Paul was delighted that the "fame of [their] obedience" had "spread everywhere" (v. 19, NEB; cf. Rom 1:8). That they were swift to obey gave the apostle great joy. In what appears to be a popular aphorism, Paul counseled the Roman believers to be "well versed in all that is good" (TCNT) but innocent in regard to what is evil. Somewhat the same contrast is seen in Jesus' admonition to the Twelve, "Be as shrewd as snakes and as innocent as doves" (Matt 10:16).[67] In a culture that increasingly reveals the active presence of spiritual forces at war against the church (cf. Rev 12:17), it is critical that the followers of Christ live lives of uncompromising holiness. God never intended his children to become intimate with evil in order to communicate the gospel to those in its grasp. To Timothy, Paul advised the opposite; "Flee the evil desires of youth" (2 Tim 2:2).

Verse 20 is a benediction. Some copies of the letter might have ended at this point.[68] In view of the divisions created by false brethren (v. 17),

---

[64] δουλεύω means "to serve as a slave" (δοῦλος). It is much stronger than διακονέω, which means "to serve," e.g., as a deacon (1 Tim 3:10).

[65] Black, *Romans*, 212–13.

[66] εὐλογία means "fine words, flattery" (cf. our Eng. word "eulogy"). Of the fourteen occurrences in the NT only here is it used in a negative sense.

[67] Cf. also Paul's counsel to the Corinthians, "In regard to evil be infants, but in your thinking be adults" (1 Cor 14:20).

[68] The benediction at 15:33 could indicate yet another possible stopping point for some copies of the epistle.

God is again designated a "God of peace" (cf. 15:33). Before long God would crush Satan under their feet.[69] While there is an obvious allusion to Gen 3:15,[70] in context Paul apparently referred to the work of Satan in and through those who were spreading dissension.[71] This evil work would not continue. So, "May the grace of our Lord Jesus be with you."[72] The personal pronoun "our" not only binds together all believers but stresses their intimate relationship to the Lord as well.

(6) Greetings from Paul's Companions (16:21–23)

[21]Timothy, my fellow worker, sends his greetings to you, as do Lucius, Jason and Sosipater, my relatives.

[22]I, Tertius, who wrote down this letter, greet you in the Lord.

[23]Gaius, whose hospitality I and the whole church here enjoy, sends you his greetings.

Erastus, who is the city's director of public works, and our brother Quartus send you their greetings.

16:21–23   Earlier (vv. 4–15) Paul greeted a number of the Christians he knew who were living in Rome. Then he sent them the greetings of those who were with him. Timothy, Paul's "fellow worker" (cf. vv. 3, 9), sent his greetings.[73] Timothy occupied a very special place in Paul's heart and ministry. He joined Paul at Lystra on the second missionary journey (Acts 16:1) and labored side by side with the veteran evangelist. Paul wrote two of his last three extant letters to Timothy, whom he had left at Ephesus to carry on the work there. In the first letter he addressed him as "my true son in the faith" (1 Tim 1:2) and in the second as "my dear son" (2 Tim 1:2). No other young man had quite the same personal attention from the aging apostle, who was nearing the close of his ministry. Lucius, Jason, and Sosipater, fellow countrymen with Paul, also added their greetings. This Lucius probably should not be identified with the Lucius of Cyrene mentioned in Acts 13:1, although some have argued that he may have been Luke, the author of Luke-Acts.[74]

---

[69] Believers share in the victory won by God. Cf. Ps 91:13 ("You will tread upon the lion and the cobra; you will trample the great lion and the serpent").

[70] In the MT, not the LXX, which reads αὐτός σου τηρήσει κεφαλήν, "he shall watch against thy head."

[71] Morris maintains that although some see this as a reference to the parousia, "it is better to see the promise of a victory over Satan in the here and now" (*Romans,* 541).

[72] Cf. 1 Cor 16:23; 1 Thess 5:28; 2 Thess 3:18. For a full trinitarian benediction see 2 Cor 13:14.

[73] Black calls him "the inseparable aide-de-camp of the Apostle" (*Romans,* 215).

[74] οἱ συγγενεῖς μου, "my countrymen," refers to all three men mentioned, which would make this Lucius a Jew. Lucius of Cyrene would be a Gentile.

Although Jason was a common Greek, name it could well be that this was the Jason who was Paul's host at Thessalonica (Acts 17:6).[75] It also is possible that Sosipater was the Sopater, son of Pyrrhus, who accompanied Paul as far as Asia on his journey to Jerusalem (Acts 20:4).[76]

Verse 22 identifies Tertius as the scribe who wrote down Paul's letter.[77] Scribal assistants were widely used in antiquity. Denney notes that the use of the first person "is a striking indication of Paul's courtesy."[78] Tertius was more than simply a scribe brought in for the occasion; he was a Christian brother free to add his personal greetings to those of the others. F. F. Bruce thinks that "at this point Tertius may have handed the pen to Paul," and "we may envisage Paul writing the remainder of the letter himself"[79] (cf. 2 Thess 3:17; Gal 6:11). Gaius, the next to send his greetings, probably was the man Paul identified as one of the few he had baptized (1 Cor 1:14).[80] Paul said that he himself as well as the whole church had enjoyed his hospitality.

Two others added their greetings: Erastus and Quartus (v. 23b). An inscription in Latin discovered at Corinth in 1929 reads, "Erastus, in return for his aedileship, laid the pavement at his own expense."[81] This could be the same Erastus who here sent his greetings to the believers in Rome.[82] We know little of Quartus except that he was a brother in Christ living in Corinth.[83] Since his name is Latin, he may have had some personal contact with the church in Rome.

---

[75] Many Jews with the name "Joshua" would have used the Greek name "Jason."

[76] Σώπατρος is a shortened form of Σωσίπατρος.

[77] Since his name is Latin, we may conjecture that he may have had some personal connection with the church at Rome. Fitzmyer notes that later legends indicate that Tertius became the bishop of Iconium (*Romans,* 749).

[78] Denney, "Romans," 723.

[79] F. F. Bruce, *The Letter of Paul to the Romans,* 2d ed. TNTC (Grand Rapids: Eerdmans, 1985), 265.

[80] E. J. Goodspeed identified Gaius with Titius Justus of Acts 18:7 (*JBL* 69 [1950]: 382–83). Since Titius is a *gens* name (nomen gentile), it probably would have been preceded by a praenomen. His full name could have been Gaius Titius Justus.

[81] See Fitzmyer, *Romans,* 750, for bibliographic references.

[82] Paul referred to him as ὁ οἰκονόμος, "the city treasurer" (BAGD, 560, 1b), while an aedile would have been the more important office of "commissioner for public works." Perhaps, having served well in the more modest position, he later was promoted to the more significant office and laid the pavement as an expression of appreciation for his new role.

[83] That he alone among those greeting the church was given the more affectionate title "brother" has led some to conjecture that he may have been the blood brother of Erastus or perhaps Tertius. (Tertius is Latin for "third" and Quartus for "fourth." Could Quartus have been the younger brother of Tertius?)

(7) Doxology (16:25–27)

²⁵Now to him who is able to establish you by my gospel and the procla-mation of Jesus Christ, according to the revelation of the mystery hidden for long ages past, ²⁶but now revealed and made known through the prophetic writings by the command of the eternal God, so that all nations might believe and obey him— ²⁷to the only wise God be glory forever through Jesus Christ! Amen.

The NIV does not have a v. 24. It is not adequately supported by the better Greek manuscripts.[84] The final three verses of Romans (one sentence in Greek) form a doxology that is liturgical in character.[85] Its authenticity and location in the text are often questioned.[86] For our purposes, however, we will take it as it is and see what we can learn from it.[87]

16:25–27 Paul closed his letter with a magnificent doxology. In it are found many of the major themes of the Epistle to the Romans. God is described as the one who is able to establish and strengthen the believer. This was promised in the gospel that Paul so faithfully had proclaimed.[88] It was a gospel not taught by men but received by direct revelation from Jesus Christ (Gal 1:12). It centered in the life, death, and resurrection of Jesus Christ. He is the focal point of the gospel. Apart from him there could be no "good news" in the ultimate sense of that term. In times past it existed as a sacred secret in the eternal counsels of God. With Christ that mystery has been made known (Eph 1:9; 3:5,9; Col 1:26). Now it has been revealed through the prophetic writings according to the command of the eternal God.[89] The purpose of the mys-

---

[84] Some MSS maintain v. 24 but place it after v. 27 so the epistle will close with a benediction.

[85] Dunn lays out the Greek text in graphic form to show the orderly relationship between clauses (*Romans*, 2:913).

[86] Black writes, "That the closing doxology is of later literary vintage than the original letter to the Romans is widely recognized" (*Romans*, 215). After considering the "extremely complicated evidence" Cranfield concludes: "This doxology, either in its present form or in a somewhat briefer form, was first added to a short form of Romans (ending with 14:23 and due to the heresiarch Marcion), in order to round off what was obviously incomplete, and was subsequently (in its present form) added, because its intrinsic merit commended it, both to the full form of the epistle and also to a form ending with 15:23" (*Romans*, 2:808).

[87] See Introduction for a full treatment of the problem.

[88] By "my gospel" Paul meant the gospel that had been revealed to him and that he had made his own (cf. Rom 2:16; 2 Tim 2:8).

[89] Morris comments that while this refers naturally to the writings of the OT prophets, "it seems that Paul is saying that the real meaning of the Old Testament has become apparent only through the coming of Christ" (*Romans*, 547).

tery now revealed was to promote obedience to the faith among all nations (cf. Rom 1:5). The gospel is universal in its purpose. It reaches out to all and promises deliverance to all who respond in faith.[90]

Breaking syntax, Paul returned to what he was on the verge of saying when he began v. 25. To God, who alone is wise,[91] be glory forever through Jesus Christ (v. 27).[92] The ascription of glory to God[93] is, according to the shorter Westminster catechism, the "chief end of man." In the coming ages the songs of the redeemed will ring throughout the courts of heaven. Redemption will be complete. The eternal purposes of God will reach their fulfillment. God will be forever praised. Amen.

---

[90] εἰς πάντα τὰ ἔθνη means "as far as all the nations," i.e., throughout the entire world.

[91] A more natural rendering than "the only wise God."

[92] Newman and Nida say that this phrase "does not specify the agency for praising, but rather the one who causes such praise to be given to God" (*A Handbook on Paul's Letter to the Romans,* 300).

[93] ᾧ (see the Greek text) refers to God, not to Jesus Christ.

Selected Subject Index

Person Index

Scripture Index